For Chris,
Cable on!

Mark Gaughan

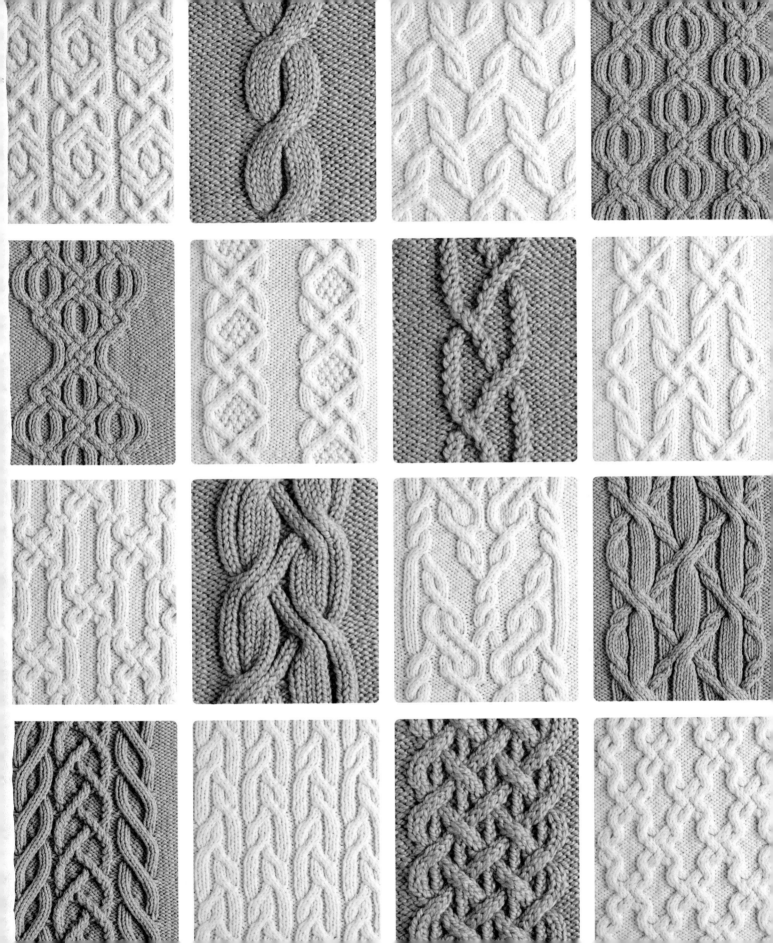

Norah Gaughan's
Knitted Cable
Sourcebook

A Breakthrough Guide to Knitting with Cables and Designing Your Own

Photographs by Jared Flood

Abrams / New York

Contents

4 Expanding PAGE 122

Introduction

I learned to knit the summer after I turned fourteen during a week-long visit with family friends in Princeton, New Jersey. The weather outside was unbearably hot, so my friend Grace and I retreated to her air-conditioned living room, where she taught me the basics.

I caught on quickly, and my first project—completed during that week—was a two-color hat worked in the round on size 4 needles. I returned home excited to knit more and quickly started trying out textural stitches and cables, and then designing my own garments.

My first experience with cables came when I knit an Aran sampler and framed it like a piece of art for a school social-studies project. Ever since then, I have been hooked. Today I love knitting cables, designing with cables, and, most of all, creating new cable patterns. I also love wearing cabled garments. My wardrobe tends to be monochromatic, but cables and other textural work keep it from being dull. It probably doesn't hurt that I am proud of my Irish heritage; though several generations have passed since my relatives found thier way across the sea, the attraction to cabled fisherman sweaters has persisted.

While I am often inspired to knit because I like the finished product, I am, more than anything, a process knitter—that is, I knit at least as much for the challenge and enjoyment of the process as for the pleasure and pride of finishing. I can find a certain meditative bliss in expanses of stockinette or garter stitch, but sometimes it's hard for me to maintain my momentum. But the promise of the "next cable" is so satisfying to me that it always keeps me motivated. I always wonder what the pattern will look like after another row. And then I tell myself I'll just finish one more cross before I turn in for

the night. Because there is a logic to cables, I generally find them easy to memorize. I like when the trajectory of the stitches becomes obvious and I am freed from referencing the chart or instructions too often. Then I can breeze through the knitting and enjoy the process of watching the fabric form in my hands.

After so many years of cable knitting, I admit that what feels like a breeze to me could be more challenging for you if you have less experience. My goal for this book is to share my enthusiasm for cable knitting—and knitting in general—and to teach you what I have learned over the years so that you can uncover the underlying logic of any cable, mix and match cables in any project, and even design your own cables. I have written it to be useful and inspiring for knitters of all levels of experience, whether you are an enthusiastic beginner or a veteran designer.

This is, in the most basic sense, a stitch dictionary with 152 different cable patterns and a project book featuring 15 garments. But there is so much more. I have done my best to explain in words and photos how one cable design leads to the next—for example, how Incline Fave leads to Weeping Blossom (see right and Chapter 5), and I hope that this information will inspire you to try out many different cables and also give you the confidence to invent your own. Similarly, I designed the garments so they can be knitted as is but also serve as templates into which you can mix and match different cables. To make this easy, I have given each cable pattern what I call an SSE, or stockinette stitch equivalent, which is the number of stockinette stitches it would require to fill the same width as the cable. As long as the cables you want to use and the cables you are replacing have the same

Incline Fave (#111)

Weeping Blossom (#114)

stockinette stitch equivalent (i.e., take up the same width), you're good to go regardless of the weight of the yarn. You might replace a wide panel with several smaller cables or, conversely, use a large cable pattern in place of a mix of smaller cables. If necessary, you can also take away or add stockinette stitches from around the cables to make up any difference. I explain all of this in detail in Chapter 1, and with each set of garment instructions I also include special considerations for cable substitutions.

I designed the majority of cables featured in these pages myself, and many I am sharing here for the first time. In Chapter 1, I introduce basic cable-knitting techniques. In Chapter 2, I present small, basic cables and variations of them. As the chapters progress I make the cables wider and more complex. In Chapter 3, I introduce new crosses and in Chapter 4 the possibility of making patterns of infinite widths by working the repeat portion of a cable chart more than once and connecting the pattern seamlessly. In Chapter 5, I explore the use of motifs, or distinct elements of a pattern, and show how one

idea can blossom into many. Then, finally, in Chapter 6, I delve into drawing with cables, by which I mean creating sinuous lines with cables and "coloring in" with textures and openwork. Within each chapter I have divided the cables into numbered groups. All of the cables within the same group represent a progression of innovation. I hope seeing them together helps you to understand them better—and inspires you to innovate further.

To my mind there can be no such thing as an all-encompassing encyclopedia of cables (as much as my publisher would have loved for this book to have been called an encyclopedia) because one volume can't begin to contain all the cables in use already and all of the cables yet to be revealed by our imaginations. This book is meant to be both a resource for existing cable patterns and a jumping-off point for making new cable discoveries. Honestly, after 40-plus years of working with them, I feel as if I have barely begun to uncover their potential. It is an exciting adventure to which I welcome you.

Chapter 1

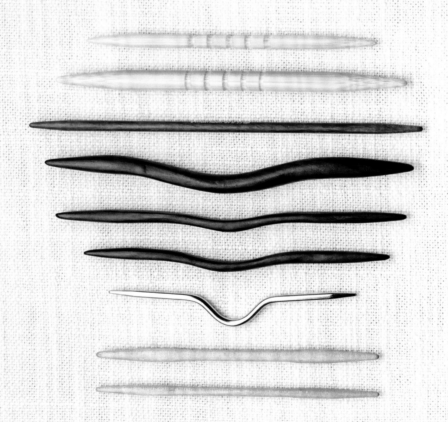

Essentials

Cables are formed when a few stitches switch places with another few stitches. Really, it's that simple. You hold some stitches aside while you knit the next few and then work the ones you were holding. The result is a lovely twist, or cross, in the fabric.

The most basic of cables are worked in stockinette stitch and the number of stitches held aside is the same as the number of stitches worked. Begin changing the pattern stitch within a cable or vary the number of stitches crossed, and the possibilities are endless.

Basics

Choosing Yarns

My favorite yarns for knitting cables are multi-ply wools. The plying makes them round and smooth, and cables knit from these yarns tend to be round and smooth as well, showing off every twist and turn clearly. Wool has a lot of natural elasticity, which is great on several levels. The stretch makes it easier to work the cable crosses. Wool is also very forgiving. Stitches tend to stay beautiful and well shaped, smoothing out little inconsistencies in tension. Many companies make beautiful yarns of this type. These are the ones I chose for the swatches in this book:

Chapter 2 Imperial Yarn Erin
Chapter 3 Blue Sky Alpacas Extra
Chapter 4 Quince & Co. Lark
Chapter 5 Jaggerspun Super Lamb
Chapter 6 Quince & Co. Chickadee

Of course, cables can look great in all sorts of yarns, not just multi-ply wools. I chose a bunch of different types for the garments in this book.

Choosing a Cable Needle

When you are holding stitches aside while cabling, typically you put them on another needle and hold them in front or in back of the work. There are small needles made for the purpose (officially called *cable needles*), but any double-pointed needle will do the job just as well. When I refer to a cable needle in this book, I mean whatever needle you choose to use.

I've seen cable needles made of wood, metal, plastic, and bamboo. Most are only a few inches long. They can be straight, have a dip in the center to aid in holding stitches, or have a few ridges or grooves meant to do the same. Some cable needles are shaped like a U to make it easier to carry stitches from the front to the back and to keep the stitches from falling off. It works best to use a cable needle that is slightly smaller in diameter than your knitting needles, just fat enough to stay in place and not slip out, leaving your stitches dangling. The best cable needle for you is entirely a matter of personal preference.

Using a Double-Pointed Needle as a Cable Needle

When I'm cabling, I like to use a double-pointed needle a size or two smaller than my working needle as my cable needle. The 4″ (10 cm) double-pointed needles are great, but I usually use 7″ (18 cm) ones because I have a lot of them around. Some people think the longer length makes using them awkward, but I have developed a system that makes it easy.

When a cable requires holding stitches in the back, I bring the cable needle to the back of the work prior to slipping the stitches onto it; that way I don't have to wrestle the longer needle from the front to the back.

After I have slipped my stitches onto the cable needle, I plant the left end of the cable needle into the body of my work. This holds everything in place a little better than leaving the cable needle hanging from the work, and it keeps the cable needle from slipping out of the stitches. Planting the cable needle into the body of the work also makes it less likely for the beginning cable knitter to twist the cable around 180°, causing the stitches to be in reverse order (meaning that the left-most stitches swing around to become the right-most stitches). If this happens to you, you'll likely notice there is a problem because the stitches will appear scrunched up and messy and will be harder to work or harder to slip onto the left-hand needle.

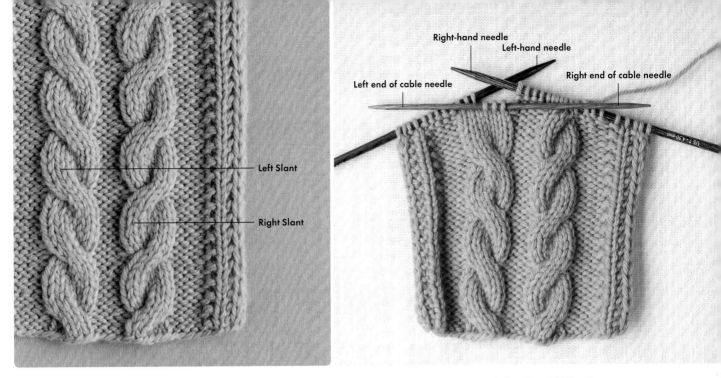

Right-hand needle
Left-hand needle
Left end of cable needle
Right end of cable needle

Where you hold your cable needle—to the front or to the back—determines whether your cable will slant to the left (front) or right (back).

Right Slant or Left Slant

You can manipulate the direction of your cable by holding stitches to the front of your work or to the back. Holding to the front makes a cable cross slant to the left. Holding to the the back makes it slant to the right. This isn't something you need to purposely memorize (though over time it will come naturally) because the chart or written instructions will always tell you what you need to do.

To hold the stitches to the front or back, you slip the stitches to be held onto a cable needle (see below). If you are going to hold the stitches to the front of your work (that's between you and your knitting) then start with the cable needle in front as well. If you want to hold the stitches to the back, bring the cable needle to the back of your work before you slip the stitches onto it. If you typically slip the stitches onto the cable needle while the needle is still in front of your work, and then bring it into the back by maneuvering it between your two main needles, then definitely give my way a try; I think it's much easier.

Slipping Stitches to Cable Needle

Always slip stitches off your left-hand needle onto the left end of your cable needle. When you work off of the cable needle (i.e., knit or purl the stitches), work off of the right end of the cable needle onto the right-hand needle.

You may want to slip all of the stitches at once rather than one at a time. No matter which way you do it, always keep them in their original orientation on the needle. This is called slipping as if to purl (or slipping purlwise), because the needle goes into the stitches on the right side and comes out the left, just as if you were purling. But don't think about this too much. When you are slipping more than 1 stitch at once, this is the intuitive choice. Note that unless stitches are to be slipped knitwise for some reason, the instructions in this book don't specify how to slip them; slipping them purlwise is the default.

Working Held Stitches

Instructions for knitting cables often tell you to knit the held stitches directly off of the cable needle. For instance, in this book, the key might say, "k4 from cn." You certainly can work directly off of your cable needle as instructed. However, I personally find it a bit awkward, so I usually slip the stitches back to my left-hand needle before working them. In some cases the left-most stitches might get stretched a bit with this method. For me, though, the comfort of slipping them back and working off of my main needle trumps any slight stretching.

Cable Terminology

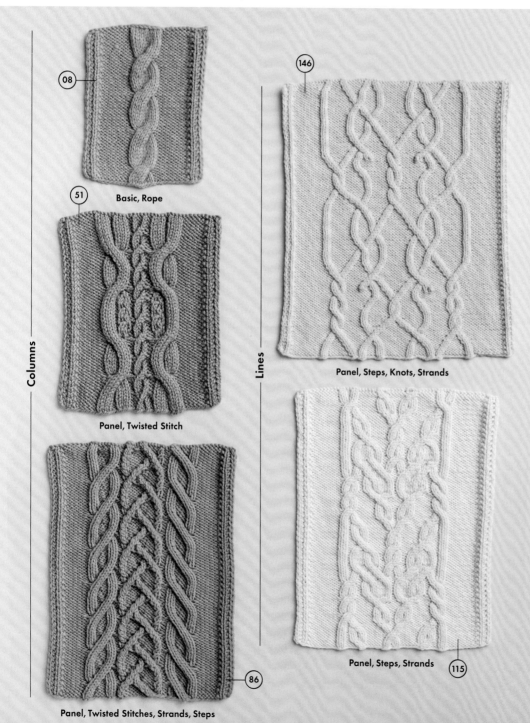

Columns

08 — Basic, Rope

51 — Panel, Twisted Stitch

86 — Panel, Twisted Stitches, Strands, Steps

Lines

146 — Panel, Steps, Knots, Strands

115 — Panel, Steps, Strands

I think of cables in two categories: columns and lines.

COLUMNS are cable crosses stacked on top of each other. The cable crosses might form ropes, braids, Xs, Os, or their infinite combinations. All of the cables in Chapters 2 and 3 fall into this category.

LINES are crosses lined up with the end of one cross becoming the beginning of a cross above it, so stitches move across the fabric diagonally. These lines can form zigzags, then diamonds and other shapes. Change how many stitches you move over and you alter the steepness of your line. Use more than one steepness and you can now form sinuous curves. I think of this as drawing with cables. There are cables with lines in all of the chapters of this book, but they figure most prominently in Chapters 5 and 6.

Both types, columns and lines, can be repeated and intertwined to form wide panels and allover patterns. For example, you might have lines within a column, or you might have a large panel of cables with both columns and lines. The possibilities are limitless.

There is no "official" terminology for cable knitting, and oftentimes people use the same words to mean different actions and results. As such, writing about cables can be challenging. To clear things up and to help you understand my instructions, here is a list of the words I use often and the way I define them.

BASIC The descriptor I use in a cable name if I know that the cable has been published in other sources and is familiar to many knitters. I only include basic cables in this book when they are the basis for one or more of my unique variations.

The most basic of cables are worked in stockinette stitch, and the number of stitches held aside (i.e., to the front or back) is the same as the number of stitches worked. For example, in the Basic 3/3 Rope (#1), 3 stockinette stitches cross over 3 stockinette stitches.

CABLE OR CABLE STITCH A combination of stitches crossing one another to form a pattern. It can refer both to the entire stitch pattern and to the individual crosses within that pattern. In some contexts I might use the word "cable" as a verb to refer to the action of crossing stitches. For example, I might write "cable 2 stitches over 2 stitches" to mean "cross 2 stitches over 2 stitches."

COLUMNS One of the 2 categories into which I divide cables (see definition at left).

CROSS(ING) OR CABLE CROSS(ING) The point at which a group of stitches is held in front or in back of another group of stitches, then worked in order to switch the positioning of the 2 groups. I sometimes refer to cable crosses as stitches moving. For instance, I might write "cross 3 stitches over 3 stitches to the left" or "work a 6-stitch cable crossing."

KNOT A smaller bobble that can be worked without turning the work. For example, see Paisley Shadow (#146).

LINES One of the 2 categories into which I divide cables (see definition at left).

PANEL A wide column or a collection of cables that are meant to be kept together.

ROPE When basic crosses such as 3/3 or 4/4 are stacked up in a column and give the appearance of a rope. See Basic 3/3 Rope (#1) or Basic 4/4 Rope (#8).

STEP When a group of stitches moves in a line and it takes several right-side rows to complete its action (to go from the beginning of the line to the end), I call each cable cros-

sing needed to make the action a *step*. In a right-traveling line, you might have a number of right-side rows in which you work a right cross that moves the top (visible) stitches of each cable crossing to the right; each of these right-side crosses is considered a step in the line. For example, see Purl Center 2-Step (#6) or 4-Step Swing (#30).

STRAND A strand is a number of stitches that travel together through the cable pattern, either for a short distance or through the entire pattern. You can usually pick out a strand within a particular pattern and follow the stitches of that strand from the beginning of the column/line to the end. To illustrate this, picture hand-braiding 3 different-color strands of yarn together, then choosing a strand/color and following it from beginning to end as it weaves over and under the other strands/colors. A strand can be made up of all knit stitches, all purl stitches, a combination of knit and purl stitches, or even yarn-overs paired with decreases. A strand can divide, with the separate new strands traveling in different directions. Or it might divide and combine with the pieces of another strand, either temporarily or for the remainder of the piece.

TWISTED STITCH When referred to in the singular, a twisted stitch is a stitch that is worked into the back loop on both the right and wrong sides. The plural twisted stitches involves 2 stitches (described below).

TWISTED STITCHES A method of making 2 stitches look as if they have been cabled, without using a cable needle. The instructions for working right twists and left twists are in the key for each applicable cable pattern.

Written Instructions and Charts

If you are what I call a spreadsheet thinker, your ideal pattern is written out row by row. When you're done with a row, you cross it off on your pattern. When instructions aren't detailed enough for you, you make a spreadsheet, or even write out each row yourself.

If you are what I call a chart thinker, you like to see a visual representation of what you are creating. Following a symbol that looks like the cable you are knitting is much easier for you than reading words that describe each action.

In my experience, most knitters lean one way or the other. That is why in this book, whenever possible, I included both written-out and charted instructions. I made an exception and only included a chart when the pattern was both very wide and very tall, because writing out the instructions would have been unwieldy.

I almost always prefer to work from charts rather than row-by-row instructions, especially when working cables. When using a chart, if you put your knitting down and come back later, it is much easier to see where you are in the pattern than if you are following written instructions, because you can compare your knitted fabric to the chart. When following written instructions, you can make a mark on the instructions that tells you where you are leaving off but, in practice, I have found that many knitters with the best of intentions don't succeed at doing this consistently and then have to struggle to figure out where they are in the pattern.

Charts make it so much easier than written instructions to figure out if you have made a mistake and how far you have to rip, or drop down, to fix it. Just look at your knitting and compare it to the chart. Since cable chart symbols are designed to look like the cables, once you get used to them, you can decipher them at a glance.

As hard as we might try, designers do make mistakes, and even after the technical editor and proofreader have gone over a pattern with their discerning eyes, sometimes mistakes make it into print. But once you start knitting, if you see the mistake in your knitting, by looking at the chart, you'll likely be able to figure out what to do to correct it because you'll be able to discern what was intended.

Compared to working from written words, it is much easier to understand how to decrease or increase in a cable pattern when working from a chart. Whereas written instructions may tell you to "work in pattern" and leave it up to you to understand what that means, charted instructions provide visual clues because you can easily see what came before and what comes after.

Chart Basics

Once you understand the basics, reading a chart becomes second nature. Here are some general guidelines:

- The chart is drawn to represent how your knitting will appear when you're looking at the right side of the fabric, the side that will be on the outside. All of the symbols represent how the stitches look on the right side.

- One square on a chart represents 1 stitch.

- Right-side rows are worked from right to left on the chart. Wrong-side rows are worked from left to right on the chart.

- The row number is placed on the chart where you will begin the row. Right-side rows have the numbers along the right edge of the chart, and wrong-side rows have the numbers along the left edge of the chart.

- Imagine labeling everything as if you are seeing it from the right (or public) side of your work. Picture those labels pinned to your knitting. Once the right-side row is complete, you'll need to turn the piece over to work on the wrong side. The yarn is now on the edge you have labeled as the left-hand edge. You are working from your right to your left as always, but since you are on the back of the knitted piece, the row is worked from the edge labeled left to the edge labeled right. The chart is also worked the way the piece is labeled, from left to right. If you are having trouble wrapping

Reading Rows on a Chart

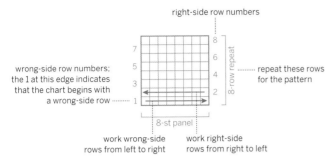

right-side row numbers

wrong-side row numbers; the 1 at this edge indicates that the chart begins with a wrong-side row

8-row repeat

repeat these rows for the pattern

8-st panel

work wrong-side rows from left to right

work right-side rows from right to left

Reading Stitch Repeats on a Chart

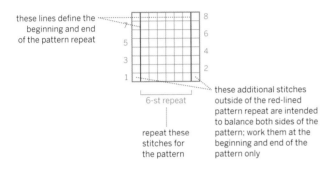

these lines define the beginning and end of the pattern repeat

6-st repeat

repeat these stitches for the pattern

these additional stitches outside of the red-lined pattern repeat are intended to balance both sides of the pattern; work them at the beginning and end of the pattern only

Keeping Your Place on a Chart

- It's fine to make a photocopy of the chart you are working on for your personal use (but not for distribution).

- Enlarge the chart when you photocopy it if your vision isn't great. Sometimes it is necessary to photocopy the chart in 2 pieces if it is long; just make sure that you don't leave out any rows when you do so. For a chart that is really wide, it might help to photocopy each half of the chart, then cut and paste the halves into one full chart so that you can read across the rows without having to consult two separate sheets; again, be sure you're not missing any stitches in the center.

- A magnet board, highlighter tape, washi tape, or a large sticky note placed above the row you're working on brings your eye right where you want it to be and makes referencing the chart much easier. However, if placing it below works better for you, that's fine, too. The one disadvantage to placing it below your current row is that you'll be obscuring the previous row, which you may need to refer to while you are working. Place a photocopy of the chart in a plastic sleeve if you plan to use any kind of adhesive tape as a row marker. That way you won't risk marring the original printed page.

your mind around this, don't worry. Sometimes a full understanding of the concept comes after you've been knitting for a while.

- The chart key may give one definition for right-side rows and another for wrong-side rows. Because the symbols on the chart represent how the fabric will appear when looking at the right side, you must do the opposite on a wrong-side row. For instance, a knit stitch is represented as an empty box on the right side. When you see an empty box while working a wrong-side row, you purl it, because when you purl on the wrong side, it will look like a knit on the right side. This is clearly defined in the key as "knit on RS" and "purl on WS."

- Sometimes the repeat line at the beginning of the repeat bisects a cable. When this happens, the repeat line at the end of the repeat will also bisect a cable. The leftover cable stitches at the beginning and end of the repeat will add up to a whole cable. Note that the chart and written stitch pattern do not always present the

repeats in exactly the same manner, however, the end result will be the same.

- If you are working in the round, your round always begins on the right. The charts in this book can all be worked in the round, and the keys have been written with that in mind. (Note that the text has been written for working back and forth in rows, not in the round; if you wish to work in the round, you will need to work from the charts.) If you see a symbol with an explanation for working both on the wrong side and on the right side, but the symbol appears to be placed on a wrong-side row, work that symbol following the directions for working on a right-side row; since if you are working in the round, there are no wrong-side rows.

Symbol Anatomy

The symbols in this book were designed to tell you as much as possible at a glance about the cable crosses that you are to work. They are based on standard symbols generally used within the knitting community but were tweaked to accommodate the unique stitch manipulations I present here. They are meant to make the chart look as much like your knitting as possible so you can easily differentiate one cable cross from another. By looking at a symbol, you can determine the direction of the cross, how the stitches were worked before the cable, and how they are worked as you are working the cable. There is a key to each symbol used in the chart on the same page for easy reference, so there is no need to memorize the details.

There are 3 basic parts of a cable symbol, as shown in the chart below.

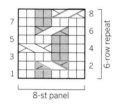

 Knit on RS, purl on WS. ☐ Purl on RS, knit on WS.

 2/2 RC (2 over 2 right cross): Slip 2 sts to cn, hold to back, k2, k2 from cn.

2/2 LC (2 over 2 left cross): Slip 2 sts to cn, hold to front, k2, k2 from cn.

2/2 RPC (2 over 2 right purl cross): Slip 2 sts to cn, hold to back, k2, p2 from cn.

2/2 LPC (2 over 2 left purl cross): Slip 2 sts to cn, hold to front, p2, k2 from cn.

Part A, outlined in red, is the most important part, since it shows you what the visible part of the cable will look like, and in which direction the cable will cross. This is a right-cross cable, where you will hold your cable needle to the back to work the cable. The stitches are worked as knit stitches.

The second most important part, Part B, shown in blue, is the portion of the cable that is worked behind the first part. Part B stitches will always be shown above the first diagonal line of Part A in a left-cross cable (like this one) or above the second diagonal line of Part A in a right-cross cable (like the cable at the top of the chart). Since the cable is crossing to the left, your cable needle will be held to the front to work the cable. These Part B stitches will be worked as purl stitches; the Part B stitches in the top cable will be worked as knit stitches.

Part C, shown in green, is not essential to how the cable is worked on the current row. Rather, it indicates how the stitches that will form the cable were worked on the preceding row. Part C stitches will always be shown below the diagonal section of Part A. In this example, the stitches were worked as purl stitches on the preceding row. For cables (like the one in this example) where you are taking purl stitches and crossing them to be worked as purl stitches on the opposite side of the cable (or crossing knits to knits as in the red-outlined cable), this part of the symbol won't be an important one to pay attention to. However, there will be instances where the stitches from the preceding row are all knit stitches (or all purl stitches, or some combination thereof), but you will work some or all of them differently when you cross the cable. Understanding that fact will enable you to a) verify that you are working the cable in the correct place in your knitting by reading the preceding row and matching it to the Part C stitches, and b) not wonder if there is an error in the cable. In other words, yes, you really are supposed to turn those knits into purls or vice versa. You can, if you'd like, ignore Part C of the symbol and just focus on Parts A and B, since those tell you what you actually need to do; Part C is just there to give you clarity. Note that unlike Part C, Part A will not tell you what the stitches were on the preceding row, only how they will be worked on the current row.

You will note that in some charts, there will be more than one symbol for the same cable cross. You will begin to see a few of these in Chapter 4, but the majority of them are in Chapters 5 and 6.

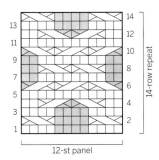

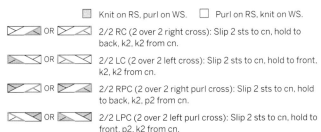

In the example above, there are two symbols for each of the cable crosses. Taking the first symbol (2/2 RC) as an example, note that in Part C on the right-hand symbol, the original stitches were knit stitches, whereas in the left-hand symbol, the stitches shown in Part C were purl stitches, so you will be crossing 2 purl stitches to the back to become 2 knit stitches. Compare the outlined Part C for each of the other symbol sets. This type of knit-to-purl or purl-to-knit cross is used often in line cables (see page 14) that are progressing across the fabric, rather than column cables, which just progress vertically.

Following are additional symbols that you will encounter. These give you an idea of the variety of ribbed cables included in this book. Some have the ribbing at the front of the cable, and some at the back. In some cases, ribs are crossed over ribs, and in others, ribs are crossed over knit or purl stitches. Again, pay close attention to the Part A and B stitches, but also note what the Part C stitches reveal about how the stitches were worked on the preceding row.

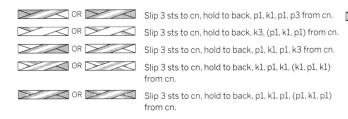

For some cable patterns, again mostly in Chapters 5 and 6, there are numerous symbols that are similar enough to each other that it might be hard to distinguish them while you're working the cable. In cases such as this, the cables are color-coded to make it easier to understand. Since it was essential to maintain the gray shading for purl stitches, only the Part A section of the cable, and only the knit stitches of that section, not the purls, are colored. As with the previous example, some of these cables have multiple symbols, depending on what the Part C stitches were on the previous row. Each version of the cable is colored the same, so you can just pay attention to the color and ignore the Part C section of the symbol if you choose. Also note that for each color, there are right-cross cables and left-cross cables. So for the green cables, the top symbol set is for *2/2 right* cross and the bottom symbol set is for *2/2 left* cross.

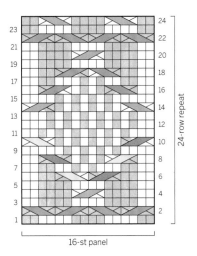

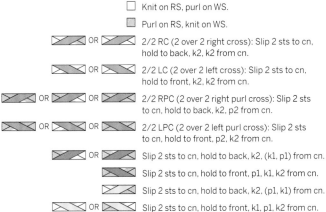

Stockinette Stitch Equivalent System (SSE)

I designed the 15 sweaters and accessories in this book so they can be knit as is, with the cable shown, or with a different cable of your choice. If the width of the cable shown and the one you are substituting are the same and they're both worked on the same number of stitches, then you're good to go. If the two cables have different widths, then you'll need to add or take away background stitches accordingly. If your garment ends up with a different number of stitches because of your cable choice (cables of the same width can have a different stitch count), you'll need to adjust your stitch count. Notes about how to handle this are included in the garment instructions.

To make mixing and matching cables easy, I developed a system called Stockinette Stitch Equivalent (SSE). A cable's SSE, which is included with the instructions, tells you how many stockinette stitches are needed to achieve the same width as the cable in any weight yarn. So, for example, if you want to make the Skirt on page 265 but you want to substitute O Knot Singles (#94) for Macramé (#145), you're good to go because you can see in the instructions that both have an SSE of 32. But let's say you want to substitute Elaborate Rib & Rope (#82), which has an SSE of 18. Even though they don't have the same SSE, you can make this work by adding 14 extra stockinette stitches in the background (7 on each side of the cable).

Here are a few more examples to show you how SSE works within this book:

- If the pattern uses a cable with an SSE of 9, you can substitute another cable with an SSE of 9, or use a cable with an SSE of 7 and add 2 background stitches, or you can use a cable with an SSE of 13 and take away 4 background stitches.

  In many of my garment patterns, a wide panel of cables is surrounded by stockinette stitch. If the cables you choose to knit have a lower SSE than the original cables, then you can add evenly to the existing stockinette stitch on either side to make up the difference. If the cables you choose are a bit wider than the original cable (they have a higher SSE), then you'll take away some stockinette stitches from each side. How much wider your chosen cable can be depends on the garment instructions, and in some cases on the size you are making. I've included some specific notes about this within each set of instructions.

- If the cable in the pattern has an SSE of 42, you can substitute a cable with an SSE of 14 + another cable with an SSE of 8, used twice (one on either side of the larger cable) + 12 background stitches (14 + 8 + 8 + 12 = 42). You might use 4 reverse stockinette stitches between the cables and add 2 reverse stockinette stitches at either end. Or you could add a 2 x 2 rib between the cables to use up the extra 12 stitches: smaller cable, p2, k2, p2, larger cable, p2, k2, p2, smaller cable again. The 2 x 2 rib gauge will not be exactly the same as the stockinette stitch gauge, but it will be close enough in this small space, especially since ribbing tends to stretch.

- Some cables have SSEs with a half stitch. Don't let this throw you. I included the fraction so the SSE would be as accurate as possible. But it's not a problem to be ½ or 1 stitch off thanks to knitting's natural stretchiness. If you are using only 1 cable, round up or down to the nearest whole number with confidence and don't fret if you need to add or subtract 1 more stitch to make things work out. (For instance, you may need an even number of stitches, but have an odd number, or vice versa.) When you're using a combination of several cables, wait until you've added all the SSEs together before rounding up or down.

If you want to use the cable stitch patterns in this book *in a project of your own design* rather than one from this book, here are some guidelines:

- Use the SSE to determine how wide the cable will be based on your stockinette stitch gauge. First work a gauge swatch in stockinette stitch, then divide the SSE by the gauge per inch (cm). For instance, Cruller Chevron (#115) has an SSE of 27.5; if your stockinette stitch gauge is 4½ stitches per inch (1.8 stitches per cm), then to find the width of Cruller Chevron in your yarn, divide 27.5 by 4½ = 6.11″ (27.5 ÷ 1.8 = 15.28 cm), which I would round to 6″ (15 cm).

When designing your own projects, remember that the SSE calculation is just a starting point. There may be other considerations. For instance, multiple cables separated by reverse stockinette stitch might begin to pull in like ribbing. In other words, you'll still need to swatch copiously.

If you want to use the cable stitch patterns in this book *in a project from another designer,* here are some guidelines:

- If your project instructions tell you both the stockinette stitch gauge and how wide the cable is supposed to be, you can calculate the SSE. For instance, if your project's stockinette stitch gauge is 5 stitches per inch (2 sts per cm) and the original cable has a width of 3½″ (9 cm), then the original cable has an SSE of 17.5 (18) [5 x 3½ = 17.5 (2 x 9 = 18)]. You can replace the original cable with any cable in this book that has an SSE of 17–18. Note that the SSE may differ slightly when calculating it in inches vs centimeters, but it likely won't differ by more than half a stitch, which is fine.

    If the pattern you're working from gives the cable gauge but not the stockinette stitch gauge, then you'll need to knit the cable to gauge to find the correct needle size first, then knit a stockinette swatch with that nee-

dle to determine the stockinette stitch gauge, before you can calculate the SSE. For example, if your pattern says that the original cable should be 5″ (12.5 cm) wide, and you find that a size 8 needle (5 mm) gives you the right width when you swatch the cable, you'll then knit a stockinette swatch on 8s to find the stockinette gauge. Say for instance that you find your stockinette gauge is 4½ sts per inch (1.8 sts per cm), then the SSE is 22½ because it would take 22.5 sts of stockinette to get the 5″ (12.5 cm) width of the original cable. [4½ x 5 = 22.5 (1.8 x 12.5 = 22.5)].

Troubleshooting

Swatching

Swatching is important when learning a new cable and trying out a cable and yarn combination. It is crucial for determining your gauge (stitches and rows per inch) before starting a project.

In the instructions for the projects in this book that are not worked entirely in a cable pattern(s), you will see that I give gauge information for both the cables and the background stitches. It is important to swatch both. And don't skimp. For background stitches, such as stockinette or reverse stockinette, make the swatches a minimum of 5″ (12.5 cm) square—the larger the swatch, the more accurate the gauge reading. For the cables, work one full width of a cable column or the number of stitches given in the gauge instructions for a larger cable pattern. Make a separate swatch for each stitch. Wash each swatch and lay it flat to dry; in other words, treat it like you will treat the finished knitted piece. Some yarns bloom (plump up and fill in) when washed and some (like superwash) tend to stretch out. If you skip this step, you may be unhappily surprised when you wash your finished project.

To fully realize the potential of any yarn or of any cable pattern, you have to test the possibilities. I find that the best surprises occur when I am testing the boundaries of what I think is possible. Don't think of swatching as a chore, but rather as an adventure in which you can make new discoveries and surprise yourself.

Fixing a Cable Crossed in the Wrong Direction

It happens. You mean to cross a cable in one direction (such as right to left) and you accidentally cross it in the opposite direction (meaning left to right). If you catch your mistake right away, while you are working the row, it's a simple matter of unknitting back to the error and making the correction. But if you don't see the error until later, the fix is a bit more complicated but still doable. Here are the methods I use:

- Rip back to the mistake and reknit. Either keep track of how many rows you rip out so you can find your place,

or figure out where you are by comparing your knitted fabric to the chart.

- To avoid having to reknit large portions of your project, drop down just the stitches involved in the mistake. This is a fairly advanced technique, but it's amazing how fast you can learn something new if it means not having to reknit half of a sweater front. Besides, you have nothing to lose by trying, since messing up means you have to rip back to the mistake, which you were going to do anyway. To do this, drop the stitches involved in the mistake by sliding them off of your needle and tugging them gently to make them run down, leaving a loose ladder. Patiently rework the dropped stitches row by row with the help of a spare needle. I work all of the rows from the right side, because it's easier to knit than purl with the small loop of yarn, and why bother to turn the piece over? If you've never picked up dropped stitches before, I suggest that you refer to your favorite basic knitting reference book or video. Note: This technique only works if the stitchwork above the cable you are correcting rips down freely, as it would if you were correcting a single cable cross in a simple 4-stitch cable column. If another cable cross was worked above the one you want to correct and included only some of the stitches you are trying to drop, you won't be able to drop down past that cable cross. This would be the case in a cable pattern that uses lines rather than columns (see page 14). You might have to rip out a cable or two on either side of the one that is incorrect, which would likely make it easier to just rip the entire piece down to the error.

When it's impossible to drop down, or when you can't bear the thought of ripping out or ripping down, there are three options, one advanced, one easy, and one easier.

- The advanced way involves clipping a stitch in the row above the offending cable, ripping back to the edge of the cable in both directions, then ripping out the cable row. Reknit the cable row with the ripped-out yarn. Once the cable cross is reknit, you have to use Kitch-

Here I worked duplicate stitch (in white so you can see it) to hide a miscrossed cable.

Use your fingertip to spread out rows between cable crosses to make them easier to count.

ener stitch to attach the new row of knitting to the row above it. I've done this a few times and I have to admit it's nerve-wracking. Finding the correct row to clip is difficult, and the number of stitches ripped back in each direction has to be big enough to leave an end that can be securely woven in later.

- The easy option, my favorite trick for correcting a wrongly turned cable, is to fake it with a row or two of duplicate stitch worked over the top (see above). The duplicate stitch lies across of the top of the incorrect cross, masking it and making it appear as if the cable is crossed correctly.

- The final option is to leave the mistake and not worry about it.

Counting Rows Between Cable Crosses

If you are like me and are not good at keeping track in your head of how many rows you've worked after you've made a cable cross, it's helpful to know how to count them. At the point where your cable crosses, there is always a small hole. For some reason the hole tends to be larger on the left side of the cable for most people, so that's the

hole I use in my counting technique. I put a finger into the opening from the back of my knitting, then use the same finger to open the ladders above the hole so I can more easily count the ladders. When counting ladders, the first one is the cable crossing and then each remaining ladder is a row worked after the crossing. So, if you count 7 rows above the hole as in the photo above, you've worked the cable row + 6 more rows.

Chapter 2

Basics
Ropes, Braids, and Horseshoes

For this chapter I chose familiar cables in narrow columns: basic ropes with one twist repeated every few rows; braids, where the alternation of cables mimics a plait of hair; and horseshoes formed by placing two mirrored columns side by side. I then varied these cables by adding twists; swapping out stitches; incorporating openwork; adjusting stitch placement to reveal new shapes; playing with mirrored sections; and combining different cables.

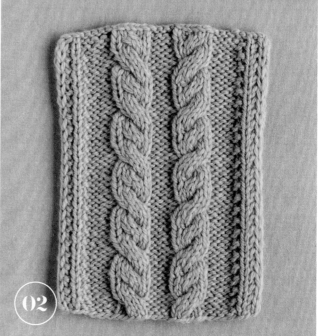

Basic 3/3 Rope GROUP 1

The 2 cables shown on this swatch are both Basic 3/3 Ropes. The one on the left twists to the left and the one on the right twists to the right. Often mirrored cables are placed on each side of a wider panel of cables. This all-stockinette 6-stitch cable is very useful on its own, or as a bold and easy separator between more complicated columns. The version shown here crosses every 8 rows for a classic look. You may want to experiment with crossing every 6, 10, or 12 rows. There are no rules for the perfect number of rows between crosses. The choice depends on personal preference based upon the yarn and the stitches around your cable.

LEFT CROSS
(panel of 6 sts; 8-row repeat)
SSE: 5.5 sts

ROW 1 AND ALL WS ROWS (WS): Purl.
ROW 2: Knit.
ROW 4: 3/3 LC.
ROWS 6 AND 8: Knit.
Repeat Rows 1–8 for pattern.

RIGHT CROSS
(panel of 6 sts; 8-row repeat)
SSE: 5.5 sts

ROW 1 AND ALL WS ROWS (WS): Purl.
ROW 2: Knit.
ROW 4: 3/3 RC.
ROWS 6 AND 8: Knit.
Repeat Rows 1–8 for pattern.

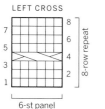

Knit on RS, purl on WS.

3/3 RC (3 over 3 right cross): Slip 3 sts to cn, hold to back, k3, k3 from cn.

3/3 LC (3 over 3 left cross): Slip 3 sts to cn, hold to front, k3, k3 from cn.

Cable Center 3/3 GROUP 1

This cable differs from Basic 3/3 (#1) because I've added a 2/2 cable in the center where it was previously only stockinette stitch.

LEFT CROSS
(panel of 6 sts; 8-row repeat)
SSE: 5 sts

ROW 1 AND ALL WS ROWS (WS): Purl.
ROW 2: Knit.
ROW 4: 3/3 LC.
ROW 6: Knit.
ROW 8: K1, 2/2 LC, k1.
Repeat Rows 1–8 for pattern.

RIGHT CROSS
(panel of 6 sts; 8-row repeat)
SSE: 5 sts

ROW 1 AND ALL WS ROWS (WS): Purl.
ROW 2: Knit.
ROW 4: 3/3 RC.
ROW 6: Knit.
ROW 8: K1, 2/2 RC, k1.
Repeat Rows 1–8 for pattern.

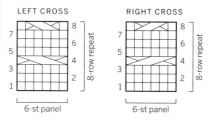

Knit on RS, purl on WS.

2/2 RC (2 over 2 right cross): Slip 2 sts to cn, hold to back, k2, k2 from cn.

2/2 LC (2 over 2 left cross): Slip 2 sts to cn, hold to front, k2, k2 from cn.

3/3 RC (3 over 3 right cross): Slip 3 sts to cn, hold to back, k3, k3 from cn.

3/3 LC (3 over 3 left cross): Slip 3 sts to cn, hold to front, k3, k3 from cn.

Rib Twist 3/3 GROUP 1

Substituting ribbing for stockinette stitch is one of the basic tenets of my cable explorations. In this version of Basic 3/3 Rope (#1), a twisted knit, flanked by a purl on each side, takes the place of 3 stockinette stitches. I've found that twisting the rib stitches gives a consistently attractive result; of course, you can work the rib without twisting the stitches. I think the latter looks good when the yarn is round or bulky; otherwise the stitches tend to splay out and appear messy.

LEFT CROSS
(panel of 6 sts; 8-row repeat)
SSE: 5 sts

ROW 1 AND ALL WS ROWS (WS):
K1, p1-tbl, k2, p1-tbl, k1.
ROW 2: P1, k1-tbl, p2, k1-tbl, p1.
ROW 4: Slip 3 sts to cn, hold to front, p1, k1-tbl, p1, (p1, k1-tbl, p1) from cn.
ROWS 6 AND 8: Repeat Row 2.
Repeat Rows 1–8 for pattern.

RIGHT CROSS
(panel of 6 sts; 8-row repeat)
SSE: 5 sts

ROW 1 AND ALL WS ROWS (WS):
K1, p1-tbl, k2, p1-tbl, k1.
ROW 2: P1, k1-tbl, p2, k1-tbl, p1.
ROW 4: Slip 3 sts to cn, hold to back, p1, k1-tbl, p1, (p1, k1-tbl, p1) from cn.
ROWS 6 AND 8: Repeat Row 2.
Repeat Rows 1–8 for pattern.

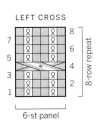

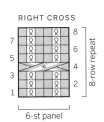

☐ Knit on RS, purl on WS.   ☐ Purl on RS, knit on WS.
☑ K1-tbl on RS, p1-tbl on WS.

Slip 3 sts to cn, hold to back, p1, k1-tbl, p1, (p1, k1-tbl, p1) from cn.

Slip 3 sts to cn, hold to front, p1, k1-tbl, p1, (p1, k1-tbl, p1) from cn.

Mini Twist 3/3 GROUP 1

This cable takes 2 leaps forward from Basic 3/3 Rope (#1). First, I substituted k1, p1, k1 for each group of 3 stockinette stitches. Then, halfway between the main twists, I added a smaller twist (worked without a cable needle) to give the center definition.

LEFT CROSS
(panel of 6 sts; 8-row repeat)
SSE: 5 sts

ROW 1 (WS): P1, k1, p2, k1, p1.
ROWS 2 AND 3: Knit the knit sts and purl the purl sts as they face you.
ROW 4: Slip 3 sts to cn, hold to front, k1, p1, k1, (k1, p1, k1) from cn.
ROWS 5–7: Repeat Row 2.
ROW 8: K1, p1, LT, p1, k1.
Repeat Rows 1–8 for pattern.

RIGHT CROSS
(panel of 6 sts; 8-row repeat)
SSE: 5 sts

ROW 1 (WS): P1, k1, p2, k1, p1.
ROWS 2 AND 3: Knit the knit sts and purl the purl sts as they face you.
ROW 4: Slip 3 sts to cn, hold to back, k1, p1, k1, (k1, p1, k1) from cn.
ROWS 5–7: Repeat Row 2.
ROW 8: K1, p1, RT, p1, k1.
Repeat Rows 1–8 for pattern.

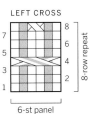

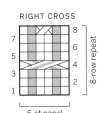

☐ Knit on RS, purl on WS.   ☐ Purl on RS, knit on WS.

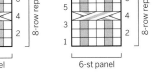 RT (right twist): K2tog, but do not drop sts from left needle; insert right needle between 2 sts just worked and knit first st again, slip both sts from left needle together.

LT (left twist): Insert needle from back to front between first and second sts on left needle and knit the second st through the front loop; knit first st, slip both sts from left needle together.

Slip 3 sts to cn, hold to front, k1, p1, k1, (k1, p1, k1) from cn.

Slip 3 sts to cn, hold to back, k1, p1, k1, (k1, p1, k1) from cn.

Broken Mini Twist 3/3 GROUP 1

Breaking the line formed by the outside rib of Mini Twist 3/3 (#4) leaves an interesting X shape. To give the Xs enough room, I skipped every other big cross, replacing it with smaller twists.

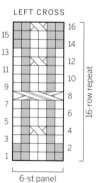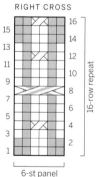

LEFT CROSS
(panel of 6 sts; 16-row repeat)
SSE: 5 sts

ROW 1 (WS): K2, p2, k2.
ROW 2: Knit the knit sts and purl the purl sts as they face you.
ROW 3: P1, k1, p2, k1, p1.
ROW 4: K1, p1, LT, p1, k1.
ROWS 5–7: Repeat Row 2.
ROW 8: Slip 3 sts to cn, hold to front, k1, p1, k1, (k1, p1, k1) from cn.
ROWS 9–11: Repeat Row 2.
ROW 12: Repeat row 4.
ROW 13: Repeat row 2.
ROW 14: P2, k2, p2.
ROW 15: Repeat Row 2.
ROW 16: P2, LT, p2.
Repeat Rows 1–16 for pattern.

RIGHT CROSS
(panel of 6 sts; 16-row repeat)
SSE: 5 sts

ROW 1 (WS): K2, p2, k2.
ROW 2: Knit the knit sts and purl the purl sts as they face you.
ROW 3: P1, k1, p2, k1, p1.
ROW 4: K1, p1, RT, p1, k1.
ROWS 5–7: Repeat Row 2.
ROW 8: Slip 3 sts to cn, hold to back, k1, p1, k1, (k1, p1, k1) from cn.
ROWS 9–11: Repeat Row 2.
ROW 12: Repeat row 4.
ROW 13: Repeat row 2.
ROW 14: P2, k2, p2.
ROW 15: Repeat Row 2.
ROW 16: P2, RT, p2.
Repeat Rows 1–16 for pattern.

□ Knit on RS, purl on WS. ▨ Purl on RS, knit on WS.

⧄ RT (right twist): K2tog, but do not drop sts from left needle; insert right needle between 2 sts just worked and knit first st again, slip both sts from left needle together.

⧅ LT (left twist): Insert needle from back to front between first and second sts on left needle and knit the second st through the front loop; knit first st, slip both sts from left needle

⧄ Slip 3 sts to cn, hold to back, k1, p1, k1, (k1, p1, k1) from cn.together.

⧅ Slip 3 sts to cn, hold to front, k1, p1, k1, (k1, p1, k1) from cn.

Purl Center 2-Step GROUP 2

All of the cables up to this point have been 6-stitch cables worked by crossing 3 stitches over 3 stitches. Another way to make a 6-stitch cable is to cross 2 sts over 2 sts twice (over 2 right-side rows). This cable starts with 2 x 2 rib (before the cable crosses). I could have started with stockinette stitch, which would look similar, but I think using rib is better because it has more depth.

LEFT CROSS
(panel of 6 sts; 6-row repeat)
SSE: 5 sts

ROW 1 (WS): P2, k2, p2.
ROW 2: K2, p2, k2.
ROW 3: Repeat Row 1.
ROW 4: 2/2 LC, k2.
ROW 5: Purl.
ROW 6: K2, 2/2 LPC.
Repeat Rows 1–6 for pattern.

RIGHT CROSS
(panel of 6 sts; 6-row repeat)
SSE: 5 sts

ROW 1 (WS): P2, k2, p2.
ROW 2: K2, p2, k2.
ROW 3: Repeat Row 1.
ROW 4: K2, 2/2 RC.
ROW 5: Purl.
ROW 6: 2/2 RPC, k2.
Repeat Rows 1–6 for pattern.

LEFT CROSS / RIGHT CROSS charts, 6-st panel, 6-row repeat.

□ Knit on RS, purl on WS.   ▨ Purl on RS, knit on WS.

2/2 RC (2 over 2 right cross): Slip 2 sts to cn, hold to back, k2, k2 from cn.

2/2 LC (2 over 2 left cross): Slip 2 sts to cn, hold to front, k2, k2 from cn.

2/2 RPC (2 over 2 right purl cross): Slip 2 sts to cn, hold to back, k2, p2 from cn.

2/2 LPC (2 over 2 left purl cross): Slip 2 sts to cn, hold to front, p2, k2 from cn.

Eyelet 2-Step GROUP 2

In this variation of the Purl Center 2-Step (#6), large eyelets replace reverse stockinette stitch. The double yarnovers and their companion decreases used to create the eyelets are worked on the wrong side so they appear centered vertically within the cable crossing without interfering with it.

LEFT CROSS
(panel of 6 sts; 6-row repeat)
SSE: 5 sts

ROW 1 (WS): Purl.
ROW 2: 2/2 LC, k2.
ROW 3: Purl.
ROW 4: K2, 2/2 LC.
ROW 5: P1, p2tog, yo2, ssp, p1.
ROW 6: K2, (k1, p1) into yo2, k2.
Repeat Rows 1–6 for pattern.

RIGHT CROSS
(panel of 6 sts; 6-row repeat)
SSE: 5 sts

ROW 1 (WS): Purl.
ROW 2: K2, 2/2 RC.
ROW 3: Purl.
ROW 4: 2/2 RC, k2.
ROW 5: P1, p2tog, yo2, ssp, p1.
ROW 6: K2, (k1, p1) into yo2, k2.
Repeat Rows 1–6 for pattern.

LEFT CROSS / RIGHT CROSS charts, 6-st panel, 6-row repeat.

□ Knit on RS, purl on WS.

○○ Yo2

☒ K2tog on RS, p2tog on WS.

⊠ Ssk on RS, ssp on WS.

▨ (K1, p1) into yo2.

2/2 RC (2 over 2 right cross): Slip 2 sts to cn, hold to back, k2, k2 from cn.

2/2 LC (2 over 2 left cross): Slip 2 sts to cn, hold to front, k2, k2 from cn.

Basic 4/4 Rope GROUP 3

I like the proportions of this bold cable, where the crosses are worked every 12th row. You can easily extend it by crossing every 14 rows or even every 16 rows or more. Many designers like to coordinate the row repeats of different cables within a garment so they have common multiples. For example, cables that repeat every 6th row, every 8th row and every 12th row all have 24 rows as the common multiple. The 6-row pattern repeats 4 times within 24 rows, the 8-row cable repeats 3 times, and the 12-row cable repeats twice. That way, the knitter can think of all of the cables combined as a 24-row repeat. The next 4 swatches show how switching out the stockinette stitches on each side of the cable with other stitches opens up new possibilities. For more about stitch substitutions, see page 42.

(panel of 8 sts; 12-row repeat)
SSE: 7 sts

ROW 1 AND ALL WS ROWS (WS): Purl.
ROWS 2 AND 4: Knit.
ROW 6: 4/4 RC.
ROWS 8, 10, AND 12: Knit.
Repeat Rows 1–12 for pattern.

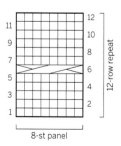

8-st panel

☐ Knit on RS, purl on WS.

4/4 RC (4 over 4 right cross): Slip 4 sts to cn, hold to back, k4, k4 from cn.

Rib 4/4 GROUP 3

In this variation of the Basic 4/4 Rope (#8), 4 stitches again cross over 4 stitches, but this time a 2-stitch rib is flanked by a purl on each side, automatically forming a carved-out center and giving the cross a lot of dimension.

LEFT CROSS
(panel of 8 sts; 12-row repeat)
SSE: 7 sts

ROW 1 (WS): K1, p2, k2, p2, k1.
ROWS 2–5: Knit the knit sts and purl the purl sts as they face you.
ROW 6: Slip 4 sts to cn, hold to front, p1, k2, p1, (p1, k2, p1) from cn.
ROWS 7–12: Repeat Row 2.
Repeat Rows 1–12 for pattern.

RIGHT CROSS
(panel of 8 sts; 12-row repeat)
SSE: 7 sts

ROW 1 (WS): K1, p2, k2, p2, k1.
ROWS 2–5: Knit the knit sts and purl the purl sts as they face you.
ROW 6: Slip 4 sts to cn, hold to back, p1, k2, p1, (p1, k2, p1) from cn.
ROWS 7–12: Repeat Row 2.
Repeat Rows 1–12 for pattern.

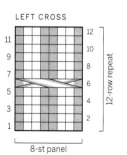

LEFT CROSS   RIGHT CROSS

8-st panel   8-st panel

☐ Knit on RS, purl on WS.

▨ Purl on RS, knit on WS.

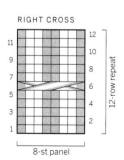

Slip 4 sts to cn, hold to back, p1, k2, p1, (p1, k2, p1) from cn.

Slip 4 sts to cn, hold to front, p1, k2, p1, (p1, k2, p1) from cn.

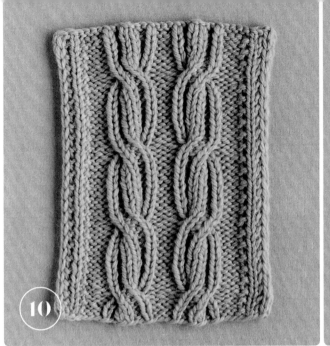
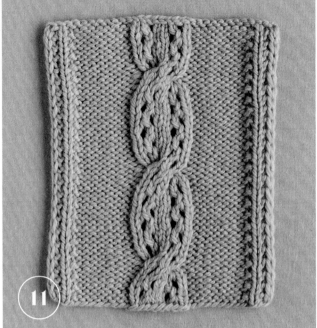

Reverse Rib 4/4 GROUP 3

This is the "wrong" side of Rib 4/4 (#9). It has 8 stitches. If you think of it as having 2 identical vertical halves, you can see that each of those halves is k1, p2, k1. The 2 halves cross each other every 12 rows. The single knit outlines the cable while 2 knits come together to form a solid center. These 2 stitches are fair game for twisting again. For an example of how these twists work, see Twist 1/1 Travel Share (#77).

LEFT CROSS
(panel of 8 sts; 12-row repeat)
SSE: 7 sts

ROW 1 (WS): P1, k2, p2, k2, p1.
ROWS 2–5: Knit the knit sts and purl the purl sts as they face you.
ROW 6: Slip 4 sts to cn, hold to front, k1, p2, k1, (k1, p2, k1) from cn.
ROWS 7–12: Repeat Row 2.
Repeat Rows 1–12 for pattern.

RIGHT CROSS
(panel of 8 sts; 12-row repeat)
SSE: 7 sts

ROW 1 (WS): P1, k2, p2, k2, p1.
ROWS 2–5: Knit the knit sts and purl the purl sts as they face you.
ROW 6: Slip 4 sts to cn, hold to back, k1, p2, k1, (k1, p2, k1) from cn.
ROWS 7–12: Repeat Row 2.
Repeat Rows 1–12 for pattern.

Lace 4/4 GROUP 3

A simple lace pattern takes the place of stockinette stitch in this variation of Basic 4/4 Rope (#8). I purposely chose a lace pattern with an all-purl resting row to simplify the knitting. I added a few more rows between the cable crosses so the eyelets would open up and could be seen clearly.

(panel of 8 sts; 16-row repeat)
SSE: 8 sts
ROW 1 AND ALL WS ROWS (WS): Purl.
ROW 2: K1, k2tog, yo, k2, k2tog, yo, k1.
ROW 4: K1, yo, ssk, k2, yo, ssk, k1.

ROW 6: Repeat Row 2.
ROW 8: Slip 4 sts to cn, hold to back, k1, yo, ssk, k1, (k1, yo, ssk, k1) from cn.
ROWS 9–16: Repeat Rows 1–4 twice.
Repeat Rows 1–10 for pattern.

LEFT CROSS
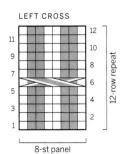
8-st panel

RIGHT CROSS
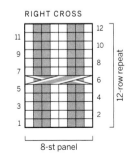
8-st panel

☐ Knit on RS, purl on WS.

▨ Purl on RS, knit on WS.

▱ Slip 4 sts to cn, hold to back, k1, p2, k1, (k1, p2, k1) from cn.

▱ Slip 4 sts to cn, hold to front, k1, p2, k1, (k1, p2, k1) from cn.

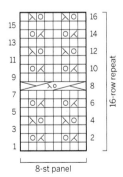
8-st panel

☐ Knit on RS, purl on WS.

⊡ Yo

⊠ K2tog on RS

⊠ Ssk on RS

▱ Slip 4 sts to cn, hold to back, k1, yo, ssk, k1, (k1, yo, ssk, k1) from cn.

Basic Flat Braid GROUP 4

Two-over-two crosses are used to make this flat yet well-defined braid. The full crossing happens in 2 subsequent right-side rows, which means that the original 2 stitches move over 4 stitches. Switching out the stitches in the center yields the ribbed or punctured versions coming up next.

(panel of 8 sts; 8-row repeat)
SSE: 7 sts

ROW 1 AND ALL WS ROWS (WS): Purl.
ROW 2: K2, 2/2 LC, k2.
ROW 4: K4, 2/2 LC.
ROW 6: K2, 2/2 RC, k2.
ROW 8: 2/2 RC, k4.
Repeat Rows 1–8 for pattern.

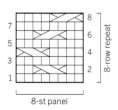

8-st panel

8-row repeat

☐ Knit on RS, purl on WS.

2/2 RC (2 over 2 right cross): Slip 2 sts to cn, hold to back, k2, k2 from cn.

2/2 LC (2 over 2 left cross): Slip 2 sts to cn, hold to front, k2, k2 from cn.

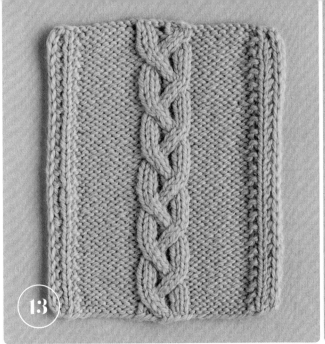

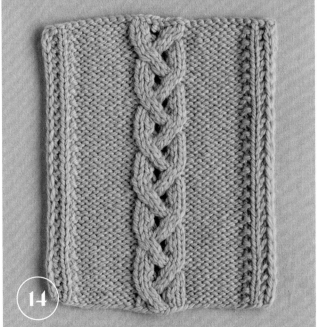

Purl Center Flat Braid GROUP 4

As in Purl Center 2-Step (#6), as the stitches are slipped onto and worked off of the cable needles, they sometimes switch from reverse stockinette to stockinette (or vice versa). The switch is hidden by the stitches passing over the top at the point where the cross happens. The receding purls make the stitches of the braid appear to be raised from the background, almost as if they have been carved with a chisel. This cable looks especially nice on the wrong side (see page 51).

(panel of 8 sts; 8-row repeat)
SSE: 7 sts

ROW 1 (WS): P2, k2, p4.
ROW 2: K2, 2/2 LPC, k2.
ROW 3 AND ALL FOLLOWING WS ROWS: Knit the knit sts and purl the purl sts as they face you.

ROW 4: K2, p2, 2/2 LC.
ROW 6: K2, 2/2 RPC, k2.
ROW 8: 2/2 RC, p2, k2.
Repeat Rows 1–8 for pattern.

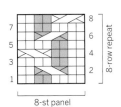

☐ Knit on RS, purl on WS.   ▨ Purl on RS, knit on WS.

⬋ 2/2 RC (2 over 2 right cross): Slip 2 sts to cn, hold to back, k2, k2 from cn.

⬊ 2/2 LC (2 over 2 left cross): Slip 2 sts to cn, hold to front, k2, k2 from cn.

⬋ 2/2 RPC (2 over 2 right purl cross): Slip 2 sts to cn, hold to back, k2, p2 from cn.

⬊ 2/2 LPC (2 over 2 left purl cross): Slip 2 sts to cn, hold to front, p2, k2 from cn.

Open Flat Braid GROUP 4

The addition of double yarnovers forms open centers in this variation of Basic Flat Braid (#12). These yarnovers and their companion decreases are worked on wrong-side rows. The decreases may be a bit more difficult to manipulate on the wrong side, but it's worth it to avoid having to work cable twists and decreases simultaneously on the right side.

(panel of 8 sts; 8-row repeat)
SSE: 7 sts

ROW 1 (WS): Purl.
ROW 2: K2, 2/2 LC, k2.
ROW 3: P3, ssp, yo2, p2tog, p1.
ROW 4: K2, (k1, p1) into yo2, 2/2 LC.

ROW 5: Purl.
ROW 6: K2, 2/2 RC, k2.
ROW 7: P1, ssp, yo2, p2tog, p3.
ROW 8: 2/2 RC, (k1, p1) into yo2, k2.
Repeat Rows 1–8 for pattern.

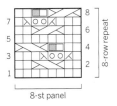

☐ Knit on RS, purl on WS.

○○ Yo2

☒ K2tog on RS, p2tog on WS.

⊠ Ssk on RS, ssp on WS.

▭ (K1, p1) into yo2.

⬋ 2/2 RC (2 over 2 right cross): Slip 2 sts to cn, hold to back, k2, k2 from cn.

⬊ 2/2 LC (2 over 2 left cross): Slip 2 sts to cn, hold to front, k2, k2 from cn.

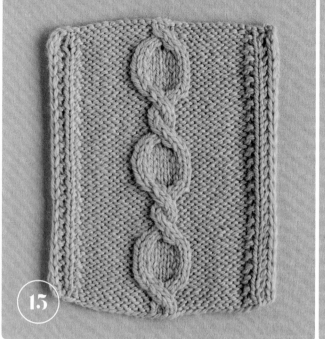

Basic Globe GROUP 5

Here we begin to see how versatile working with 2/2 crosses can be. Not only can they form simple ropes and straight lines, they can also make rounded shapes.

(panel of 8 sts; 16-row repeat)
SSE: 7 sts

ROW 1 (WS): K2, p4, k2.
ROW 2: P2, k4, p2.
ROW 3 AND ALL FOLLOWING WS ROWS: Knit the knit sts and purl the purl sts as they face you.

ROW 4: P2, 2/2 LC, p2.
ROW 6: 2/2 RC, 2/2 LC.
ROWS 8, 10, AND 12: Knit.
ROW 14: 2/2 LPC, 2/2 RPC.
ROW 16: Repeat Row 4.
Repeat Rows 1–16 for pattern.

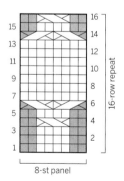

8-st panel

Knit on RS, purl on WS.

Purl on RS, knit on WS.

2/2 RC (2 over 2 right cross): Slip 2 sts to cn, hold to back, k2, k2 from cn.

OR 2/2 LC (2 over 2 left cross): Slip 2 sts to cn, hold to front, k2, k2 from cn.

2/2 RPC (2 over 2 right purl cross): Slip 2 sts to cn, hold to back, k2, p2 from cn.

2/2 LPC (2 over 2 left purl cross): Slip 2 sts to cn, hold to front, p2, k2 from cn.

Lace Globe GROUP 5

A few openwork stitches make this variation of Basic Globe (#15) ideal for laceweight or summer yarns. For more examples of openwork cables worked in alternate yarns, see page 95.

(panel of 8 sts; 18-row repeat)
SSE: 7 sts

ROW 1 AND ALL WS ROWS (WS): Purl.
ROW 2: K1, ssk, yo, k2, yo, k2tog, k1.
ROW 4: 2/2 LC, 2/2 RC.
ROW 6: Ssk, yo, 2/2 LC, yo, k2tog.
ROW 8: Ssk, yo, k4, yo, k2tog.

ROW 10: Repeat Row 6.
ROW 12: 2/2 RC, 2/2 LC.
ROWS 14, 16, AND 18: K1, ssk, yo, k2, yo, k2tog, k1.
Repeat Rows 1–18 for pattern.

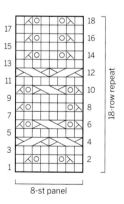

8-st panel

Knit on RS, purl on WS.

Yo

K2tog on RS, p2tog on WS.

Ssk on RS, ssp on WS.

2/2 RC (2 over 2 right cross): Slip 2 sts to cn, hold to back, k2, k2 from cn.

2/2 LC (2 over 2 left cross): Slip 2 sts to cn, hold to front, k2, k2 from cn.

(17)

Globe Braid GROUP 5

When I started working on this book I explored a lot of different cable ideas by swatching on a continuous piece of fabric (rather than binding off after each new cable and then casting on with new yarn for the next). Basic Globe (#15) serendipitously landed above a tightly braided cable, and I loved the way the two looked together. I decided not to feature the tightly braided cable on its own, but you can easily do that by following Rows 12–15 of this chart.

(panel of 8 sts; 28-row repeat)
SSE: 7 sts

ROW 1 (WS): K2, p4, k2.

ROW 2: P2, k4, p2.

ROW 3 AND ALL FOLLOWING WS ROWS: Knit the knit sts and purl the purl sts as they face you.

ROW 4: P2, 2/2 LC, p2.

ROW 6: 2/2 RC, 2/2 LC.

ROWS 8 AND 10: Knit.

ROW 12: K2, 2/2 LC, k2.

ROW 14: [2/2 RC] twice.

ROWS 16–19: Repeat Rows 12–15.

ROW 20: Repeat Row 12.

ROWS 22 AND 24: Knit.

ROW 26: 2/2 LPC, 2/2 RPC.

ROW 28: P2, 2/2 LC, p2.
Repeat Rows 1–28 for pattern.

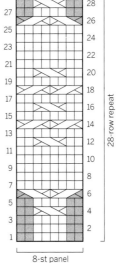

8-st panel

28-row repeat

☐ Knit on RS, purl on WS.

▨ Purl on RS, knit on WS.

OR 2/2 RC (2 over 2 right cross): Slip 2 sts to cn, hold to back, k2, k2 from cn.

OR 2/2 LC (2 over 2 left cross): Slip 2 sts to cn, hold to front, k2, k2 from cn.

 2/2 RPC (2 over 2 right purl cross): Slip 2 sts to cn, hold to back, k2, p2 from cn.

 2/2 LPC (2 over 2 left purl cross): Slip 2 sts to cn, hold to front, p2, k2 from cn.

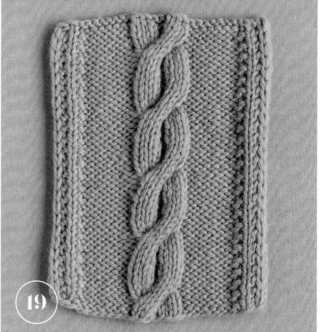

Large 2-Step GROUP 6

The gracious carved-out swoops of this cable are formed simply by crossing 3 stitches over 3 stitches, 2 times, in a line. The more stitches you cross, the deeper and more carved out the cable becomes.

(panel of 9 sts; 10-row repeat)
SSE: 8 sts

ROW 1 AND ALL WS ROWS (WS): Purl.
ROW 2: Knit.
ROW 4: K3, 3/3 RC.
ROW 6: 3/3 RC, k3.
ROWS 8 AND 10: Knit.
Repeat Rows 1–10 for pattern.

Large Purl Center 2-Step GROUP 6

Here I added reverse stockinette stitch to the center of Large 2-Step (#18) to create even more depth. You might also think of this cable as being born out of 3 x 3 ribbing because before you make any cable crosses, your swatch will be a 3 x 3 rib. Check out the reverse side of this pattern on page 51.

(panel of 9 sts; 10-row repeat)
SSE: 7 sts

ROW 1 (WS): P3, k3, p3.
ROW 2: K3, p3, k3.
ROW 3 AND ALL FOLLOWING WS ROWS:
Knit the knit sts and purl the purl sts as they face you.
ROW 4: K3, 3/3 RC.
ROW 6: 3/3 RPC, k3.
ROWS 8 AND 10: Repeat Row 2.
Repeat Rows 1–10 for pattern.

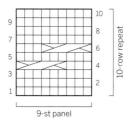

9-st panel

10-row repeat

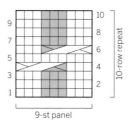

9-st panel

10-row repeat

☐ Knit on RS, purl on WS.

▨ Purl on RS, knit on WS.

⬦ 3/3 RC (3 over 3 right cross): Slip 3 sts to cn, hold to back, k3, k3 from cn.

⬦ 3/3 RPC (3 over 3 right purl cross): Slip 3 sts to cn, hold to back, k3, p3 from cn.

☐ Knit on RS, purl on WS.

⬦ 3/3 RC (3 over 3 right cross): Slip 3 sts to cn, hold to back, k3, k3 from cn.

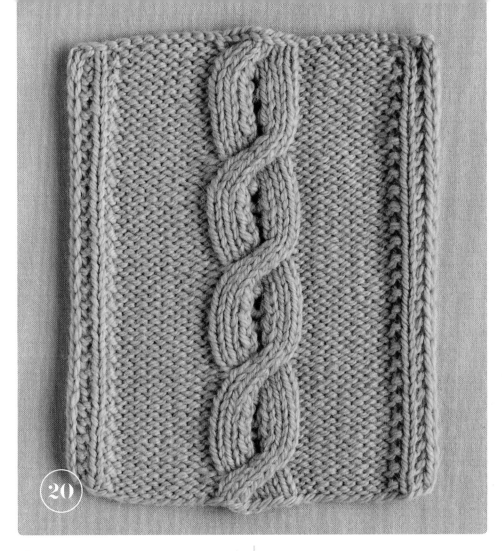

Ladder 2-Step GROUP 6

This very open variation of Large 2-Step (#18) has several rows of double yarnovers and their companion decreases. The open stitches are worked on wrong-side rows to keep the cable crosses simple. Watch the key carefully. This is the first cable in which the number of stitches crossing each other is not equal. In this case, you are crossing 3 stitches over 2 stitches on Row 6.

(panel of 8 sts; 12-row repeat)

SSE: 7 sts

ROW 1 (WS): Purl.
ROW 2: Knit.
ROW 3: Purl.
ROW 4: K2, 3/3 RC.
ROW 5: Purl.
ROW 6: 3/2 RC, k3.
ROW 7: P2, ssp, yo2, p2tog, p2.
ROW 8: K3, (k1, p1) into yo2, k3.
ROWS 9–12: Repeat Rows 7 and 8.
Repeat Rows 1–12 for pattern.

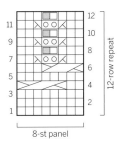

12-row repeat

8-st panel

☐ Knit on RS, purl on WS.

▢▢ Yo2

▭ (K1, p1) into yo2.

☒ K2tog on RS, p2tog on WS.

☒ Ssk on RS, ssp on WS.

▱ 3/2 RC (3 over 2 right cross): Slip 2 sts to cn, hold to back, k3, k2 from cn.

▱ 3/3 RC (3 over 3 right cross): Slip 3 sts to cn, hold to back, k3, k3 from cn.

(21)

Garter Fill 3-Step GROUP 7

While appearing very similar in form and size to the Large 2-Step (#18), this variation takes 3 cable crosses to get where it's going. Four stitches, composed of 2 garter stitches flanked by stockinette stitch, travel. The garter is worked on wrong-side rows to keep the cable crosses themselves easy.

(panel of 10 sts; 12-row repeat)
SSE: 8.5 sts

ROW 1 (WS): [P1, k2] 3 times, p1.
ROW 2: K4, p2, k4.
ROWS 3 AND 4: Repeat Rows 1 and 2.
ROW 5: Repeat Row 1.
ROW 6: K4, 4/2 RC.

ROW 7: P1, k1, p1, k2, p2, k2, p1.
ROW 8: K2, 4/2 RC, k2.
ROW 9: P1, k2, p2, k2, p1, k1, p1.
ROW 10: 4/2 RPC, k4.
ROWS 11 AND 12: Repeat Rows 1 and 2.
Repeat Rows 1–12 for pattern.

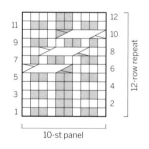

10-st panel

12-row repeat

☐ Knit on RS, purl on WS.

▨ Purl on RS, knit on WS.

4/2 RC (4 over 2 right cross): Slip 2 sts to cn, hold to back, k4, k2 from cn.

4/2 RPC (4 over 2 right purl cross): Slip 2 sts to cn, hold to back, k4, p2 from cn.

(22)

Twist 3-Step GROUP 7

This cable provides an introduction to one of my favorite concepts: using a mini cable and flanking purls as the 4 stitches to be placed on the cable needle. Alternating stockinette stitch with the mini cable shows off the little twisted columns by contrasting skinny versus wide, flat versus dimensional.

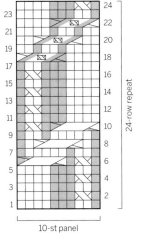

24-row repeat

10-st panel

(panel of 10 sts; 24-row repeat)
SSE: 7 sts

ROW 1 (WS): P4, k3, p2, k1.

ROW 2: P1, LT, p3, k4.

ROW 3 AND ALL FOLLOWING WS ROWS: Knit the knit sts and purl the purl sts as they face you.

ROW 4: Repeat Row 2.

ROW 6: P1, LT, p1; slip 2 sts to cn, hold to back, k4, (k1, p1) from cn.

ROW 8: P1, k1; slip 2 sts to cn, hold to back, k4, (p1, k1) from cn, k1, p1.

ROW 10: Slip 2 sts to cn, hold to back, k4, p2 from cn; p1, LT, p1.

ROWS 12, 14, AND 16: K4, p3, LT, p1.

ROW 18: K4; slip 2 sts to cn, hold to back, p1, LT, p1, k2 from cn.

ROW 20: K2; slip 2 sts to cn, hold to back, p1, LT, p1, k2 from cn; k2.

ROW 22: Slip 2 sts to cn, hold to back, p1, LT, p1, p2 from cn; k4.

ROW 24: P1, LT, p3, k4.

Repeat Rows 1–24 for pattern.

☐ Knit on RS, purl on WS.

▨ Purl on RS, knit on WS.

⧄ LT (left twist): Insert needle from back to front between first and second sts on left needle and knit the second st through the front loop; knit first st, slip both sts from left needle together.

⧄⧄⧄ Slip 2 sts to cn, hold to back, k4, (k1, p1) from cn.

⧄⧄⧄ Slip 2 sts to cn, hold to back, k4, (p1, k1) from cn.

⧄⧄⧄ 4/2 RPC (4 over 2 right purl cross): Slip 2 sts to cn, hold to back, k4, p2 from cn.

 OR ⧄⧄⧄ Slip 2 sts to cn, hold to back, p1, LT, p1, k2 from cn.

⧄⧄⧄ Slip 2 sts to cn, hold to back, p1, LT, p1, p2 from cn.

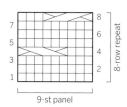

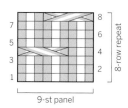

Basic 3/3/3 Braid GROUP 8

In this basic cable, 3 sets of stitches interweave just like a braid of hair. This is a classic stitch that's easy to vary by making substitutions as shown in #24–#26. For more flexibility, you can also make versions crossing groups of 2, 4, or more stitches. Play with the distance between the crosses to get a look you like.

(panel of 9 sts; 8-row repeat)
SSE: 7 sts

ROW 1 AND ALL WS ROWS: Purl.
ROW 2: Knit.
ROW 4: K3, 3/3 LC.
ROW 6: Knit.
ROW 8: 3/3 RC, k3.
Repeat Rows 1–8 for pattern.

Rib 3/3/3 GROUP 8

This is just like Basic 3/3/3 Braid (#23) except each set of 3 stockinette stitches has been replaced by the simplest of ribs—p1, k1, p1. Having a purl stitch on either side of the knit stitch makes the knit stitch stand up tall. See the reverse side on page 51.

(panel of 9 sts; 8-row repeat)
SSE: 7 sts

ROW 1 (WS): K1, [p1, k2] twice, p1, k1.
ROWS 2 AND 3: Knit the knit sts and purl the purl sts as they face you.
ROW 4: P1, k1, p1; slip 3 sts to cn, hold to front, p1, k1, p1, (p1, k1, p1) from cn.
ROWS 5–7: Repeat Row 2.
ROW 8: Slip 3 sts to cn, hold to back, p1, k1, p1, (p1, k1, p1) from cn; p1, k1, p1.
Repeat Rows 1–8 for pattern.

8-row repeat

9-st panel

8-row repeat

9-st panel

☐ Knit on RS, purl on WS.

⬛ 3/3 RC (3 over 3 right cross): Slip 3 sts to cn, hold to back, k3, k3 from cn.

⬛ 3/3 LC (3 over 3 left cross): Slip 3 sts to cn, hold to front, k3, k3 from cn.

☐ Knit on RS, purl on WS.

▨ Purl on RS, knit on WS.

▨ Slip 3 sts to cn, hold to back, p1, k1, p1, (p1, k1, p1) from cn.

▨ Slip 3 sts to cn, hold to front, p1, k1, p1, (p1, k1, p1) from cn.

3/3/3 Mix GROUP 8

While it may look complicated, this wild intertwining mélange of stitches is a simple variation of Basic 3/3/3 Braid (#23). Each set of 3 stitches used in the braid is a different stitch. One strand remains in stockinette, one is rib, and one is garter. The patterns don't change as you cable—garter stays garter, rib stays rib, and so on, so once you get started it is very easy to work.

(panel of 9 sts; 24-row repeat)
SSE: 7 sts

ROW 1 (WS): P6, k1, p1, k1.

ROW 2: P1, k1, p4, k3.

ROW 3: Repeat Row 1.

ROW 4: P1, k1, p1; slip 3 sts to cn, hold to front, k3, p3 from cn.

ROW 5: Repeat Row 1.

ROW 6: P1, k1, p1, k3, p3.

ROW 7: Repeat Row 1.

ROW 8: Slip 3 sts to cn, hold to back, k3, (p1, k1, p1) from cn; p3.

ROW 9: P3, k1, p1, k1, p3.

ROW 10: K3, p1, k1, p4.

ROW 11: Repeat Row 9.

ROW 12: K3; slip 3 sts to cn, hold to front, p3, (p1, k1, p1) from cn.

ROW 13: K1, p1, k1, p6.

ROW 14: K3, p4, k1, p1.

ROW 15: Repeat Row 13.

ROW 16: Slip 3 sts to cn, hold to back, p3, k3 from cn; p1, k1, p1.

ROW 17: Repeat Row 13.

ROW 18: P3, k3, p1, k1, p1.

ROW 19: Repeat row 13.

ROW 20: P3, slip 3 sts to cn, hold to front, p1, k1, p1, k3 from cn.

ROW 21: Repeat Row 9.

ROW 22: P4, k1, p1, k3.

ROW 23: Repeat Row 9.

ROW 24: Slip 3 sts to cn, hold to back, p1, k1, p1, p3 from cn; k3.
Repeat Rows 1–24 for pattern.

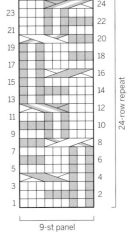

9-st panel

24-row repeat

☐ Knit on RS, purl on WS.

▨ Purl on RS, knit on WS.

⬲ Slip 3 sts to cn, hold to back, p3, k3 from cn.

⬲ Slip 3 sts to cn, hold to front, k3, p3 from cn.

⬲ Slip 3 sts to cn, hold to back, k3, (p1, k1, p1) from cn.

⬲ Slip 3 sts to cn, hold to front, p1, k1, p1, k3 from cn.

⬲ Slip 3 sts to cn, hold to back, p1, k1, p1, p3 from cn.

⬲ Slip 3 sts to cn, hold to front, p3, (p1, k1, p1) from cn.

Substitution

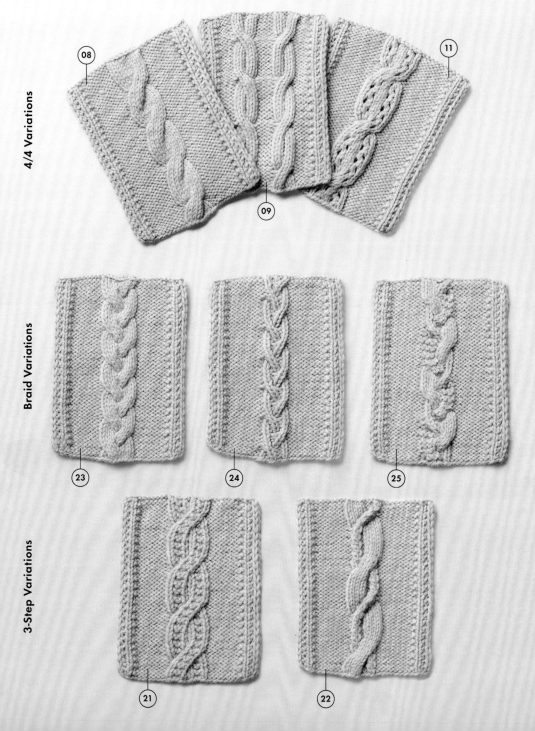

4/4 Variations

Braid Variations

3-Step Variations

Swapping ribs, texture, twisted stitches, and even lace for stockinette stitch within a cable can yield exciting new results.

4/4 VARIATIONS

All three cables in the top row are 4/4 cables. The familiar **BASIC 4/4 ROPE (#8)**, knit in stockinette stitch, starts out the group on the left. Changing the 4 stitches to a simple rib for **RIB 4/4 (#9)** or an easy lace pattern for **LACE 4/4 (#11)** creates a new cable. Any 4-stitch pattern is fair game to try. While I usually keep the pattern within the 4 stitches symmetrical, you might want to experiment with asymmetry.

BRAID VARIATIONS

Here a group of 3 stockinette stitches in **BASIC 3/3/3 BRAID (#23)** is replaced with p1, k1, p1 in **RIB 3/3/3 (#24)**. You don't have to replace all of the original stockinette stitch or even stick to just one substitution within a cable. **3/3/3 MIX (#25)** intertwines garter, rib, and stockinette stitch.

3-STEP VARIATIONS

The **GARTER FILL 3-STEP (#21)** on the left and **TWIST 3-STEP (#22)** on the right are closely related to each other. Both cables are built on the same basic structure: 4 stitches are moved over 2 stitches at a time, in 3 steps. The switch of stitches within that structure makes all the difference. Four-stitch substitutions are again the basis for invention with these 3-step variations.

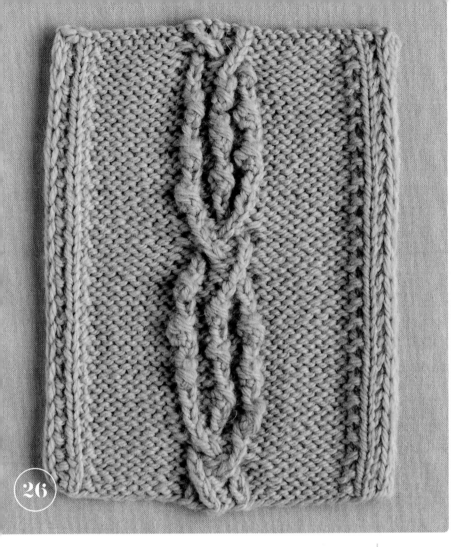

(26)

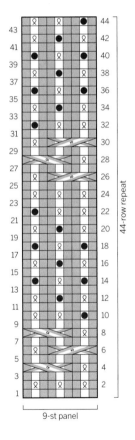

Knot 3/3/3 GROUP 8

This variation of Rib 3/3/3 (#24) is embellished with small knots that resemble strings of beads. The space between triplets (the 3 cable crosses that happen over the course of 5 rows) is stretched out over 17 rows to make room for the adornment. In contrast, there are only 3 rows between crosses in the Basic 3/3/3 Braid (#23). Not liking to turn my work around mid-row, the knots are worked by slipping stitches back onto the left needle.

(panel of 9 sts; 44-row repeat)
SSE: 7 sts

ROW 1 AND ALL WS ROWS (WS): K1, [p1, k2] twice, p1, k1.
ROW 2: P1, [k1-tbl, p2] twice, k1-tbl, p1.
ROW 4: P1, k1-tbl, p1; slip 3 sts to cn, hold to front, p1, k1-tbl, p1, (p1, k1-tbl, p1) from cn.
ROW 6: Slip 3 sts to cn, hold to back, p1, k1-tbl, p1, (p1, k1-tbl, p1) from cn; p1, k1-tbl, p1.
ROW 8: Repeat Row 4.
ROW 10: P1, MK, [p2, k1-tbl] twice, p1.

ROW 12: P1, k1-tbl, p2, MK, p2, k1-tbl, p1.
ROW 14: P1, MK, p2, k1-tbl, p2, MB, p1.
ROWS 16–19: Repeat Rows 12–15.
ROW 20: Repeat Row 12.
ROW 22: P1, [k1-tbl, p2] twice, MK, p1.
ROW 24: Repeat Row 2.
ROWS 26–29: Repeat Rows 6–9.
ROW 30: Repeat Row 6.
ROW 32: Repeat Row 22.
ROWS 34–42: Repeat Rows 12–20.
ROW 44: Repeat Row 10.
Repeat Rows 1–44 for pattern.

44-row repeat

9-st panel

□ Knit on RS, purl on WS.

▨ Purl on RS, knit on WS.

⧖ K1-tbl on RS, p1-tbl on WS.

● MK (make knot): Knit into front, back, then front of st to increase to 3 sts, slip these 3 sts back to left needle, k3, then pass third and second sts over first to decrease back to 1 st.

⬲ Slip 3 sts to cn, hold to back, p1, k1-tbl, p1, (p1, k1-tbl, p1) from cn.

⬳ Slip 3 sts to cn, hold to front, p1, k1-tbl, p1, (p1, k1-tbl, p1) from cn.

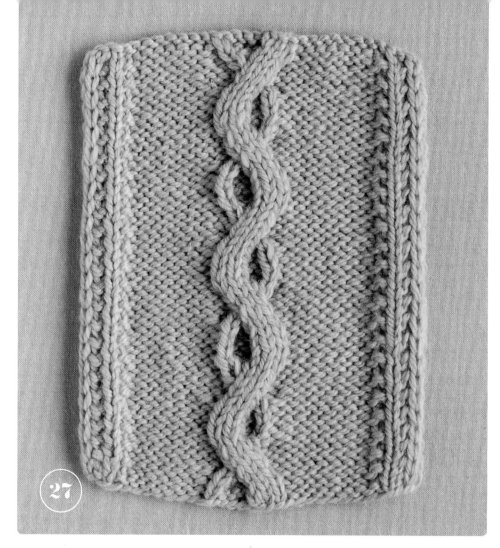

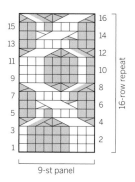

Double Zigzag GROUP 9

Here a bold zigzag overlays a more delicate ribbed zigzag. Moving 3 stockinette stitches over by 2 stitches results in an open, loose angle. Moving over fewer stitches with each cross would produce a steeper angle and even more languorous turn, while moving over more at once would result in a very sharp turn. Watch the key carefully because the number of stitches crossing each other is not always equal. For example, in Row 4, the first cable cross moves 3 stitches over 2 and the second cable cross moves 2 stitches over 2.

(panel of 9 sts; 16-row repeat)
SSE: 6 sts

ROW 1 (WS): P1, k5, p3.

ROW 2: K3, p5, k1.

ROW 3 AND ALL FOLLOWING WS ROWS: Knit the knit sts and purl the purl sts as they face you.

ROW 4: 3/2 LPC; slip 2 sts to cn, hold to back, p1, k1, p2 from cn.

ROW 6: P2; slip 3 sts to cn, hold to front, p1, k1, k3 from cn; p2.

ROW 8: Slip 2 sts to cn, hold to back, p1, k1, p2 from cn; 3/2 LPC.

ROW 10: P1, k1, p4, k3.

ROW 12: Slip 2 sts to cn, hold to front, p2, (p1, k1) from cn; 3/2 RPC.

ROW 14: P2; slip 2 sts to cn, hold to back, k3, (p1, k1) from cn; p2.

ROW 16: 3/2 RPC; slip 2 sts to cn, hold to front, p2, (p1, k1) from cn. Repeat Rows 1–16 for pattern.

□ Knit on RS, purl on WS.   ▨ Purl on RS, knit on WS.

Slip 2 sts to cn, hold to back, p1, k1, p2 from cn.

Slip 2 sts to cn, hold to front, p2, (p1, k1) from cn.

Slip 2 sts to cn, hold to back, k3, (p1, k1) from cn.

Slip 3 sts to cn, hold to front, p1, k1, k3 from cn.

3/2 RPC (3 over 2 right purl cross): Slip 2 sts to cn, hold to back, k3, p2 from cn.

3/2 LPC (3 over 2 left purl cross): Slip 3 sts to cn, hold to front, p2, k3 from cn.

9-st panel

16-row repeat

Zigzag Atop Twists GROUP 9

Using the bold stockinette stitch cable in Double Zigzag (#27) as a starting point, I experimented with leaving more stockinette stitches at each elbow (the point where the zig meets the zag) and defined the outside edges with columns of right twists. Watch the key carefully; while the large cables are always made up of 5 stitches, the number of stitches held on the cable needle is not always the same.

(panel of 9 sts; 16-row repeat)
SSE: 6 sts

ROW 1 (WS): P2, k2, p5.
ROW 2: K5, p2, LT.
ROW 3 AND ALL FOLLOWING WS ROWS: Knit the knit sts and purl the purl sts as they face you.
ROW 4: 3/2 LC, p2, LT.

ROW 6: RT, 3/2 LPC, LT.
ROW 8: RT, p2, 3/2 LC.
ROW 10: RT, p2, k5.
ROW 12: RT, p2, 3/2 RC.
ROW 14: RT, 3/2 RPC, LT.
ROW 16: 3/2 RC, p2, LT.
Repeat Rows 1–16 for pattern.

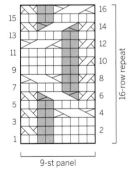

9-st panel

16-row repeat

☐ Knit on RS, purl on WS.

▨ Purl on RS, knit on WS.

⬚ **RT (right twist):** K2tog, but do not drop sts from left needle; insert right needle between 2 sts just worked and knit first st again, slip both sts from left needle together.

⬚ **LT (left twist):** Insert needle from back to front between first and second sts on left needle and knit the second st through the front loop; knit first st, slip both sts from left needle together.

⬚ **3/2 RC (3 over 2 right cross):** Slip 2 sts to cn, hold to back, k3, k2 from cn.

⬚ **3/2 LC (3 over 2 left cross):** Slip 3 sts to cn, hold to front, k2, k3 from cn.

⬚ **3/2 RPC (3 over 2 right purl cross):** Slip 2 sts to cn, hold to back, k3, p2 from cn.

⬚ **3/2 LPC (3 over 2 left purl cross):** Slip 3 sts to cn, hold to front, p2, k3 from cn.

Basics

45

Basic 4-Step GROUP 10

Two stitches travel from one side of the column to the other in what looks like a continuous swoop but is actually made up of 4 separate cable crosses. Each new cable begins on the left as the one preceding it ends on the right.

(panel of 10 sts; 6-row repeat)
SSE: 8 sts

ROW 1 AND ALL WS ROWS (WS): Purl.
ROW 2: 2/2 RC, k2, 2/2 RC.
ROW 4: K4, 2/2 RC, k2.
ROW 6: K2, 2/2 RC, k4.
Repeat Rows 1–6 for pattern.

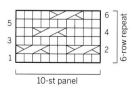

10-st panel

6-row repeat

☐ Knit on RS, purl on WS.

⬙ 2/2 RC (2 over 2 right cross): Slip 2 sts to cn, hold to back, k2, k2 from cn.

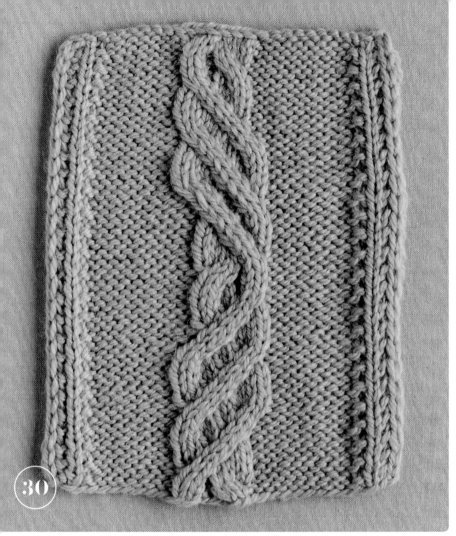

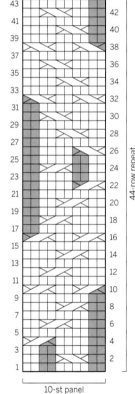

4-Step Swing GROUP 10

This variation of Basic 4-Step (#29) begins with 3 of the swoops from the original and then reverses itself. A simple 2/2 cable is placed at the point where the change in direction happens.

(panel of 10 sts; 44-row repeat)
SSE: 7 sts

ROW 1 (WS): P2, k2, p4, k2.
ROW 2: P2, 2/2 LC, p2, k2.
ROW 3 AND ALL FOLLOWING WS ROWS:
Knit the knit sts and purl the purl sts as they face you.
ROW 4: P2, k4, 2/2 RC.
ROW 6: P2, k2, 2/2 RC, k2.
ROW 8: P2, 2/2 RC, k4.
ROW 10: 2/2 RC, k2, 2/2 RC.
ROW 12: K4, 2/2 RC, k2.
ROW 14: K2, 2/2 RC, k4.
ROW 16: 2/2 RC, k2, 2/2 RPC.
ROW 18: K4, 2/2 RC, p2.

ROW 20: K2, 2/2 RC, k2, p2.
ROW 22: 2/2 RPC, k4, p2.
ROW 24: K2, p2, 2/2 RC, p2.
ROW 26: 2/2 LC, k4, p2.
ROW 28: K2, 2/2 LC, k2, p2.
ROW 30: K4, 2/2 LC, p2.
ROW 32: 2/2 LC, k2, 2/2 LC.
ROW 34: K2, 2/2 LC, k4.
ROW 36: K4, 2/2 LC, k2.
ROW 38: 2/2 LPC, k2, 2/2 LC.
ROW 40: P2, 2/2 LC, k4.
ROW 42: P2, k2, 2/2 LC, k2.
ROW 44: P2, k4, 2/2 LPC.
Repeat Rows 1–44 for pattern.

10-st panel

☐ Knit on RS, purl on WS.

▨ Purl on RS, knit on WS.

⬛ OR ⬛ 2/2 RC (2 over 2 right cross): Slip 2 sts to cn, hold to back, k2, k2 from cn.

⬛ OR ⬛ 2/2 LC (2 over 2 left cross): Slip 2 sts to cn, hold to front, k2, k2 from cn.

⬛ 2/2 RPC (2 over 2 right purl cross): Slip 2 sts to cn, hold to back, k2, p2 from cn.

⬛ 2/2 LPC (2 over 2 left purl cross): Slip 2 sts to cn, hold to front, p2, k2 from cn.

Double O GROUP 11

Essentially, this is 2 smaller cables mirrored and nestled next to each other. Two stitches travel over 1 to form open centers. The purls that give depth on the right side form a delicate honeycomb of rib on the reverse side. For more about reversibility, see page 51.

(panel of 12 sts; 8-row repeat)
SSE: 9 sts

ROW 1 (WS): P2, k2, p4, k2, p2.
ROW 2: K2, p2, k4, p2, k2.
ROW 3 AND ALL FOLLOWING WS ROWS:
Knit the knit sts and purl the purl sts as they face you.
ROW 4: [2/1 LPC, 2/1 RPC] twice.
ROW 6: P1, 2/2 RC, p2, 2/2 LC, p1.
ROW 8: [2/1 RPC, 2/1 LPC] twice.
Repeat Rows 1–8 for pattern.

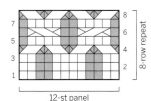

12-st panel

☐ Knit on RS, purl on WS.   ▨ Purl on RS, knit on WS.

▱ 2/1 RPC (2 over 1 right purl cross): Slip 1 st to cn, hold to back, k2, p1 from cn.

▱ 2/1 LPC (2 over 1 left purl cross): Slip 2 sts to cn, hold to front, p1, k2 from cn.

▱ 2/2 RC (2 over 2 right cross):
Slip 2 sts to cn, hold to back, k2, k2 from cn.

▱ 2/2 LC (2 over 2 left cross):
Slip 2 sts to cn, hold to front, k2, k2 from cn.

Open Double O GROUP 11

The centers of Double O (#31) provide a perfect frame for a double-sized eyelet. A pair of yarnovers along with their companion decreases is worked on the wrong side while the cables are crossed on the right side.

(panel of 12 sts; 8-row repeat)
SSE: 9.5 sts

ROW 1 (WS): P1, ssp, yo2, p2tog, p2, ssp, yo2, p2tog, p1.
ROW 2: K2, (k1, p1) into yo2, k4, (k1, p1) into yo2, k2.
ROW 3: Purl.
ROW 4: 2/1 LPC, 2/1 RC, 2/1 LC, 2/1 RPC.
ROW 5: K1, p3, ssp, yo2, p2tog, p3, k1.
ROW 6: P1, 2/2 RC, (k1, p1) into yo2, 2/2 LC, p1.
ROW 7: K1, p10, k1.
ROW 8: [2/1 RC, 2/1 LC] twice.
Repeat Rows 1–8 for pattern.

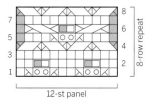

12-st panel

☐ Knit on RS, purl on WS.

▨ Purl on RS, knit on WS.

◯◯ Yo2

▨ K2tog on RS, p2tog on WS.

▨ Ssk on RS, ssp on WS.

▤ (K1, p1) into yo2.

▱ OR ▱ 2/1 RC (2 over 1 right cross): Slip 1 st to cn, hold to back, k2, k1 from cn.

▨ OR ▨ 2/1 LC (2 over 1 left cross): Slip 2 sts to cn, hold to front, k1, k2 from cn.

▱ OR ▱ 2/1 RPC (2 over 1 right purl cross): Slip 1 st to cn, hold to back, k2, p1 from cn.

▨ OR ▨ 2/1 LPC (2 over 1 left purl cross): Slip 2 sts to cn, hold to front, p1, k2 from cn.

▱ 2/2 RC (2 over 2 right cross): Slip 2 sts to cn, hold to back, k2, k2 from cn.

▨ 2/2 LC (2 over 2 left cross): Slip 2 sts to cn, hold to front, k2, k2 from cn.

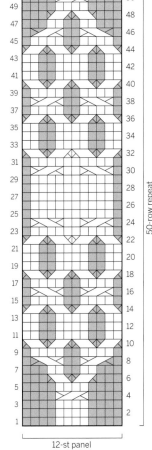

50-row repeat

12-st panel

Fancy Double O GROUP 11

While working a few repeats of Double O (#31), I came up with the idea of flipping them along the horizontal axis. The resulting rounded center is filled with stockinette stitch for simplicity. I also tapered the beginning and end of each repeat to make it appear as a discrete shape rather than one continuous column.

(panel of 12 sts; 50-row repeat)
SSE: 9 sts

ROW 1 (WS): K4, p4, k4.
ROW 2: P4, k4, p4.
ROW 3 AND ALL FOLLOWING WS ROWS: Knit the knit sts and purl the purl sts as they face you.
ROW 4: P4, 2/2 RC, p4.
ROW 6: P3, 2/1 RPC, 2/1 LPC, p3.
ROW 8: P1, 2/2 RC, p2, 2/2 LC, p1.
ROW 10: [2/1 RPC, 2/1 LPC] twice.
ROW 12: Repeat Row 3.
ROW 14: [2/1 LPC, 2/1 RPC] twice.
ROWS 16–21: Repeat Rows 8–13.
ROW 22: 2/1 LPC, 2/1 RC, 2/1 LC, 2/1 RPC.

ROW 24: P1, 2/2 RC, k2, 2/2 LC, p1.
ROWS 26 AND 28: Repeat Row 3.
ROW 30: P1, 2/2 LC, k2, 2/2 RC, p1.
ROWS 32–37: Repeat Rows 10–15.
ROW 38: P1, 2/2 LC, p2, 2/2 RC, p1.
ROWS 40–45: Repeat Rows 10–15.
ROW 46: P1, 2/2 LPC, p2, 2/2 RPC, p1.
ROW 48: P3, 2/1 LPC, 2/1 RPC, p3.
ROW 50: P4, 2/2 RC, p4.
Repeat Rows 1–50 for pattern.

☐ Knit on RS, purl on WS.

▨ Purl on RS, knit on WS.

⬚ **2/1 RC** (2 over 1 right cross): Slip 1 st to cn, hold to back, k2, k1 from cn.

⬚ **2/1 LC** (2 over 1 left cross): Slip 2 sts to cn, hold to front, k1, k2 from cn.

⬚ **2/1 RPC** (2 over 1 right purl cross): Slip 1 st to cn, hold to back, k2, p1 from cn.

⬚ **2/1 LPC** (2 over 1 left purl cross): Slip 2 sts to cn, hold to front, p1, k2 from cn.

⬚ OR ⬚ **2/2 RC** (2 over 2 right cross): Slip 2 sts to cn, hold to back, k2, k2 from cn.

⬚ OR ⬚ **2/2 LC** (2 over 2 left cross): Slip 2 sts to cn, hold to front, k2, k2 from cn.

⬚ **2/2 RPC** (2 over 2 right purl cross): Slip 2 sts to cn, hold to back, k2, p2 from cn.

⬚ **2/2 LPC** (2 over 2 left purl cross): Slip 2 sts to cn, hold to front, p2, k2 from cn.

2/2 Over 2/2 GROUP 12

Six stitches of 2 x 2 rib cross over another set of the same to form this bold dimensional cable. Ribbed cables like this one look particularly good on the wrong side and are perfect for incorporating into projects where both sides of the fabric are in view. See more on this topic on page 51.

(panel of 12 sts; 16-row repeat)
SSE: 9 sts

ROW 1 (WS): P2, k2, p4, k2, p2.

ROWS 2–9: Knit the knit sts and purl the purl sts as they face you.

ROW 10: Slip 6 sts to cn, hold to back, k2, p2, k2, (k2, p2, k2) from cn.

ROWS 11– 16: Repeat Row 2.
Repeat Rows 1–16 for pattern.

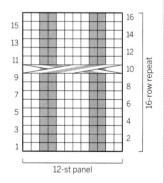

12-st panel

☐ Knit on RS, purl on WS.

▨ Purl on RS, knit on WS.

▱ Slip 6 sts to cn, hold to back, k2, p2, k2, (k2, p2, k2) from cn.

Broken X 2/2 GROUP 12

A few modifications transform 2/2 Over 2/2 (#34) into Broken X 2/2. First the center 4 stitches are twisted every few rows, forming a rope. Then, the outer rib is interrupted with reverse stockinette stitch, revealing the large X (the cable cross at its center). See the reverse side of this cable on page 51.

(panel of 12 sts; 24-row repeat)
SSE: 9 sts

ROW 1: K4, p4, k4.

ROWS 2 AND 3: Knit the knit sts and purl the purl sts as they face you.

ROW 4: K2, p2, k4, p2, k2.

ROW 5: Repeat Row 2.

ROW 6: K2, p2, 2/2 RC, p2, k2.

ROWS 7–11: Repeat Row 2.

ROW 12: Slip 6 sts to cn, hold to back, k2, p2, k2, (k2, p2, k2) from cn.

ROWS 13–17: Repeat Row 2.

ROW 18: Repeat Row 6.

ROW 19: Repeat Row 2.

ROW 20: P4, k4, p4.

ROWS 21–23: Repeat Row 2.

ROW 24: P4, 2/2 RC, p4.
Repeat Rows 1–24 for pattern.

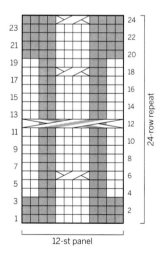

12-st panel

☐ Knit on RS, purl on WS.

▨ Purl on RS, knit on WS.

▱ 2/2 RC (2 over 2 right cross): Slip 2 sts to cn, hold to back, k2, k2 from cn.

▱ Slip 6 sts to cn, hold to back, k2, p2, k2, (k2, p2, k2) from cn.

Reversibility

(13)   (24)   (31)   (34)   (19)   (35)   (39)   (42)

When I separate out all of the swatches with reverse sides that I find visually appealing (and might work well in projects where both sides show), I see that they fall into three categories: 1) reverse-stockinette stitch centers; 2) rib-based; 3) made with naturally 2-sided stitches like seed stitch and lace.

REVERSE-STOCKINETTE STITCH CENTERS

PURL CENTER FLAT BRAID (#13), DOUBLE O (#31), and **LARGE PURL CENTER 2-STEP (#19)** all have reverse-stockinette stitch centers on the face intended to be the right side. On the wrong side they become stockinette stitch and form pleasing paths.

RIB-BASED

More often than not, ribbed cables look great, though not identical, on both sides. Check out **RIB 3/3/3 (#24)** and **2/2 OVER 2/2 (#34)** above. Even in **BROKEN X 2/2 (#35),** where the outside ribs are interrupted by stockinette stitch, there is a pleasing smaller X formation on the wrong side.

TWO-SIDED STITCHES

Simple lace patterns—for instance, a repeat of a yarnover followed by a purl-2-together or a slip-slip-knit—almost always look pleasing on both faces. With **LACE MEGA (#39),** the openwork lies on a bed of stockinette stitch on the intended right side of the fabric and is just as pleasingly nestled in reverse stockinette stitch on the so-called wrong side. Two-sided textural patterns, like garter stitch, make attractive two-sided cables as well; see **GARTER FILL BIG BRAID (#42).**

Rib Mega GROUP 13

This rather large cable, along with the next 4 in this series, are experiments with crossing 9 stitches over 9 stitches all at the same time. This is about as large a number of stitches as I like to cross at once, because more can become quite awkward and tight. Having an odd number of stitches on each side keeps the cable symmetrical when working in 1x1 rib. Notice how each half of the cable starts and ends with a purl, resulting in a carved-out center where the 2 sides meet.

(panel of 18 sts; 24-row repeat)
SSE: 12.5 sts

ROW 1 (WS): [K1, p1] 4 times, k2, [p1, k1] 4 times.

ROWS 2–13: Knit the knit sts and purl the purl sts as they face you.

ROW 14: Slip 9 sts to cn, hold to front, [p1, k1] 4 times, p1, ([p1, k1] 4 times, p1) from cn.

ROWS 15–24: Repeat Row 2. Repeat Rows 1–24 for pattern.

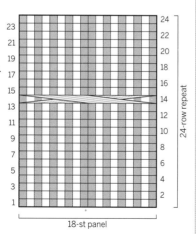

□ Knit on RS, purl on WS.

▨ Purl on RS, knit on WS.

Slip 9 sts to cn, hold to front, [p1, k1] 4 times, p1, ([p1, k1] 4 times, p1) from cn.

18-st panel

24-row repeat

Slip Mega GROUP 13

The slipped stitch in the center of each half of this cable is lifted from the stockinette and rib fabric that surrounds it, forming a visually interesting peak. As with Rib Mega (#36), the vertical center of the cable is distinguished by 2 purl stitches coming together and creating a narrow depression in the fabric.

(panel of 18 sts; 24-row repeat)
SSE: 12.5 sts

ROW 1 AND ALL WS ROWS (WS): K1, p1, k1, p3, k1, p1, k2, p1, k1, p3, k1, p1, k1.

ROWS 2, 4, 6, 8, 10, AND 12: [P1, k1] twice, slip 1, k1, p1, k1, p2, k1, p1, k1, slip 1, [k1, p1] twice.

ROW 14: Slip 9 sts to cn, hold to back, [p1, k1] twice, slip 1, [k1, p1] twice, ([p1, k1] twice, slip 1, [k1, p1] twice) from cn.

ROWS 16, 18, 20, 22, AND 24: Repeat Row 2. Repeat Rows 1–24 for pattern.

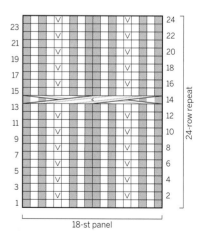

□ Knit on RS, purl on WS.

▨ Purl on RS, knit on WS.

☑ Slip 1 wyib on RS.

Slip 9 sts to cn, hold to back, [p1, k1] twice, slip 1, [k1, p1] twice, ([p1, k1] twice, slip 1, [k1, p1] twice) from cn.

18-st panel

24-row repeat

Seed Mega GROUP 13

The third in a series of 5 experiments with cabling 9 over 9,
this version places a pair of garter stitches at either side and a
seed stitch in the center of each half. These textural stitches
make a softer transition from the background and a wider, but
less pronounced, center than the other cables in this series.
The garter and seed stitches are worked on the wrong side; the
cable crosses are worked in stockinette stitch on the right side.

(panel of 18 sts; 24-row repeat)
SSE: 12.5 sts

ROW 1 AND ALL WS ROWS (WS):
K2, p2, k1, p2, k4, p2, k1, p2, k2.
ROWS 2, 4, 6, 8, 10, AND 12: Knit.
ROW 14: 9/9 RC.
ROWS 16, 18, 20, 22, AND 24: Repeat
Row 2.
Repeat Rows 1–24 for pattern.

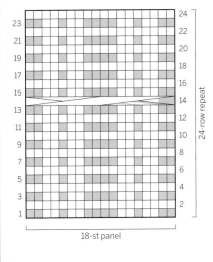

☐ Knit on RS, purl on WS.

▨ Purl on RS, knit on WS.

9/9 RC (9 over 9 right cross): Slip 9 sts to cn, hold to back, k9, k9 from cn.

Lace Mega GROUP 13

Keeping the edges in stockinette stitch makes this mega cable variation seem especially large. Lace and purl stitches give the center of each half of the cable textural interest on both the right and wrong sides. You can see a photo of the opposite side of this swatch on page 51. Instead of the carved-out center we see in the other Mega variations, here the stockinette stitch center poofs outward.

(panel of 18 sts; 24-row repeat)
SSE: 12.5 sts

ROW 1 AND ALL WS ROWS (WS):
P4, yo, p2tog, p7, yo, p2tog, p3.
ROWS 2, 4, 6, 8, 10, AND 12: K2, p1, k1, yo, ssk, p1, k4, p1, k1, yo, ssk, p1, k2.
ROW 14: Slip 9 sts to cn, hold to front, k2, p1, k1, yo, ssk, p1, k2, (k2, p1, k1, yo, ssk, p1, k2) from cn.
ROWS 16, 18, 20, 22, AND 24: Repeat Row 2.
Repeat Rows 1–24 for pattern.

18-st panel

☐ Knit on RS, purl on WS.   ▨ Purl on RS, knit on WS.   ⊙ Yo

⊠ K2tog on RS, p2tog on WS.

⊠ Ssk on RS, ssp on WS.

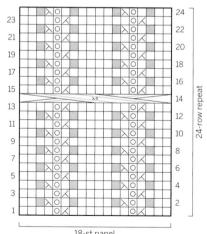

Slip 9 sts to cn, hold to front, k2, p1, k1, yo, ssk, p1, k2, (k2, p1, k1, yo, ssk, p1, k2) from cn.

Braid Mega GROUP 13

This is the most elaborate of the mega cable variations. Twisted stitches are worked on all right-side rows, forming a braid up the center of each half; this means that you have to pay attention to the twisted stitches even on the cable cross rows, which is not uncommon in this book but is uncommon in other cable collections.

(panel of 18 sts; 24-row repeat)
SSE: 12.5 sts

ROW 1 (WS): K1, p1, k1, p3, k1, p1, k2, p1, k1, p3, k1, p1, k1.

ROW 2: P1, k1, p1, RT, k1, p1, k1, p2, k1, p1, RT, [k1, p1] twice.

ROW 3 AND ALL FOLLOWING WS ROWS: Knit the knit sts and purl the purl sts as they face you.

ROW 4: [P1, k1] twice, LT, p1, k1, p2, k1, p1, k1, LT, p1, k1, p1.

ROWS 5–12: Repeat Rows 1–4 twice.

ROW 13: Repeat Row 1.

ROW 14: Slip 9 sts to cn, hold to front, p1, k1, p1, RT, [k1, p1] twice, (p1, k2, p1, RT, [k1, p1] twice) from cn.

ROWS 15–22: Repeat Rows 3–6 twice.

ROWS 23 AND 24: Repeat Rows 3 and 4.

Repeat Rows 1–24 for pattern.

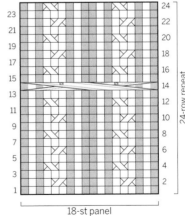

☐ Knit on RS, purl on WS. ▧ Purl on RS, knit on WS.

▧ **RT (right twist):** K2tog, but do not drop sts from left needle; insert right needle between 2 sts just worked and knit first st again, slip both sts from left needle together.

▧ **LT (left twist):** Insert needle from back to front between first and second sts on left needle and knit the second st through the front loop; knit first st, slip both sts from left needle together.

Slip 9 sts to cn, hold to front, p1, k1, p1, RT, [k1, p1] twice, (p1, k1, p1, RT, [k1, p1] twice) from cn.

Big Braid GROUP 14

This oversized braid crosses groups of 6 stockinette stitches. Cabling every 8 rows forms a fairly tight and rounded braid. Add more rows between crosses if you'd prefer a looser, lankier plait.

(panel of 18 sts; 16-row repeat)
SSE: 13.5 sts

ROW 1 AND ALL WS ROWS (WS): Purl.
ROWS 2 AND 4: Knit.
ROW 6: 6/6 RC, k6.
ROWS 8, 10, AND 12: Knit.
ROW 14: K6, 6/6 LC.
ROW 16: Knit.
Repeat Rows 1–16 for pattern.

Garter Fill Big Braid GROUP 14

In this variant of Big Braid (#41) the center of each section is filled with garter stitch. Working the garter pattern on the wrong-side rows as knits means the cable crosses themselves can be worked very easily in stockinette stitch on the right-side rows. See the reverse side of this cable on page 51.

(panel of 18 sts; 16-row repeat)
SSE: 12.5 sts

ROW 1 AND ALL WS ROWS (WS): P1, [k4, p2] twice, k4, p1.
ROWS 2 AND 4: Knit.

ROW 6: 6/6 RC, k6.
ROWS 8, 10, AND 12: Knit.
ROW 14: K6, 6/6 LC.
ROW 16: Knit.
Repeat Rows 1–16 for pattern.

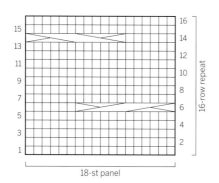

18-st panel

16-row repeat

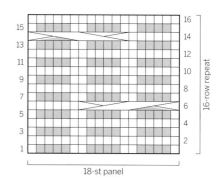

18-st panel

16-row repeat

☐ Knit on RS, purl on WS.

6/6 RC (6 over 6 right cross): Slip 6 sts to cn, hold to back, k6, k6 from cn.

6/6 LC (6 over 6 left cross): Slip 6 sts to cn, hold to front, k6, k6 from cn.

☐ Knit on RS, purl on WS.

▨ Purl on RS, knit on WS.

6/6 RC (6 over 6 right cross): Slip 6 sts to cn, hold to back, k6, k6 from cn.

6/6 LC (6 over 6 left cross): Slip 6 sts to cn, hold to front, k6, k6 from cn.

Horseshoe Combo GROUP 15

Here a vertical slip-stitch welt serves as the central anchor for 2 flanking Basic 3/3 Ropes (#1). I like the way the 3 distinct elements merge together visually to create the look of a unified whole.

(panel of 17 sts; 8-row repeat)
SSE: 13.5 sts

ROW 1 AND ALL WS ROWS (WS):
P6, k1, p3, k1, p6.
ROW 2: K6, p1, k1, slip 1, k1, p1, k6.
ROW 4: 3/3 RC, p1, k1, slip 1, k1, p1, 3/3 LC.
ROWS 6 AND 8: Repeat Row 2.
Repeat Rows 1–8 for pattern.

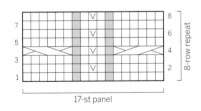

17-st panel

8-row repeat

☐ Knit on RS, purl on WS.

▨ Purl on RS, knit on WS.

Ⓥ Slip 1 wyib on RS.

⬚ 3/3 RC (3 over 3 right cross): Slip 3 sts to cn, hold to back, k3, k3 from cn.

⬚ 3/3 LC (3 over 3 left cross): Slip 3 sts to cn, hold to front, k3, k3 from cn.

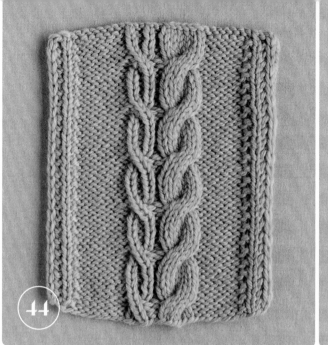

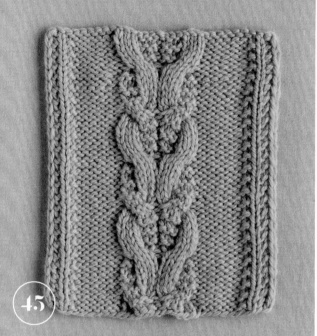

Contrast Horseshoe GROUP 15

Working a 3/3 ribbed cable next to its stockinette-stitch cousin calls out their differences and forms an interesting asymmetrical horseshoe. Identical in both stitches and rows, the ribbed side is slender and delicate, while the stockinette side is more solid and round. One reverse stockinette stitch separates the pair, alleviating the tension of the opposing crosses.

(panel of 13 sts; 8-row repeat)
SSE: 10 sts

ROW 1 AND ALL WS ROWS (WS):
K1, [p1, k2] twice, p6.
ROW 2: K6, [p2, k1] twice, p1.
ROW 4: 3/3 RC, p1; slip 3 sts to cn, hold to front, p1, k1, p1, (p1, k1, p1) from cn.
ROWS 6 AND 8: Repeat Row 2.
Repeat Rows 1–8 for pattern.

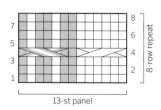

8-row repeat

13-st panel

☐ Knit on RS, purl on WS.

▦ Purl on RS, knit on WS.

▱ 3/3 RC (3 over 3 right cross): Slip 3 sts to cn, hold to back, k3, k3 from cn.

▱ Slip 3 sts to cn, hold to front, p1, k1, p1, (p1, k1, p1) from cn.

Horseshoe Mix GROUP 15

In this cable, 3 garter stitches and 3 stockinette stitches change places every 8 rows on each side of a single column of reverse stockinette stitch. The textural contrast between the garter and the stockinette stitches gives this simple cable a complex look.

(panel of 13 sts; 12-row repeat)
SSE: 10 sts

ROW 1 (WS): P3, k7, p3.
ROW 2: K6, p1, k6.
ROW 3: Repeat Row 1.
ROW 4: 3/3 RC, p1, 3/3 LC.
ROW 5: K3, p3, k1, p3, k3.
ROW 6: Repeat Row 2.
ROWS 7–10: Repeat Rows 5 and 6.
ROW 11: Repeat Row 5.
ROW 12: Repeat Row 4.
Repeat Rows 1–12 for pattern.

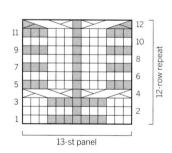

12-row repeat

13-st panel

☐ Knit on RS, purl on WS.

▦ Purl on RS, knit on WS.

▱ OR ▱ 3/3 RC (3 over 3 right cross): Slip 3 sts to cn, hold to back, k3, k3 from cn.

▱ OR ▱ 3/3 LC (3 over 3 left cross): Slip 3 sts to cn, hold to front, k3, k3 from cn.

Rib Triplet Horseshoe   GROUP 15

Taking the idea of combinations one step further, here 2 mirrored ribbed cables flank a central stockinette stitch cable of the same size. Each is divided by one column of reverse stockinette to distinguish the crosses a bit.

(panel of 18 sts; 24-row repeat)
SSE: 13.5 sts

ROW 1 (WS): K1, [p1, k2] twice, p4, [k2, p1] twice, k1.

ROWS 2, 3, AND ALL FOLLOWING WS ROWS: Knit the knit sts and purl the purl sts as they face you.

ROW 4: P1, [k1, p2] twice, 2/2 LC, [p2, k1] twice, p1.

ROW 6: Slip 3 sts to cn, hold to back, p1, k1, p1, (p1, k1, p1) from cn; p1, k4, p1; slip 3 sts to cn, hold to front, p1, k1, p1, (p1, k1, p1) from cn.

ROW 8: Repeat Row 2.
ROW 10: Repeat Row 4.
ROW 12: Repeat Row 2.
ROW 14: Repeat Row 6.
ROW 16: Repeat Row 4.
ROWS 18 AND 20: Repeat Row 2.
ROW 22: Slip 3 sts to cn, hold to back, p1, k1, p1, (p1, k1, p1) from cn; p1, 2/2 LC, p1; slip 3 sts to cn, hold to front, p1, k1, p1, (p1, k1, p1) from cn.
ROW 24: Repeat Row 2.
Repeat Rows 1–24 for pattern.

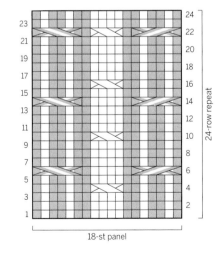

☐ Knit on RS, purl on WS. ▓ Purl on RS, knit on WS.

2/2 LC (2 over 2 left cross): Slip 2 sts to cn, hold to front, k2, k2 from cn.

Slip 3 sts to cn, hold to back, p1, k1, p1, (p1, k1, p1) from cn.

Slip 3 sts to cn, hold to front, p1, k1, p1, (p1, k1, p1) from cn.

Vest

SIZES
To fit bust 30 (34, 38, 42, 46, 50, 54)" [76 (86.5, 96.5, 106.5, 117, 127, 137) cm]

FINISHED MEASUREMENTS
32 (36, 40½, 44, 48, 52, 56½)" [81.5 (91.5, 103, 112, 122, 132, 143.5) cm] bust, with fronts over-lapped

YARN
Berroco Maya [85% cotton/15% alpaca; 137 yards (125 meters)/50 grams]: **10 (11, 12, 13, 14, 16, 17) hanks #5651 Lavanda**

NEEDLES
One 32" (80 cm) long or longer circular needle size US 7 (4.5 mm)

One 32" (80 cm) long or longer circular needle size US 5 (3.75 mm)

Change needle size if necessary to obtain correct gauge.

NOTIONS
Stitch markers; stitch holder; cable needle

GAUGE
21 sts and 30 rows = 4" (10 cm) in St st, using larger needle

9-st panel from Cable Pattern measures 1¾" (4.5 cm), using larger needle.

Steam or wet block your swatch before taking the measurements.

STITCH PATTERNS
2 x 2 Rib
(multiple of 4 sts + 2; 1-row repeat)
ROW 1 (WS): **P2, *k2, p2; repeat from * to end.**
ROW 2: **Knit the knit sts and purl the purl sts as they face you.**
Repeat Row 2 for pattern.

Cable: Knot 3/3/3 (#26)

PATTERN NOTES
This Vest is worked seamlessly from the top down. The right half of the collar is worked first, then the left half is picked up and worked from the cast-on edge of the right half. When the left half is complete, stitches are picked up along one edge of both halves for the Yoke, which is worked down to the armholes with raglan shaping. The Fronts and Back are divided at the armholes and all three pieces are worked simultaneously to the base of the armholes. Then the pieces are joined again and the body is worked in one piece to the bottom edge.

✂ If you'd like to make a cable substitution, see page 63.

Collar
RIGHT HALF
Using larger needle, CO 16 sts.
ROW 1 (WS): Slip 2, k1, work Cable Pattern over 9 sts, k1, p3.
ROW 2: K3, p1, work Cable Pattern, p1, k2.
Work even until piece measures 5½ (5½, 6, 6, 6¼, 6¼, 6¼)" [11 (11, 12, 12, 12.5, 12.5, 12.5) cm] from the beginning, measured along longer edge (opposite slipped sts), ending with a WS row. Cut yarn and place sts on holder.

LEFT HALF
With RS of Right Half facing, using larger needle, pick up and knit 16 sts along CO edge of Right Half.
ROW 1 (WS): P3, k1, work Cable Pattern over 9 sts, k1, p2.
ROW 2: Slip 2, p1, work Cable Pattern, p1, k3.
Work even until piece measures 5½ (5½, 6, 6, 6¼, 6¼, 6¼)" [11 (11, 12, 12, 12.5, 12.5, 12.5) cm] from pick-up row, measured along longer edge, ending with a WS row. Do not cut yarn.

Yoke
NEXT ROW (RS): Continuing in pattern as established, work across Left Half of Collar; working along St st edge of Collar, pick up and knit 58 (58, 62, 62, 66, 66, 66) sts along edge; work across Right Half of Collar—90 (90, 94, 94, 98, 98, 98) sts.
SET-UP ROW (WS): Work 15 sts as established, k1, [p1, k1] twice, pm p2, pm for end of Right Front, k1, p1, k1, p4, k1, p1, k1, pm for end of right raglan, p26 (26, 30, 30, 34, 34, 34), pm for end of Back, k1, p1, k1, p4, k1, p1, k1, pm for end of left raglan, pm, p2, pm, k1, [p1, k1] twice, work 15 sts as established.

SHAPE RAGLAN AND FRONT NECK
Note: Raglan and Front neck shaping are worked at the same time; Front neck shaping begins on third RS row of raglan shaping and will not be completed until after hip shaping has begun; please read entire section through before beginning.
RAGLAN SINGLE INCREASE ROW (RS): Work 15 sts, p1, [k1-tbl, p1] twice, sm, [knit to next marker, M1R, sm, p1, k1-tbl, p1, k4, p1, k1-tbl, p1, sm, M1L] twice, knit to next marker, sm, p1, [k1-tbl, p1] twice, work to end—4 sts increased.
Work 1 row even.
RAGLAN DOUBLE INCREASE ROW (RS): Continuing in patterns as established, work to first marker, sm, [knit to 2 sts before next marker, M1R, k2, M1R, sm, p1, k1-tbl, p1, k4, p1, k1-tbl, p1, sm, M1L, k2, M1L] twice, knit to next marker, sm, work to end—8 sts increased.
Work 1 row even.

Repeat Raglan Double Increase Row every RS row - (-, -, 1, 6, 13, 22) time(s).

Work 1 row even.

ALL SIZES

Repeat Raglan Single Increase Row once.

Work 1 row even.

Repeat Raglan Double Increase Row once.

Work 1 row even.

Repeat last 4 rows 2 (6, 10, 13, 11, 8, 4) times.

SIZES 32, 36, AND 40½" (81.5, 91.5, AND 103 CM) ONLY

Repeat Raglan Single Increase Row once.

Work 1 row even.

Repeat last 2 rows 19 (12, 5, -, -, -, -) times.

ALL SIZES

AT THE SAME TIME, beginning on third RS row of raglan shaping, work Front neck shaping as follows:

FRONT NECK INCREASE ROW (RS): Continuing to work raglan shaping as established, work to first marker, sm, k1, M1L, work to 1 st before last marker, M1R, k1, sm, work to end—2 sts increased.

Continuing to work raglan shaping as established, repeat Front Neck Increase Row every 6 rows 16 (16, 18, 22, 24, 26, 26) times, then every 8 rows 7 (7, 6, 3, 2, 1, 1) time(s).

AT THE SAME TIME, when raglan shaping is complete, ending with a WS row, divide for armholes as follows. *Note: When raglan shaping is complete, you will have 236 (256, 282, 302, 322, 344, 368) sts; 90 (100, 114, 124, 136, 146, 158) sts for Back, 63 (68, 74, 79, 83, 89, 95) sts each Front, and 10 sts each raglan.*

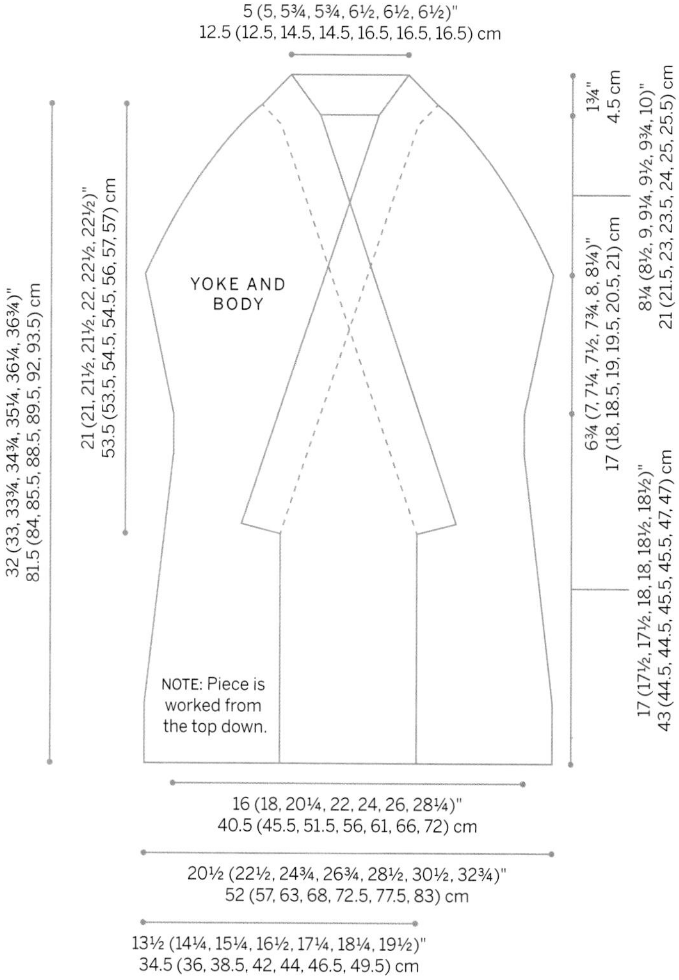

Body

DIVIDE FOR ARMHOLES

Note: Continue to work Front neck shaping as established while working armhole shaping.

NEXT ROW (RS): Work to second marker, sm, p1, k1-tbl, p1, slip 2 sts to cn, hold to back, k2, join a second ball of yarn, k2 from cn, p1, k1-tbl, p1, work to next marker, p1, k1-tbl, p1, slip 2 sts to cn, hold to front, k2, join a third ball of yarn, k2 from cn, p1, k1-tbl, p1, sm, work to end.

NEXT ROW: Working all 3 pieces at the same time with separate balls of yarn, on Right Front, work to second marker, sm, k1, p1, k1, p2; on Back, p2, k1, p1, k1, sm, purl to next marker, sm, k1, p1, k1, p2; on Left Front, p2, k1, p1, k1, sm, purl to next marker, sm, work to end.

NEXT ROW: On Left Front, work to second marker, sm, p1, k1-tbl, p1, k2; on Back, k2, p1, k1-tbl, p1, sm, knit to next marker, sm, p1, k1-tbl, p1, k2; on Right Front, k2, p1, k1-tbl, p1, sm, knit to next marker, sm, work to end.

Work 3 rows even.

ARMHOLE DECREASE ROW (RS): On Left Front, work to 2 sts before second marker, ssk, sm, k1, p1, k1, p2; on Back, p2, k1, p1, k1, sm, k2tog, purl to 2 sts before next marker, ssk, sm, k1, p1, k1, p2; on Right Front, p2, k1, p1, k1, sm, k2tog, purl to end, sm, work to end—4 sts

decreased, 1 st on each side of each armhole edge.

Repeat Armhole Decrease Row every 6 rows 5 (4, 7, 6, 9, 9, 8) times, then every 8 rows 2 (3, 1, 2, 0, 0, 1) time(s)—84 (94, 106, 116, 126, 136, 148) sts remain for Back, 69 (74, 79, 85, 89, 94, 101) sts each Front. Work 1 row even.

JOIN FRONTS AND BACK

Note: Continue to work Front neck shaping as established while rejoining pieces and working body.

NEXT ROW (RS): Working across all sts with 1 ball of yarn (cut second and third balls as you come to them), work to second marker, remove marker, knit to end of Left Front, pm for side, [knit to marker, remove marker] twice, knit to end of Back, pm for side, knit to marker, remove marker, knit to last marker, sm, work to end—222 (242, 264, 286, 306, 324, 352) sts.

NEXT ROW: Work to marker, sm, purl to last marker, sm, work to end. Work in patterns as established until piece measures 2" (5 cm) from underarms, ending with a WS row.

SHAPE HIPS AND FINISH FRONT EDGING

Note: Continue to work Front neck shaping as established while

5 (5, 5¾, 5¾, 6½, 6½, 6½)"
12.5 (12.5, 14.5, 14.5, 16.5, 16.5, 16.5) cm

1¾"
4.5 cm

YOKE AND BODY

8¾ (8½, 9, 9¼, 9½, 9¾, 10)"
21 (21.5, 23, 23.5, 24, 25, 25.5) cm

6¾ (7, 7¼, 7½, 7¾, 8, 8¼)"
17 (18, 18.5, 19, 19.5, 20.5, 21) cm

21 (21, 21½, 21½, 22, 22½, 22½)"
53.5 (53.5, 54.5, 54.5, 55, 56.5, 57) cm

32 (33, 33¾, 34¾, 35¼, 36¼, 36¾)"
81.5 (84, 85.5, 88.5, 89.5, 92, 93.5) cm

NOTE: Piece is worked from the top down.

17 (17½, 17½, 18, 18, 18½, 18½)"
43 (44.5, 44.5, 45.5, 45.5, 47, 47) cm

16 (18, 20¼, 22, 24, 26, 28¼)"
40.5 (45.5, 51.5, 56, 61, 66, 72) cm

20½ (22½, 24¾, 26¾, 28½, 30½, 32¾)"
52 (57, 63, 68, 72.5, 77.5, 83) cm

13½ (14¼, 15¼, 16½, 17¼, 18¼, 19½)"
34.5 (36, 38.5, 42, 44, 46.5, 49.5) cm

working hip shaping. Neck shaping will be completed before edging is finished; hip shaping will be completed after edging is finished.

HIP INCREASE ROW (RS): Work to 2 sts before second marker, M1R, k2, sm, k2, M1L, work to 2 sts before next marker, M1R, k2, sm, k2, M1L, work to end—4 sts increased.

Repeat Hip Increase Row every 6 (6, 6, 8, 8, 8, 8) rows 4 (2, 2, 11, 11, 11, 11) times, then every 8 (8, 8, 0, 0, 0, 0) rows 7 (9, 9, 0, 0, 0, 0) times. AT THE SAME TIME, when Front neck shaping is complete, ending with a WS row, finish Front edging as follows:

NEXT ROW (RS): Continuing to work hip shaping as established, slip 2, p1, p2sso, bind off sts until 7 sts remain on left needle before first marker, slip 2 sts, pass first st on right needle over these 2 sts, work to marker, remove marker, work to end—13 sts decreased.

NEXT ROW: S2kp2, bind off sts until 7 sts remain on left needle before first marker, slip 2 sts, pass first st on right needle over these 2 sts, work to marker, remove marker, work to end—13 sts decreased.

Slipping first 2 sts of every row, continue until hip shaping is complete—256 (276, 298, 320, 338, 360, 384) sts when all shaping is complete: 108 (118, 130, 140, 150, 160, 172) sts for Back, 74 (79, 84, 90, 94, 100, 106) sts each Front.

Work even until piece measures 14 (14½, 14½, 15, 15, 15½, 15½)" [35.5 (37, 37, 38, 38, 39.5, 39.5) cm] from underarm, ending with a WS row.

Change to smaller needle.

NEXT ROW (RS): Work 7 sts as established, k2, M1L, [k8 (9, 9, 8, 7, 7, 9), M1L] 2 (5, 8, 6, 4, 1, 11) time(s), [k9 (8, 8, 9, 8, 8, 8), M1L] 22 (21, 17, 22, 33, 41, 21) times, [k8 (9, 9, 8, 7, 7, 9), M1L] 3 (5, 8, 7, 4, 1, 11) time(s), k2, work as established to end—284 (308, 332, 356, 380, 404, 428) sts.

NEXT ROW: Work 7 sts, work 2x2 Rib to last 7 sts, work to end.

Work even for 3" (7.5 cm).

BO all sts in pattern.

Block as desired.

Cable Substitution

Before getting started, review Stockinette Stitch Equivalent System on page 20.

CHOOSING CABLES

The width of the collar doesn't affect any other design elements, so it's fine to choose a cable with a different width than the one shown here. I recommend looking for a cable with an SSE of 14 or lower, which you'll find in Chapters 2 and 3. With an SSE of 7, as shown, the collar is about 1¾" (4.5 cm) wide. A cable with an SSE of 14 will make the collar about 3" (7.5 cm) wide.

MANAGING A CHANGE IN STITCH COUNT

The cable chosen will affect the number of stitches you cast on for the right half of the collar and pick up for the left half. Make note of the difference between your cast-on/pick-up numbers and the cast-on/pick-up called for in the pattern and remember to add or subtract this difference in all stitch counts until the collar is bound off.

CABLE PATTERN
(panel of 9 sts; 44-row repeat)
SSE: 7 sts

ROW 1 AND ALL WS ROWS (WS): K1, [p1, k2] twice, p1, k1.
ROW 2: P1, [k1-tbl, p2] twice, k1-tbl, p1.
ROW 4: P1, k1-tbl, p1; slip 3 sts to cn, hold to front, p1, k1-tbl, p1, (p1, k1-tbl, p1) from cn.
ROW 6: Slip 3 sts to cn, hold to back, p1, k1-tbl, p1, (p1, k1-tbl, p1) from cn; p1, k1-tbl, p1.
ROW 8: Repeat Row 4.
ROW 10: P1, MB, [p2, k1-tbl] twice, p1.

ROW 12: P1, k1-tbl, p2, MB, p2, k1-tbl, p1.
ROW 14: P1, MB, p2, k1-tbl, p2, MB, p1.
ROWS 16–19: Repeat Rows 12–15.
ROW 20: Repeat Row 12.
ROW 22: P1, [k1-tbl, p2] twice, MB, p1.
ROW 24: Repeat Row 2.
ROWS 26–29: Repeat Rows 6–9.
ROW 30: Repeat Row 6.
ROW 32: Repeat Row 22.
ROWS 34–42: Repeat Rows 12–20.
ROW 44: Repeat Row 10.
Repeat Rows 1–44 for pattern.

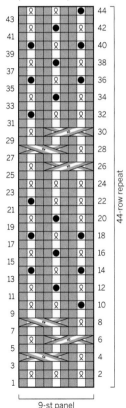

CABLE PATTERN
(KNOT 3/3/3)

9-st panel

44-row repeat

☐ Knit on RS, purl on WS.

▨ Purl on RS, knit on WS.

🙾 K1-tbl on RS, p1-tbl on WS.

● MK (make knot): Knit into front, back, then front of st to increase to 3 sts, slip these 3 sts back to left needle, k3, then pass third and second sts over first to decrease back to 1 st.

◥◣ Slip 3 sts to cn, hold to back, p1, k1-tbl, p1, (p1, k1-tbl, p1) from cn.

◥◣ Slip 3 sts to cn, hold to front, p1, k1-tbl, p1, (p1, k1-tbl, p1) from cn.

Hat

FINISHED MEASUREMENTS

Brim circumference: 17" (43 cm)

Body circumference: 21" (53.5 cm)

Length: 10" (25.5 cm)

Note: Brim is intended to fit with 2–4" (5–10 cm) negative ease.

YARN

Yarn Stories Fine Merino DK [100% fine merino; 131 yards (120 meters)/ 50 grams]: 2 balls Taupe

NEEDLES

Needle(s) in preferred style for small circumference knitting in the rnd, size US 4 (3.5 mm)

Needle(s) in preferred style for small circumference knitting in the rnd, size US 2 (2.75 mm)

Set of five double-pointed needles size US 4 (3.5 mm)

Change needle size if necessary to obtain correct gauge.

NOTIONS

Cable needle; stitch marker

GAUGE

26 sts and 36 rows = 4" (10 cm) in Texture Pattern, using larger needle

8-st panel from Cable A measures 1¼" (3 cm), using larger needle

9-st panel from Cable B measures 1" (2.5 cm), using larger needle

Steam or wet block your swatch before taking the measurements.

ABBREVIATION

S3K2P3: **Slip the next 3 stitches together to the right-hand needle as if to knit 3 together, k2tog, pass the 3 slipped stitches over.**

STITCH PATTERNS

1x1 Rib

(even number of sts; 1-rnd repeat)

ALL RNDS: *K1, p1; repeat from * to end.

Texture Pattern

(odd number of sts; 4-rnd repeat)

RND 1: **Purl.**

RNDS 2 AND 3: **K1, *p1, k1; repeat from * to end.**

RND 4: **Knit.**

Repeat Rnds 1–4 for Texture Pattern.

Cable A: Basic Globe (#15)

Cable B: Zigzag Atop Twists (#28)

PATTERN NOTES

Hat is worked in the rnd.

If you'd like to make a cable substitution, see page 66.

Hat

BRIM

Using smaller needle, CO 150 sts. Join for working in the rnd, being careful not to twist sts; pm for beginning of rnd.

Work in 1x1 Rib until piece measures 1½" (4 cm).

Change to larger circular needle; knit 1 rnd, increasing 3 sts evenly spaced—153 sts.

BODY

NEXT RND: *Work 13 sts in Texture Pattern, p2, work 8 sts of Cable A, p2, work 13 sts in Texture Pattern, p2, work 9 sts of Cable B, p2; repeat from * to end.

Work even until piece measures 7½" (19 cm) from beginning, ending with Rnd 2 of Texture Pattern.

SHAPE CROWN

DECREASE RND 1: *K3tog, work 7 sts in Texture Pattern, sssk, p2, work Cable A, p2, k3tog, work 7 sts in Texture Pattern, sssk, p2, work Cable B, p2; repeat from * to end—129 sts remain.

Work 7 rnds even.

DECREASE RND 2: Continuing in patterns as established, *k3tog, work 3 sts, sssk, work 12 sts, k3tog, work 3 sts, sssk, work 13 sts; repeat from * to end—105 sts remain.

Work 7 rnds even.

DECREASE RND 3: *S3k2p3, work 12 sts, s3k2p3, work 13 sts; repeat from * to end—81 sts remain.

Work 3 rnds even.

DECREASE RND 4: *Work 1 st, p2tog, work 8 sts, p2tog, work 1 st, p2tog, work 9 sts, p2tog; repeat from * to end—69 sts remain.

NEXT RND: Work to last st, pm for new beginning of rnd.

DECREASE RND 5: *S2kp2 (last st of previous rnd together with first 2 sts of current rnd, removing marker), work 8 sts, s2kp2, work 9 sts; repeat from * to end—57 sts remain.

Work 1 rnd even.

Purl 1 rnd.

DECREASE RND 6: *K1, k2tog; repeat from * to end—38 sts remain.

Purl 1 rnd.

DECREASE RND 7: *K2tog; repeat from * to end—19 sts remain.

Purl 1 rnd.

DECREASE RND 9: *K2tog; repeat from * to last st, k1—10 sts remain.

Cut yarn, leaving a long tail. Thread tail through remaining sts, pull tight and fasten off.

Finishing

Steam or wet-block piece to finished measurements.

✂ Cable Substitution

Before getting started, review Stockinette Stitch Equivalent System on page 20.

CHOOSING CABLES

To maintain the shaping at the crown, stick with cables of the same or similar width as the original. For Cable A, substitute a cable with an SSE of 6.5–7.5. For Cable B, substitute a cable with an SSE of 5.5–6.5 and keep the reverse stockinette stitch and texture stitch counts as they are. Or, if you're up for a more challenging substitution, for Cable A, substitute a cable with an SSE of 8.5–9.5 and for Cable B, substitute a cable with an SSE of 7.5–8.5, then take away 1 reverse stockinette stitch from each side of every cable.

MANAGING A CHANGE IN STITCH COUNT

Keep the ribbing as written. If you decide to work different cables, adjust the stitch count if necessary when working the knit round after the ribbing. Remember that the stitch counts following each Decrease Round will be changed. For Decrease Rounds 6–9, stay as close as you can to the instructions, but don't worry if you have a few more or fewer stitches left to work at the end of each Decrease Round.

CABLE A
(panel of 8 sts; 16-row repeat)
SSE: 7 sts

ROW 1 (WS): K2, p4, k2.
ROW 2: P2, k4, p2.
ROW 3 AND ALL FOLLOWING WS ROWS: Knit the knit sts and purl the purl sts as they face you.
ROW 4: P2, 2/2 LC, p2.
ROW 6: 2/2 RC, 2/2 LC.
ROWS 8, 10, AND 12: Knit.
ROW 14: 2/2 LC, 2/2 RC.
ROW 16: Repeat Row 4.
Repeat Rows 1–16 for pattern.

CABLE B
(panel of 9 sts; 16-row repeat)
SSE: 6 sts

ROW 1 (WS): P2, k2, p5.
ROW 2: K5, p2, LT.
ROW 3 AND ALL FOLLOWING WS ROWS: Knit the knit sts and purl the purl sts as they face you.
ROW 4: 3/2 LC, p2, LT.
ROW 6: RT, 3/2 LPC, LT.
ROW 8: RT, p2, 3/2 LC.
ROW 10: RT, p2, k5.
ROW 12: RT, p2, 3/2 RC.
ROW 14: RT, 3/2 RPC, LT.
ROW 16: 3/2 RC, p2, LT.
Repeat Rows 1–16 for pattern.

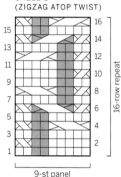

CABLE A
(BASIC GLOBE)

8-st panel

16-row repeat

CABLE B
(ZIGZAG ATOP TWIST)

9-st panel

16-row repeat

☐ Knit on RS, purl on WS.

▨ Purl on RS, knit on WS.

▨ **RT (right twist):** K2tog, but do not drop sts from left needle; insert right needle between 2 sts just worked and knit first st again, slip both sts from left needle together.

▨ **LT (left twist):** Insert needle from back to front between first and second sts on left needle and knit the second st through the front loop; knit first st, slip both sts from left needle together.

▨ **2/2 RC (2 over 2 right cross):** Slip 2 sts to cn, hold to back, k2, k2 from cn.

▨ **2/2 LC (2 over 2 left cross):** Slip 2 sts to cn, hold to front, k2, k2 from cn.
OR

▨ **2/2 RPC (2 over 2 right purl cross):** Slip 2 sts to cn, hold to back, k2, p2 from cn.

▨ **2/2 LPC (2 over 2 left purl cross):** Slip 2 sts to cn, hold to front, p2, k2 from cn.

▨ **3/2 RC (3 over 2 right cross):** Slip 2 sts to cn, hold to back, k3, k2 from cn.

▨ **3/2 LC (3 over 2 left cross):** Slip 3 sts to cn, hold to front, k2, k3 from cn.

▨ **3/2 RPC (3 over 2 right purl cross):** Slip 2 sts to cn, hold to back, k3, p2 from cn.

▨ **3/2 LPC (3 over 2 left purl cross):** Slip 3 sts to cn, hold to front, p2, k3 from cn.

Sideways Pullover

SIZES
To fit bust 30 (34, 38, 42, 46, 50, 54)" [76 (86.5, 96.5, 106.5, 117, 127, 137) cm]

FINISHED MEASUREMENTS
37 (41, 44, 49, 53, 57, 61)" [94 (104, 112, 124.5, 134.5, 145, 155) cm] bust

YARN
Valley Yarns Northfield [70% merino/20% baby alpaca/10% silk; 124 yards (113 meters)/50 grams]: 11 (12, 14, 15, 16, 17, 18) balls #10 Seaspray

NEEDLES
One 32" (80 cm) long circular needle size US 6 (4 mm)

One pair straight needles size US 4 (3.5 mm)

One 16" (40 cm) long circular needle size US 4 (3.5 mm), for Turtleneck

Change needle size if necessary to obtain correct gauge.

NOTIONS
Stitch markers; cable needle; stitch holder or waste yarn

GAUGE
22 sts and 32 rows = 4" in Rev St st, using larger needle

12-st panel from Cable A measures 1¾" (4.5 cm), using larger needle

8-st panel from Cable B measures 1½" (4 cm), using larger needle

18-st panel Cable C measures 2¾" (7 cm), using larger needle

Steam or wet block your swatch before taking the measurements.

Note: Because piece is worked from side to side, the row gauge will affect the bust measurements given and the stitch gauge will affect the length.

STITCH PATTERNS
2 x 2 Rib
(multiple of 4 sts + 2; 1-row repeat)
ROW 1 (WS): P2, *k2, p2; repeat from * to end.
ROW 2: Knit the knit sts and purl the purl sts as they face you.
Repeat Row 2 for pattern.

2 x 1 Rib
(multiple of 3 sts; 1-rnd repeat)
ALL RNDS: *K2, p1; repeat from * to end.

Cable A: Double O (#31)
Cable B: Basic Globe (#15)
Cable C: Braid Mega (#40)

PATTERN NOTES
Pullover is worked in one piece from left sleeve to right sleeve. A circular needle is used to accommodate the large number of stitches.

⅋ If you'd like to make a cable substitution, see page 70.

Left Sleeve

Using smaller needles, CO 74 (78, 82, 90, 94, 98, 106) sts.
Begin 2 x 2 Rib; work even until piece measures 5" (12.5 cm), ending with a WS row.
Change to larger circular needle.
NEXT ROW (RS): K12 (14, 16, 12, 14, 16, 12), [k2, k2tog] 12 (12, 12, 16, 16, 16, 20) times, knit to end—62 (66, 70, 74, 78, 82, 86) sts remain.

SHAPE GUSSET

NEXT ROW (WS): Using Cable CO, CO 16 sts, k2, work Cable B over 8 sts, k3, p2, k3, work Cable A over 12 sts, k3, p2, k24 (28, 32, 36, 40, 44, 48), p2, k3, work Cable A over 12 sts, k2—78 (82, 86, 90, 94, 98, 102) sts.
NEXT ROW (RS): P2, work Cable A, p2, k4, p22 (26, 30, 34, 38, 42, 46), k4, p2, work Cable A, p2, k4, p2, work Cable B, p2.
Work even until gusset measures 3" (7.5 cm), ending with a WS row.

Body

NEXT ROW (RS): CO 81 sts, knit across CO sts, work in patterns as established to end—159 (163, 167, 171, 175, 179, 183) sts.
Note: On next row, continue to work existing cables as established; begin all new cables with Row 1 of pattern.
NEXT ROW: CO 65 sts; working across CO sts, k1, p1, k3, work Cable A over 12 sts, k3, p2, k3, work Cable B over 8 sts, k3, p2, k3, work Cable C over 18 sts, k3, p2, k3, work Cable B over 8 sts, k3, p2, k3, work Cable A over 12 sts, k3, p2, k24 (28, 32, 36, 40, 44, 48), p2, k3, work Cable A over 12 sts, k3, p2, k3, work Cable B over 8 sts, k3, p2, k3, work Cable C over 18 sts, k3, p2, k3, work Cable B over 8 sts, k3, p2, k3, work Cable A over 12 sts, k3, p1, k1—224 (228, 232, 236, 240, 244, 248) sts.
Work even until piece measures 5¾ (6¾, 7¼, 8, 8¾, 9¾, 10¾)" [14.5 (17, 18.5, 20.5, 22, 25, 27.5) cm] from beginning of Body, ending with a WS row. Pm either side of center 30 (34, 38, 42, 46, 50, 54) sts. Make note of how many rows were worked since the end of the gusset so that you can match the row count when working the right shoulder.

SHAPE NECK

NEXT ROW (RS): Work to marker, sm, k4, p11 (13, 15, 17, 19, 21, 23), transfer 112 (114, 116, 118, 120, 122, 124) Back sts to st holder or waste yarn, BO 3 (4, 4, 4, 4, 4, 4) sts, work to end.
Working on Front sts only, BO 2 (3, 3, 3, 3, 3, 3) sts at neck edge 2 (1, 2, 1, 1, 2, 2) time(s), then 0 (2, 2, 2, 2, 2, 2) sts 0 (1, 1, 2, 2, 2, 3) time(s), then decrease 1 st every RS row 7 (7, 6, 8, 9, 7, 6) times—98 (98, 98, 99, 100, 101, 102) sts remain.

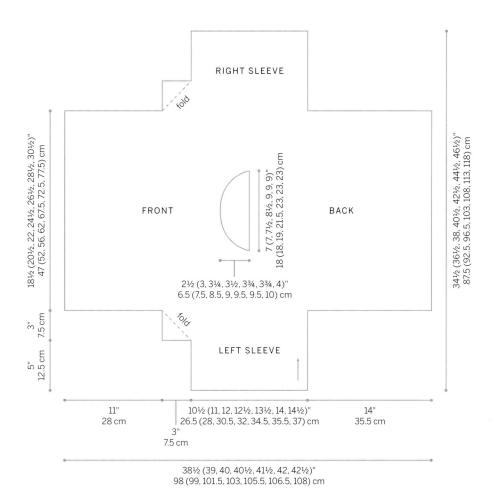

Work even for 2¼ (2¼, 2¾, 2¾, 2¾, 3¼, 3¼)" [5.5 (5.5, 7, 7, 7, 8.5, 8.5) cm], ending with a WS row.

NEXT ROW (RS): Inc 1 st at neck edge this row, then every RS row 6 (6, 5, 7, 8, 6, 5) times. CO 2 st(s) at beginning of next 2 (1, 1, 2, 2, 2, 3) RS row(s), then 3 (4, 4, 4, 4, 4, 4) sts at beginning of next 1 (1, 2, 1, 1, 2, 2) RS row(s), then 4 sts at beginning of next 0 (1, 1, 1, 1, 1, 1) RS row(s), working new sts in Rev St st—112 (114, 116, 118, 120, 122, 124) sts. Work even for 1 WS row. Cut yarn and transfer sts to st holder or waste yarn.

With RS facing, return Back sts to needle. Join yarn and work in pattern as established across Back sts for 7 (7, 7½, 8½, 9, 9, 9)" [18 (18, 19, 21.5, 23, 23, 23) cm], ending with a WS row. Transfer Front sts back to needle.

JOIN BACK AND FRONT

NEXT ROW (RS): Work to end of Back (removing marker); continuing across Front sts with same ball of yarn, purl to marker, remove marker, work in pattern as established to end—224 (228, 232, 236, 240, 244, 248) sts.

Work even until piece measures 5½ (6½, 7, 7¾, 8½, 9½, 10½)" [14 (16.5, 18, 19.5, 21.5, 24, 26.5) cm] from end of neck shaping, ending with a WS row, and having worked 2 fewer rows than you worked for left shoulder.

BO 81 sts at beginning of next row, then 65 sts at beginning of next row—78 (82, 86, 90, 94, 98, 102) sts remain.

Right Sleeve

Work even for 3" (7.5 cm), ending with a RS row.

NEXT ROW (WS): BO 16 sts, work to end—62 (66, 70, 74, 78, 82, 86) sts remain.

Change to smaller needles.

NEXT ROW: K12 (14, 16, 12, 14, 16, 12), [k2, M1] 12 (12, 12, 16, 16, 16, 20) times, knit to end—74 (78, 82, 90, 94, 98, 106) sts.

Begin 2 x 2 Rib; work even for 5" (12.5 cm), ending with a RS row.

BO all sts in pattern.

Finishing

Block piece as desired.

BOTTOM RIBBING

Using smaller needles, pick up and knit 114 (126, 138, 150, 162, 178, 190) sts across bottom edge of Front. Begin 2 x 2 Rib; work even for 3" (7.5 cm). BO all sts in pattern. Repeat for Back.

Sew side seam from Bottom Ribbing to gusset. Fold gusset along diagonal and sew to Sleeve and Back, then sew Sleeve seam,

reversing seam to RS approximately 3" (7.5) from end of Sleeve, so seam doesn't show when cuff is turned up.

TURTLENECK

With RS facing, using smaller circular needle and beginning at left shoulder, pick up and knit 81 (93, 102, 108, 114, 114, 117) sts around neck shaping. Join for working in the rnd; pm for beginning of rnd. Begin 2x1 Rib; work even for 2" (5 cm).

NEXT RND: *K2, M1P, p1; repeat from * to end—108 (124, 136, 144, 152, 152, 156) sts.

NEXT RND: *K2, p2; repeat from * to end.

Work even until piece measures 9" (23 cm).

BO ROW: K2, *insert left needle into fronts of sts just knit, then knit them again through the back loops, k1; repeat from * until 1 st remains, omitting final k1. Fasten off.

✗ Cable Substitution

Before getting started, review Stockinette Stitch Equivalent System on page 20.

CHOOSING CABLES

Cable A has an SSE of 9. Cable B has an SSE of 7. You can vary the widths of Cables A and B as long as the SSE of both combined is close to 16. Cable C has an SSE of 12.5 so you can substitute a cable or cables with a total SSE of 11 to 14. The substitution for Cable C can be wider or narrower, but remember that since this piece is worked sideways, this change will affect the length of the garment.

MANAGING A CHANGE IN STITCH COUNT

If, after substituting, your stitch count has changed, make note of the difference between your cast-on numbers and the cast-on called for in the pattern and remember to add or subtract those stitches throughout the instructions. Cables A and B affect both the number of stitches cast on at the beginning and for the body, and the stitch counts throughout. Any change in the number of stitches used for Cables A and B together also affects the number of stitches bound off before beginning the right sleeve, and at the end of the cabled portion of the right sleeve, before beginning the ribbing. You may also need to adjust the number of stitches to a multiple of 4 stitches plus

CABLE A

(panel of 12 sts; 8-row repeat)
SSE: 9 sts

ROW 1 (WS): P2, k2, p4, k2, p2.
ROW 2: K2, p2, k4, p2, k2.
ROW 3 AND ALL FOLLOWING WS ROWS: Knit the knit sts and purl the purl sts as they face you.
ROW 4: [2/1 LPC, 2/1 RPC] twice.
ROW 6: P1, 2/2 RC, p2, 2/2 LC, p1.
ROW 8: [2/1 RPC, 2/1 LPC] twice.
Repeat Rows 1–8 for pattern.

CABLE B

(panel of 8 sts; 16-row repeat)
SSE: 7 sts

ROW 1 (WS): K2, p4, k2.
ROW 2: P2, k4, p2.
ROW 3 AND ALL FOLLOWING WS ROWS: Knit the knit sts and purl the purl sts as they face you.
ROW 4: P2, 2/2 LC, p2.
ROW 6: 2/2 RC, 2/2 LC.
ROWS 8, 10, AND 12: Knit.
ROW 14: 2/2 LPC, 2/2 RPC.
ROW 16: Repeat Row 4.
Repeat Rows 1–16 for pattern.

CABLE C

(panel of 18 sts; 24-row repeat)
SSE: 12.5 sts

ROW 1 (WS): K1, p1, k1, p3, k1, p1, k2, p1, k1, p3, k1, p1, k1.
ROW 2: P1, k1, p1, RT, k1, p1, k1, p2, k1, p1, RT, [k1, p1] twice.
ROW 3 AND ALL FOLLOWING WS ROWS: Knit the knit sts and purl the purl sts as they face you.
ROW 4: [P1, k1] twice, LT, p1, k1, p2, k1, p1, k1, LT, p1, k1, p1.
ROWS 6–13: Repeat Rows 2–5.
ROW 14: Slip 9 sts to cn, hold to front, p1, k1, p1, RT, [k1, p1] twice, (p1, k1, p1, RT, [k1, p1] twice) from cn.
ROWS 16–23: Repeat Rows 4–7.
ROW 24: Repeat Row 4.
Repeat Rows 1–24 for pattern.

CABLE C (BRAID MEGA)

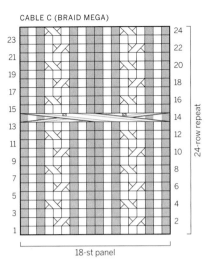

18-st panel

CABLE B (BASIC GLOBE)

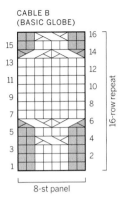

8-st panel

CABLE A (DOUBLE O)

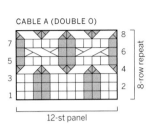

12-st panel

☐ Knit on RS, purl on WS.

▨ Purl on RS, knit on WS.

▨ **RT (right twist):** K2tog, but do not drop sts from left needle; insert right needle between 2 sts just worked and knit first st again, slip both sts from left needle together.

▨ **LT (left twist):** Insert needle from back to front between first and second sts on left needle and knit the second st through the front loop; knit first st, slip both sts from left needle together.

▨ **2/1 RPC (2 over 1 right purl cross):** Slip 1 st to cn, hold to back, k2, p1 from cn.

▨ **2/1 LPC (2 over 1 left purl cross):** Slip 2 sts to cn, hold to front, p1, k2 from cn.

▨ OR ▨ **2/2 RC (2 over 2 right cross):** Slip 2 sts to cn, hold to back, k2, k2 from cn.

▨ OR ▨ **2/2 LC (2 over 2 left cross):** Slip 2 sts to cn, hold to front, k2, k2 from cn.

▨ **2/2 RPC (2 over 2 right purl cross):** Slip 2 sts to cn, hold to back, k2, p2 from cn.

▨ **2/2 LPC (2 over 2 left purl cross):** Slip 2 sts to cn, hold to front, p2, k2 from cn.

 Slip 9 sts to cn, hold to front, p1, k1, p1, RT, [k1, p1] twice, (p1, k1, p1, RT, [k1, p1] twice) from cn.

Chapter **3**

Adding

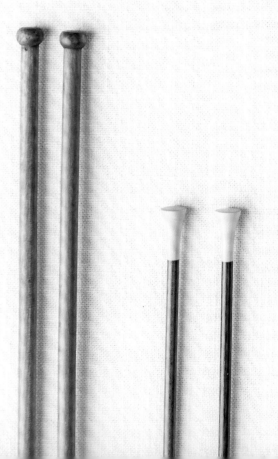

Breadth

In this chapter, I introduce two concepts that lead to wider and more complex cables: a center stable cross and stitch sharing. In a center stable cross, stitches are divided into 3 sections, one on the right, one in the center, and one on the left. After the cable cross is completed, the stitches that were on the right and the stitches that were on the left have switched positions, but the stitches in the center have remained stable (i.e., they haven't moved). In stitch sharing, the cable pattern starts out very much like the ribbed cables in Chapter 2 (see page 24), but, as these new cables develop, stitches are distributed, or shared, between them, creating the look of many crosses with just a few. Stitch sharing appears to be intricate and complicated, but it is actually deceptively simple because there are almost always multiple resting rows between the crossing rows.

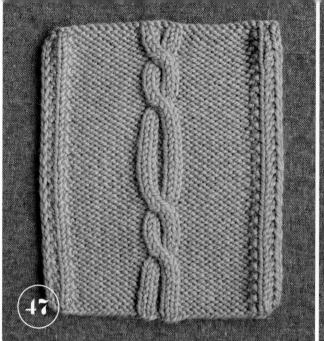

Small Center Stable GROUP 1

In this cable's main cross, the 2 stockinette stitches on the right swap places with the 2 stockinette stitches on the left, while the 2 center stitches remain stable in the center.

(panel of 6 sts; 26-row repeat)
SSE: 5.5 sts

ROW 1 (WS): P2, k2, p2.
ROWS 2–11: Knit the knit sts and purl the purl sts as they face you.
ROW 12: 2/2/2 LPC.
ROWS 14–19: Repeat Row 2.
ROW 20: Repeat Row 12.
ROWS 21–26: Repeat Row 2.
Repeat Rows 1–26 for pattern.

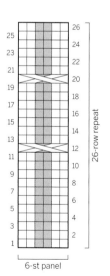

6-st panel

☐ Knit on RS, purl on WS.

▨ Purl on RS, knit on WS.

⬭ 2/2/2 LPC (2 over 2 over 2 left purl cross): Slip 4 sts to cn, hold to front, k2, slip last 2 sts from cn back to left needle, p2, k2 from cn.

Expanded 4/4 GROUP 1

A larger version of Small Center Stable (#47), here the 4 stockinette stitches on the right swap places with the 4 stockinette stitches on the left. One purl stitch remains stable in the center, which is what differentiates this cable from Basic 4/4 Rope (#8).

(panel of 11 sts; 14-row repeat)
SSE: 8.5 sts

ROW 1 (WS): P4, k3, p4.
ROWS 2–7: Knit the knit sts and purl the purl sts as they face you.
ROW 8: 4/1 LPC, p1, 4/1 RPC.
ROW 9: Repeat Row 2.
ROW 10: P1, 4/1/4 RPC, p1.
ROW 11: Repeat Row 2.
ROW 12: 4/1 RPC, p1, 4/1 LPC.
ROWS 13 AND 14: Repeat Row 2.
Repeat Rows 1–14 for pattern.

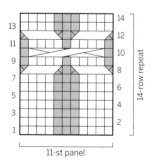

11-st panel

☐ Knit on RS, purl on WS.

▨ Purl on RS, knit on WS.

⬭ 4/1 RPC (4 over 1 right purl cross): Slip 1 st to cn, hold to back, k4, p1 from cn.

⬭ 4/1 LPC (4 over 1 left purl cross): Slip 4 sts to cn, hold to front, p1, k4 from cn.

⬭ 4/1/4 RPC (4 over 1 over 4 right purl cross): Slip 5 sts to cn, hold to back, k4, slip last st from cn back to left needle, p1, k4 from cn.

Garter Center Stable GROUP 1

In this cousin of Expanded 4/4 (#48), 2 garter stitches replace the 2 center stockinette stitches on each strand of the cable; there are 2 reverse stockinette stitches in between the 2 strands throughout, and these remain stable during the cross. See the reverse side of this cable on page 83.

(panel of 10 sts; 16-row repeat)
SSE: 8.5 sts

ROW 1 AND ALL WS ROWS (WS): [P1, k2] 3 times, p1.
ROWS 2, 4, AND 6: K4, p2, k4.
ROW 8: 4/2/4 LPC.
ROWS 10, 12, 14, AND 16: Repeat Row 2.
Repeat Rows 1–16 for pattern.

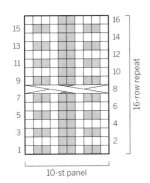

10-st panel

☐ Knit on RS, purl on WS.

▨ Purl on RS, knit on WS.

4/2/4 LPC (4 over 2 over 4 left purl cross): Slip 6 sts to cn, hold to front, k4, slip last 2 sts from cn back to left needle, p2, k4 from cn.

Lace Center Stable GROUP 1

In Expanded 4/4 (#48) you can see that each strand of the cable is made up of 4 stockinette stitches that change places on the cross row. Here those stockinette stitches become a small lace pattern. Two reverse stockinette stitches remain constant in the center.

(panel of 16 sts; 14-row repeat)
SSE: 8.5 sts

ROW 1 (WS): K1, p4, k6, p4, k1.
ROW 2: P1, k1, k2tog, yo, k1, p6, k1, yo, ssk, k1, p1.
ROW 3: Repeat Row 1.
ROW 4: P1, k1, yo, ssk, k1, p6, k1, k2tog, yo, k1, p1.
ROW 5: Repeat Row 1.
ROW 6: P1, M1P, k1, yo, ssk, k1, p2tog, p2, p2tog, k1, k2tog, yo, k1, M1P, p1.
ROW 7: K2, p4, k4, p4, k2.
ROW 8: P2, M1P, k1, k2tog, yo, k1, [p2tog] twice, k1, yo, ssk, k1, M1P, p2.
ROW 9: K3, p4, k2, p4, k3.
ROW 10: P3; slip 6 sts to cn, hold to front, k1, k2tog, yo, k1, slip last 2 sts from cn back to left needle, p2, (k1, k2tog, yo, k1) from cn; p3.
ROW 11: Repeat Row 9.
ROW 12: P1, p2tog, k1, k2tog, yo, k1, M1P, p2, M1P, k1, yo, ssk, k1, p2tog, p1.
ROW 13: Repeat Row 7.
ROW 14: P2tog, k1, yo, ssk, k1, M1P, p4, M1P, k1, k2tog, yo, k1, p2tog.
Repeat Rows 1–14 for pattern.

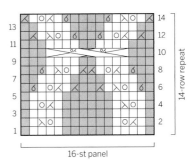

16-st panel

☐ Knit on RS, purl on WS.

▨ Purl on RS, knit on WS.

Ɓ M1P

⊙ Yo

◹ K2tog on RS, p2tog on WS.

◺ Ssk on RS, ssp on WS.

◿ P2tog on RS, k2tog on WS.

Slip 6 sts to cn, hold to front, k1, k2tog, yo, k1, slip last 2 sts from cn back to left needle, p2, (k1, k2tog, yo, k1) from cn.

Big O Sampler GROUP 1

To fully understand this cable, think of it as 3 separate columns placed next to each other. The 2 outside columns mirror each other. Both are made with center stable crosses. The columns serpentine back and forth like a snake because the cable crosses alternate moving to the right with moving to the left. At one point 1 strand of each of the mirrored cables is replaced with a twisted-stitch braid and that becomes the focal point, appearing to be surrounded by a big O of stockinette. A simple Rib Twist 3/3 (#3) from Chapter 2 separates the 2 sides.

(panel of 24 sts; 54-row repeat)
SSE: 18 sts

ROW 1 AND ALL WS ROWS (WS):
[P3, k2] twice, [p1-tbl, k2] twice, p3, k2, p3.

ROW 2: [K3, p2] twice, [k1-tbl, p2] twice, k3, p2, k3.

ROW 4: Repeat Row 2.

ROW 6: K3, p2, k3, p1; slip 3 sts to cn, hold to back, p1, k1-tbl, p1, (p1, k1-tbl, p1) from cn; p1, k3, p2, k3.

ROWS 8 AND 10: Repeat Row 2.

ROW 12: 3/2/3 LPC, p1; slip 3 sts to cn, hold to back, p1, k1-tbl, p1, (p1, k1-tbl, p1) from cn; p1, 3/2/3 RPC.

ROWS 14 AND 16: Repeat Row 2.

ROW 18: Repeat Row 6.

ROWS 20 AND 22: Repeat Row 2.

ROW 24: 3/2/3 RPC, p1; slip 3 sts to cn, hold to back, p1, k1-tbl, p1, (p1, k1-tbl, p1) from cn; p1, 3/2/3 LPC.

ROW 26: K3, p2, k1, RT, [p2, k1-tbl] twice, p2, LT, k1, p2, k3.

ROW 28: K3, p2, LT, k1, [p2, k1-tbl] twice, p2, k1, RT, p2, k3.

ROW 30: K3, p2, k1, RT, p1; slip 3 sts to cn, hold to back, p1, k1-tbl, p1, (p1, k1-tbl, p1) from cn; p1, LT, k1, p2, k3.

ROW 32: Repeat Row 28.

ROW 34: Repeat Row 26.

ROW 36: K3, p2, LT, k1, p1; slip 3 sts to cn, hold to back, p1, k1-tbl, p1, (p1, k1-tbl, p1) from cn; p1, k1, RT, p2, k3.

ROWS 38 AND 40: Repeat Rows 26 and 28.

ROWS 42–54: Repeat Rows 12–24. Repeat Rows 1–54 for pattern.

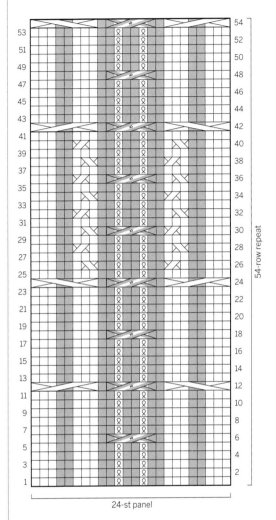

24-st panel

□ Knit on RS, purl on WS.

▨ Purl on RS, knit on WS.

⧖ K1-tbl on RS, p1-tbl on WS.

▱◪ RT (right twist): K2tog, but do not drop sts from left needle; insert right needle between 2 sts just worked and knit first st again, slip both sts from left needle together.

◪▱ LT (left twist): Insert needle from back to front between first and second sts on left needle and knit the second st through the front loop; knit first st, slip both sts from left needle together.

▱▱ Slip 3 sts to cn, hold to back, p1, k1-tbl, p1, (p1, k1-tbl, p1) from cn.

▱▱ 3/2/3 RPC (3 over 2 over 3 right purl cross): Slip 5 sts to cn, hold to back, k3, slip last 2 sts from cn back to left needle, p2, k3 from cn.

▱▱ 3/2/3 LPC (3 over 2 over 3 left purl cross): Slip 5 sts to cn, hold to front, k3, slip last 2 sts from cn back to left needle, p2, k3 from cn.

Seed Ridge Horseshoe GROUP 2

This horseshoe cable is made up of 2 mirrored columns of center stable cables. In each column, the outer strands swap places while 1 reverse stockinette stitch remains unmoved in the center. Each strand is made up of seed, stockinette, seed. Seed stitch adds an interesting texture and also lifts the stockinette stitch like the crest of a mountain chain. If the columns weren't separated from each other by the stable reverse stockinette stitch, the seed stitches from each column would meet and become garter stitch (something to try).

(panel of 15 sts; 8-row repeat)
SSE: 10 sts

ROW 1 AND ALL WS ROWS (WS):
K1, [p1, k3] 3 times, p1, k1.
ROWS 2 AND 4: [K3, p1] 3 times, k3.
ROW 6: 3/1/3 RPC, p1, 3/1/3 LPC.
ROW 8: Repeat Row 2.
Repeat Rows 1–8 for pattern.

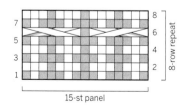

15-st panel

8-row repeat

☐ Knit on RS, purl on WS.

▨ Purl on RS, knit on WS.

✕ 3/1/3 RPC (3 over 1 over 3 right purl cross): Slip 4 sts to cn, hold to back, k3, slip last st from cn back to left needle, p1, k3 from cn.

✕ 3/1/3 LPC (3 over 1 over 3 left purl cross): Slip 4 sts to cn, hold to front, k3, slip last st from cn back to left needle, p1, k3 from cn.

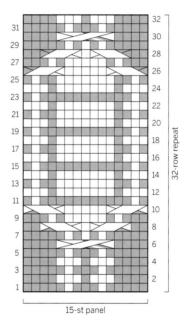

Seed Ridge Expansion GROUP 2

This expanded version of Seed Ridge Horseshoe (#52) features a single column rather than 2 mirrored columns. The seed and stockinette make up each side of the cable and move outward and then inward, creating a generous rounded space filled with garter ridges. Check out the reverse side of this cable on page 83.

(panel of 15 sts; 32-row repeat)
SSE: 12 sts

ROW 1 (WS): K5, p1, k3, p1, k5.
ROW 2: P4, k3, p1, k3, p4.
ROWS 3 AND 4: Repeat Rows 1 and 2.
ROW 5: Repeat Row 1.
ROW 6: P4, 3/1/3 RPC, p4.
ROW 7: K5, [p1, k1] twice, p1, k5.
ROW 8: P2, 3/2 RC, k1, 3/2 LC, p2.
ROW 9: K3, p1, k1, p5, k1, p1, k3.
ROW 10: 3/2 RC, k5, 3/2 LC.
ROW 11: K1, p1, k11, p1, k1.
ROW 12: K3, p1, k7, p1, k3.

ROW 13: K1, p1, k2, p7, k2, p1, k1.
ROW 14: Repeat Row 12.
ROWS 15–22: Repeat Rows 11–14 twice.
ROWS 23–25: Repeat Rows 11–13.
ROW 26: 3/2 LPC, k5, 3/2 RPC.
ROW 27: K3, p1, k1, p5, k1, p1, k3.
ROW 28: P2, 3/2 LPC, k1, 3/2 RPC, p2.
ROW 29: Repeat Row 7.
ROW 30: Repeat Row 6.
ROWS 31 AND 32: Repeat Rows 1 and 2.
Repeat Rows 1–32 for pattern.

☐ Knit on RS, purl on WS.

▨ Purl on RS, knit on WS.

3/2 RC (3 over 2 right cross): Slip 2 sts to cn, hold to back, k3, k2 from cn.

3/2 LC (3 over 2 left cross): Slip 3 sts to cn, hold to front, k2, k3 from cn.

3/2 RPC (3 over 2 right purl cross): Slip 2 sts to cn, hold to back, k3, p2 from cn.

3/2 LPC (3 over 2 left purl cross): Slip 3 sts to cn, hold to front, p2, k3 from cn.

3/1/3 RPC (3 over 1 over 3 right purl cross): Slip 4 sts to cn, hold to back, k3, slip last st from cn back to left needle, p1, k3 from cn.

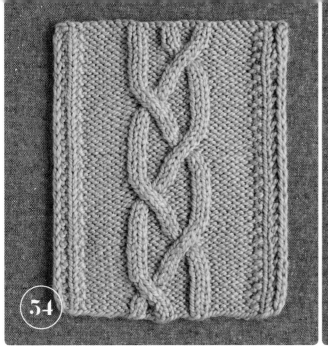

Stable Braid GROUP 3

Three strands of 2 stockinette stitches weave around each other in this loose braid. This differs from the 3/3/3 braids (#23–#26) in Chapter 2 because the strands being braided are not lying next to each other; instead, they are separated by reverse stockinette. There is always 1 stable reverse stockinette stitch in the center on the rows where the strands cross each other.

(panel of 12 sts; 16-row repeat)
SSE: 9.5 sts

ROW 1 (WS): [P2, k3] twice, p2.
ROW 2: [K2, p3] twice, k2.
ROW 3 AND ALL FOLLOWING WS ROWS: Knit the knit sts and purl the purl sts as they face you.
ROW 4: K2, p3, 2/1 LPC, p1, 2/1 RPC.
ROW 6: K2, p4, 2/1/2 LPC, p1.
ROW 8: K2, p3, 2/1 RPC, p1, 2/1 LPC.
ROW 10: Repeat Row 2.
ROW 12: 2/1 LPC, p1, 2/1 RPC, p3, k2.
ROW 14: P1, 2/1/2 RPC, p4, k2.
ROW 16: 2/1 RPC, p1, 2/1 LPC, p3, k2.
Repeat Rows 1–16 for pattern.

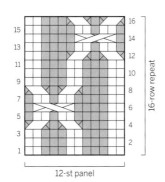

12-st panel

☐ Knit on RS, purl on WS.

▨ Purl on RS, knit on WS.

▨ 2/1 RPC (2 over 1 right purl cross): Slip 1 st to cn, hold to back, k2, p1 from cn.

▨ 2/1 LPC (2 over 1 left purl cross): Slip 2 sts to cn, hold to front, p1, k2 from cn.

▨ 2/1/2 RPC (2 over 1 over 2 right purl cross): Slip 3 sts to cn, hold to back, k2, slip last st from cn back to left needle, p1, k2 from cn.

▨ 2/1/2 LPC (2 over 1 over 2 left purl cross): Slip 3 sts to cn, hold to front, k2, slip last st from cn back to left needle, p1, k2 from cn.

Twist Stable Braid GROUP 3

By substituting a series of right twists for the stockinette stitch in Stable Braid (#54), I created Twist Stable Braid, which looks like 3 tiny twisted ropes loosely braided together.

(panel of 12 sts; 16-row repeat)
SSE: 9 sts

ROW 1 (WS): [P2, k3] twice, p2.
ROW 2: [RT, p3] twice, RT.
ROW 3 AND ALL FOLLOWING WS ROWS: Knit the knit sts and purl the purl sts as they face you.
ROW 4: RT, p3; slip 2 sts to cn, hold to front, p1, RT from cn; p1; slip 1 st to cn, hold to back, RT, p1 from cn.
ROW 6: RT, p4; slip 3 sts to cn, hold to front, RT, slip last st from cn back to left needle, p1, RT from cn; p1.
ROW 8: RT, p3; slip 1 st to cn, hold to back, RT, p1 from cn; p1; slip 2 sts to cn, hold to front, p1, RT from cn.
ROW 10: Repeat Row 2.
ROW 12: Slip 2 sts to cn, hold to front, p1, RT from cn; p1; slip 1 st to cn, hold to back, RT, p1 from cn; p3, RT.
ROW 14: P1; slip 3 sts to cn, hold to back, RT, slip last st from cn back to left needle, p1, RT from cn; p4, RT.
ROW 16: Slip 1 st to cn, hold to back, RT, p1 from cn; p1; slip 2 sts to cn, hold to front, p1, RT from cn; p3, RT.
Repeat Rows 1–16 for pattern.

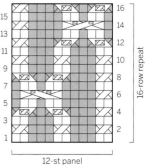

12-st panel

☐ Knit on RS, purl on WS.

▨ Purl on RS, knit on WS.

▨ RT (right twist): K2tog, but do not drop sts from left needle; insert right needle between 2 sts just worked and knit first st again, slip both sts from left needle together.

▨ Slip 1 st to cn, hold to back, RT, p1 from cn.

▨ Slip 2 sts to cn, hold to front, p1, RT from cn.

▨ Slip 3 sts to cn, hold to back, RT, slip last st from cn back to left needle, p1, RT from cn.

▨ Slip 3 sts to cn, hold to front, RT, slip last st from cn back to left needle, p1, RT from cn.

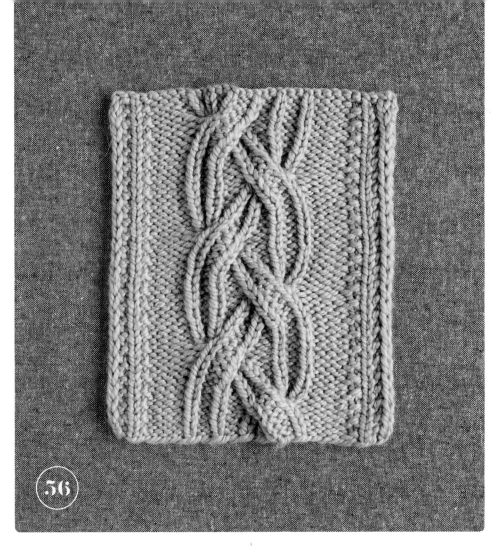

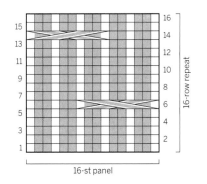

Rib Braid GROUP 3

This braid starts out as a simple rib of k1, p2. Every 8th row 4 rib stitches switch places with another group of 4 rib stitches while 2 purls remain stable in the center. Those 2 purls (reverse stockinette stitches) keep the ribs separated and allow them to pop out more from the fabric and become more well defined than they would otherwise.

(panel of 16 sts; 16-row repeat)
SSE: 11 sts

ROW 1 (WS): [P1, k2] 5 times, p1.

ROWS 2–5: Knit the knit sts and purl the purl sts as they face you.

ROW 6: Slip 6 sts to cn, hold to front, k1, p2, k1, slip last 2 sts from cn back to left needle, p2, (k1, p2, k1) from cn; [p2, k1] twice.

ROWS 7–13: Repeat Row 2.

ROW 14: [K1, p2] twice; slip 6 sts to cn, hold to back, k1, p2, k1, slip last 2 sts from cn back to left needle, p2, (k1, p2, k1) from cn.

ROWS 15 AND 16: Repeat Row 2
Repeat Rows 1–16 for pattern.

☐ Knit on RS, purl on WS.

▨ Purl on RS, knit on WS.

⬭ Slip 6 sts to cn, hold to back, k1, p2, k1, slip last 2 sts from cn back to left needle, p2, (k1, p2, k1) from cn.

⬭ Slip 6 sts to cn, hold to front, k1, p2, k1, slip last 2 sts from cn back to left needle, p2, (k1, p2, k1) from cn.

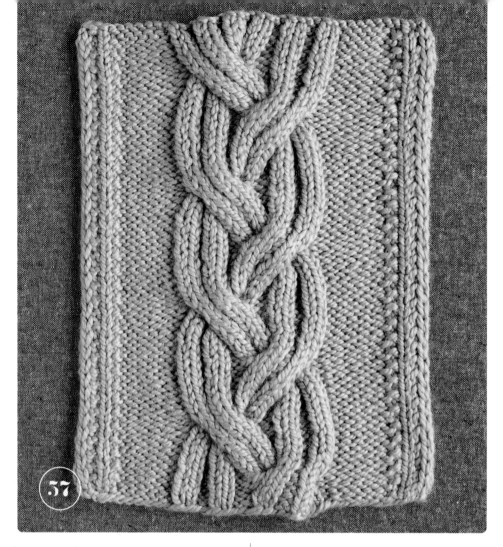

Mega Rib Braid GROUP 3

Doubling the knit stitches of Rib Braid (#56) (k1, p2 becomes k2, p2) gives us Mega Rib Braid. The crosses are worked every 8th row in both versions. Since there are a greater number of stitches being crossed, Mega Rib Braid appears to be a tighter braid. To loosen it up, you could cross every 10th or 12th row instead.

(panel of 22 sts; 16-row repeat)
SSE: 14.5 sts

ROW 1 (WS): [P2, k2] 5 times, p2.

ROWS 2–5: Knit the knit sts and purl the purl sts as they face you.

ROW 6: Slip 8 sts to cn, hold to back, k2, p2, k2, slip last 2 sts from cn back to left needle, p2, (k2, p2, k2) from cn; [p2, k2] twice.

ROWS 7–13: Repeat Row 2.

ROW 14: [K2, p2] twice; slip 8 sts to cn, hold to front, k2, p2, k2, slip last 2 sts from cn back to left needle, p2, (k2, p2, k2) from cn.

ROWS 15 AND 16: Repeat Row 2. Repeat Rows 1–16 for pattern.

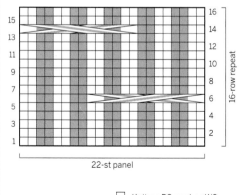

☐ Knit on RS, purl on WS.

▨ Purl on RS, knit on WS.

Slip 8 sts to cn, hold to back, k2, p2, k2, slip last 2 sts from cn back to left needle, p2, (k2, p2, k2) from cn.

Slip 8 sts to cn, hold to front, k2, p2, k2, slip last 2 sts from cn back to left needle, p2, (k2, p2, k2) from cn.

Reversibility

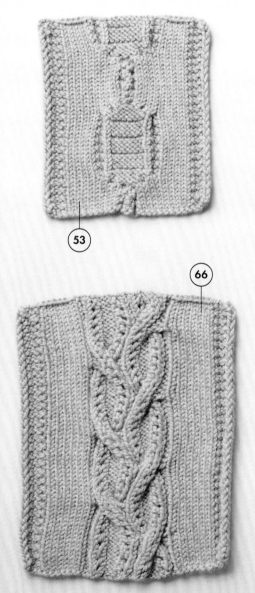

Here are more stitch patterns that look good on both sides. The attractive reverse sides shown here fall into the categories I introduced on page 51.

I like the quirky combinations of textures and shapes on the reverse side of **SEED RIDGE EXPANSION (#53).**

CHEVRON SHARE TIGHT (#72) follows the rib-based reversibility rule. It's difficult to tell the right side from the wrong side of this cable.

The eyelets nestled in reverse stockinette stitch on the right side of **EYELET 2/2 SHARE (#66)** look equally good on the wrong side.

The reversibility of garter stitch means that **GARTER CENTER STABLE (#49)** looks good on both sides. The center stable cable cross adds to its success because the stitches that remain in the center are underneath the garter stitches on both sides.

Double Twist Braid GROUP 3

It took me a while to realize that this cable is essentially a braid and is closely related to Mega Rib Braid (#57). In this case the rib base is k3, p2. This is difficult to see as a braid because 2 right crosses are followed by 2 left crosses, with 7 straight rows of rib in between all of the crosses. More typically, braids are created by crossing once to the right and then once to the left or vice versa (as seen in #54–#57).

(panel of 13 sts; 32-row repeat)
SSE: 10 sts

ROW 1 (WS): [P3, k2] twice, p3.
ROWS 2 AND 3: Knit the knit sts and purl the purl sts as they face you.
ROW 4: K3, p2, 3/2/3 LPC.
ROWS 5–11: Repeat Row 2.

ROW 12: Repeat Row 4.
ROWS 13–19: Repeat Row 2.
ROW 20: 3/2/3/RPC, p2, k3.
ROWS 21–27: Repeat Row 2.
ROW 28: Repeat Row 20.
ROWS 29–32: Repeat Row 2.
Repeat Rows 1–32 for pattern.

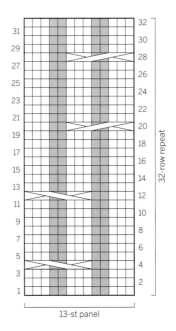

13-st panel

32-row repeat

☐ Knit on RS, purl on WS.

▦ Purl on RS, knit on WS.

3/2/3 RPC (3 over 2 over 3 right purl cross): Slip 5 sts to cn, hold to back, k3, slip last 2 sts from cn back to left needle, p2, k3 from cn.

3/2/3 LPC (3 over 2 over 3 left purl cross): Slip 5 sts to cn, hold to front, k3, slip last 2 sts from cn back to left needle, p2, k3 from cn.

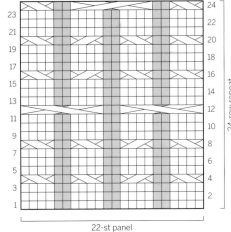

Rope Braid GROUP 3

As in the 3 previous braids, this braid begins as rib. In this case, it's k4, p2. The addition of 2/2 crosses changes the four k4 strands into ropes. The ropes switch places when you work the larger center stable crosses, but the p2 remains stable in the center. I usually like to continue any pattern stitch I've begun while I'm working the cable cross row, but in this case I skipped the 2/2 cross and switched to stockinette. I made this choice because I like the way the flat stockinette fabric looks and also because it would be very difficult to perform both of these crosses at once.

(panel of 22 sts; 24-row repeat)
SSE: 16 sts

ROW 1 (WS): [P4, k4] 3 times, p4.

ROWS 2 AND 3: Knit the knit sts and purl the purl sts as they face you.

ROW 4: 2/2 LC, p2, 2/2 RC, [p2, 2/2 LC] twice.

ROWS 5–8: Repeat Rows 1–4.

ROWS 9–11: Repeat Row 2.

ROW 12: 4/2/4 LC, p2, 4/2/4 LRC.

ROWS 13–15: Repeat Row 2.

ROW 16: [2/2 LC, p2] twice, 2/2 RC, p2, 2/2 LC.

ROWS 17–20: Repeat Rows 13–16.

ROWS 21–23: Repeat Row 2.

ROW 24: 2/2 LC, p2, 4/2/4 RC, p2, 2/2 LC.
Repeat Rows 1–24 for pattern.

□ Knit on RS, purl on WS. ▨ Purl on RS, knit on WS.

▨ **2/2 RC (2 over 2 right cross):** Slip 2 sts to cn, hold to back, k2, k2 from cn.

▨ **2/2 LC (2 over 2 left cross):** Slip 2 sts to cn, hold to front, k2, k2 from cn.

▨ **4/2/4 RPC (4 over 2 over 4 right purl cross):** Slip 6 sts to cn, hold to back, k4, slip last 2 sts from cn back to left needle, p2, k4 from cn.

▨ **4/2/4 LPC (4 over 2 over 4 left purl cross):** Slip 6 sts to cn, hold to front, k4, slip last 2 sts from cn back to left needle, p2, k4 from cn.

Stable Lace GROUP 4

Here a stable 2-stitch lace pattern forms a strong vertical element in the center of the cable, while each side of the cable is p2, k2 rib. Those ribbed sides swap places at the cross while the 2 lace stitches remain in the center.

(panel of 14 sts; 16-row repeat)
SSE: 9 sts

ROW 1 AND ALL WS ROWS (WS):
K2, p2, k2, ssk, yo, k2, p2, k2.
ROWS 2, 4, 6, AND 8: P2, k2, p2,
p2tog, yo, p2, k2, p2.
ROW 10: Slip 8 sts to cn, hold to
back, p2, k2, p2, slip last 2 sts
from cn back to left needle, p2,
(p2, k2, p2) from cn.
ROWS 12, 14, AND 16: Repeat Row 2.
Repeat Rows 1–16 for pattern.

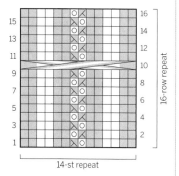

14-st repeat

☐ Knit on RS, purl on WS.

◻ Purl on RS, knit on WS.

⧀ Yo

⧅ P2tog on RS, k2tog on WS.

⧄ Ssp on RS, ssk on WS.

 Slip 8 sts to cn, hold to back, p2, k2, p2, slip last 2 sts from cn back to left needle, p2, (p2, k2, p2) from cn.

Stable Twist GROUP 4

The strong vertical element in the center of this cable is a column of right twists. Three stockinette stitches form the strands of the cable. After the large center stable cable cross, these 3 stitches are moved outward and reverse stockinette is introduced on each side of the center twists.

(panel of 12 sts; 16-row repeat)
SSE: 9 sts

ROW 1 (WS): P3, k2, p2, k2, p3.
ROW 2: K3, p2, RT, p2, k3.
ROW 3 AND ALL FOLLOWING WS ROWS:
Knit the knit sts and purl the purl
sts as they face you.
ROWS 4 AND 6: Repeat Row 2.
ROW 8: 3/2 LPC, RT, 3/2 RPC.
ROW 10: P2, 3/2/3 LC, p2.
ROW 12: 3/2 RPC, RT, 3/2 LPC.
ROWS 14 AND 16: Repeat Row 2.
Repeat Rows 1–16 for pattern.

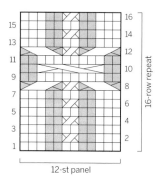

12-st panel

☐ Knit on RS, purl on WS.

◻ Purl on RS, knit on WS.

⧄⧅ RT (right twist): K2tog, but do not drop sts from left needle; insert right needle between 2 sts just worked and knit first st again, slip both sts from left needle together.

⟋ 3/2 RPC (3 over 2 right purl cross): Slip 2 sts to cn, hold to back, k3, p2 from cn.

⟍ 3/2 LPC (3 over 2 left purl cross): Slip 3 sts to cn, hold to front, p2, k3 from cn.

⟋⟍ 3/2/3 LC (3 over 2 over 3 left cross): Slip 5 sts to cn, hold to front, k3, slip last 2 sts from cn back to left needle, k2, k3 from cn.

(62)

Twist Center Lattice GROUP 4

Essentially, this lattice is an expanded version of Stable Twist (#61). To understand how this cable is structured, picture placing 2 repeats of Stable Twist next to each other, separated by a column of right twists, and then adding a center stable cross each time a k3, RT, and k3 meet up (which is every 6 rows).

(panel of 14 sts + 12; 12-row repeat)
TOTAL SSE: 17 sts
REPEAT SSE: 9 sts

ROW 1 (WS): P3, k2, p2, *k2, p8, k2, p2; repeat from * to last 5 sts, k2, p3.

ROW 2: 3/1 LPC, p1, *RT, p1, 3/1 RPC, RT, 3/1 LPC, p1; repeat from * to last 7 sts, RT, p1, 3/1 RPC.

ROW 3 AND ALL FOLLOWING WS ROWS: Knit the knit sts and purl the purl sts as they face you.

ROW 4: P1, 3/1 LPC, *RT, 3/1 RPC, p1, RT, p1, 3/1 LPC; repeat from * to last 7 sts, RT, 3/1 RPC, p1.

ROW 6: P2, 3/2/3 RC, *p2, RT, p2, 3/2/3 RC; repeat from * to last 2 sts, p2.

ROW 8: P1, 3/1 RPC, *RT, 3/1 LPC, p1, RT, p1, 3/1 RPC; repeat from * to last 7 sts, RT, 3/1 LPC, p1.

ROW 10: 3/1 RPC, p1, *RT, p1, 3/1 LPC, RT, 3/1 RPC, p1; repeat from * to last 7 sts, RT, p1, 3/1 LPC.

ROW 12: K3, p2, *RT, p2, 3/2/3 LC, p2; repeat from * to last 7 sts, RT, p2, k3.

Repeat Rows 1–12 for pattern.

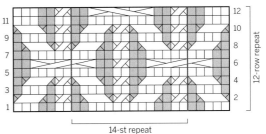

14-st repeat

12-row repeat

☐ Knit on RS, purl on WS.　▨ Purl on RS, knit on WS.

❘ Pattern Repeat

⬖ RT (right twist): K2tog, but do not drop sts from left needle; insert right needle between 2 sts just worked and knit first st again, slip both sts from left needle together.

◰ 3/1 RPC (3 over 1 right purl cross): Slip 1 st to cn, hold to back, k3, p1 from cn.

◰ 3/1 LPC (3 over 1 left purl cross): Slip 3 sts to cn, hold to front, p1, k3 from cn.

⬒ 3/2/3 RC (3 over 2 over 3 right cross): Slip 5 sts to cn, hold to back, k3, slip last 2 sts from cn back to left needle, k2, k3 from cn.

⬒ 3/2/3 LC (3 over 2 over 3 left cross): Slip 5 sts to cn, hold to front, k3, slip last 2 sts from cn back to left needle, k2, k3 from cn.

(63)

Stretch Twist Lattice GROUP 4

This variation of Twist Center Lattice (#62) opens up the lattice both vertically and horizontally. Width is added by introducing a second set of cable crosses that move the stockinette stitches over by 2 while also adding 4 rows in height.

(multiple of 18 + 16 sts; 24-row repeat)

TOTAL SSE: 25 sts

REPEAT SSE: 12.5 sts

ROW 1 (WS): *K2, p3, k2, p2; repeat from * to last 7 sts, k2, p3, k2.

ROW 2: P2, k3, p2, *RT, p2, k3, p2; repeat from * to end.

ROW 3 AND ALL FOLLOWING WS ROWS: Knit the knit sts and purl the purl sts as they face you.

ROW 4: P2, 3/1 LPC, p1, *RT, p1, 3/1 RPC, p2, RT, p2, 3/1 LPC, p1; repeat from * to last 9 sts, RT, p1, 3/1 RPC, p2.

ROW 6: P3, 3/1 LPC, *RT, 3/1 RPC, p3, RT, p3, 3/1 LPC; repeat from * to last 9 sts, RT, 3/1 RPC, p3.

ROW 8: P4, 3/2/3 RC, *p4, RT, p4, 3/2/3 RC; repeat from * to last 4 sts, p4.

ROW 10: P3, 3/1 RPC, *RT, 3/1 LPC, p3, RT, p3, 3/1 RPC; repeat from * to last 9 sts, RT, 3/1 LPC, p3.

ROW 12: P2, 3/1 RPC, p1, *RT, p1, 3/1 LPC, p2, RT, p2, 3/1 RPC, p1; repeat from * to last 9 sts, RT, p1, 3/1 LPC, p2.

ROW 14: Repeat Row 2.

ROW 16: P1, 3/1 RPC, p2, *RT, p2, 3/1 LPC, p1, RT, p1, 3/1 RPC, p2; repeat from * to last 9 sts RT, p2, 3/1 LPC, p1.

ROW 18: 3/1 RPC, p3, *RT, p3, 3/1 LPC, RT, 3/1 RPC, p3; repeat from * to last 9 sts RT, p3, 3/1 LPC.

ROW 20: K3, p4, *RT, p4, 3/2/3 LC, p4; repeat from * to last 9 sts, RT, p4, k3.

ROW 22: 3/1 LPC, p3, *RT, p3, 3/1 RPC, RT, 3/1 LPC, p3; repeat from * to last 9 sts, RT, p3, 3/1 RPC.

ROW 24: P1, 3/1 LPC, p2, *RT, p2, 3/1 RPC, p1, RT, p1, 3/1 LPC, p2; repeat from * to last 9 sts, RT, p2, 3/1 RPC, p1.

Repeat Rows 1–24 for pattern.

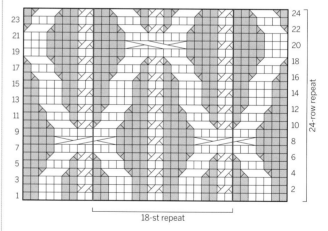

□ Knit on RS, purl on WS. ▨ Purl on RS, knit on WS.

Ι Pattern Repeat

▨ RT (right twist): K2tog, but do not drop sts from left needle; insert right needle between 2 sts just worked and knit first st again, slip both sts from left needle together.

▱ 3/1 RPC (3 over 1 right purl cross): Slip 1 st to cn, hold to back, k3, p1 from cn.

▱ 3/1 LPC (3 over 1 left purl cross): Slip 3 sts to cn, hold to front, p1, k3 from cn.

▱ 3/2/3 RC (3 over 2 over 3 right cross): Slip 5 sts to cn, hold to back, k3, slip last 2 sts from cn back to left needle, k2, k3 from cn.

▱ 3/2/3 LC (3 over 2 over 3 left cross): Slip 5 sts to cn, hold to front, k3, slip last 2 sts from cn back to left needle, k2, k3 from cn.

(64)

Snug Lattice GROUP 4

A shrunken-down version of Twist Center Lattice (#62), Snug Lattice is worked with 2 stitches instead of 3, forming diagonals. The stable center is reduced to 1 twisted knit stitch.

(multiple of 10 sts +19; 8-row repeat)

TOTAL SSE: 19 sts

REPEAT SSE: 6 sts

ROW 1 (WS): *K2, p2, p1-tbl, p2, k2, p1-tbl; repeat from * to last 9 sts, k2, p2, p1-tbl, p2, k2.

ROW 2: *P2, 2/1/2 RC, p2, k1-tbl; repeat from * to last 9 sts, p2, 2/1/2 RC, p2.

ROW 3: Repeat Row 1.

ROW 4: *2/2 RPC, k1-tbl, 2/2 LPC, k1-tbl; repeat from * to last 9 sts, 2/2 RPC, k1-tbl, 2/2 LPC.

ROW 5: *P2, k2, p1-tbl, k2, p2, p1-tbl; repeat from * to last 9 sts, p2, k2, p1-tbl, k2, p2.

ROW 6: K2, *p2, k1-tbl, p2, 2/1/2 LC; repeat from * to last 7 sts, p2, k1-tbl, p2, k2.

ROW 7: Repeat Row 5.

ROW 8: *2/2 LPC, k1-tbl, 2/2 RPC, k1-tbl; repeat from * to last 9 sts, 2/2 LPC, k1-tbl, 2/2 RPC. Repeat Rows 1–8 for pattern.

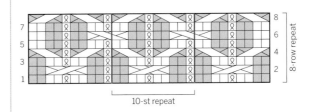

10-st repeat

8-row repeat

☐ Knit on RS, purl on WS.

▨ Purl on RS, knit on WS.

⧖ K1-tbl on RS, p1-tbl on WS.

❘ Pattern repeat

2/2 RPC (2 over 2 right purl cross): Slip 2 sts to cn, hold to back, k2, p2 from cn.

2/2 LPC (2 over 2 left purl cross): Slip 2 sts to cn, hold to front, p2, k2 from cn.

2/1/2 RC (2 over 1 over 2 right cross): Slip 3 sts to cn, hold to back, k2, slip last st from cn back to left needle, k1, k2 from cn.

2/1/2 LC (2 over 1 over 2 left cross): Slip 3 sts to cn, hold to front, k2, slip last st from cn back to left needle, k1, k2 from cn.

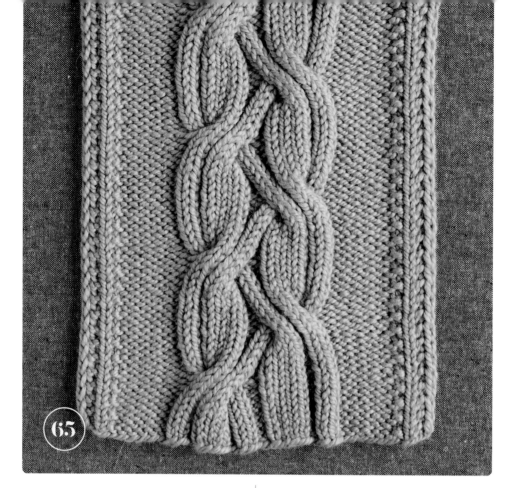

(65)

2/2 Share GROUP 5

The crosses in this pattern are identical to the crosses in 2/2 Over 2/2 (#34). K2, p2, k2 crosses over k2, p2, k2. This occurs on the left first, and then a few rows later on the right as a mirror image. The mirrored crosses share 2 knit stitches. The rib formed by the 2 shared stitches appears to move diagonally from one cable crossing to the next. It's hard to believe that all of the perceived movement is made by 2 simple cables separated by 7 rows of ribbing.

(panel of 22 sts; 16-row repeat)
SSE: 16 sts

ROW 1 (WS): [P2, k2, p4, k2] twice, p2.
ROWS 2–7: Knit the knit sts and purl the purl sts as they face you.
ROW 8: K2, p2, k4, p2; slip 6 sts to cn, hold to back, k2, p2, k2, (k2, p2, k2) from cn.

ROWS 9–15: Repeat Row 2.
ROW 16: Slip 6 sts to cn, hold to front, k2, p2, k2, (k2, p2, k2) from cn; p2, k4, p2, k2.
Repeat Rows 1–16 for pattern.

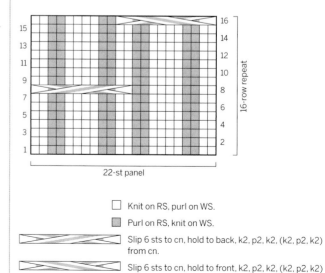

22-st panel

16-row repeat

☐ Knit on RS, purl on WS.

▨ Purl on RS, knit on WS.

Slip 6 sts to cn, hold to back, k2, p2, k2, (k2, p2, k2) from cn.

Slip 6 sts to cn, hold to front, k2, p2, k2, (k2, p2, k2) from cn.

Eyelet 2/2 Share GROUP 5

In this variation of the 2/2 Share (#65), a column of yarnovers and decreases opens up the reverse-stockinette-stitch spaces between the ribs. See the reverse side of this cable on page 83.

(panel of 22 sts; 16-row repeat)
SSE: 16 sts

ROW 1 AND ALL WS ROWS (WS):
[P2, k2, p4, k2] twice, p2.
ROWS 2, 4, AND 6: [K2, p1, yo, k2tog, k2, ssk, yo, p1] twice, k2.
ROW 8: K2, p1, yo, k2tog, k2, ssk, yo, p1; slip 6 sts to cn, hold to back, k2, p2, k2, (k2, p2, k2) from cn.

ROWS 10, 12, AND 14: Repeat Row 2.
ROW 16: Slip 6 sts to cn, hold to front, k2, p2, k2, (k2, p2, k2) from cn; p1, yo, k2tog, k2, ssk, yo, p1, k2. Repeat Rows 1–16 for pattern.

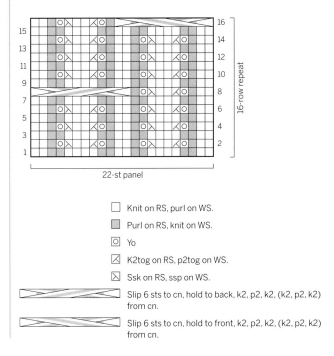

22-st panel

☐ Knit on RS, purl on WS.

▨ Purl on RS, knit on WS.

☑ Yo

◪ K2tog on RS, p2tog on WS.

◩ Ssk on RS, ssp on WS.

Slip 6 sts to cn, hold to back, k2, p2, k2, (k2, p2, k2) from cn.

Slip 6 sts to cn, hold to front, k2, p2, k2, (k2, p2, k2) from cn.

Rope 2/2 Share GROUP 5

This cable starts out in the same way as 2/2 Share (#65) with k2, p2, k2 next to k2, p2, k2, forming 4 stockinette stitches where the ribs meet up. The addition of a few 2/2 crosses worked over those 4 stockinette stitches gives the appearance of 2 ropes.

(panel of 22 sts; 16-row repeat)
SSE: 16.5 sts

ROW 1 (WS): [P2, k2, p4, k2] twice, p2.

ROWS 2 AND 3: Knit the knit sts and purl the purl sts as they face you.

ROW 4: K2, p2, 2/2 LC, p2, k2, p2, 2/2 RC, p2, k2.

ROWS 5–7: Repeat Row 2.

ROW 8: K2, p2, 2/2 LC, p2; slip 6 sts to cn, hold to back, k2, p2, k2, (k2, p2, k2) from cn.

ROWS 9–11: Repeat Row 2.

ROW 12: Repeat Row 4.

ROWS 13–15: Repeat Row 2.

ROW 16: Slip 6 sts to cn, hold to front, k2, p2, k2, (k2, p2, k2) from cn; p2, 2/2 RC, p2, k2.
Repeat Rows 1–16 for pattern.

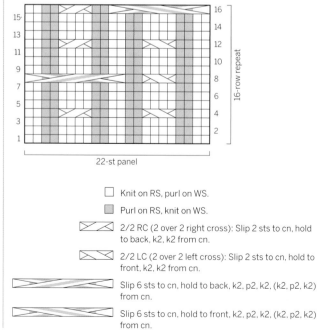

22-st panel

16-row repeat

☐ Knit on RS, purl on WS.

▨ Purl on RS, knit on WS.

2/2 RC (2 over 2 right cross): Slip 2 sts to cn, hold to back, k2, k2 from cn.

2/2 LC (2 over 2 left cross): Slip 2 sts to cn, hold to front, k2, k2 from cn.

Slip 6 sts to cn, hold to back, k2, p2, k2, (k2, p2, k2) from cn.

Slip 6 sts to cn, hold to front, k2, p2, k2, (k2, p2, k2) from cn.

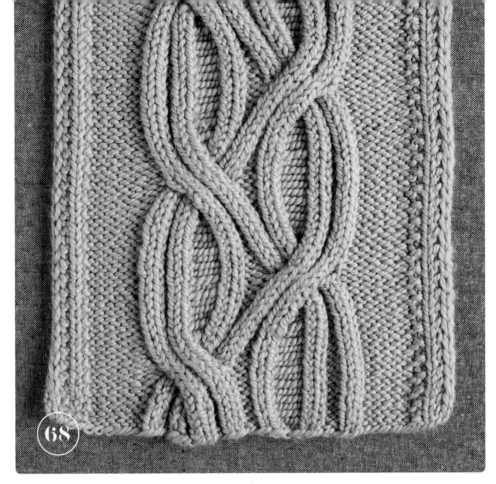

(68)

Drop Center 2/2 Share GROUP 5

Here an additional purl separates the central 4 stockinette stitches of 2/2 Share (#65). This stitch is later dropped down to the yarnover at its base. The "run" that results forms what looks like a ladder and opens up the fabric. To keep the ladder in place, knit stitches on either side of the dropped stitch are twisted. Without twists, the stitches next to the ladder would take in extra yarn and become fatter and, as a result, the ladder would be less defined.

(panel of 26 sts; decreases to 24 sts; 24-row repeat)
SSE: 20 sts

CO 26 sts.

ROW 1 (SET-UP ROW) (WS): P2, k2, p1, p2tog, yo, p2tog, p1, k2, p2, k2, p1, p2tog, yo, p2tog, p1, k2, p2—24 sts remain.

ROW 2: K2, p2, k1, k1-tbl, p1, k1-tbl, k1, p2, k2, p2, k1, k1-tbl, p1, k1-tbl, k1, p2, k2.

ROW 3 AND ALL FOLLOWING WS ROWS: P2, k2, p1, p1-tbl, k1, p1-tbl, p1, p2, k2, p1, p1-tbl, k1, p1-tbl, p1, k2, p2.

ROWS 4, 6, AND 8: Repeat Row 2.

ROW 10: K2, p2, k1, k1-tbl, p1, k1-tbl, k1, p2; slip 7 sts to cn, hold to front, k2, p2, k2, slip next from cn back to left needle, p1, (k2, p2, k2) from cn.

ROWS 12, 14, 16, 18, AND 20: Repeat Row 2.

ROW 22: Slip 7 sts to cn, hold to back, k2, p2, k2, slip next from cn back to left needle, p1, (k2, p2, k2) from cn; p2, k1, k1-tbl, p1, k1-tbl, k1, p2, k2.

ROWS 24 AND 25: Repeat Rows 2 and 3.
Repeat Rows 2–25 for pattern.

ROW 26 (BIND-OFF ROW): BO sts as you go, working as follows: K2, p2, k2, yo, drop next st and unravel, [k2, p2] twice, k2, yo, drop next st and unravel, k2, p2, k2.

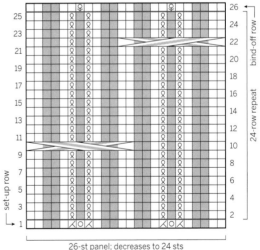

26-st panel; decreases to 24 sts

NOTE: Cast on 26 sts. Work Row 1 (Set-Up Row) once; work Rows 2–25 for main pattern. Bind off sts following Row 26 (Bind-Off Row).

☐ Knit on RS, purl on WS.

▦ Purl on RS, knit on WS.

𝒬 K1-tbl on RS, p1-tbl on WS.

○ Yo

⧄ K2tog on RS, p2tog on WS.

𝒬 Yo, drop next st and unravel.

▎ Pattern repeat

Slip 7 sts to cn, hold to back, k2, p2, k2, slip next st from cn back to left needle, p1, (k2, p2, k2) from cn.

Slip 7 sts to cn, hold to front, k2, p2, k2, slip next st from cn back to left needle, p1, (k2, p2, k2) from cn.

Adding Breadth

93

1/1 Share Drop GROUP 6

This cable introduces the concept of dropping stitches to create ladders within a strand. In contrast, in Drop Center 2/2 Share (#68), the dropped stitches happen between the strands (in what looks like the carved-out area).

(panel of 27 sts; decreases to 25 sts; 12-row repeat)
SSE: 21 sts

CO 27 sts.

ROW 1 (SET-UP ROW) (WS): P1, k1, p1, k3, p1, k1, p2tog, yo, p2tog, k3, p2tog, yo, p2tog, k1, p1, k3, p1, k1, p1—25 sts remain.

ROW 2: K1, p1, k1, p3, k1, [p1, k1-tbl] twice, p3, [k1-tbl, p1] twice, k1, p3, k1, p1, k1.

ROW 3 AND ALL FOLLOWING WS ROWS: P1, k1, p1, k3, p1, [k1, k1-tbl] twice, k3, [p1-tbl, k1] twice, p1, k3, p1, k1, p1.

ROW 4: Repeat Row 2.

ROW 6: K1, p1, k1, p3, k1, p1; slip 6 sts to cn, hold to front, k1, p1, k1, slip last 3 sts from cn back to left needle, p3, (k1, p1, k1) from cn; p1, k1, p3, k1, p1, k1.

ROWS 8 AND 10: Repeat Row 2.

ROW 12: Slip 6 sts to cn, hold to back, k1, p1, k1, slip last 3 sts from cn back to left needle, p3, (k1, p1, k1) from cn; p1, k1-tbl, p3, k1-tbl, p1; slip 6 sts to cn, hold to back, k1, p1, k1, slip last 3 sts from cn back to left needle, p3, (k1, p1, k1) from cn.

ROW 13: Repeat Row 3.
Repeat Rows 2–13 for pattern.

ROW 14 (BIND-OFF ROW): BO sts as you go, working as follows: K1, p1, k1, p3, k1, p1, k1-tbl, yo, drop next st and unravel, k1-tbl, p3, k1-tbl, drop next st and unravel, k1-tbl, p1, k1, p3, k1, p1, k1.

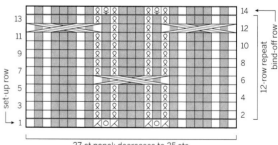

27-st panel; decreases to 25 sts

NOTE: Cast on 27 sts. Work Row 1 (Set-Up Row) once, then work Rows 2–13 for main pattern. Bind off sts following Row 14 (Bind-Off Row).

- ☐ Knit on RS, purl on WS.
- ▨ Purl on RS, knit on WS.
- ⊠ K1-tbl on RS, p1-tbl on WS.
- ⊙ Yo
- ⊠ K2tog on RS, p2tog on WS.

⊉ Yo, drop next st and unravel.

| Pattern repeat

Slip 6 sts to cn, hold to back, k1, p1, k1, slip last 3 sts from cn back to left needle, p3, (k1, p1, k1) from cn.

Slip 6 sts to cn, hold to front, k1, p1, k1, slip last 3 sts from cn back to left needle, p3, (k1, p1, k1) from cn.

Alternate Yarns

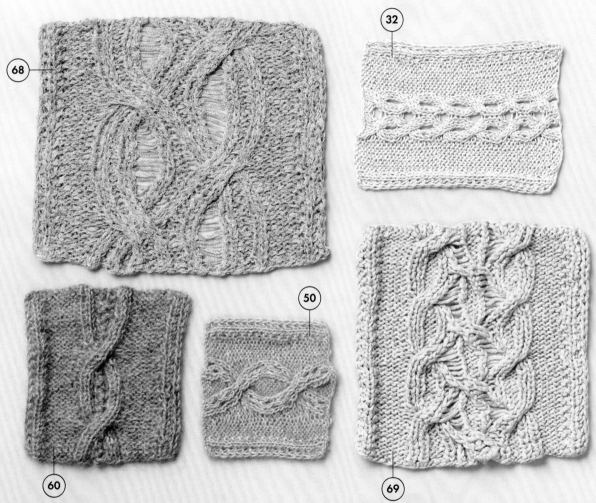

68

32

50

60

69

For the sake of consistency, I began by swatching all of the cables in this book in a wool or wool-blend yarn. In real life, of course, there are many other options. Featured here are 4 cables from this chapter and one from Chapter 2 worked in a second yarn. All four feature openwork of some sort, including small lace patterns, double yarnovers, or dropped stitches.

The dropped stitches of **DROP CENTER 2/2 SHARE (#68)** stand out in a lightweight, acrylic-linen railroad ribbon (Berroco Linus).

The double yarnovers of **OPEN DOUBLE O (#32)** pair well with a crisp linen yarn (Quince Sparrow) for garments worn in warm weather.

The openwork interior of **STABLE LACE (#60)** is shown off well in this sport weight but high-loft Gotland wool from the Island of Bornholm in Denmark (a souvenir of my visit).

A laceweight cashmere-and-possum blend with a soft halo (Zealana Air) works well

with the openwork of **LACE CENTER STABLE (#50).**

The dropped stitches of **1/1 SHARE DROP (#69)** look especially nice in this flat, pure linen knit ribbon (Quince Kestral).

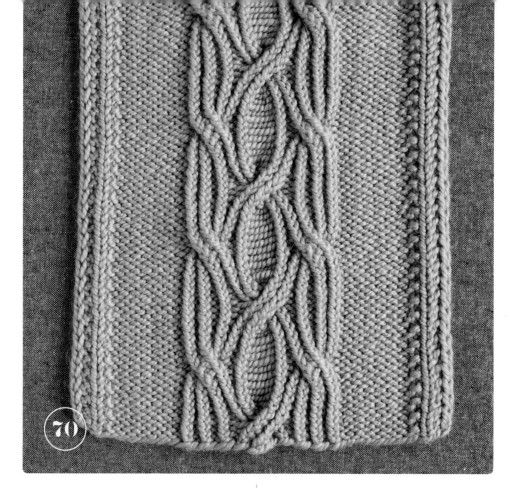

Share Center Drop GROUP 6

Although the ribbing in Share Center Drop is similar to 1/1 Share Drop (#69), in this case, it is twisted. In addition, the dropped stitches in this cable happen in the center of the center column rather than as part of the strands.

(multiple of 13 sts + 7; decreases to 12 sts + 7; 16-row repeat)
SSE: 14.5 sts

CO a multiple of 13 sts + 7.
ROW 1 (SET-UP ROW) (WS): P1-tbl, k1, p1-tbl, *[k1, p1-tbl] twice, k1, p2tog, yo, p2tog, [k1, p1-tbl] twice; repeat from * to last 4 sts, [k1, p1-tbl] twice—1 st decreased.
ROW 2: *K1-tbl, p1; repeat from * to last st, k1-tbl.
ROW 3 AND ALL FOLLOWING WS ROWS: *P1-tbl, k1; repeat from * to last st, p1-tbl.
ROW 4: [K1-tbl, p1] twice, *k1-tbl, p1; slip 4 sts to cn, hold to back, k1-tbl, p1, k1-tbl, slip last st from cn back to left needle, p1, (k1-tbl, p1, k1-tbl) from cn; p1, k1-tbl, p1; repeat from * to last 3 sts, k1-tbl, p1, k1-tbl.

ROWS 6, 8, AND 10: Repeat Row 2.
ROW 12: Slip 4 sts to cn, hold to front, k1-tbl, p1, k1-tbl, slip last st from cn back to left needle, p1, (k1-tbl, p1, k1-tbl) from cn; *[p1, k1-tbl] twice, p1; slip 4 sts to cn, hold to front, k1-tbl, p1, k1-tbl, slip last st from cn back to left needle, p1, (k1-tbl, p1, k1-tbl) from cn; repeat from * to end.
ROWS 14 AND 16: Repeat Row 2.
ROW 17: Repeat Row 3.
Repeat Rows 2–17 for pattern.

ROW 18 (BIND-OFF ROW): BO sts as you go, working as follows: [K1-tbl, p1] twice, *[k1-tbl, p1] twice, k1-tbl, yo, drop next st and unravel, [k1-tbl, p1] 3 times; repeat from * to last 3 sts, k1-tbl, p1, k1-tbl.

13-st repeat; decrease to 12 sts

NOTE: Cast on 20 sts. Work Row 1 (Set-Up Row) once, then work Rows 2–16 for main pattern. Bind off sts following Row 18 (Bind-Off Row).

☐ Knit on RS, purl on WS.

▨ Purl on RS, knit on WS.

Ⓠ K1-tbl on RS, p1-tbl on WS.

Ⓞ Yo

⊠ K2tog on RS, p2tog on WS.

Ⓠ Yo, drop next st and unravel.

│ Pattern repeat

Slip 4 sts to cn, hold to back, k1-tbl, p1, k1-tbl, slip last st from cn back to left needle, p1, (k1-tbl, p1, k1-tbl) from cn.

Slip 4 sts to cn, hold to front, k1-tbl, p1, k1-tbl, slip last st from cn back to left needle, p1, (k1-tbl, p1, k1-tbl) from cn.

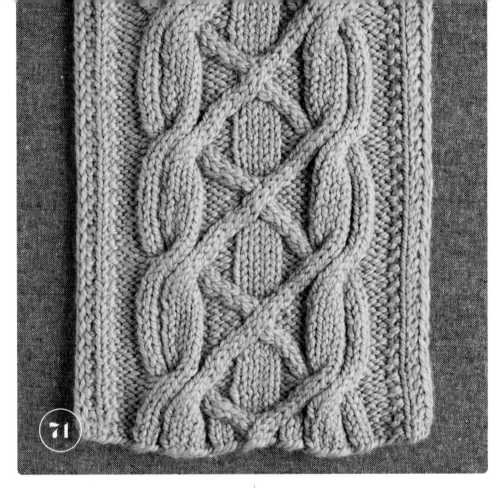

2/2 Share Extend GROUP 7

Just like the 2/2 Share (#65), this cable starts out with a pair of 2/2 Over 2/2 cables (#34). In this case the 2 cables are placed a little farther away from each other (i.e., extended) than they were in 2/2 Share. Two lines, each made of 2 stockinette stitches, extend out from the cable crosses on each side and crisscross in the center.

(panel of 32 sts; 16-row repeat)
SSE: 22.5 sts

ROW 1 (WS): P2, k2, p4, k2, p2, k2, p4, k2, p2, k2, p4, p2.

ROW 2: K2, p2, k4, p2, k2, p2, 2/2 RC, p2, k2, p2, k4, p2, k2.

ROW 3 AND ALL FOLLOWING WS ROWS: Knit the knit sts and purl the purl sts as they face you.

ROW 4: K2, p2, k4, p2, k2, 2/2 RC, 2/2 LC, k2, p2, k4, p2, k2.

ROW 6: K2, p2, k4, p2, 2/2 RPC, k4, 2/2 LPC, p2, k4, p2, k2.

ROW 8: [K2, p2, k4, p2] 3 times, k2.

ROW 10: Slip 6 sts to cn, hold to back, k2, p2, k2, (k2, p2, k2) from cn; p2, k4, p2; slip 6 sts to cn, hold to back, k2, p2, k2, (k2, p2, k2) from cn.

ROW 12: Repeat Row 8.

ROW 14: K2, p2, k4, p2, 2/2 LPC, k4, 2/2 RPC, p2, k4, p2, k2.

ROW 16: K2, p2, k4, p4, 2/2 LPC, 2/2 RPC, p4, k4, p2, k2.

ROW 18: K2, p2, k4, p6, 2/2 RC, p6, k4, p2, k2.

ROW 20: K2, p2, k4, p4, 2/2 RC, 2/2 LC, p4, k4, p2, k2.

ROW 22: Repeat Row 6.

ROW 24: Repeat Row 8.
Repeat Rows 9–24 for pattern.

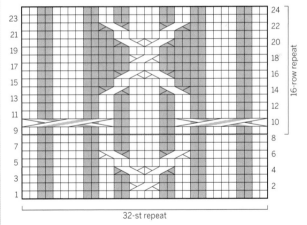

☐ Knit on RS, purl on WS. ▨ Purl on RS, knit on WS.

Ι Pattern repeat

2/2 RC (2 over 2 right cross): Slip 2 sts to cn, hold to back, k2, k2 from cn.

2/2 LC (2 over 2 left cross): Slip 2 sts to cn, hold to front, k2, k2 from cn.

2/2 RPC (2 over 2 right purl cross): Slip 2 sts to cn, hold to back, k2, p2 from cn.

2/2 LPC (2 over 2 left purl cross): Slip 2 sts to cn, hold to front, p2, k2 from cn.

Slip 6 sts to cn, hold to back, k2, p2, k2, (k2, p2, k2) from cn.

Slip 6 sts to cn, hold to front, k2, p2, k2, (k2, p2, k2) from cn.

Chevron Share Tight

GROUP 7

This cable pattern looks complicated, but is surprisingly simple to work. Once again, this cable starts out just like the 2/2 Over 2/2 cables from Chapter 2 (#34–35). If you look at Row 8 of this cable chart, you can see that there are 3 crosses placed 4 stitches apart. In the first row of cables, k2, p2, k2 crosses over k2, p2, k2. After 7 blissfully easy rows working straight in rib, there are 2 more cable crosses, but this time they start with purls: p2, k2, p2 crosses over p2, k2, p2. This cross places the k2 in the center and makes it look a lot like the 4-stitch line of cable crosses in 2/2 Share Extend (#71), but with less work. Check out the reverse side of this cable on page 83.

(panel of 44 sts; 16-row repeat)
SSE: 29 sts

ROW 1 (WS): [P2, k2, p4, k2, p2, k4] twice, p2, k2, p4, k2, p2.

ROWS 2–7: Knit the knit sts and purl the purl sts as they face you.

ROW 8: [Slip 6 sts to cn, hold to back, k2, p2, k2, (k2, p2, k2) from cn; p4] twice; slip 6 sts to cn, hold to front, k2, p2, k2, (k2, p2, k2) from cn.

ROWS 9–15: Repeat Row 2.

ROW 16: K2, p2, k4; slip 6 sts to cn, hold to back, p2, k2, p2, (p2, k2, p2) from cn; k4; slip 6 sts to cn, hold to front, p2, k2, p2, (p2, k2, p2) from cn; k4, p2, k2. Repeat Rows 1–16 for pattern.

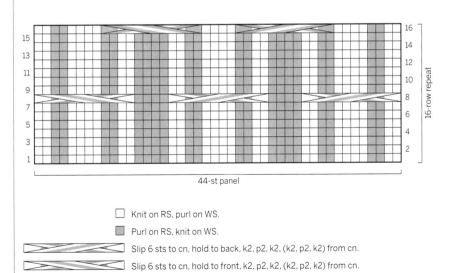

44-st panel

16-row repeat

☐ Knit on RS, purl on WS.

▨ Purl on RS, knit on WS.

▧ Slip 6 sts to cn, hold to back, k2, p2, k2, (k2, p2, k2) from cn.

▧ Slip 6 sts to cn, hold to front, k2, p2, k2, (k2, p2, k2) from cn.

▧ Slip 6 sts to cn, hold to back, p2, k2, p2, (p2, k2, p2) from cn.

▧ Slip 6 sts to cn, hold to front, p2, k2, p2, (p2, k2, p2) from cn.

(73)

Chevron Share Loose

GROUP 7

While working those easy ribbed rows in Chevron Share Tight (#72), I started to plan this variation. The major crosses of Chevron Share Loose have 11 rows between them, where before there were 7, and a few 2/2 crosses have been added to break up the stockinette stitches. I began this cable pattern with 1 cable rather than 3, which gives it the feeling of a tree trunk merging into branches. If you don't want the "trunk," you can start with Row 25.

(panel of 44 sts; 24-row repeat)
SSE: 29 sts

ROW 1 (WS): [P2, k2, p4, k2, p2, k4] twice, p2, k2, p4, k2, p2.

ROWS 2–7: Knit the knit sts and purl the purl sts as they face you.

ROW 8: K2, p2, k4, p2, k2, p4, k2, p2, 2/2 RC, p2, k2, p4, k2, p2, k4, p2, k2.

ROWS 9–15: Repeat Row 2.

ROW 16: K2, p2, k4, p2, k2, p4; slip 6 sts to cn, hold to back, k2, p2, k2, (k2, p2, k2) from cn; p4, k2, p2, k4, p2, k2.

ROWS 17–24: Repeat Rows 1–8.

ROWS 25–27: Repeat Row 2.

ROW 28: K2, p2, k4; slip 2 sts to cn, hold to back, p2, k2, p2, (p2, k2, p2) from cn; k4, slip 6 sts to cn, hold to front, p2, k2, p2, (p2, k2, p2) from cn; k4, p2, k2.

ROWS 29–31: Repeat Row 2.

ROW 32: [K2, p2, 2/2 RC, p2, k2, p4] twice, k2, p2, 2/2 LC, p2, k2.

ROWS 33–39: Repeat Row 2.

ROW 40: [Slip 6 sts to cn, hold to back, k2, p2, k2, (k2, p2, k2) from cn; p4] twice; slip 6 sts to cn, hold to front, k2, p2, k2, (k2, p2, k2) from cn.

ROWS 41–47: Repeat Row 2.

ROW 48: Repeat Row 32.
Repeat Rows 25–48 for pattern.

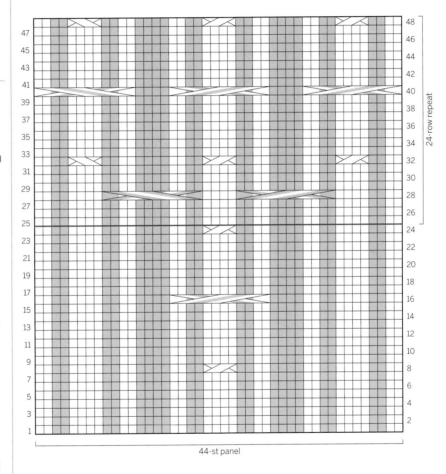

24-row repeat

44-st panel

☐ Knit on RS, purl on WS.

▨ Purl on RS, knit on WS.

❘ Pattern repeat

▧ 2/2 RC (2 over 2 right cross): Slip 2 sts to cn, hold to back, k2, k2 from cn.

▨ 2/2 LC (2 over 2 left cross): Slip 2 sts to cn, hold to front, k2, k2 from cn.

▱ Slip 6 sts to cn, hold to back, k2, p2, k2, (k2, p2, k2) from cn.

▱ Slip 6 sts to cn, hold to front, k2, p2, k2, (k2, p2, k2) from cn.

▱ Slip 6 sts to cn, hold to back, p2, k2, p2, (p2, k2, p2) from cn.

▱ Slip 6 sts to cn, hold to front, p2, k2, p2, (p2, k2, p2) from cn.

Medallion GROUP 8

Just like 2/2 Share (#65) and Chevron Share Tight (#72) and their variations, in this cable pattern, k2, p2, k2 rib over k2, p2, k2 rib is the largest, most dominant cross. The outermost ribs then go on to be shared with smaller 2/2 crosses. Those smaller crosses later switch direction, and that reversal helps create the illusion of an oval medallion in the center. I didn't set out to make this rounded shape. I was playing around with charts on my computer looking for variations of 2/2 Share and thought I was making a narrow column. Although years of experience means I am good at visualizing how a chart will look when knit, there are still happy surprises like this one.

(panel of 16 sts; 24-row repeat)
SSE: 13.5 sts

ROW 1 (WS): [P4, k2] twice, p4.
ROWS 2 AND 3: Knit the knit sts and purl the purl sts as they face you.
ROW 4: 2/2 LC, p2, k4, p2, 2/2 RC.
ROWS 5–8: Repeat Rows 1–4.
ROWS 9–11: Repeat Row 2.

ROW 12: K2; slip 6 sts to cn, hold to front, k2, p2, k2, (k2, p2, k2) from cn; k2.
ROWS 13–15: Repeat Row 2.
ROW 16: 2/2 RC, p2, k4, p2, 2/2 LC.
ROWS 17–20: Repeat Rows 13–16.
ROWS 21–24: Repeat Row 2.
Repeat Rows 1–24 for pattern.

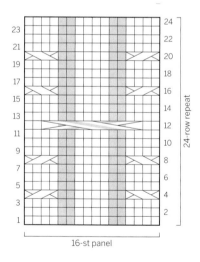

16-st panel

24-row repeat

☐ Knit on RS, purl on WS.

▨ Purl on RS, knit on WS.

⬚ 2/2 RC (2 over 2 right cross): Slip 2 sts to cn, hold to back, k2, k2 from cn.

⬚ 2/2 LC (2 over 2 left cross): Slip 2 sts to cn, hold to front, k2, k2 from cn.

⬚ Slip 6 sts to cn, hold to front, k2, p2, k2, (k2, p2, k2) from cn.

Rope & Lasso GROUP 8

Rope & Lasso and Medallion (#74) share the same large cable cross and overall shape. The 2 center stitches on the outer strands are worked as right twists and look like mini ropes. The mini ropes move outward and back inward to create the oval lasso that surrounds the central rope.

(panel of 18 sts; 24-row repeat)
SSE: 12.5 sts

ROW 1 (WS): K1, p2, k4, p4, k4, p2, k1.

ROW 2: Slip 4 sts to cn, hold to front, p1, (p1, RT, p1) from cn; p2, k4, p2; slip 1 st to cn, hold to back, p1, RT, p1, p1 from cn.

ROW 3 AND ALL FOLLOWING WS ROWS: Knit the knit sts and purl the purl sts as they face you.

ROW 4: P1; slip 4 sts to cn, hold to front, p1, (p1, RT, p1) from cn; p1, k4, p1; slip 1 st to cn, hold to back, p1, RT, p1, p1 from cn; p1.

ROW 6: P3, RT, p2, k4, p2, RT, p3.

ROW 8: P3; slip 6 sts to cn, hold to back, k2, p2, k2, (k2, p2, k2) from cn; p3.

ROW 10: Repeat Row 6.

ROW 12: P1; slip 1 st to cn, hold to back, p1, RT, p1, p1 from cn; p1, k4, p1; slip 4 sts to cn, hold to front, p1, (p1, RT, p1) from cn; p1.

ROW 14: Slip 1 st to cn, hold to back, p1, RT, p1, p1 from cn; p2, k4, p2; slip 4 sts to cn, hold to front, p1, (p1, RT, p1) from cn.

ROW 16: P1, RT, p4, 2/2 RC, p4, RT, p1.

ROWS 18, 20, AND 22: P1, RT, p4, k4, p4, RT, p1.

ROW 24: Repeat Row 16.
Repeat Rows 1–24 for pattern.

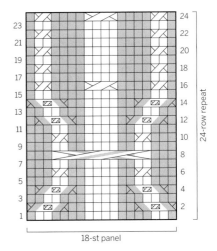

18-st panel

☐ Knit on RS, purl on WS.

▨ Purl on RS, knit on WS.

 RT (right twist): K2tog, but do not drop sts from left needle; insert right needle between 2 sts just worked and knit first st again, slip both sts from left needle together.

2/2 RC (2 over 2 right cross): Slip 2 sts to cn, hold to back, k2, k2 from cn.

Slip 1 st to cn, hold to back, p1, RT, p1, p1 from cn.

Slip 4 sts to cn, hold to front, p1, (p1, RT, p1) from cn.

Slip 6 sts to cn, hold to back, k2, p2, k2, (k2, p2, k2) from cn.

1/1 Travel Share GROUP 9

Up to this point most of the shared cables in this chapter have been based on 2×2 rib, but 1/1 Travel Share is based on 1×1 rib. If you glance at this photo quickly, you might think that the ribs are traveling every right-side row but, in actuality, they're traveling every 4th row (which you can see clearly on the chart).

(panel of 22 sts; 16-row repeat)
SSE: 16 sts

ROW 1 (WS): [P1, k1, p2, k1, p1, k2] twice, p1, k1, p2, k1, p1.

ROW 2: Knit the knit sts and purl the purl sts as they face you.

ROW 4: K1, p1, k2, p1, k1, p2; slip 3 sts to cn, hold to back, k1, p1, k1, (k1, p1, k1) from cn; p2, k1, p1, k2, p1, k1.

ROWS 5–7: Repeat Row 2.

ROW 8: K1, p1, k2; slip 3 sts to cn, hold to back, p1, k1, p1, (p1, k1, p1) from cn; k2; slip 3 sts to cn, hold to front, p1, k1, p1, (p1, k1, p1) from cn; k2, p1, k1.

ROWS 9–11: Repeat Row 2.

ROW 12: Slip 3 sts to cn, hold to back, k1, p1, k1, (k1, p1, k1) from cn; p2, k1, p1, k2, p1, k1, p2; slip 3 sts to cn, hold to front, k1, p1, k1, (k1, p1, k1) from cn.

ROWS 13–15: Repeat Row 2.

ROW 16: K1, p1, k2; slip 3 sts to cn, hold to front, p1, k1, p1, (p1, k1, p1) from cn; k2; slip 3 sts to cn, hold to back, p1, k1, p1, (p1, k1, p1) from cn; k2, p1, k1.

Repeat Rows 1–16 for pattern.

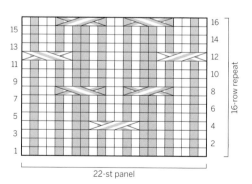

☐ Knit on RS, purl on WS.

▨ Purl on RS, knit on WS.

▨▨ Slip 3 sts to cn, hold to back, k1, p1, k1, (k1, p1, k1) from cn.

▨▨ Slip 3 sts to cn, hold to front, k1, p1, k1, (k1, p1, k1) from cn.

▨▨ Slip 3 sts to cn, hold to back, p1, k1, p1, (p1, k1, p1) from cn.

▨▨ Slip 3 sts to cn, hold to front, p1, k1, p1, (p1, k1, p1) from cn.

Twist 1/1 Travel Share GROUP 9

The addition of right and left twists changes 1/1 Travel Share (#76) into Twist 1/1 Travel Share. The twists are added in all of the places where 2 knits come together, making it look like there are 3 mini ropes intertwined with the ribbing. Working these twists doesn't require a cable needle, which makes this pattern deceptively simple to execute.

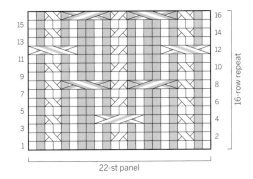

22-st panel

(panel of 22 sts; 16-row repeat)
SSE: 14.5 sts

ROW 1 AND ALL WS ROWS (WS): [P1, k1, p2, k1, p1, k2] twice, p1, k1, p2, k1, p1.

ROW 2: K1, p1, LT, p1, k1, p2, k1, p1, RT, p1, k1, p2, k1, p1, LT, p1, k1.

ROW 4: K1, p1, LT, p1, k1, p2; slip 3 sts to cn, hold to back, k1, p1, k1, (k1, p1, k1) from cn; p2, k1, p1, LT, p1, k1.

ROW 6: Repeat Row 2.

ROW 8: K1, p1, LT; slip 3 sts to cn, hold to back, p1, k1, p1, (p1, k1, p1) from cn; RT; slip 3 sts to cn, hold to front, p1, k1, p1, (p1, k1, p1) from cn; LT, p1, k1.

ROW 10: Repeat Row 2.

ROW 12: Slip 3 sts to cn, hold to front, k1, p1, k1, (k1, p1, k1) from cn; p2, k1, p1, RT, p1, k1, p2; slip 3 sts to cn, hold to front, k1, p1, k1, (k1, p1, k1) from cn.

ROW 14: Repeat Row 2.

ROW 16: K1, p1, LT; slip 3 sts to cn, hold to front, p1, k1, p1, (p1, k1, p1) from cn; RT; slip 3 sts to cn, hold to back, p1, k1, p1, (p1, k1, p1) from cn; LT, p1, k1.

Repeat Rows 1–16 for pattern.

☐ Knit on RS, purl on WS.

▨ Purl on RS, knit on WS.

⧄ **RT (right twist):** K2tog, but do not drop sts from left needle; insert right needle between 2 sts just worked and knit first st again, slip both sts from left needle together.

⧅ **LT (left twist):** Insert needle from back to front between first and second sts on left needle and knit the second st through the front loop; knit first st, slip both sts from left needle together.

Slip 3 sts to cn, hold to back, k1, p1, k1, (k1, p1, k1) from cn.

Slip 3 sts to cn, hold to front, k1, p1, k1, (k1, p1, k1) from cn.

Slip 3 sts to cn, hold to back, p1, k1, p1, (p1, k1, p1) from cn.

Slip 3 sts to cn, hold to front, p1, k1, p1, (p1, k1, p1) from cn.

Adding Breadth

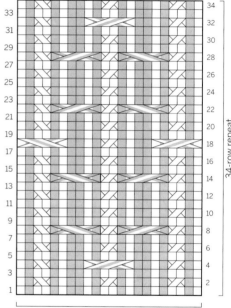

22-st panel

☐ Knit on RS, purl on WS.

▨ Purl on RS, knit on WS.

◩ RT (right twist): K2tog, but do not drop sts from left needle; insert right needle between 2 sts just worked and knit first st again, slip both sts from left needle together.

◪ LT (left twist): Insert needle from back to front between first and second sts on left needle and knit the second st through the front loop; knit first st, slip both sts from left needle together.

▱ Slip 3 sts to cn, hold to back, k1, p1, k1, (k1, p1, k1) from cn.

▱ Slip 3 sts to cn, hold to front, k1, p1, k1, (k1, p1, k1) from cn.

▱ Slip 3 sts to cn, hold to back, p1, k1, p1, (p1, k1, p1) from cn.

▱ Slip 3 sts to cn, hold to front, p1, k1, p1, (p1, k1, p1) from cn.

Fancy 1/1 Travel Share GROUP 9

This cable starts out like the Twist 1/1 Travel Share (#77), but the p1, k1, p1 cable cross is worked a second time, 6 rows later, elongating the diamond and adding fanciful detail. The central cable cross is worked in the same manner, forming a rounded separation between the large, elaborate diamond shapes.

(panel of 22 sts; 34-row repeat)
SSE: 16 sts

ROW 1 AND ALL WS ROWS (WS):
[P1, k1, p2, k1, p1, k2] twice, p1, k1, p2, k1, p1.

ROW 2: [K1, p1, RT, p1, k1, p2] twice, k1, p1, LT, p1, k1.

ROW 4: K1, p1, RT, p1, k1, p2; slip 3 sts to cn, hold to back, k1, p1, k1, (k1, p1, k1) from cn; p2, k1, p1, LT, p1, k1.

ROW 6: Repeat Row 2.

ROW 8: K1, p1, RT; slip 3 sts to cn, hold to back, p1, k1, p1, (p1, k1, p1) from cn; RT; slip 3 sts to cn, hold to front, p1, k1, p1, (p1, k1, p1) from cn; LT, p1, k1.

ROWS 10 AND 12: Repeat Row 2.

ROW 14: Repeat Row 8.

ROW 16: Repeat Row 2.

ROW 18: Slip 3 sts to cn, hold to back, k1, p1, k1, (k1, p1, k1) from cn; p2, k1, p1, RT, p1, k1, p2; slip 3 sts to cn, hold to front, k1, p1, k1, (k1, p1, k1) from cn.

ROW 20: Repeat Row 2.

ROW 22: K1, p1, RT; slip 3 sts to cn, hold to front, p1, k1, p1, (p1, k1, p1) from cn; RT; slip 3 sts to cn, hold to back, p1, k1, p1, (p1, k1, p1) from cn; LT, p1, k1.

ROWS 24 AND 26: Repeat Row 2.

ROW 28: Repeat Row 22.

ROW 30: Repeat Row 2.

ROW 32: Repeat Row 4.

ROW 34: Repeat Row 2.
Repeat Rows 1–34 for pattern.

Travel Share Variations

76

77

78

For me, the most exciting time when making up new cables is when the ideas for variations come fast and furious. Sometimes variations come to me when I am charting a cable, but most often new ideas pop into my head when I am knitting. There is something about the act of making stitches that settles my brain's nervous chatter and allows creative thoughts to surface.

This set of three variations started with the swatch on the left, **1/1 TRAVEL SHARE (#76).** I began by charting this stitch on my computer; then when I started to knit, it occurred to me that the k2 columns could easily be worked as right twists; that idea became **TWIST 1/1 TRAVEL SHARE (#77),** the swatch in the center. The third variation, **FANCY 1/1 TRAVEL SHARE (#78),** was born of a happy accident later in that same swatch. After working straight for 5 rows, my mind wandered and I absent-mindedly worked one of the

cable crosses a second time before moving to the next cross, which led to me doubling a few more of the cable crosses as well. Next I worked expanded allover versions of these cables, which I present in Chapter 4: See 1/1 Diamonds, 1/1 Diamond Twist, and 1/1 Diamond Fancy (#104–#106).

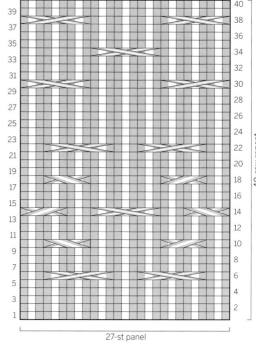

40-row repeat

27-st panel

Rib Fantasy GROUP 10

Visually, you can see that there is a relationship between the 1/1 Travel cables (#76–#78) and this one. Some of the crosses are the same—p1, k1, p1 crosses over itself again here—and the idea that a central knit stitch forms a line is also integral. The rib base of this cable is a bit different though. Instead of starting with a mix of ribs, this cable starts with a base of p1, k1, p1 repeated across the panel. Two new center-stable crosses are introduced as well. They each intertwine 3 sets of p1, k1, p1 rib. Ribbed braids surround a fancy diamond, but there is so much going on, it can take a second to see the diamond. The overall effect is quite rococo.

☐ Knit on RS, purl on WS.

▨ Purl on RS, knit on WS.

◩ Slip 3 sts to cn, hold to back, p1, k1, p1, (p1, k1, p1) from cn.

◩ Slip 3 sts to cn, hold to front, p1, k1, p1, (p1, k1, p1) from cn.

◩ Slip 6 sts to cn, hold to back, p1, k1, p1, slip last 3 sts from cn back to left needle, p1, k1, p1, (p1, k1, p1) from cn.

◩ Slip 6 sts to cn, hold to front, p1, k1, p1, slip last 3 sts from cn back to left needle, p1, k1, p1, (p1, k1, p1) from cn.

(panel of 27 sts; 40-row repeat)
SSE: 16 sts

ROW 1 (WS): K1, [p1, k2] 8 times, p1, k1.

ROWS 2–5: Knit the knit sts and purl the purl sts as they face you.

ROW 6: P1, k1, p1; slip 6 sts to cn, hold to front, p1, k1, p1, slip last 3 sts from cn back to left needle, p1, k1, p1, (p1, k1, p1) from cn; p1, k1, p1; slip 6 sts to cn, hold to back, p1, k1, p1, slip last 3 sts from cn back to left needle, p1, k1, p1, (p1, k1, p1) from cn; p1, k1, p1.

ROWS 7–9: Repeat Row 2.

ROW 10: P1, k1, p1; slip 3 sts to cn, hold to back, p1, k1, p1, (p1, k1, p1)

from cn; p1, [k1, p2] twice, k1, p1; slip 3 sts to cn, hold to front, p1, k1, p1, (p1, k1, p1) from cn; p1, k1, p1.

ROWS 11–13: Repeat Row 2.

ROW 14: Slip 3 sts to cn, hold to front, p1, k1, p1, (p1, k1, p1) from cn; p1, k1, p1; slip 6 sts to cn, hold to back, p1, k1, p1, slip last 3 sts from cn back to left needle, p1, k1, p1, (p1, k1, p1) from cn; p1, k1, p1; slip 3 sts to cn, hold to back, p1, k1, p1, (p1, k1, p1) from cn.

ROWS 15–17: Repeat Row 2.

ROW 18: Repeat Row 10.

ROWS 19–21: Repeat Row 2.

ROW 22: P1, k1, p1; slip 6 sts to cn, hold to back, p1, k1, p1, slip last

3 sts from cn back to left needle, p1, k1, p1, (p1, k1, p1) from cn; p1, k1, p1; slip 6 sts to cn, hold to front, p1, k1, p1, slip last 3 sts from cn back to left needle, p1, k1, p1, (p1, k1, p1) from cn; p1, k1, p1.

ROWS 23–29: Repeat Row 2.

ROW 30: Slip 6 sts to cn, hold to back, p1, k1, p1, slip last 3 sts from cn back to left needle, p1, k1, p1, (p1, k1, p1) from cn; p1, [k1, p2] twice, k1, p1; slip 6 sts to cn, hold to front, p1, k1, p1, slip last 3 sts from cn back to left needle, p1, k1, p1, (p1, k1, p1) from cn.

ROWS 31–33: Repeat Row 2.

ROW 34: P1, [k1, p2] twice, k1, p1; slip 6 sts to cn, hold to front, p1,

k1, p1, slip last 3 sts from cn back to left needle, p1, k1, p1, (p1, k1, p1) from cn; p1, [k1, p2] twice, k1, p1.

ROWS 35–37: Repeat Row 2.

ROW 38: Slip 6 sts to cn, hold to front, p1, k1, p1, slip last 3 sts from cn back to left needle, p1, k1, p1, (p1, k1, p1) from cn; p1, [k1, p2] twice, k1, p1; slip 6 sts to cn, hold to back, p1, k1, p1, slip last 3 sts from cn back to left needle, p1, k1, p1, (p1, k1, p1) from cn.

ROWS 39–40: Repeat Row 2.
Repeat Rows 1–40 for pattern.

79

Duel Rib Diamond GROUP 10

While experimenting with Rib Fantasy (#79), I decided to add a k2 rib within the ribbed braids to emphasize the diamond shape, to simplify the diamond by removing the large cross, and to make the diamond smaller.

(panel of 29 sts; 24-row repeat)
SSE: 17 sts

ROW 1 (WS): K1, [p1, k2] twice, p2, [k2, p1] 3 times, k2, p2, [k2, p1] twice, k1.

ROWS 2 AND 3: Knit the knit sts and purl the purl sts as they face you.

ROW 4: P1, k1, p2, k1, p1; slip 4 sts to cn, hold to front, p1, k1, p1, (p1, k2, p1) from cn; p1, k1, p1; slip 3 sts to cn, hold to back, p1, k2, p1, (p1, k1, p1) from cn; p1, k1, p2, k1, p1.

ROWS 5–7: Repeat Row 2.

ROW 8: P1, k1, p1; slip 3 sts to cn, hold to back, p1, k1, p1, (p1, k1, p1) from cn; p1, k2, p2, k1, p2, k2, p1; slip 3 sts to cn, hold to front, p1, k1, p1, (p1, k1, p1) from cn; p1, k1, p1.

ROWS 9–11: Repeat Row 2.

ROW 12: Slip 3 sts to cn, hold to front, p1, k1, p1, (p1, k1, p1) from cn; p1, k1, p1; slip 7 sts to cn, hold to front, p1, k2, p1, slip last 3 sts from cn back to left needle, p1, k1, p1, (p1, k2, p1) from cn; p1, k1, p1; slip 3 sts to cn, hold to back, p1, k1, p1, (p1, k1, p1) from cn.

ROWS 13–15: Repeat Row 2.

ROW 16: Repeat Row 8.

ROWS 17–19: Repeat Row 2.

ROW 20: P1, k1, p2, k1, p1; slip 3 sts to cn, hold to back, p1, k2, p1, (p1, k1, p1) from cn; p1, k1, p1; slip 4 sts to cn, hold to front, p1, k1, p1, (p1, k2, p1) from cn; p1, k1, p2, k1, p1.

ROWS 21–23: Repeat Row 2.

ROW 24: Slip 3 sts to cn, hold to front, p1, k1, p1 (p1, k1, p1) from cn; p1, k2 [p2, k1] 3 times, p2, k2, p1; slip 3 sts to cn, hold to back, p1, k1, p1, (p1, k1, p1) from cn. Repeat Rows 1–24 for pattern.

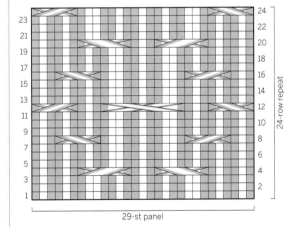

☐ Knit on RS, purl on WS.

▦ Purl on RS, knit on WS.

Slip 3 sts to cn, hold to back, p1, k1, p1, (p1, k1, p1) from cn.

Slip 3 sts to cn, hold to front, p1, k1, p1, (p1, k1, p1) from cn.

Slip 3 sts to cn, hold to back, p1, k2, p1, (p1, k1, p1) from cn.

Slip 4 sts to cn, hold to front, p1, k1, p1, (p1, k2, p1) from cn.

Slip 7 sts to cn, hold to front, p1, k2, p1, slip last 3 sts from cn back to left needle, p1, k1, p1, (p1, k2, p1) from cn.

81

Rib & Rope GROUP 11

I've broken my own rule with this one. Usually when a cable changes stitches during a cross, I hide the switch behind the forward part of the cable. In this case, the switch from stockinette stitch to 2 x 2 rib happens in full sight on the larger cable cross. This switch keeps the rib in the center and the 3/3 cables to the outside throughout the pattern. Although this cable doesn't actually exhibit stitch sharing, I've included it here because its variation, Elaborate Rib & Rope (#82), is all about sharing.

(panel of 26 sts; 30-row repeat)
SSE: 20 sts

ROW 1 (WS): P8, [k2, p2] twice, k2, p8.

ROWS 2–5: Knit the knit sts and purl the purl sts as they face you.

ROW 6: 3/3 LC, [k2, p2] 3 times, k2, 3/3 RC.

ROWS 7–11: Repeat Row 2.

ROW 12: Slip 6 sts to cn, hold to front, k6, (k2, p2, k2) from cn; p2; slip 6 sts to cn, hold to back, k2, p2, k2, k6 from cn.

ROWS 13–17: Repeat Row 2.

ROW 18: 3/3 RC, [k2, p2] 3 times, k2, 3/3 LC.

ROWS 19–23: Repeat Row 2.

ROWS 24–29: Repeat Rows 18–23.

ROW 30: Repeat Row 18.
Repeat Rows 1–30 for pattern.

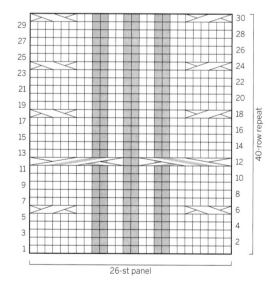

26-st panel

40-row repeat

☐ Knit on RS, purl on WS.

▨ Purl on RS, knit on WS.

⬚ 3/3 RC (3 over 3 right cross): Slip 3 sts to cn, hold to back, k3, k3 from cn.

⬚ 3/3 LC (3 over 3 left cross): Slip 3 sts to cn, hold to front, k3, k3 from cn.

⬚ Slip 6 sts to cn, hold to back, k2, p2, k2, k6 from cn.

⬚ Slip 6 sts to cn, hold to front, k6, (k2, p2, k2) from cn.

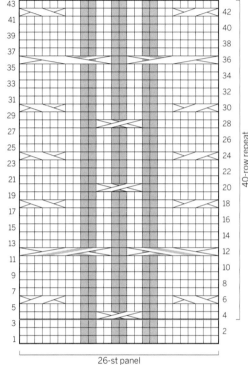

Elaborate Rib & Rope   GROUP 11

In the original Rib & Rope (#81), all of the large major cables travel from the outside of the panel in toward the center. Here they first travel inward and then travel outward. The 2 central ribs are cabled over each other, then share some of their stitches with the cabled Xs and Os. As a result, what was basically a large horseshoe cable is transformed into a very different composition.

(panel of 26 sts; 40-row repeat)
SSE: 18 sts

ROW 1: P8, [k2, p2] twice, k2, p8.

ROWS 2 AND 3: Knit the knit sts and purl the purl sts as they face you.

ROW 4: K8, p2, 2/2/2 RPC, p2, k8.

ROW 5: Repeat Row 2.

ROW 6: 3/3 LC, [k2, p2] 3 times, k2, 3/3 RC.

ROWS 7–11: Repeat Row 2.

ROW 12: Slip 6 sts to cn, hold to front, k6, (k2, p2, k2) from cn; p2; slip 6 sts to cn, hold to back, k2, p2, k2, k6 from cn.

ROWS 13–17: Repeat Row 2.

ROW 18: 3/3 RC, [k2, p2] 3 times, k2, 3/3 LC.

ROW 19: Repeat Row 2.

ROW 20: Repeat Row 4.

ROWS 21–23: Repeat Row 2.

ROWS 24–29: Repeat Rows 18–23.

ROW 30: Repeat Row 18.

ROWS 31–35: Repeat Row 2.

ROW 36: Slip 6 sts to cn, hold to back, 6, (k2, p2, k2) from cn; p2; slip 6 sts to cn, hold to front, k2, p2, k2, k6 from cn.

ROWS 37–41: Repeat Row 2.

ROW 42: Repeat Row 18.

ROW 43: Repeat Row 2.

Repeat Rows 4–43 for pattern.

---

43 | 42
41 | 40
39 | 38
37 | 36
35 | 34
33 | 32
31 | 30
29 | 28
27 | 26
25 | 24
23 | 22
21 | 20
19 | 18
17 | 16
15 | 14
13 | 12
11 | 10
9 | 8
7 | 6
5 | 4
3 | 2
1

40-row repeat

26-st panel

☐ Knit on RS, purl on WS.

▨ Purl on RS, knit on WS.

❘ Pattern repeat

⤫ **3/3 RC (3 over 3 right cross):** Slip 3 sts to cn, hold to back, k3, k3 from cn.

⤫ **3/3 LC (3 over 3 left cross):** Slip 3 sts to cn, hold to front, k3, k3 from cn.

⤫ **2/2/2 RPC (2 over 2 over 2 right purl cross):** Slip 4 sts to cn, hold to back, k2, slip last 2 sts from cn back to left needle, p2, k2 from cn.

⤬ Slip 6 sts to cn, hold to back, k2, p2, k2, k6 from cn.

⤬ Slip 6 sts to cn, hold to front, k6, (k2, p2, k2) from cn.

⤬ Slip 6 sts to cn, hold to back, k6, (k2, p2, k2) from cn.

⤬ Slip 6 sts to cn, hold to front, k2, p2, k2, k6 from cn.

Cloche

FINISHED MEASUREMENTS

Brim circumference: 20" (51 cm)

Body circumference: 22" (56 cm)

Length: 9¾" (25 cm)

YARN

Zealana Kauri Worsted Weight [60% New Zealand merino/30% brushtail possum/10% mulberry silk; 94 yards (86 meters)/50 grams]: 3 hanks K01 Natural

NEEDLES

One pair straight needles size US 8 (5 mm)

One 16" (40 cm) long circular needle size US 7 (4.5 mm)

Change needle size if necessary to obtain correct gauge.

NOTIONS

Stitch marker; cable needle

GAUGE

18 sts and 24 rows = 4" (10 cm) in St st, using larger needles

22-st panel from Cable Pattern measures 3½" (9 cm), using larger needles

Steam or wet block your swatch before taking the measurements.

STITCH PATTERNS

1x1 Rib

(worked in rows over an odd number of sts; 1-row repeat)

ROW 1 (WS): **K1, *p1, k1; repeat from * to end.**

ROW 2: **Knit the knit sts and purl the purl sts as they face you.**

Repeat Row 2 for pattern.

1x1 Rib

(worked in rnds over an even number of sts; 1-rnd repeat)

ALL RNDS: ***K1, p1; repeat from * to end.**

Cable: Fancy 1/1 Travel Share (#78)

PATTERN NOTES

The Cloche begins with the Cable Panel, worked side to side to form main body. The Crown is picked up from the Cable Panel and worked back and forth to top, with short rows and decreases to shape it. The remaining stitches are worked in rib until piece is long enough to reach opposite long side edge of Cable Panel. Stitches are picked up along Cable Panel and Brim is worked in round, then side edges of ribbing are sewn to CO and BO edges of Cable Panel.

⚇ If you'd like to make a cable substitution, see page 114.

Hat

CABLE PANEL

Using larger needles, CO 40 sts. Do not join.

ROW 1 (WS): Slip 2, k2, p2, k3, work Cable Pattern over 22 sts, k3, p2, k2, p2.

ROW 2: Slip 2, p2, k2, p3, work Cable Pattern, p3, k2, p2, k2.

Work even until piece measures approximately 22" (56 cm) from the beginning, ending with a RS row. BO all sts, working p2tog several times across row to keep edge from flaring. Do not cut yarn. Pull ball through last st.

CROWN

With WS facing, working into center of third st in from edge, pick up and knit 73 sts (approximately 1 st for every 2 rows) along long side edge of Cable Panel. If necessary, you may adjust your st count on the next row.

SHORT ROW 1 (RS): Knit to last 5 sts.

SHORT ROW 2 (WS): Turn, yo, purl to last 5 sts, turn.

SHORT ROW 3: Yo, knit to 5 sts before yo from previous RS row, turn.

SHORT ROW 4: Yo, purl to 5 sts before yo from previous WS row, turn.

SHORT ROWS 5–14: Repeat Short Rows 3 and 4 five times.

SHORT ROW 15: Yo, k3, k2tog (yo and following st), [k4, k2tog (yo and following st)] 6 times, knit to end.

NEXT ROW: P45, [ssp (yo and following st)] 7 times, purl to end.

Knit 1 row. Purl 1 row.

SHAPE CROWN

DECREASE ROW 1 (RS): *K4, k2tog; repeat from * to last st, k1—61 sts remain.

Work 5 rows even.

DECREASE ROW 2: *K3, k2tog; repeat from * to last st, k1—49 sts remain.

Work 3 rows even.

DECREASE ROW 3: *K2, k2tog; repeat from * to last st, k1—37 sts remain.

Purl 1 row.

DECREASE ROW 4: *K1, k2tog; repeat from * to last st, k1—25 sts remain.

Purl 1 row.

DECREASE ROW 5: *K2tog; repeat from * to last st, k1—13 sts remain.

Purl 1 row.

DECREASE ROW 6: *K2tog; repeat from * to last st, k1—7 sts remain.

RIBBED BACK PANEL

Change to circular needle and 1 x 1 Rib; do not join.
Work even for 5" (12.5 cm), ending with a WS row. Do not turn.

BRIM

Continuing on the WS, pick up and knit 95 sts along second long side edge of Cable Panel, working into center of third st from edge—102 sts. Join for working in the rnd; pm for beginning of rnd. Begin 1 x 1 Rib; work even for 1¾" (4.5 cm). BO all sts in pattern. Sew CO and BO edges of Cable Panel to sides of Ribbed Back Panel.

Block as desired.

---

❽ Cable Substitution

Before getting started, review Stockinette Stitch Equivalent System on page 20.

CHOOSING CABLES

The SSE of the cable in the Cloche is 16. If you want to work a larger cable, you have 5 stitches of rib on either side of the current cable that can be replaced, giving you 10 more stitches with which to work. You'll want to keep the remaining 4 stitches at each end of the Cable Panel as is. So, the SSE of your cable can be as large as 26.

MANAGING A CHANGE IN STITCH COUNT

If, after substituting, your stitch count has changed, adjust the cast-on for the Cable Panel to accommodate your stitch count.

CABLE PATTERN
(panel of 22 sts; 34-row repeat)
SSE: 16 sts

ROW 1 AND ALL WS ROWS (WS): [P1, k1, p2, k1, p1, k2] twice, p1, k1, p2, k1, p1.
ROW 2: [K1, p1, RT, p1, k1, p2] twice, k1, p1, LT, p1, k1.
ROW 4: K1, p1, RT, p1, k1, p2; slip 3 sts to cn, hold to back, k1, p1, k1, (k1, p1, k1) from cn; p2, k1, p1, LT, p1, k1.
ROW 6: Repeat Row 2.
ROW 8: K1, p1, RT; slip 3 sts to cn, hold to back, p1, k1, p1, (p1, k1, p1) from cn; RT; slip 3 sts to cn, hold to front, p1, k1, p1, (p1, k1, p1) from cn; LT, p1, k1.
ROWS 10 AND 12: Repeat Row 2.
ROW 14: Repeat Row 8.
ROW 16: Repeat Row 2.

ROW 18: Slip 3 sts to cn, hold to back, k1, p1, k1, (k1, p1, k1) from cn; p2, k1, p1, RT, p1, k1, p2; slip 3 sts to cn, hold to front, k1, p1, k1, (k1, p1, k1) from cn.
ROW 20: Repeat Row 2.
ROW 22: K1, p1, RT; slip 3 sts to cn, hold to front, p1, k1, p1, (k1, p1, p1) from cn; RT; slip 3 sts to cn, hold to back, p1, k1, p1, (p1, k1, p1) from cn; LT, p1, k1.
ROWS 24 AND 26: Repeat Row 2.
ROW 28: Repeat Row 22.
ROW 30: Repeat Row 2.
ROW 32: Repeat Row 4.
ROW 34: Repeat Row 2.
Repeat Rows 1–34 for pattern.

CABLE PATTERN (FANCY 1/1 TRAVEL SHARE)

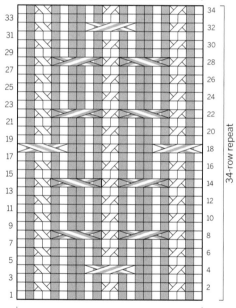

34-row repeat

22-st panel

 Knit on RS, purl on WS.

▨ Purl on RS, knit on WS.

RT (right twist): K2tog, but do not drop sts from left needle; insert right needle between 2 sts just worked and knit first st again, slip both sts from left needle together.

LT (left twist): Insert needle from back to front between first and second sts on left needle and knit the second st through the front loop; knit first st, slip both sts from left needle together.

Slip 3 sts to cn, hold to back, k1, p1, k1, (k1, p1, k1) from cn.

Slip 3 sts to cn, hold to front, k1, p1, k1, (k1, p1, k1) from cn.

Slip 3 sts to cn, hold to back, p1, k1, p1, (p1, k1, p1) from cn.

Slip 3 sts to cn, hold to front, p1, k1, p1, (p1, k1, p1) from cn.

Scarf

FINISHED MEASUREMENTS
Approximately 8" (20.5 cm) wide x 78" (198 cm) long, not including fringe

YARN
Blue Sky Alpacas Techno [68% alpaca/22% silk/ 10% extra fine merino; 120 yards (109 meters)/ 50 grams]: 7 hanks #1971 Metro Silver

Note: Scarf used exactly 6 hanks. An additional hank is required for your gauge swatch.

NEEDLES
One pair straight needles size US 10 (6 mm)

Change needle size if necessary to obtain correct gauge.

NOTIONS
Cable needle; crochet hook size US J-10 (6 mm) or larger, for fringe

GAUGE
25 sts and 21 rows = 4" (10 cm) in Cable Pattern, after blocking

44-st panel from Cable Pattern measures 7" (18 cm) wide

Steam or wet block your swatch before taking the measurements.

STITCH PATTERNS
Cable: Chevron Share Loose (#73)

🔗 If you'd like to make a cable substitution, see page 116.

Scarf

CO 54 sts.

ROW 1 (WS): Slip 3 wyif, k2, work Cable Pattern to last 5 sts, k2, p3.

ROW 2: Slip 3 wyib, p2, work Cable Pattern to last 5 sts, p2, k3.

Work even until piece measures about 77" (195.5 cm), ending with Row 48 of Cable Pattern.

Repeat Rows 1 and 2 of Cable Pattern once.

BIND-OFF ROW (RS): S2kp2, BO in pattern to last 2 sts, p2tog, BO remaining st. Fasten off.

Finishing

Steam or wet-block piece to measurements.

FRINGE

Cut 112 lengths of yarn 17" (43 cm) long (I wrapped yarn around an 8½" (21.5 cm) wide booklet). Using 4 strands of yarn per fringe, work 14 fringes evenly spaced across CO and BO edges.

🔗 Cable Substitution

Before getting started, review Stockinette Stitch Equivalent System on page 20.

CHOOSING CABLES

When knitting a scarf, in general, I like to use cables that look attractive on both sides. See pages 51, 83, and 131 for some great examples. To keep your scarf the same width, you'll want an SSE of about 29. However, since scarves look great in many widths, use any combination of cables you like. Separate smaller cables with 1 or 2 reverse stockinette stitches and add 10 stitches (5 for each end). An exception to the rule in this book: Gauge doesn't matter here as long as you are flexible about the width of your scarf.

MANAGING A CHANGE IN STITCH COUNT

Cast on the number of stitches you need for your version and follow the instructions for the scarf as written.

CABLE PATTERN

(panel of 44 sts; 24-row repeat
SSE: 29 sts

ROW 1 (WS): [P2, k2, p4, k2, p2, k4] twice, p2, k2, p4, k2, p2.

ROWS 2–7: Knit the knit sts and purl the purl sts as they face you.

ROW 8: K2, p2, k4, p2, k2, p4, k2, p2, 2/2 RC, p2, k2, p4, k2, p2, k4, p2, k2.

ROWS 9–15: Repeat Row 2.

ROW 16: K2, p2, k4, p2, p4; slip 6 sts to cn, hold to back, k2, p2, k2, (k2, p2, k2) from cn; p4, k2, p2, k4, p2, k2.

ROWS 17–24: Repeat Rows 1–8.

ROWS 25–27: Repeat Row 2.

ROW 28: K2, p2, k4; slip 2 sts to cn, hold to back, p2, k2, p2, (p2, k2, p2) from cn; k4, slip 6 sts to cn, hold to front, p2, k2, p2, (p2, k2, p2) from cn; k4, p2, k2.

ROWS 29–31: Repeat Row 2.

ROW 32: [K2, p2, 2/2 RC, p2, k2, p4] twice, k2, p2, 2/2 LC, p2, k2.

ROWS 33–39: Repeat Row 2.

ROW 40: [Slip 6 sts to cn, hold to back, k2, p2, k2, (k2, p2, k2) from cn; p4] twice; slip 6 sts to cn, hold to front, k2, p2, k2, (k2, p2, k2) from cn.

ROWS 41–47: Repeat Row 2.

ROW 48: Repeat Row 32.
Repeat Rows 25–48 for pattern.

CABLE PATTERN (CHEVRON SHARE LOOSE)

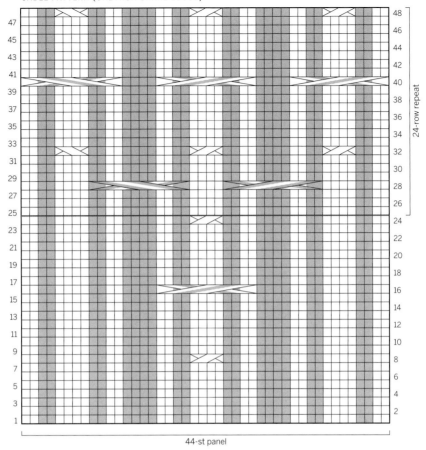

44-st panel

24-row repeat

☐ Knit on RS, purl on WS.

▨ Purl on RS, knit on WS.

| Pattern repeat

⬔ 2/2 RC (2 over 2 right cross): Slip 2 sts to cn, hold to back, k2, k2 from cn.

⬔ 2/2 LC (2 over 2 left cross): Slip 2 sts to cn, hold to front, k2, k2 from cn.

⬔ Slip 6 sts to cn, hold to back, k2, p2, k2, (k2, p2, k2) from cn.

⬔ Slip 6 sts to cn, hold to front, k2, p2, k2, (k2, p2, k2) from cn.

⬔ Slip 6 sts to cn, hold to back, p2, k2, p2, (p2, k2, p2) from cn.

⬔ Slip 6 sts to cn, hold to front, p2, k2, p2, (p2, k2, p2) from cn.

Top-Down Pullover

SIZES
To fit bust 30 (34, 38, 42, 46, 50, 54)" [76 (86.5, 96.5, 106.5, 117, 127, 137) cm]

FINISHED MEASUREMENTS
32 (36¼, 40, 44¼, 48, 52¼, 56)" [81.5 (92, 101.5, 112.5, 122, 132.5, 142) cm] bust

YARN
Berroco Inca Tweed [50% wool/30% alpaca/14% acrylic/6% rayon viscose; 153 yards (140 meters)/100 grams]: 6 (6, 7, 8, 8, 9, 10) hanks #8915 Andes

NEEDLES
One 24" (60 cm) long circular needle size US 9 (5.5 mm)

One 32" (80 cm) long or longer circular needle size US 9 (5.5 mm)

One 32" (80 cm) long or longer circular needle size US 7 (4.5 mm)

Needle(s) in preferred style for small circumference knitting in the rnd, size US 9 (5.5 mm)

Needle(s) in preferred style for small circumference knitting in the rnd, size US 7 (4.5 mm)

Change needle size if necessary to obtain correct gauge.

NOTIONS
Stitch markers; stitch holders or waste yarn

GAUGE
15 sts and 22 rnds = 4" (10 cm) in St st, using larger needle

6-st panel from Cable A or C measures 1¼" (3 cm), using larger needle

16-st panel from Cable B measures 3½" (9 cm) wide, using larger needle

Steam or wet block your swatch before taking the measurements.

STITCH PATTERNS
2x2 Rib
(multiple of 4 sts; 1-rnd repeat)
ALL RNDS: *K2, p2; repeat from * to end.

Cable A: Cable Center 3/3 (Left Cross) (#2)

Cable B: Medallion (#74)

Cable C: Cable Center 3/3 (Right Cross) (#2)

PATTERN NOTES
This pullover is worked in one piece from the top down to the armholes with circular yoke shaping. The sleeves are placed on hold while the body is worked. Then the sleeves are worked in the round. The neckband is worked in the round, with yarnover short rows to shape the back neck.

§ If you'd like to make a cable substitution, see page 120.

Yoke

Using larger 24" (60 cm) circular needle, CO 76 (84, 92, 92, 100, 100, 108) sts. Join for working in the rnd, being careful not to twist sts; pm for beginning of rnd. *Note: Beginning of rnd is at center Back.*

SET-UP RND: K20 (24, 28, 28, 32, 32, 36), pm, p2, work Cable A over 6 sts, p2, work Cable B over 16 sts, p2, work Cable C over 6 sts, p2, pm, knit to end.

NEXT RND: Knit to marker, sm, p2, work Cable A, p2, work Cable B, p2, work Cable C, p2, sm, knit to end.

SHAPE YOKE

Note: Change to larger 32" (80 cm) circular needle when desired for number of sts on needle.

INCREASE RND 1: K0 (0, 2, 0, 0, 0, 2), [k2, M1L] 9 (11, 12, 13, 15, 15, 16) times, k2, sm, p2, work to next marker, sm, k2, [M1L, k2] 9 (11, 12, 13, 15, 15, 16) times, knit to end—94 (106, 116, 118, 130, 130, 140) sts. Work 4 (5, 6, 6, 7, 7, 8) rnds even.

INCREASE RND 2: K3 (1, 6, 1, 3, 1, 4), [k2 (2, 2, 2, 3, 2, 2), M1L] 12 (16, 16, 19, 14, 22, 23) times, k2, sm, work to next marker, sm, k2, [M1, k2 (2, 2, 2, 3, 2, 2)] 12 (16, 16, 19, 14, 22, 23) times, knit to end—118 (138, 148, 156, 158, 174, 186) sts. Work 9 (9, 10, 10, 11, 11, 12) rnds even.

INCREASE RND 3: K5 (1, 3, 1, 2, 1, 7), [k2 (3, 3, 3, 3, 3, 3), M1L] 17 (16, 17, 19, 19, 22, 22) times, k2, sm, work to next marker, sm, k2, [M1L, k2 (3, 3, 3, 3, 3, 3)] 17 (16, 17, 19, 19, 22, 22) times, knit to end—152 (170, 182, 194, 196, 218, 230) sts. Work 12 (13, 13, 14, 14, 15, 16) rnds even.

INCREASE RND 4: K5 (1, 3, 1, 3, 1, 3), [k3 (4, 4, 4, 3, 4, 4), M1L] 17 (16, 17, 19, 25, 22, 23) times, k2, sm, work to next marker, sm, k2, [M1L, k3 (4, 4, 4, 3, 4, 4)] 17 (16, 17, 19, 25, 22, 23) times, knit to end—186 (202, 216, 232, 246, 262, 276) sts. Work even until piece measures 8¾ (9, 9¼, 9½, 10, 10½, 10¾)" [22 (23, 23.5, 24, 25.5, 26, 27.5) cm] from the beginning.

DIVIDE FOR BODY AND SLEEVES

NEXT RND: K27 (29, 31, 33, 35, 37, 39), place next 36 (38, 40, 42, 44, 46, 48) sts on holder or waste yarn for Sleeve, CO 4 (5, 6, 7, 8, 9, 10) sts for underarm using Knitted CO, pm for side, CO 4 (5, 6, 7, 8, 9, 10) sts for underarm, knit to marker, sm, work to next marker, sm, k12 (16, 19, 23, 26, 30, 33), place next 36 (38, 40, 42, 44, 46, 48) sts on holder or waste yarn for Sleeve, CO 4 (5, 6, 7, 8, 9, 10) sts for underarm, pm for side, CO 4 (5, 6, 7, 8, 9, 10) sts for underarm, knit to end—130 (146, 160, 176, 190, 206, 220) sts; 62 (68, 74, 80, 86, 92, 98) sts for Back, 68 (78, 86, 96, 104, 114, 122) sts for Front. Beginning of rnd remains at center Back.

Body

Continuing to work cables between Front markers and St st on remaining sts, work even for 9 (9, 9, 10, 10, 10) rnds.

SHAPE BODY

INCREASE RND: Knit to 1 st before marker, M1R, k1, sm, k1, M1L, knit to next marker, sm, work to next marker, sm, knit to 1 st before next marker, M1R, k1, sm, k1, M1L, knit to end—4 sts increased.

Repeat Increase Rnd every 10 (10, 10, 11, 11, 11) rnds 6 times—158 (174, 188, 204, 218, 234, 248) sts.

Work even until piece measures 14 (14, 14½, 14½, 15, 15, 15½)" [35.5 (35.5, 37, 37, 38, 38, 39.5) cm] from underarm.

Change to smaller 32" (80 cm) circular needle.

NEXT RND: K5 (6, 4, 8, 8, 2, 3), M1L, *k9 (8, 8, 7, 7, 8, 7), M1L; repeat from * to last 0 (0, 0, 7, 7, 0, 0) sts, knit to end—176 (196, 212, 232, 248, 264, 284) sts.

Change to 2 x 2 Rib; work even for 2" (5 cm).

BO all sts in pattern.

Sleeves

Using larger needle(s) in preferred style for small circumference knitting in the rnd, and beginning at center underarm, pick up and knit 4 (5, 6, 7, 8, 9, 10) sts from sts CO for underarm, knit across 36 (38, 40, 42, 44, 46, 48) Sleeve sts from holder, pick up and knit 4 (5, 6, 7, 8, 9, 10) sts from sts CO for underarm. Join for working in the rnd; pm for beginning of rnd—44 (48, 52, 56, 60, 64, 68) sts. Knit 11 (9, 7, 8, 6, 7, 5) rnds.

SHAPE SLEEVE

DECREASE RND: K1, k2tog, knit to 3 sts before marker, ssk, k1—2 sts decreased.

Repeat Decrease Rnd every 13 (11, 10, 7, 7, 6, 6) rnds 3 (4, 5, 7, 8, 9, 10) times—36 (38, 40, 40, 42, 44, 46) remain.

Work even until piece measures 12½ (12½, 13, 13, 13½, 13½, 14)" [32 (32, 33, 33, 34.5, 34.5, 35.5) cm] from underarm, increase 0 (2, 0, 0, 2, 0, 2) sts evenly on last rnd—36 (40, 40, 40, 44, 44, 48) sts.

Change to smaller needle(s) in preferred style for small circumference knitting in the rnd.

Change to 2 x 2 Rib; work even for 2½" (6.5 cm).

BO all sts in pattern.

Finishing

Block piece as desired.

NECKBAND

With RS facing, using smaller needle(s) in preferred style for small circumference knitting in the rnd, and beginning at right edge of Cable B, pick up and knit 13 sts across Cable B to beginning of Cable A (including 2 purl sts between cables), pick up and knit 7 sts across Cable A to beginning of St st (including 2 purl sts after Cable A), pick up and knit 40 (48, 56, 56, 64, 64, 72) sts (1 st in each CO st to 2 purl sts before Cable C), pick up and knit 9 sts to beginning of rnd (including 2 purl sts before and after Cable C)—69 (77, 85, 85, 93, 93, 101) sts.

SHAPE NECKBAND

SHORT ROW 1 (WS): Turn, yo, knit to marker.

SHORT ROW 2 (RS): Turn, yo, knit to 4 (4, 5, 5, 6, 6, 7) sts before yo from previous WS row.

SHORT ROW 3: Turn, yo, knit to 4 (4, 5, 5, 6, 6, 7) sts before yo from previous RS row.

SHORT ROW 4: Turn, yo, knit to 4 (4, 5, 5, 6, 6, 7) sts before yo from previous WS row.

SHORT ROW 5: Turn, yo, purl to 4 (4, 5, 5, 6, 6, 7) sts before yo from previous RS row.

SHORT ROW 6: Turn, knit to 4 (4, 5, 5, 6, 6, 7) sts before yo from previous WS row.

SHORT ROWS 7 AND 8: Repeat Short Rows 5 and 6.

SHORT ROW 9: Turn, yo, purl to 4 sts before yo from previous RS row.

SHORT ROW 10: Turn, yo, knit to center Back neck, pm for new beginning of rnd.

NEXT RND: [Purl to yo, p2tog (yo and following st)] 5 times, [purl to 1 st before yo, p2tog (yo and st before it)] 5 times, purl to end.

Purl 1 rnd.

BO all sts purlwise.

⚭ Cable Substitution

Before getting started, review Stockinette Stitch Equivalent System on page 20.

CHOOSING CABLES

You can use multiple cables or one single cable to make the panel in the front of this pullover.

EASY SUBSTITUTION: Cable A has an SSE of 5. Cable B has an SSE of 13.5. The total SSE for the panel is 27.5 (5 + p2 + 13.5 + p2 + 5), not including the 2 reverse stockinette stitches (p2) on either outside end of the panel. If you'd like your cables to be next to the stockinette stitch (with no purl stitches between the cables and the stockinette stitch), aim for a total SSE of 31.5; in this case, any SSE between 30 and 33 will work well.

ADVANCED SUBSTITUTION: If you adjust the width of the cable panel in the center, you'll also need to adjust the number of stitches between the increases on each Increase Round, so that you can fit in the required number of increases before and after working the panel. (The number of increases will remain the same.) I recommend limiting any additional width beyond the SSE of 31.5 to an SSE of 8 (4 on each side of the panel).

MANAGING A CHANGE IN STITCH COUNT

If, after substituting, your stitch count has changed, make note of the difference between your required cast-on numbers and the cast-on called for in the pattern and remember to add or subtract those stitches for the rest of the instructions. When you divide for body and sleeves, the extra stitches will be on the front.

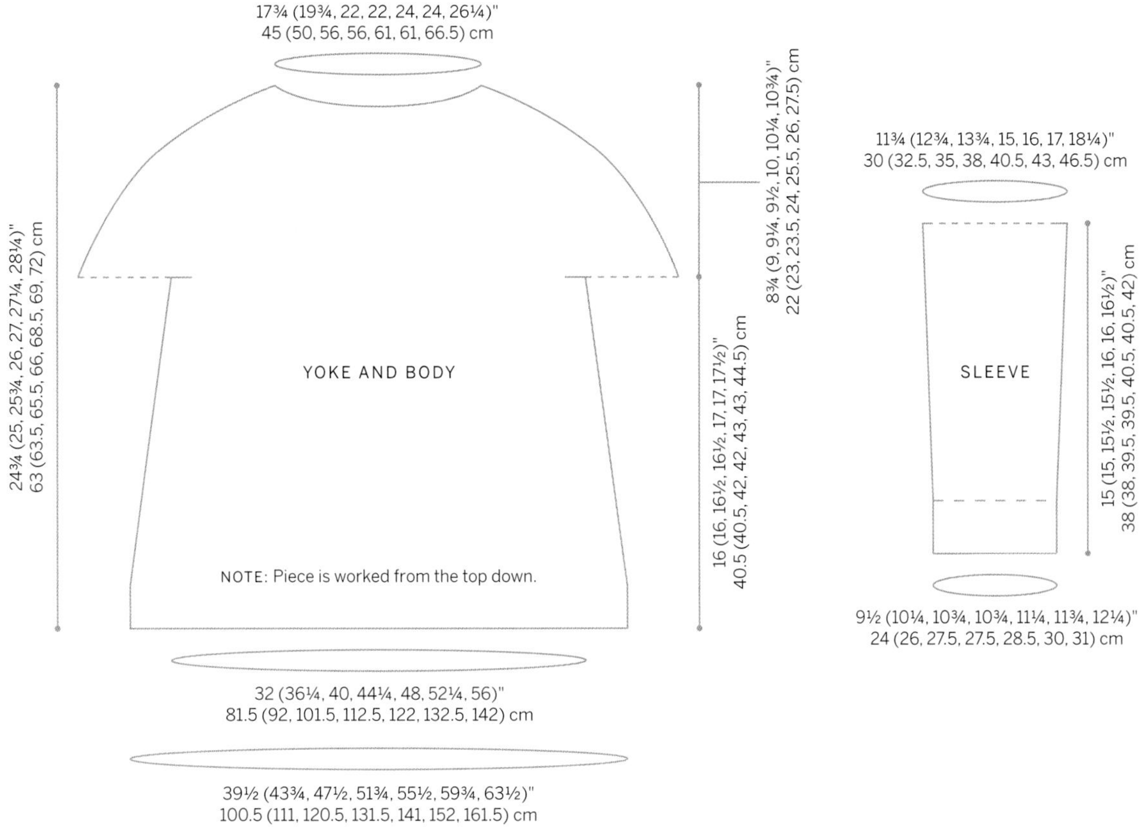

17¾ (19¾, 22, 22, 24, 24, 26¼)"
45 (50, 56, 56, 61, 61, 66.5) cm

8¾ (9, 9¼, 9½, 10, 10¼, 10¾)"
22 (23, 23.5, 24, 25.5, 26, 27.5) cm

11¾ (12¾, 13¾, 15, 16, 17, 18¼)"
30 (32.5, 35, 38, 40.5, 43, 46.5) cm

24¾ (25, 25¾, 26, 27, 27¼, 28¼)"
63 (63.5, 65.5, 66, 68.5, 69, 72) cm

YOKE AND BODY

SLEEVE

15 (15, 15½, 15½, 16, 16, 16½)"
38 (38, 39.5, 39.5, 40.5, 40.5, 42) cm

16 (16, 16½, 16½, 17, 17, 17½)"
40.5 (40.5, 42, 42, 43, 43, 44.5) cm

NOTE: Piece is worked from the top down.

9½ (10¼, 10¾, 10¾, 11¼, 11¾, 12¼)"
24 (26, 27.5, 27.5, 28.5, 30, 31) cm

32 (36¼, 40, 44¼, 48, 52¼, 56)"
81.5 (92, 101.5, 112.5, 122, 132.5, 142) cm

39½ (43¾, 47½, 51¾, 55½, 59¾, 63½)"
100.5 (111, 120.5, 131.5, 141, 152, 161.5) cm

CABLE A
(panel of 6 sts; 8-rnd repeat)
SSE: 5 sts

RND 1 AND ALL ODD-NUMBERED RNDS:
Purl.
RND 2: Knit.
RND 4: 3/3 LC.
RND 6: Knit.
RND 8: K1, 2/2 LC, k1.
Repeat Rnds 1–8 for pattern.

CABLE B
(panel of 16 sts; 24-rnd repeat)
SSE: 13.5 sts

RND 1: [P4, k2] twice, p4.
RNDS 2 AND 3: Knit the knit sts and purl the purl sts as they face you.
RND 4: 2/2 LC, p2, k4, p2, 2/2 RC.
RNDS 5–8: Repeat Rnds 1–4.
RNDS 9–11: Repeat Rnd 2.
RND 12: K2; slip 6 sts to cn, hold to front, k2, p2, k2, (k2, p2, k2) from cn; k2.
RNDS 13–15: Repeat Rnd 2.
RND 16: 2/2 RC, p2, k4, p2, 2/2 LC.
RNDS 17–20: Repeat Rnds 13–16.
RNDS 21–24: Repeat Rnd 2.
Repeat Rnds 1–24 for pattern.

CABLE C
(panel of 6 sts; 8-rnd repeat)
SSE: 5 sts

RND 1 AND ALL ODD-NUMBERED RNDS:
Purl.
RND 2: Knit.
RND 4: 3/3 RC.
RND 6: Knit.
RND 8: K1, 2/2 RC, k1.
Repeat Rnds 1–8 for pattern.

CABLE A
(CABLE CENTER 3/3
[LEFT CROSS])

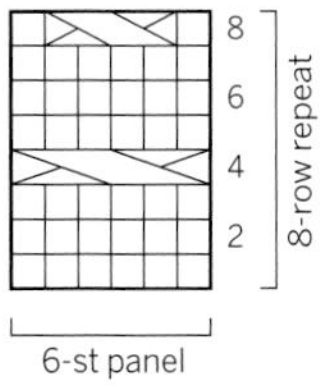

8-row repeat

6-st panel

CABLE B
(CABLE CENTER 3/3
[RIGHT CROSS])

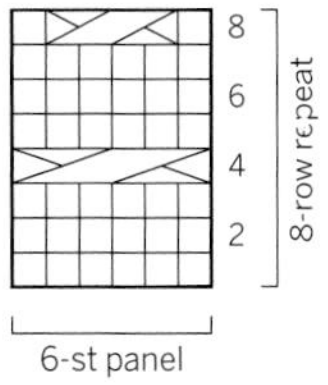

8-row repeat

6-st panel

CABLE B (MEDALLION)

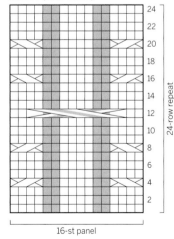

24-row repeat

16-st panel

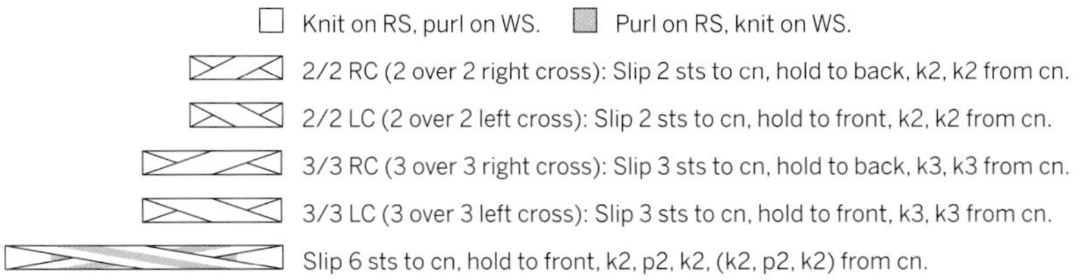

□ Knit on RS, purl on WS.   ▨ Purl on RS, knit on WS.

2/2 RC (2 over 2 right cross): Slip 2 sts to cn, hold to back, k2, k2 from cn.

2/2 LC (2 over 2 left cross): Slip 2 sts to cn, hold to front, k2, k2 from cn.

3/3 RC (3 over 3 right cross): Slip 3 sts to cn, hold to back, k3, k3 from cn.

3/3 LC (3 over 3 left cross): Slip 3 sts to cn, hold to front, k3, k3 from cn.

 Slip 6 sts to cn, hold to front, k2, p2, k2, (k2, p2, k2) from cn.

Chapter

This chapter explores making wider cable panels. Some of these are brand new and some are expansions of cables introduced in earlier chapters. For instance, Rib Mock Mega (#84) expands on the idea of cabling with p1, k2, p1 from Rib 4/4 (#9) in Chapter 2. A few of the wider cable panels are formed by putting pieces together to construct a wider panel

Expanding

(e.g., Rib Braid Combo [#86] and Dolled-Up Separates [#109]). Most are the result of repeating a defined portion of the chart to make a cable panel that is flexible in width because the defined portion can be repeated as many times as desired. The minimum number of stitches that can be used is shown on the chart along with the repeat, the number of stitches you can add (as many times as you'd like). Some of these repeatable panels are expanded versions of cables we've seen in the previous chapters. For instance, 1/1 Diamonds (#104) is the expanded version of 1/1 Travel Share (#76). The same is true for Medallion Expansion (#107) and Medallion (#74). Ribbon Weave (#96) and Cross Wave Rib (#102) are ideas we haven't seen before.

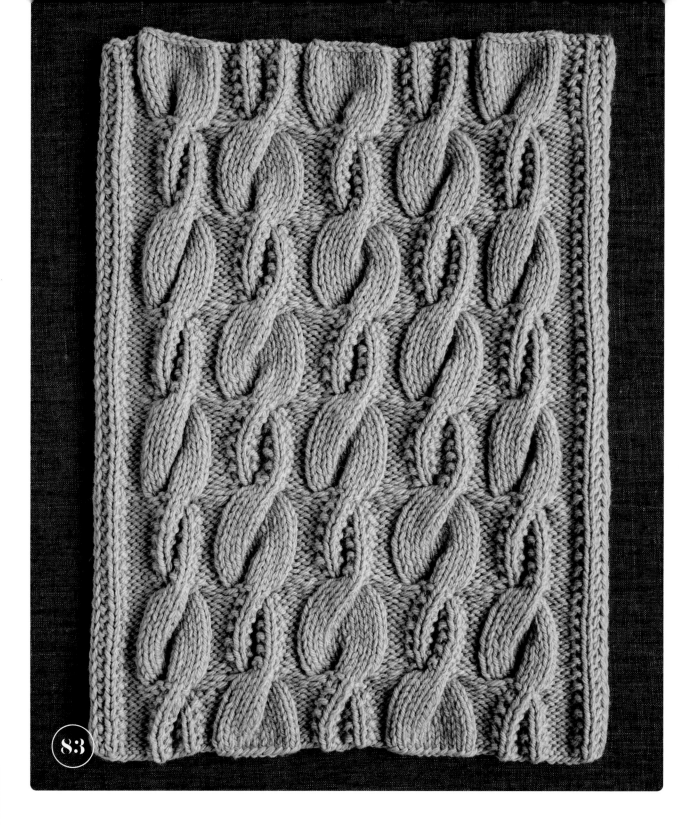

Seed Rib Half Drop

GROUP 1

Seed Rib Half Drop starts out as a basic 5/5 cable and is then transformed and expanded in a few steps. In the swatch shown, there are 5 separate columns (2 columns are repeated 2½ times). In each column, seeded rib alternates with stockinette stitch. The columns are set up so that every other one starts halfway through the row repeat of the one next to it; as a result, the columns look staggered.

(multiple of 24 sts + 10; 28-row repeat)

TOTAL SSE: 25 sts
REPEAT SSE: 18 sts

ROW 1 (WS): K2, *[p1, k4] twice, p10, k4; repeat from * to last 8 sts, p1, k4, p1, k2.
ROW 2: P1, k3, p2, k3, *p3, k10, p3, k3, p2, k3; repeat from * to last st, p1.
ROWS 3–10: Repeat Rows 1 and 2 four times.
ROW 11: Repeat Row 1.
ROW 12: 5/5 RC, *p2, 5/5 RC; repeat from * to end.
ROW 13: P10, *[k4, p1] twice, k4, p10; repeat from * to end.
ROW 14: K10, *p3, k3, p2, k3, p3, k10; repeat from * to end.
ROWS 15–24: Repeat Rows 13 and 14 five times.
ROW 25: Repeat Row 13.
ROW 26: 5/5 RC, *p2, 5/5 RC; repeat from * to end.
ROWS 27 AND 28: Repeat Rows 1 and 2.
Repeat Rows 1–28 for pattern.

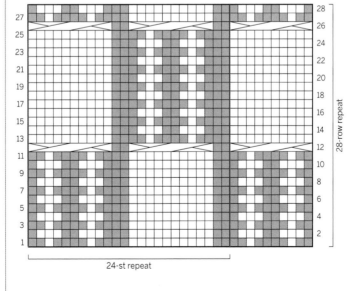

24-st repeat

28-row repeat

□ Knit on RS, purl on WS.

▨ Purl on RS, knit on WS.

| Pattern repeat

⬦ 5/5 RC (5 over 5 right cross): Slip 5 sts to cn, hold to back, k5, k5 from cn.

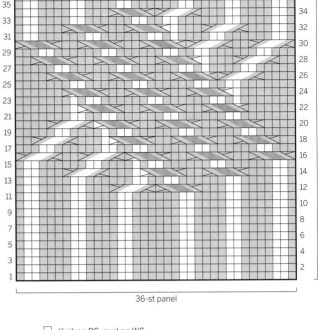

36-st panel

38-row repeat

Rib Mock Mega GROUP 2

This pattern appears to be one large cable but is a combination of multiple small cable crosses. With every cross, 4 stitches cross over 2 stitches, creating the diagonal lines that together mimic a huge cable crossing. Crossing p1, k2, p1 lifts the cables higher and more dramatically off the rest of the fabric than moving only the 2 knit stitches in the center (as is the case for Herringbone Lattice (#88) and numerous cables in other chapters).

(panel of 36 sts; 38-row repeat)
SSE: 23.5 sts

ROW 1 (WS): K1, [p2, k4] twice, p2, k6, [p2, k4] twice, p2, k1.

ROW 2: P1, [k2, p4] twice, k2, p6, [k2, p4] twice, k2, p1.

ROW 3 AND ALL FOLLOWING WS ROWS: Knit the knit sts and purl the purl sts as they face you.

ROWS 4, 6, 8, AND 10: Repeat Row 2.

ROW 12: P1, k2, p4, k2, p3; slip 4 sts to cn, hold to front, p2, (p1, k2, p1) from cn; slip 2 sts to cn, hold to back, p1, k2, p1, p2 from cn; p3, k2, p4, k2, p1.

ROW 14: P1, k2, p3; slip 4 sts to cn, hold to front, p2, (p1, k2, p1) from cn; p2; slip 4 sts to cn, hold to front, p2, (p1, k2, p1) from cn; k1, p3; slip 2 sts to cn, hold to back, p1, k2, p1, p2 from cn; p3, k2, p1.

ROW 16: [Slip 4 sts to cn, hold to front, p2, (p1, k2, p1) from cn; p2] twice; slip 4 sts to cn, hold to front, p2, (p1, k2, p1) from cn; slip 2 sts to cn, hold to back, p1, k2, p1, p2 from cn; p2; slip 2 sts to cn, hold to back, p1, k2, p1, p2 from cn.

ROW 18: [P2; slip 4 sts to cn, hold to front, p2, (p1, k2, p1) from cn] 3 times; k1, p3; slip 2 sts to cn, hold to back, p1, k2, p1, p2 from cn; p2.

ROW 20: P4; [slip 4 sts to cn, hold to front, p2, (p1, k2, p1) from cn; p2] twice; slip 4 sts to cn, hold to front, p2, (p1, k2, p1) from cn; slip 2 sts to cn, hold to back, p1, k2, p1, p2 from cn; p4.

ROW 22: P6; slip 4 sts to cn, hold to front, p1, k1, (p1, k2, p1) from cn; [p2, slip 4 sts to cn, hold to front, p2, (p1, k2, p1) from cn] twice; k1, p7.

ROW 24: P7, k1; slip 4 sts to cn, hold to front, k1, p1, (p1, k2, p1) from cn; [p2; slip 4 sts to cn, hold to front, p2, (p1, k2, p1) from cn] twice; p6.

ROW 26: P4; slip 2 sts to cn, hold to back, p1, k2, p1, p2 from cn; slip 4 sts to cn, hold to front, p1, k1, (p1, k2, p1) from cn; [p2; slip 4 sts to cn, hold to front, p2, (p1, k2, p1) from cn] twice; p4.

ROW 28: P2; slip 2 sts to cn, hold to back, p1, k2, p1, p2 from cn; p3, k1; slip 4 sts to cn, hold to front, k1, p1, (p1, k2, p1) from cn; [p2; slip 4 sts to cn, hold to front, p2, (p1, k2, p1) from cn] twice; p2.

ROW 30: Slip 2 sts to cn, hold to back, p1, k2, p1, p2 from cn; p2; slip 2 sts to cn, hold to back, p1, k2, p1, p2 from cn; slip 4 sts to cn, hold to front, p1, k1, (p1, k2, p1) from cn; [p2; slip 4 sts to cn, hold to front, p2, (p1, k2, p1) from cn] twice.

ROW 32: P1, k2, p3; slip 2 sts to cn, hold to back, p1, k2, p1, p2 from cn; p3, k1; slip 4 sts to cn, hold to front, k1, p1, (p1, k2, p1) from cn; p2; slip 4 sts to cn, hold to front, p2, (p1, k2, p1) from cn; p3, k2, p1.

ROW 34: P1, k2, p4, k2, p3; slip 2 sts to cn, hold to back, p1, k2, p1, p2 from cn; slip 4 sts to cn, hold to front, p2, (p1, k2, p1) from cn; p3, k2, p4, k2, p1.

ROWS 36 AND 38: Repeat Row 2. Repeat Rows 1–38 for pattern.

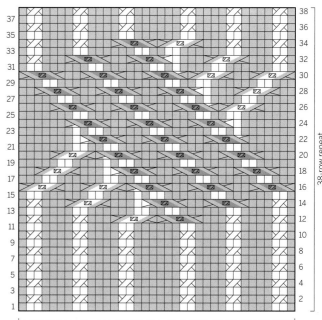

Twist Mock Mega GROUP 2

Replacing the k2 of Rib Mock Mega (#84) transforms the ribs into mini ropes.

□ Knit on RS, purl on WS.

▨ Purl on RS, knit on WS.

▨ RT (right twist): K2tog, but do not drop sts from left needle; insert right needle between 2 sts just worked and knit first st again, slip both sts from left needle together.

Slip 2 sts to cn, hold to back, p1, RT, p1, p2 from cn.

Slip 4 sts to cn, hold to front, p1, k1, (p1, RT, p1) from cn.

Slip 4 sts to cn, hold to front, k1, p1, (p1, RT, p1) from cn.

OR
OR

Slip 4 sts to cn, hold to front, p2, (p1, RT, p1) from cn.

(panel of 36 sts; 38-row repeat)
SSE: 23.5 sts

ROW 1 (WS): K1, [p2, k4] twice, p2, k6, [p2, k4] twice, p2, k1.

ROW 2: P1, [RT, p4] twice, RT, p6, [RT, p4] twice, RT, p1.

ROW 3 AND ALL FOLLOWING WS ROWS: Knit the knit sts and purl the purl sts as they face you.

ROWS 4, 6, 8, AND 10: Repeat Row 2.

ROW 12: P1, RT, p4, RT, p3; slip 4 sts to cn, hold to front, p2, (p1, RT, p1) from cn; slip 2 sts to cn, hold to back, p1, RT, p1, p2 from cn; p3, RT, p4, RT, p1.

ROW 14: P1, RT, p3; slip 4 sts to cn, hold to front, p2, (p1, RT, p1) from cn; p2; slip 4 sts to cn, hold to front, p2, (p1, RT, p1) from cn; k1, p3; slip 2 sts to cn, hold to back, p1, RT, p1, p2 from cn; p3, RT, p1.

ROW 16: [Slip 4 sts to cn, hold to front, p2, (p1, RT, p1) from cn; p2] twice; slip 4 sts to cn, hold to front, p2, (p1, RT, p1) from cn; slip 2 sts to cn, hold to back, p1, RT, p1, p2 from cn; p2; slip 2 sts to cn, hold to back, p1, RT, p1, p2 from cn; p4.

ROW 18: [P2; slip 4 sts to cn, hold to front, p2, (p1, RT, p1) from cn] 3 times; k1, p3; slip 2 sts to cn, hold to back, p1, RT, p1, p2 from cn, p2.

ROW 20: P4; [slip 4 sts to cn, hold to front, p2, (p1, RT, p1) from cn; p2] twice; slip 4 sts to cn, hold to front, p2, (p1, RT, p1) from cn; slip 2 sts to cn, hold to back, p1, RT, p1, p2 from cn; p4.

ROW 22: P6; slip 4 sts to cn, hold to front, p1, k1, (p1, RT, p1) from cn; [p2; slip 4 sts to cn, hold to front, p2, (p1, RT, p1) from cn] twice, k1, p7.

ROW 24: P7, k1; slip 4 sts to cn, hold to front, k1, p1, (p1, RT, p1) from cn; [p2; slip 4 sts to cn, hold to front, p2, (p1, RT, p1) from cn] twice; p6.

ROW 26: P4; slip 2 sts to cn, hold to back, p1, RT, p1, p2 from cn; slip 4 sts to cn, hold to front, p1, k1, (p1,

RT, p1) from cn; [p2; slip 4 sts to cn, hold to front, p2, (p1, RT, p1) from cn] twice; p4.

ROW 28: P2; slip 2 sts to cn, hold to back, p1, RT, p1, p2 from cn; p3, k1; slip 4 sts to cn, hold to front, k1, p1, (p1, RT, p1) from cn; [p2; slip 4 sts to cn, hold to front, p2, (p1, RT, p1) from cn] twice; p2.

ROW 30: Slip 2 sts to cn, hold to back, p1, RT, p1, p2 from cn; p2; slip 2 sts to cn, hold to back, p1, RT, p1, p2 from cn; slip 4 sts to cn, hold to front, p1, k1, (p1, RT, p1) from cn; [p2; slip 4 sts to cn, hold to front, p2, (p1, RT, p1) from cn] twice.

ROW 32: P1, RT, p3; slip 2 sts to cn, hold to back, p1, RT, p1, p2 from cn; p3, k1; slip 4 sts to cn, hold to front, k1, p1, (p1, RT, p1) from cn;

p2; slip 4 sts to cn, hold to front, p2, (p1, RT, p1) from cn; p3, RT, p1.

ROW 34: P1, RT, p4, RT, p3; slip 2 sts to cn, hold to back, p1, RT, p1, p2 from cn; slip 4 sts to cn, hold to front, p2, (p1, RT, p1) from cn; p3, RT, p4, RT, p1.

ROWS 36 AND 38: Repeat Row 2.
Repeat Rows 1–38 for pattern.

Rib Braid Combo GROUP 3

In this cable pattern 3 columns—a center braid and 2 flanking cables—nestle together to form a wide panel. The left-slanted portion of the braid and the cable to its right start at the same time as do the right-slanted portion of the braid and the cable to its left. This allows the 3 cables to nestle together perfectly and makes the pattern easy to memorize.

(panel of 42 sts; 12-row repeat)
SSE: 25 sts

ROW 1 (WS): K1, [p2, k6, p2, k2] twice, p2, k1, p1, k2, p2, k4, p2, k1, p1, k1.

ROW 2: P1, k1; slip 4 sts to cn, hold to front, k1, p1, (k1, p2, k1) from cn; p1, k2, p2, k1; slip 4 sts to cn, hold to front, k1, p1, (p1, k2, p1) from cn; k1, p6, k2, p2, k2, p6, k2, p1.

ROW 3 AND ALL FOLLOWING WS ROWS: Knit the knit sts and purl the purl sts as they face you.

ROW 4: P1, k2, p1; slip 4 sts to cn, hold to front, p2, (p1, k2, p1) from cn; k1, p2, k2, p1; slip 4 sts to cn, hold to front, p2, (p1, k2, p1) from cn; p5, k2, p2, k2, p6, k2, p1.

ROW 6: P1, k2, p3; slip 4 sts to cn, hold to front, p2, (p1, k2, p1) from cn; p1, k2, p3; slip 4 sts to cn, hold to front, p2, (p1, k2, p1); from cn slip 2 sts to cn, hold to back, p1, k2, p1, (k1, p1) from cn; p1, k2, p3; slip 2 sts to cn, hold to back, p1, k2, p1, (k1, p1) from cn.

ROW 8: P1, k2, p6, k2, p2, k2, p6, k1; slip 2 sts to cn, hold to back, p1, k2, p1, (p1, k1) from cn; k1, p2, k2, p1; slip 2 sts to cn, hold to back, p1, k2, p1, (p1, k1) from cn; k1, p1.

ROW 10: P1, k2, p6, k2, p2, k2, p5; slip 2 sts to cn, hold to back, p1, k2, p1, p2 from cn; p1, k2, p2, k1; slip 2 sts to cn, hold to back, p1, k2, p1, p2 from cn; p1, k2, p1.

ROW 12: Slip 4 sts to cn, hold to front, p1, k1, (p1, k2, p1) from cn; p3, k2, p1; slip 4 sts to cn, hold to front, p1, k1, (p1, k2, p1) from cn; slip 2 sts to cn, hold to back, p1, k2, p1, p2 from cn; p3, k2, p1; slip 2 sts to cn, hold to back, p1, k2, p1, p2 from cn; p3, k2, p1.
Repeat Rows 1–12 for pattern.

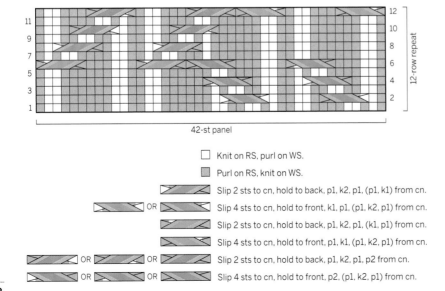

42-st panel

□ Knit on RS, purl on WS.

▨ Purl on RS, knit on WS.

Slip 2 sts to cn, hold to back, p1, k2, p1, (p1, k1) from cn.

OR   Slip 4 sts to cn, hold to front, k1, p1, (p1, k2, p1) from cn.

Slip 2 sts to cn, hold to back, p1, k2, p1, (k1, p1) from cn.

Slip 4 sts to cn, hold to front, p1, k1, (p1, k2, p1) from cn.

OR   OR   Slip 2 sts to cn, hold to back, p1, k2, p1, p2 from cn.

OR   OR   Slip 4 sts to cn, hold to front, p2, (p1, k2, p1) from cn.

Twist Braid Combo GROUP 3

In this variation on Rib Braid Combo (#86), right and left twists are substituted for the k2 in the center braid, giving it a ropy look. I tried substituting right twists in the cables that surround the braid as well, but I thought it looked too busy. Also, I like the contrast of the ropy center braid with the smooth cables that surround it.

(panel of 42 sts; 12-row repeat)
SSE: 25 sts

ROW 1 (WS): K1, [p2, k6, p2, k2] twice, p2, k1, p1, k2, p2, k4, p2, k1, p1, k1.

ROW 2: P1, k1; slip 4 sts to cn, hold to front, k1, p1, (k1, p2, k1) from cn; p1, k2, p2, k1; slip 4 sts to cn, hold to front, k1, p1, (p1, RT, p1) from cn; k1, p6, LT, p2, k2, p6, k2, p1.

ROW 3 AND ALL FOLLOWING WS ROWS: Knit the knit sts and purl the purl sts as they face you.

ROW 4: P1, k2, p1; slip 4 sts to cn, hold to front, p2, (p1, k2, p1) from cn; k1, p2, RT, p1; slip 4 sts to cn, hold to front, p2, (p1, RT, p1) from cn; p5, LT, p2, k2, p6, k2, p1.

ROW 6: P1, k2, p3; slip 4 sts to cn, hold to front, p2, (p1, k2, p1) from

cn; p1, RT, p3; slip 4 sts to cn, hold to front, p2, (p1, RT, p1) from cn; slip 2 sts to cn, hold to back, p1, LT, p1, (k1, p1) from cn; p1, k2, p3; slip 2 sts to cn, hold to back, p1, k2, p1, (k1, p1) from cn.

ROW 8: P1, k2, p6, k2, p2, RT, p6, k1; slip 2 sts to cn, hold to back, p1, LT, p1, (p1, k1) from cn; k1, p2, k2, p1; slip 2 sts to cn, hold to back, p1, k2, p1, (p1, k1) from cn; k1, p1.

ROW 10: P1, k2, p6, k2, p2, RT, p5; slip 2 sts to cn, hold to back, p1, LT, p1, p2 from cn; p1, LT, p2, k1; slip 2 sts to cn, hold to back, p1, k2, p1, p2 from cn; p1, k2, p1.

ROW 12: Slip 4 sts to cn, hold to front, p1, k1, (p1, k2, p1) from cn; p3, k2, p1; slip 4 sts to cn, hold to front, p1, k1, (p1, RT, p1) from cn; slip 2 sts to cn, hold to back, p1, LT, p1, p2 from cn; p3, LT, p1; slip 2 sts to cn, hold to back, p1, k2, p1, p2 from cn; p3, k2, p1.

Repeat Rows 1–12 for pattern.

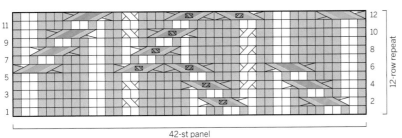

42-st panel

☐ Knit on RS, purl on WS. ▨ Purl on RS, knit on WS.

RT (right twist): K2tog, but do not drop sts from left needle; insert right needle between 2 sts just worked and knit first st again, slip both sts from left needle together.

LT (left twist): Insert needle from back to front between first and second sts on left needle and knit the second st through the front loop; knit first st, slip both sts from left needle together.

Slip 2 sts to cn, hold to back, p1, k2, p1, (p1, k1) from cn.

Slip 4 sts to cn, hold to front, k1, p1, (p1, k2, p1) from cn.

Slip 2 sts to cn, hold to back, p1, k2, p1, (k1, p1) from cn.

Slip 4 sts to cn, hold to front, p1, k1, (p1, k2, p1) from cn.

OR Slip 2 sts to cn, hold to back, p1, k2, p1, p2 from cn.

OR Slip 4 sts to cn, hold to front, p2, (p1, k2, p1) from cn.

Slip 2 sts to cn, hold to back, p1, LT, p1, (p1, k1) from cn.

Slip 4 sts to cn, hold to front, k1, p1, (p1, RT, p1) from cn.

Slip 2 sts to cn, hold to back, p1, LT, p1, (k1, p1) from cn.

Slip 4 sts to cn, hold to front, p1, k1, (p1, RT, p1) from cn.

OR Slip 2 sts to cn, hold to back, p1, LT, p1, p2 from cn.

OR Slip 4 sts to cn, hold to front, p2, (p1, RT, p1) from cn.

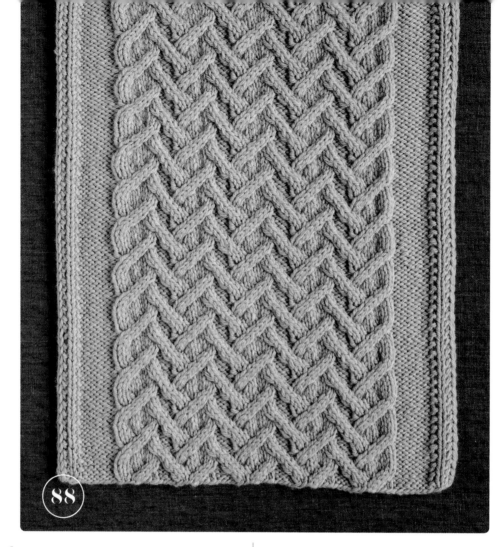

Herringbone Lattice GROUP 4

The diagonal lines in Herringbone Lattice are made by combining 2/2 cable crosses. I made this simulation of a herringbone weave by alternating right- and left-slanting cable lines. Stockinette stitch fills the spaces above and below the right-slanting lines, while the space between the left-slanting lines is filled with reverse stockinette stitch. You can skip the reverse stockinette, but you will lose some of the textural depth.

(multiple of 12 sts + 8; 8-row repeat)

TOTAL SSE: 14.5 sts

REPEAT SSE: 8.5 sts

ROW 1 AND ALL WS ROWS (WS): P8, *k4, p8; repeat from * to end.

ROW 2: *K2, 2/2 RC, k2, p4; repeat from * to last 8 sts, k2, 2/2 RC, k2.

ROW 4: *2/2 RC, k2, 2/2 LC, p2; repeat from * to last 8 sts, 2/2 RC, k4.

ROW 6: *K8, 2/2 LPC; repeat from * to last 8 sts, k8.

ROW 8: K4, *2/2 RC, p2, 2/2 LPC, k2; repeat from * to last 4 sts, 2/2 RC.

Repeat Rows 1–8 for pattern.

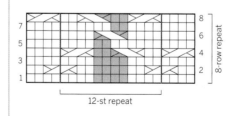

☐ Knit on RS, purl on WS.

▨ Purl on RS, knit on WS.

| Pattern repeat

2/2 RC (2 over 2 right cross): Slip 2 sts to cn, hold to back, k2, k2 from cn.

2/2 LC (2 over 2 left cross): Slip 2 sts to cn, hold to front, k2, k2 from cn.

OR 2/2 LPC (2 over 2 left purl cross): Slip 2 sts to cn, hold to front, p2, k2 from cn.

Reversibility

I find the "wrong" sides of these cable patterns so attractive that I would consider using them as "right" sides.

The wrong side of **LINKED (#91)** resembles a checkerboard of parentheses. I am not surprised that **1/1 DIAMONDS (#104)** is reversible since most ribbed cables look good on both sides,

but in this case, the wrong side, in which delicate Xs nestle among serpentine waves, is especially graphic and interesting. The wrong sides of both **PERFORATED RIB SHARE (#103)** and **DISTANT SHARE LATTICE (#100)** look very different than their right sides.

Herringbone Composition

In this variation of Herring-bone Lattice (#88), I began with the same 2/2 stitch panel but eliminated the center cables over a rectangular section in the center, creating an empty space. I filled that space with garter stitch and a small honeycomb pattern.

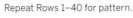

(panel of 44 sts; 40-row repeat)
SSE: 34 sts

ROW 1 (WS): P8, k2, p24, k2, p8.
ROW 2: K4, 2/2 RC, p2, k24, p2, k4, 2/2 RC.
ROW 3: P8, k28, p8.
ROW 4: K2, 2/2 RC, k2, p2, k24, p2, k2, 2/2 RC, k2.
ROW 5: Repeat Row 3.
ROW 6: 2/2 RC, k4, p2, k24, p2, 2/2 RC, k4.
ROW 7: Repeat Row 3.
ROW 8: K8, p2, k24, p2, k8.
ROW 9: Repeat Row 1.
ROW 10: K4, 2/2 RC, p2, k6, 2/2 RC, k8, 2/2 RC, k2, p2, k4, 2/2 RC.
ROW 11: Repeat Row 1.
ROW 12: K2, 2/2 RC, k2, p2, k4, 2/2 RC, k8, 2/2 RC, k4, p2, k2, 2/2 RC, k2.
ROW 13: Repeat Row 1.
ROW 14: [2/2 RC, k2, 2/2 LC, k2] twice, 2/2 RC, k2, 2/2 LC, p2, 2/2 RC, k4.
ROW 15: P8, k2, p34.
ROW 16: [K8, 2/2 LC] 3 times, k8.
ROW 17: Purl.
ROW 18: K4, [2/2 RC, k2, 2/2 LC, k2] 3 times, 2/2 RC.
ROW 19: Purl.
ROW 20: K2, [2/2 RC, k8] 3 times, 2/2 RC, k2.
ROW 21: Purl.
ROW 22: [2/2 RC, k2, 2/2 LC, k2] 3 times, 2/2 RC, k4.
ROW 23: Purl.
ROW 24: K8, 2/2 LPC, [k8, 2/2 LC] twice, k8.
ROW 25: P34, k2, p8.
ROW 26: K4, 2/2 RC, p2, [2/2 LC, k8] twice, 2/2 LPC, k2, 2/2 RC.
ROW 27: P8, k2, p24, k2, p8.
ROW 28: K2, 2/2 RC, k2, p2, k24, p2, k2, 2/2 RC, k2.
ROW 29: P8, k28, p8.
ROW 30: 2/2 RC, k4, p2, k24, p2, 2/2 RC, k4.

ROW 31: Repeat Row 29.
ROW 32: K8, p2, k24, p2, k8.
ROW 33: Repeat Row 29.
ROW 34: K4, 2/2 RC, p2, k24, p2, k4, 2/2 RC.
ROW 35: Repeat Row 27.
ROW 36: K2, 2/2 RC, k2, p2, [RT, LT] 6 times, p2, k2, 2/2 RC, k2.
ROW 37: Repeat Row 27.
ROW 38: 2/2 RC, k4, p2, [LT, RT] 6 times, p2, 2/2 RC, k4.
ROW 39: Repeat Row 27.
ROW 40: Repeat Row 32.
Repeat Rows 1–40 for pattern.

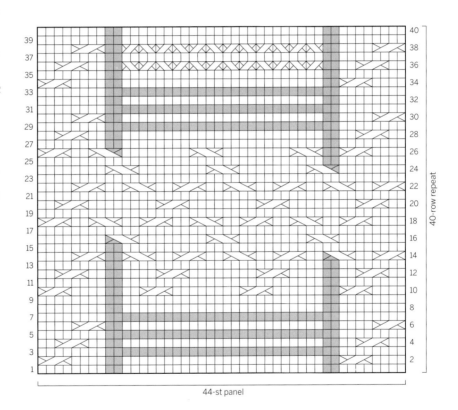

44-st panel

40-row repeat

☐ Knit on RS, purl on WS.

▨ Purl on RS, knit on WS.

❘ Pattern repeat

 RT (right twist): K2tog, but do not drop sts from left needle; insert right needle between 2 sts just worked and knit first st again, slip both sts from left needle together.

LT (left twist): Insert needle from back to front between first and second sts on left needle and knit the second st through the front loop; knit first st, slip both sts from left needle together.

2/2 RC (2 over 2 right cross): Slip 2 sts to cn, hold to back, k2, k2 from cn.

OR 2/2 LC (2 over 2 left cross): Slip 2 sts to cn, hold to front, k2, k2 from cn.

2/2 LPC (2 over 2 left purl cross): Slip 2 sts to cn, hold to front, p2, k2 from cn.

Swing Diamonds GROUP 4

Swing Diamonds uses the same 2/2 crosses as Herringbone Lattice (#88) and Herringbone Composition (#89) to create diagonal lines. In this case, the diagonal lines are stacked and mirror-imaged to create the outline of a large diamond.

(multiple of 34 sts + 1; 68-row repeat)

TOTAL SSE: 26 sts

REPEAT SSE: 25 sts

ROW 1 (WS): K1, *p2, k6, p4, k2, p2, k1, p2, k2, p4, k6, p2, k1; repeat from * to end.

ROW 2: P1, *k2, p6, 2/2 LC, p2, k2, p1, k2, p2, 2/2 RC, p6, k2, p1; repeat from * to end.

ROW 3 AND ALL FOLLOWING WS ROWS: Knit the knit sts and purl the purl sts as they face you.

ROW 4: P1, *k2, p6, k4, 2/2 RC, p1, 2/2 LC, k4, p6, k2, p1; repeat from * to end.

ROW 6: P1, *k2, p6, k2, 2/2 RC, k2, p1, k2, 2/2 LC, k2, p6, k2, p1; repeat from * to end.

ROW 8: P1, *k2, p6, 2/2 RC, k4, p1, k4, 2/2 LC, p6, k2, p1; repeat from * to end.

ROW 10: P1, *k2, p4, 2/2 RC, k2, 2/2 LC, p1, 2/2 RC, k2, 2/2 LC, p4, k2, p1; repeat from * to end.

ROW 12: P1, *k2, p4, k4, 2/2 RPC, k2, p1, k2, 2/2 LPC, k4, p4, k2, p1; repeat from * to end.

ROW 14: P1, *k2, p4, k2, 2/2 RC, p2, k2, p1, k2, p2, 2/2 LC, k2, p4, k2, p1; repeat from * to end.

ROW 16: P1, *k2, p4, 2/2 RC, k2, p2, k2, p1, k2, p2, k2, 2/2 LC, p4, k2, p1; repeat from * to end.

ROW 18: Repeat Row 3.

ROW 20: P1, *k2, p4, k2, 2/2 RPC, p2, k2, p1, k2, p2, 2/2 LPC, k2, p4, k2, p1; repeat from * to end.

ROW 22: P1, *k2, p4, 2/2 RC, p4, k2, p1, k2, p4, 2/2 LC, p4, k2, p1; repeat from * to end.

ROW 24: P1, *k2, p2, 2/2 RC, k2, p4, k2, p1, k2, p4, k2, 2/2 LC, p2, k2, p1; repeat from * to end.

ROW 26: P1, *k2, 2/2 RC, k4, p4, k2, p1, k2, p4, k4, 2/2 LC, k2, p1; repeat from * to end.

ROW 28: P1, *2/2 RC, k2, 2/2 RPC, p4, k2, p1, k2, p4, 2/2 LPC, k2, 2/2 LC, p1; repeat from * to end.

ROW 30: P1, *k4, 2/2 RC, p6, k2, p1, k2, p6, 2/2 LC, k4, p1; repeat from * to end.

ROW 32: P1, *k2, 2/2 RC, k2, p6, k2, p1, k2, p6, k2, 2/2 LC, k2, p1; repeat from * to end.

ROW 34: P1, *2/2 RPC, k4, p6, k2, p1, k2, p6, k4, 2/2 LPC, p1; repeat from * to end.

ROW 36: P1, *k2, p2, 2/2 RC, p6, k2, p1, k2, p6, 2/2 LC, p2, k2, p1; repeat from * to end.

ROW 38: P1, *2/2 LC, k4, p6, k2, p1, k2, p6, k4, 2/2 RC, p1; repeat from * to end.

ROW 40: P1, *k2, 2/2 LC, k2, p6, k2, p1, k2, p6, k2, 2/2 RC, k2, p1; repeat from * to end.

ROW 42: P1, *k4, 2/2 LC, p6, k2, p1, k2, p6, 2/2 RC, k4, p1; repeat from * to end.

ROW 44: P1, *2/2 LC, k2, 2/2 LC, p4, k2, p1, k2, p4, 2/2 RC, k2, 2/2 RC, p1; repeat from * to end.

ROW 46: P1, *k2, 2/2 LPC, k4, p4, k2, p1, k2, p4, k4, 2/2 RPC, k2, p1; repeat from * to end.

ROW 48: P1, *k2, p2, 2/2 LPC, k2, p4, k2, p1, k2, p4, k2, 2/2 RPC, p2, k2, p1; repeat from * to end.

ROW 50: P1, *k2, p4, 2/2 LC, p4, k2, p1, k2, p4, 2/2 RC, p4, k2, p1; repeat from * to end.

ROW 52: P1, *k2, p4, k2, 2/2 LC, p2, k2, p1, k2, p2, 2/2 RC, k2, p4, k2, p1; repeat from * to end.

ROW 54: P1, *k2, p4, k6, p2, k2, p1, k2, p2, k6, p4, k2, p1; repeat from * to end.

ROW 56: P1, *k2, p4, 2/2 LC, k2, p2, k2, p1, k2, p2, k2, 2/2 RC, p4, k2, p1; repeat from * to end.

ROW 58: P1, *k2, p4, k2, 2/2 LC, p2, k2, p1, k2, p2, 2/2 RC, k2, p4, k2, p1; repeat from * to end.

ROW 60: P1, *k2, p4, k4, 2/2 LC, k2, p1, k2, 2/2 RC, k4, p4, k2, p1; repeat from * to end.

ROW 62: P1, *k2, p4, 2/2 LPC, k2, 2/2 LC, p1, 2/2 RC, k2, 2/2 RPC, p4, k2, p1; repeat from * to end.

ROW 64: P1, *k2, p6, 2/2 LC, k4, p1, k4, 2/2 RC, p6, k2, p1; repeat from * to end.

ROW 66: P1, *k2, p6, k2, 2/2 LC, k2, p1, k2, 2/2 RC, k2, p6, k2, p1; repeat from * to end.

ROW 68: P1, *k2, p6, k4, 2/2 LPC, p1, 2/2 RPC, k4, p6, k2, p1; repeat from * to end.

Repeat Rows 1–68 for pattern.

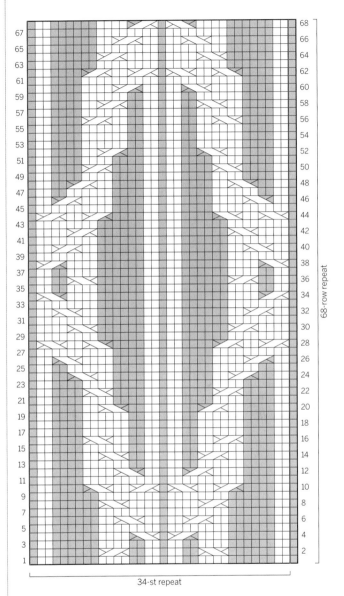

34-st repeat

68-row repeat

☐ Knit on RS, purl on WS.

▨ Purl on RS, knit on WS.

| Pattern repeat

2/2 RC (2 over 2 right cross): Slip 2 sts to cn, hold to back, k2, k2 from cn.

2/2 LC (2 over 2 left cross): Slip 2 sts to cn, hold to front, k2, k2 from cn.

2/2 RPC (2 over 2 right purl cross): Slip 2 sts to cn, hold to back, k2, p2 from cn.

2/2 LPC (2 over 2 left purl cross): Slip 2 sts to cn, hold to front, p2, k2 from cn.

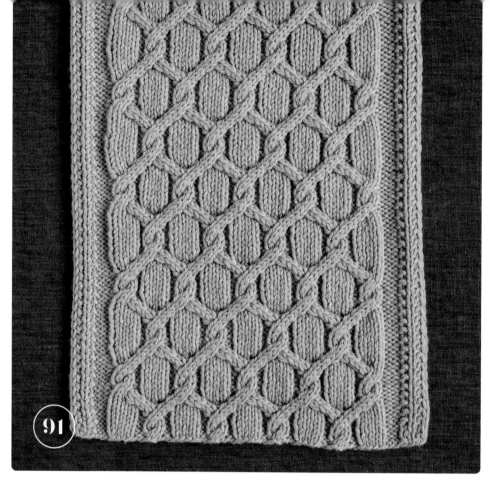

Linked GROUP 4

Here I have combined simple 2/2 crosses to make right- and left-slanting diagonal lines and combined them with short 2/2 ropes to make a pattern that looks like a chain link fence. Check out the surprise pattern on the wrong side on page 131.

(multiple of 12 sts + 16; 20-row repeat)

TOTAL SSE: 20 sts

REPEAT SSE: 8.5 sts

ROW 1 (WS): *P4, k2; repeat from * to last 4 sts, p4.

ROW 2: K4, *p2, 2/2 RC, p2, k4; repeat from * to end.

ROW 3 AND ALL FOLLOWING WS ROWS: Knit the knit sts and purl the purl sts as they face you.

ROW 4: K4, *p2, k4; repeat from * to end.

ROW 6: Repeat Row 2.

ROW 8: K4, *2/2 RC, 2/2 LC, k4; repeat from * to end.

ROW 10: K2, *2/2 RPC, k4, 2/2 LPC; repeat from * to last 2 sts, k2.

ROW 12: 2/2 RC, *p2, k4, p2, 2/2 RC; repeat from * to end.

ROW 14: Repeat Row 4,

ROW 16: Repeat Row 12.

ROW 18: K2, *2/2 LC, k4, 2/2 RC; repeat from * to last 2 sts, k2.

ROW 20: K4, *2/2 LPC, 2/2 RPC, k4; repeat from * to end.

Repeat Rows 1–20 for pattern.

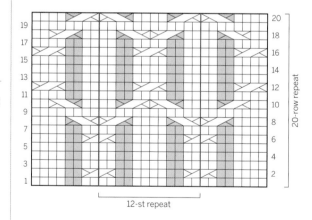

20-row repeat

12-st repeat

☐ Knit on RS, purl on WS.

▨ Purl on RS, knit on WS.

| Pattern repeat

⬚ OR ⬚ 2/2 RC (2 over 2 right cross): Slip 2 sts to cn, hold to back, k2, k2 from cn.

⬚ 2/2 LC (2 over 2 left cross): Slip 2 sts to cn, hold to front, k2, k2 from cn.

⬚ 2/2 RPC (2 over 2 right purl cross): Slip 2 sts to cn, hold to back, k2, p2 from cn.

⬚ 2/2 LPC (2 over 2 left purl cross): Slip 2 sts to cn, hold to front, p2, k2 from cn.

Knot Lattice GROUP 5

Here knots made up of 2/2 crosses intertwine with each other and then reach out on the diagonal to form a lattice. A simple rope fills the diamond made by the lattice and joins each knot to the one above it.

(multiple of 16 sts + 12; 16-row repeat)
TOTAL SSE: 19 sts
REPEAT SSE: 10 sts

ROW 1 (WS): P2, k2, p4, k2, *p8, k2, p4, k2; repeat from * to last 2 sts, p2.

ROW 2: K2, p2, k4, p2, *[2/2 RC] twice, p2, k4, p2; repeat from * to last 2 sts, k2.

ROW 3 AND ALL FOLLOWING WS ROWS: Knit the knit sts and purl the purl sts as they face you.

ROW 4: K2, p2, 2/2 RC, p2, k2, *2/2 LC, k2, p2, 2/2 RC, p2; repeat from * to last 2 sts, k2.

ROW 6: Repeat Row 2.

ROW 8: 2/2 LPC, 2/2 RC, 2/2 RPC, *2/2 LC, 2/2 LPC, 2/2 RC, 2/2 RPC; repeat from * to end.

ROW 10: P2, [2/2 LC] twice, p2, *k4, p2, [2/2 LC] twice, p2; repeat from * to end.

ROW 12: Repeat Row 4.

ROW 14: Repeat Row 10.

ROW 16: 2/2 RPC, 2/2 RC, 2/2 LPC, *2/2 LC, 2/2 RPC, 2/2 RC, 2/2 LPC; repeat from * to end.
Repeat Rows 1–16 for pattern.

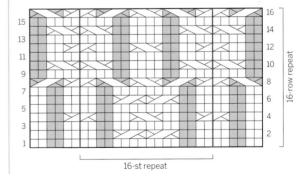

☐ Knit on RS, purl on WS.

▨ Purl on RS, knit on WS.

Ⅰ Pattern repeat

2/2 RC (2 over 2 right cross): Slip 2 sts to cn, hold to back, k2, k2 from cn.

2/2 LC (2 over 2 left cross): Slip 2 sts to cn, hold to front, k2, k2 from cn.

2/2 RPC (2 over 2 right purl cross): Slip 2 sts to cn, hold to back, k2, p2 from cn.

2/2 LPC (2 over 2 left purl cross): Slip 2 sts to cn, hold to front, p2, k2 from cn.

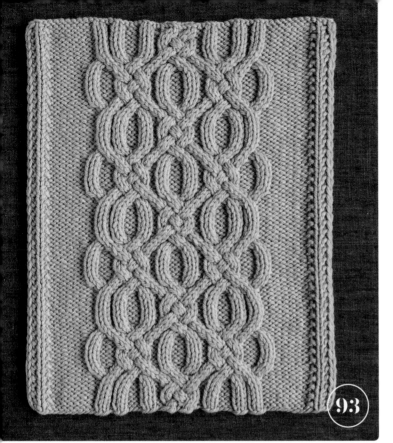

O Knot Lattice GROUP 5

In this variation of Knot Lattice (#92), the knots are spread farther apart from each other, expanding the lattice, and large Os replace the ropes. The outermost curves are not integral to the woven elements of the pattern (if you look carefully, you'll see that all of the other k2 lines intertwine with one another); I added them simply because I like the the way they complete the composition.

(multiple of 20 sts + 20; 20-row repeat)

TOTAL SSE: 27 sts
REPEAT SSE: 13 sts

ROW 1 (WS): [K2, p2] twice, k4, *p2, k2, p8, k2, p2, k4; repeat from * to last 8 sts, [p2, k2] twice.

ROW 2: [P2, k2] twice, p4, *k2, p2, [2/2 RC] twice, p2, k2, p4; repeat from * to last 8 sts, [k2, p2] twice.

ROW 3 AND ALL FOLLOWING WS ROWS: Knit the knit sts and purl the purl sts as they face you.

ROW 4: [P2, k2] twice, p4, *k2, p2, k2, 2/2 LC, k2, p2, k2, p4; repeat from * to last 8 sts, [k2, p2] twice.

ROW 6: Repeat Row 2.

ROW 8: P2, [2/2 LC] twice, *[2/2 RC] twice, [2/2 LC] 3 times; repeat from * to last 10 sts, [2/2 RC] twice, p2.

ROW 10: 2/2 RPC, 2/2 LPC, *2/2 RC, [2/2 RPC] twice, [2/2 LPC] twice; repeat from * to last 12 sts, , 2/2 RC, 2/2 RPC, 2/2 LPC.

ROW 12: K2, p4, [2/2 LC] twice, *p2, k2, p4, k2, p2, [2/2 LC] twice; repeat from * to last 6 sts, p4, k2.

ROW 14: K2, p4, k2, 2/2 RC, k2, *p2, k2, p4, k2, p2, k2, 2/2 RC, k2; repeat from * to last 6 sts, p4, k2.

ROW 16: Repeat Row 12.

ROW 18: 2/2 LPC, [2/2 RC] twice, *[2/2 LC] twice, [2/2 RC] 3 times; repeat from * to last 8 sts, 2/2 LC, 2/2 RPC.

ROW 20: P2, [2/2 RPC] twice, *[2/2 LPC] twice, 2/2 LC, [2/2 RPC] twice; repeat from * to last 10 sts, [2/2 LPC] twice, p2.
Repeat Rows 1–20 for pattern.

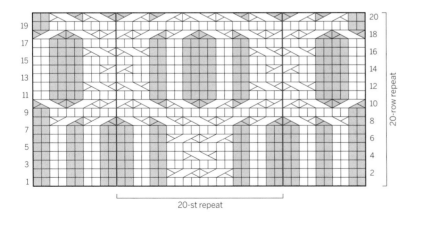

20-st repeat

20-row repeat

☐ Knit on RS, purl on WS.

▨ Purl on RS, knit on WS.

❙ Pattern repeat

OR 2/2 RC (2 over 2 right cross): Slip 2 sts to cn, hold to back, k2, k2 from cn.

OR 2/2 LC (2 over 2 left cross): Slip 2 sts to cn, hold to front, k2, k2 from cn.

OR 2/2 RPC (2 over 2 right purl cross): Slip 2 sts to cn, hold to back, k2, p2 from cn.

OR 2/2 LPC (2 over 2 left purl cross): Slip 2 sts to cn, hold to front, p2, k2 from cn.

Progression of O Knot Cables

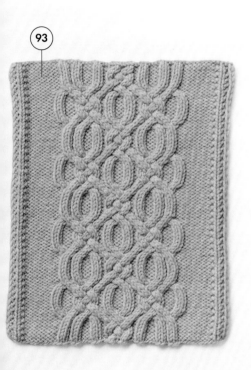

93

94

95

One cable pattern can be varied in markedly different ways as shown in this trio.

I started with **O KNOT LATTICE (#93)**, which looks like an allover panel. I then simplified it to create O Knot Singles. **O KNOT SINGLES (#94)** is an example of a cable panel composed of 3 distinct vertical columns; any one of those columns could be taken away without affecting the others. Then I decided to carve away some of the stitches in O Knot Lattice in order to achieve **O KNOT OGEE (#95).**

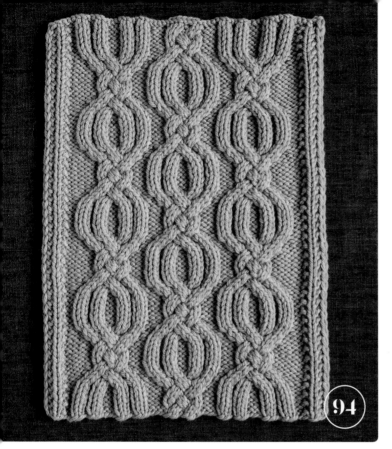

O Knot Singles GROUP 5

After knitting O Knot Lattice (#93) I came up with the idea of making this simpler version with individual columns that are nestled into each other but not interlaced.

(multiple of 32 sts + 16; 20-row repeat)

NOTE: Pattern may also be worked in panels of 16 sts (see Chart).

TOTAL SSE: 20 sts

REPEAT SSE: 10 sts

ROW 1 (WS): K4, p8, k4, *[p2, k2, p2, k4] twice, p8, k4; repeat from * to end.

ROW 2: P4, [2/2 RC] twice, p4, *[k2, p2, k2, p4] twice, [2/2 RC] twice, p4; repeat from * to end.

ROW 3 AND ALL FOLLOWING WS ROWS: Knit the knit sts and purl the purl sts as they face you.

ROW 4: P4, k2, 2/2 LC, k2, p4, *[k2, p2, k2, p4] twice, k2, 2/2 LC, k2, p4; repeat from * to end.

ROW 6: Repeat Row 2.

ROW 8: P2, 2/2 RC, [2/2 LC] twice, p2, *2/2 LPC, 2/2 LC, 2/2 RC, 2/2 RPC, p2, 2/2 RC, [2/2 LC] twice, p2; repeat from * to end.

ROW 10: [2/2 RPC] twice, [2/2 LPC] twice, p2, *2/2 LPC, 2/2 RC, 2/2 RPC, p2, [2/2 RPC] twice, [2/2 LPC] twice; repeat from * to end.

ROW 12: *[K2, p2, k2, p4] twice, [2/2 LC] twice, p4; repeat from * to last 16 sts, k2, p2, k2, p4, k2, p2, k2.

ROW 14: *[K2, p2, k2, p4] twice, k2, 2/2 RC, k2, p4; repeat from * to last 16 sts, k2, p2, k2, p4, k2, p2, k2.

ROW 16: Repeat Row 12.

ROW 18: 2/2 LPC, 2/2 LC, 2/2 RC, 2/2 RPC, *p2, [2/2 RC] twice, 2/2 LC, p2, 2/2 LPC, 2/2 LC, 2/2 RC, 2/2 RPC; repeat from * to end.

ROW 20: P2, 2/2 LPC, 2/2 LC, 2/2 RPC, p2, *[2/2 RPC] twice, [2/2 LPC] twice, p2, 2/2 LPC, 2/2 LC, 2/2 RPC, p2; repeat from * to end. Repeat Rows 1–20 for pattern.

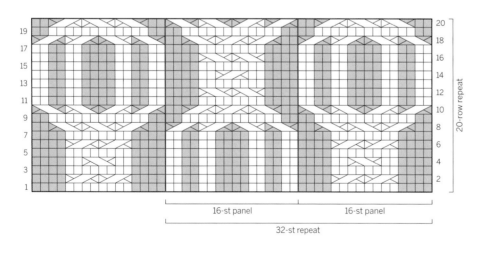

16-st panel | 16-st panel

32-st repeat

20-row repeat

☐ Knit on RS, purl on WS.

▨ Purl on RS, knit on WS.

❙ Pattern repeat

OR   2/2 RC (2 over 2 right cross): Slip 2 sts to cn, hold to back, k2, k2 from cn.

OR   2/2 LC (2 over 2 left cross): Slip 2 sts to cn, hold to front, k2, k2 from cn.

OR   2/2 RPC (2 over 2 right purl cross): Slip 2 sts to cn, hold to back, k2, p2 from cn.

OR   2/2 LPC (2 over 2 left purl cross): Slip 2 sts to cn, hold to front, p2, k2 from cn.

O Knot Ogee GROUP 5

By removing triangular sections of O Knot Lattice (#93), I revealed the gorgeous hourglass shape of O Knot Ogee.

(panel of 36 sts; 40-row repeat)
SSE: 23.5 sts

ROW 1 (WS): K10, p2, k2, p8, k2, p2, k10.

ROW 2: P10, k2, p2, [2/2 RC] twice, p2, k2, p10.

ROW 3 AND ALL FOLLOWING WS ROWS: Knit the knit sts and purl the purl sts as they face you.

ROW 4: P10, k2, p2, k2, 2/2 LC, k2, p2, k2, p10.

ROW 6: Repeat Row 2.

ROW 8: P8, [2/2 RC] twice, [2/2 LC] 3 times, p8.

ROW 10: P6, 2/2 RC, [2/2 RPC] twice, [2/2 LPC] twice, 2/2 LC, p6.

ROW 12: P4, 2/2 RC, 2/2 LC, p2, k2, p4, k2, p2, [2/2 LC] twice, p4.

ROW 14: P4, k2, 2/2 RC, k2, p2, k2, p4, k2, p2, k2, 2/2 RC, k2, p4.

ROW 16: P4, [2/2 LC] twice, p2, k2, p4, k2, p2, [2/2 LC] twice, p4.

ROW 18: P2, [2/2 RPC] twice, [2/2 LC] twice, [2/2 RC] 3 times, 2/2 LC, p2.

ROW 20: [2/2 RPC] twice, [2/2 LPC] twice, 2/2 LC, [2/2 RPC] twice, [2/2 LPC] twice.

ROW 22: K2, p2, k2, p4, k2, p2, [2/2 RC] twice, p2, k2, p4, k2, p2, k2.

ROW 24: K2, p2, k2, p4, k2, p2, k2, 2/2 LC, k2, p2, k2, p4, k2, p2, k2.

ROW 26: Repeat Row 22.

ROW 28: 2/2 LPC, 2/2 LC, [2/2 RC] twice, [2/2 LC] 3 times, 2/2 RC, 2/2 RPC.

ROW 30: P2, 2/2 LPC, 2/2 RC, [2/2 RPC] twice, [2/2 LPC] twice, 2/2 RC, 2/2 RPC, p2.

ROW 32: P4, [2/2 LC] twice, p2, k2, p4, k2, p2, [2/2 LC] twice, p4.

ROW 34: P4, k2, 2/2 RC, k2, p2, k2, p4, k2, p2, k2, 2/2 RC, k2, p4.

ROW 36: P4, 2/2 LPC, 2/2 LC, p2, k2, p4, k2, p2, 2/2 LC, 2/2 RPC, p4.

ROW 38: P6, 2/2 LPC, [2/2 LC] twice, [2/2 RC] twice, 2/2 RPC, p6.

ROW 40: P8, [2/2 LPC] twice, 2/2 LC, [2/2 RPC] twice, p8.

Repeat Rows 1–40 for pattern.

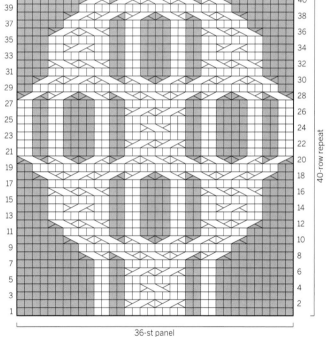

36-st panel

☐ Knit on RS, purl on WS.

▨ Purl on RS, knit on WS.

2/2 RC (2 over 2 right cross): Slip 2 sts to cn, hold to back, k2, k2 from cn.

2/2 LC (2 over 2 left cross): Slip 2 sts to cn, hold to front, k2, k2 from cn.

2/2 RPC (2 over 2 right purl cross): Slip 2 sts to cn, hold to back, k2, p2 from cn.

2/2 LPC (2 over 2 left purl cross): Slip 2 sts to cn, hold to front, p2, k2 from cn.

Ribbon Weave

GROUP 6

Here a half-twisted background of 1x1 rib (created by working the knit stitches through their back loops on right-side rows) is interwoven with "ribbons" of stockinette stitch. The ribbons cross over 2 stitches of background rib on every right-side row.

(multiple of 16 sts + 23; 32-row repeat)

TOTAL SSE: 28 sts

REPEAT SSE: 10 sts

ROW 1 (WS): [K1, p1] 3 times, k1, *p5, [k1, p1] 5 times, k1; repeat from * to end.

ROW 2: [P1, k1-tbl] 4 times, p1; slip 2 sts to cn, hold to back, k4, (k1-tbl, p1) from cn; *[k1-tbl, p1] 5 times; slip 2 sts to cn, hold to back, k4, (k1-tbl, p1) from cn; repeat from * to last 8 sts, [k1-tbl, p1] 4 times.

ROW 3: [K1, p1] 4 times, k1, p5, *[k1, p1] 5 times, k1, p5; repeat from * to last 9 sts, [k1, p1] 4 times, k1.

ROW 4: [P1, k1-tbl] 3 times, p1; *slip 2 sts to cn, hold to back, k4, (k1-tbl, p1) from cn; [k1-tbl, p1] 5 times; repeat from * to end.

ROW 5: *[K1, p1] 5 times, k1, p5; repeat from * to last 7 sts, [k1, p1] 3 times, k1.

ROW 6: [P1, k1-tbl] twice, p1; *slip 2 sts to cn, hold to front, k4, (k1-tbl, p1) from cn; [k1-tbl, p1] 5 times; repeat from * to last 2 sts, k1-tbl, p1.

ROW 7: [K1, p1] 6 times, k1, p5, *[k1, p1] 5 times, k1, p5; repeat from * to last 5 sts, [k1, p1] twice, k1.

ROW 8: P1, k1-tbl, p1; *slip 2 sts to cn, hold to back, k4, (k1-tbl, p1) from cn; [k1-tbl, p1] 5 times; repeat from * to last 4 sts, [k1-tbl, p1] twice.

ROW 9: [K1, p1] 7 times, k1, p5, *[k1, p1] 5 times, k1, p5; repeat from * to last 3 sts, k1, p1, k1.

ROW 10: *[P1, k1-tbl] 5 times, p1, k5; repeat from * to last 7 sts, [p1, k1-tbl] 3 times, p1.

ROW 11: Repeat Row 1.

ROW 12: P1, *[k1-tbl, p1] 5 times; slip 4 sts to cn, hold to front, k1-tbl, p1, k4 from cn; repeat from * to last 6 sts, [k1-tbl, p1] 3 times.

ROW 13: [K1, p1] twice, k1, *p5, [k1, p1] 5 times, k1; repeat from * to last 2 sts, p1, k1.

ROW 14: P1, k1-tbl, p1, *[k1-tbl, p1] 5 times; slip 4 sts to cn, hold to front, k1-tbl, p1, k4 from cn; repeat from * to last 4 sts, [k1-tbl, p1] twice.

ROW 15: K1, p1, k1, *p5, [k1, p1] 5 times, k1; repeat from * to last 4 sts, [p1, k1] twice.

ROW 16: P1, k5, [p1, k1-tbl] 4 times, p1; *slip 4 sts to cn, hold to back, k1-tbl, p1, k4 from cn; [k1-tbl, p1] 5 times; repeat from * to last 8 sts; slip 4 sts to cn, hold to back, k1-tbl, p1, k4 from cn; k1-tbl, p1.

ROW 17: K1, p5, *[k1, p1] 5 times, k1, p5; repeat from * to last st, k1.

ROW 18: P1; slip 4 sts to cn, hold to front, k1-tbl, p1, k4 from cn; *[k1-tbl, p1] 5 times; slip 4 sts to cn, hold to front, k1-tbl, p1, k4 from cn; repeat from * to end.

ROW 19: P4, *[k1, p1] 5 times, k1, p5; repeat from * to last 3 sts, k1, p1, k1.

ROW 20: P1, k1-tbl, p1 *slip 4 sts to cn, hold to front, k1-tbl, p1, k4 from cn; [k1-tbl, p1] 5 times; repeat from * to last 4 sts, [k1-tbl, p1] twice.

ROW 21: Repeat Row 7.

ROW 22: [P1, k1-tbl] twice, p1; *slip 4 sts to cn, hold to back, k1-tbl, p1, k4 from cn; [k1-tbl, p1] 5 times; repeat from * to last 2 sts, k1-tbl, p1.

ROW 23: Repeat Row 5.

ROW 24: [P1, k1-tbl] 3 times, p1; *slip 4 sts to cn, hold to front, k1-tbl, p1, k4 from cn; [k1-tbl, p1] 5 times; repeat from * to end.

ROW 25: Repeat Row 3.

ROW 26: [P1, k1-tbl] 8 times, p1, *k4, [k1-tbl, p1] 6 times; repeat from * to last 6 sts, p4, k1-tbl, p1.

ROW 27: K1, *p5, [k1, p1] 5 times, k1; repeat from * to last 6 sts, [p1, k1] 3 times.

ROW 28: [P1, k1-tbl] 7 times, p1; slip 2 sts to cn, hold to back, k4, (k1-tbl, p1) from cn; *[k1-tbl, p1] 5 times; slip 2 sts to cn, hold to back, k4, (k1-tbl, p1) from cn; repeat from * to last 2 sts, k1-tbl, p1.

ROW 29: K1, p1, k1, *p5, [k1, p1] 5 times, k1; repeat from * to last 4 sts, [p1, k1] twice.

ROW 30: [P1, k1-tbl] 6 times, p1; slip 2 sts to cn, hold to back, k4, (k1-tbl, p1) from cn; *[k1-tbl, p1] 5 times; slip 2 sts to cn, hold to back, k4, (k1-tbl, p1) from cn; repeat from * to last 4 sts, [k1-tbl, p1] twice.

ROW 31: [K1, p1] twice, k1, *p5, [k1, p1] 5 times, k1; repeat from * to last 2 sts, p1, k1.

ROW 32: P1, *[k1-tbl, p1] 5 times; slip 2 sts to cn, hold to front, k4, (k1-tbl, p1) from cn; repeat from * to last 6 sts, [k1-tbl, p1] 3 times. Repeat Rows 1–32 for pattern.

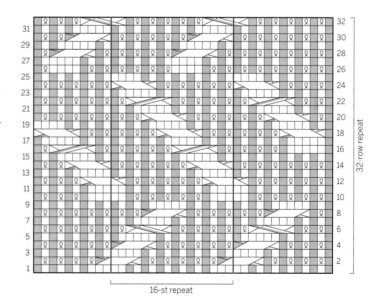

16-st repeat

32-row repeat

☐ Knit on RS, purl on WS.

▨ Purl on RS, knit on WS.

⊠ K1-tbl on RS, p1-tbl on WS.

▏ Pattern repeat

Slip 2 sts to cn, hold to back, k4, (k1-tbl, p1) from cn.

Slip 4 sts to cn, hold to front, k1-tbl, p1, k4 from cn.

Slip 4 sts to cn, hold to back, k1-tbl, p1, k4 from cn.

Slip 2 sts to cn, hold to front, k4, (k1-tbl, p1) from cn.

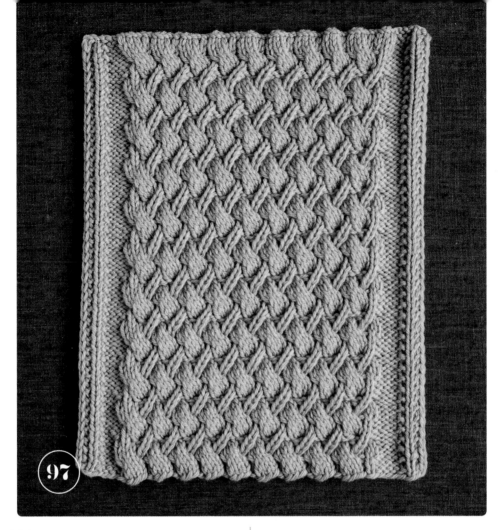

Uneven Weave GROUP 6

Perhaps I should have named this one *Faux Uneven Weave* since the cable crosses are actually all perfectly even 3/3 crosses. They appear uneven because 3 rib stitches (p1, k1, p1) are being crossed over 3 stockinette stitches, giving the impression that 1 stitch is crossing over 3.

(multiple of 6 sts + 9; 8-row repeat)

TOTAL SSE: 9 sts

REPEAT SSE: 3.5 sts

ROW 1 (WS): K1, p1, k1, *p3, k1, p1, k1; repeat from * to end.

ROWS 2 AND 3: Knit the knit sts and purl the purl sts as they face you.

ROW 4: K3; *slip 3 sts to cn, hold to front, p1, k1, p1, k3 from cn; repeat from * to end.

ROW 5: P3, *k1, p1, k1, p3; repeat from * to end.

ROWS 6 AND 7: Repeat Row 2.

ROW 8: *Slip 3 sts to cn, hold to back, p1, k1, p1, k3 from cn; repeat from * to last 3 sts, p1, k1, p1. Repeat Rows 1–8 for pattern.

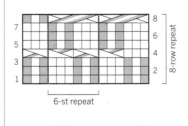

6-st repeat

8-row repeat

☐ Knit on RS, purl on WS.

▨ Purl on RS, knit on WS.

❘ Pattern repeat

Slip 3 sts to cn, hold to front, p1, k1, p1, k3 from cn.

Slip 3 sts to cn, hold to back, p1, k1, p1, k3 from cn.

Center Lattice GROUP 7

Once you've mastered the concept of the center stable cable cross (see page 73), this lattice is very easy to work. You start the pattern with 3 x 2 rib, work a row with center stable crosses, then continue with the rib for 5 more rows before working another cable cross row. The 2 reverse stockinette stitches of the rib keep the crosses separated and reinforce the illusion of a loosely woven fabric.

(multiple of 10 sts + 8; 12-row repeat)

TOTAL SSE: 14 sts

REPEAT SSE: 7 sts

ROW 1 (WS): P3, *k2, p3; repeat from * to end.

ROWS 2 AND 3: Knit the knit sts and purl the purl sts as they face you.

ROW 4: 3/2/3 RPC, * p2, 3/2/3 RPC; repeat from * to end.

ROWS 5–9: Repeat Row 2.

ROW 10: K3, p2, *3/2/3 LPC, p2; repeat from * to last 3 sts, k3.

ROWS 11 AND 12: Repeat Row 2. Repeat Rows 1–12 for pattern.

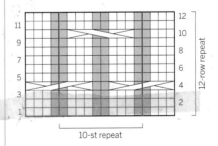

□ Knit on RS, purl on WS.

▨ Purl on RS, knit on WS.

| Pattern repeat

3/2/3 RPC (3 over 2 over 3 right purl cross): Slip 5 sts to cn, hold to back, k3, slip last 2 sts from cn back to left needle, p2, k3 from cn.

3/2/3 LPC (3 over 2 over 3 left purl cross): Slip 5 sts to cn, hold to front, k3, slip last 2 sts from cn back to left needle, p2, k3 from cn.

Rib Share Lattice GROUP 8

I began this series with an uneven rib across the panel, then added cable crosses every 10th row to create the pattern you see here.

(multiple of 10 sts + 6; 20-row repeat)

TOTAL SSE: 11 sts

REPEAT SSE: 7 sts

ROW 1 (WS): *P1, k1, p2, k1; repeat from * to last st, p1.

ROWS 2–7: Knit the knit sts and purl the purl sts as they face you.

ROW 8: Slip 3 sts to cn, hold to back, k1, p1, k1, (k1, p1, k1) from cn; *p1, k2, p1; slip 3 sts to cn, hold to back, k1, p1, k1, (k1, p1, k1) from cn; repeat from * to end.

ROWS 9–17: Repeat Row 2.

ROW 18: K1, p1, k2, p1; *slip 3 sts to cn, hold to front, k1, p1, k1, (k1, p1, k1) from cn; p1, k2, p1, k1; repeat from * to end.

ROWS 19 AND 20: Repeat Row 2. Repeat Rows 1–20 for pattern.

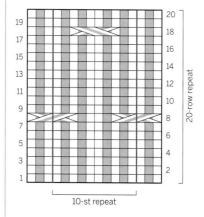

10-st repeat

20-row repeat

☐ Knit on RS, purl on WS.

▨ Purl on RS, knit on WS.

❙ Pattern repeat

▨ Slip 3 sts to cn, hold to back, k1, p1, k1, (k1, p1, k1) from cn.

▨ Slip 3 sts to cn, hold to front, k1, p1, k1, (k1, p1, k1) from cn.

Distant Share Lattice GROUP 8

Two simple changes make the difference between this cable and Rib Share Lattice (#99). All the purls are doubled, which extends the distance between the knit stitches. Also, the cable crosses are worked every 6th row instead of every 10th. See the wrong side of Distant Share Lattice on page 131.

(multiple of 14 sts + 8; 12-row repeat)

TOTAL SSE: 12.5 sts

REPEAT SSE: 8 sts

ROW 1 (WS): *P1, k2, p2, k2; repeat from * to last st, p1.

ROWS 2–5: Knit the knit sts and purl the purl sts as they face you.

ROW 6: Slip 4 sts to cn, hold to front, k1, p2, k1, (k1, p2, k1) from cn; *p2, k2, p2; slip 4 sts to cn, hold to front, k1, p2, k1, (k1, p2, k1) from cn; repeat from * to end.

ROWS 7–11: Repeat Row 2.

ROW 12: K1, p2, k2, *p2; slip 4 sts to cn, hold to back, k1, p2, k1, (k1, p2, k1) from cn; p2, k2; repeat from * to last 3 sts, p2, k1.

Repeat Rows 1–12 for pattern.

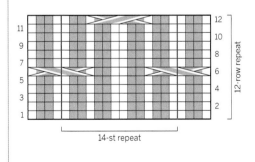

□ Knit on RS, purl on WS.

▧ Purl on RS, knit on WS.

❘ Pattern repeat

▨ Slip 4 sts to cn, hold to back, k1, p2, k1, (k1, p2, k1) from cn.

▨ Slip 4 sts to cn, hold to front, k1, p2, k1, (k1, p2, k1) from cn.

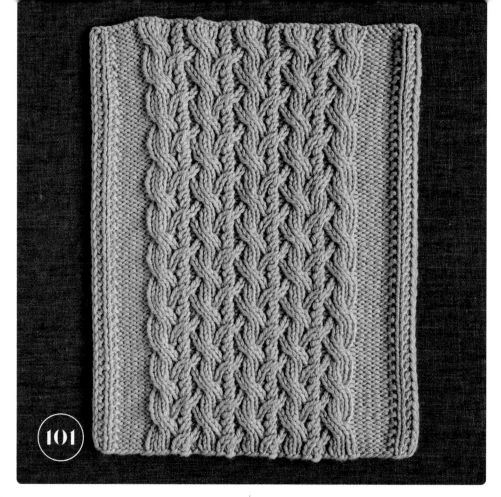

Twist Share Lattice GROUP 8

The addition of right twists and a reduction in the number of rows between cable crosses differentiate this cable from Rib Share Lattice (#99). See 4 related Shared Lattices side by side on page 149.

(multiple of 10 sts + 6;
8-row repeat)

TOTAL SSE: 10.5 sts

REPEAT SSE: 6 sts

ROW 1 AND ALL WS ROWS (WS): *P1, k1, p2, k1; repeat from * to last st, p1.

ROW 2: K1, p1, k2, *p1, k1, p1, RT, p1, k1, p1, k2; repeat from * to last 2 sts, p1, k1.

ROW 4: K1, p1, k2, *p1; slip 3 sts to cn, hold to back, k1, p1, k1, (k1, p1, k1) from cn; p1, k2; repeat from * to last 2 sts, p1, k1.

ROW 6: Repeat Row 2.

ROW 8: Slip 3 sts to cn, hold to front, k1, p1, k1, (k1, p1, k1) from cn; *p1, RT, p1; slip 3 sts to cn, hold to front, k1, p1, k1, (k1, p1, k1) from cn; repeat from * to end. Repeat Rows 1–8 for pattern.

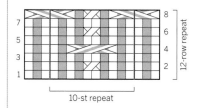

☐ Knit on RS, purl on WS.

▨ Purl on RS, knit on WS.

❘ Pattern repeat

▨ RT (right twist): K2tog, but do not drop sts from left needle; insert right needle between 2 sts just worked and knit first st again, slip both sts from left needle together.

▱ Slip 3 sts to cn, hold to back, k1, p1, k1, (k1, p1, k1) from cn.

▱ Slip 3 sts to cn, hold to front, k1, p1, k1, (k1, p1, k1) from cn.

Rib Share Lattice Variations

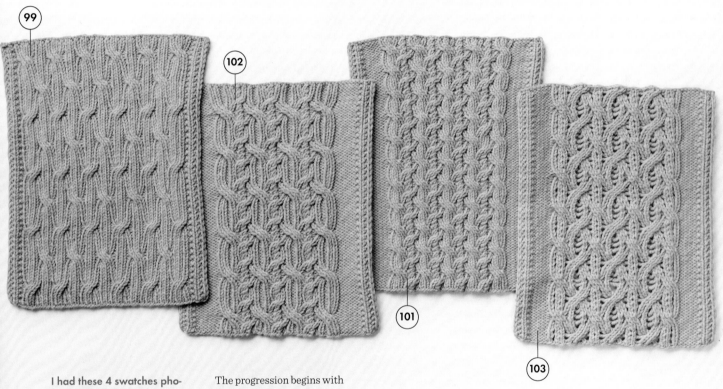

I had these 4 swatches photographed together because I wanted to highlight the breadth of variations possible by making a few simple changes to a ribbed cable pattern.

The progression begins with **RIB SHARE LATTICE (#99).** By adding right twists, openwork, and a few extra stitches, as well as varying the spacing between the cable crosses, I came up with **CROSS WAVE RIB (#102), TWIST SHARE LATTICE (#101),** and **PERFORATED RIB SHARE (#103).**

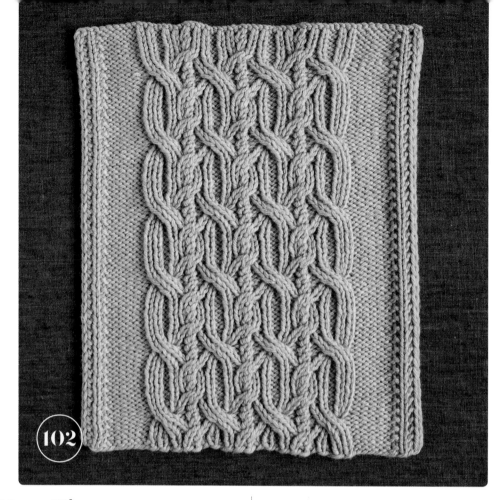

Cross Wave Rib GROUP 8

Three simple changes open up this cable and create the visually profound difference between it and Twist Share Lattice (#101). I made some of the ribs and crosses larger by adding 2 purls in the center and worked these expanded portions as a center stable cable; in addition, I repeated smaller crosses after working straight in rib and right twists for 5 rows.

(multiple of 12 sts + 20; 14-row repeat)
TOTAL SSE: 20 sts
REPEAT SSE: 7.5 sts

ROW 1 AND ALL WS ROWS (WS):
*P1, k1, p1, k2, [p1, k1] twice, p2, k1; repeat from * to last 8 sts, p1, k1, p1, k2, p1, k1, p1.
ROW 2: K1, p1, k1, p2, [k1, p1] twice, *RT, [p1, k1] twice, p2, [p1, k1] twice; repeat from * to last 11 sts, RT, [p1, k1] twice, p2, k1, p1, k1.
ROW 4: K1, p1, k1, p2, k1, p1; *slip 3 sts to cn, hold to back, k1, p1, k1, (k1, p1, k1) from cn; p1, k1, p2, k1, p1; repeat from * to last st, k1.

ROW 6: Repeat Row 2.
ROW 8: Slip 5 sts to cn, hold to front, k1, p1, k1, slip last 2 sts from cn back to left needle, p2, (k1, p1, k1) from cn; *p1, RT, p1; slip 5 sts to cn, hold to front, k1, p1, k1, slip last 2 sts from cn back to left needle, p2, (k1, p1, k1) from cn; repeat from * to end.
ROW 10: Repeat Row 2.
ROW 12: Repeat Row 4.
ROW 14: Repeat Row 2.
Repeat Rows 1–14 for pattern.

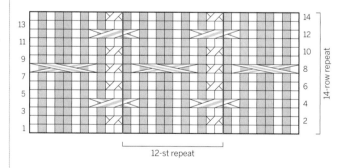

☐ Knit on RS, purl on WS.

▨ Purl on RS, knit on WS.

❘ Pattern repeat

▧ RT (right twist): K2tog, but do not drop sts from left needle; insert right needle between 2 sts just worked and knit first st again, slip both sts from left needle together.

▱ Slip 3 sts to cn, hold to back, k1, p1, k1, (k1, p1, k1) from cn.

▱ Slip 5 sts to cn, hold to front, k1, p1, k1, slip last 2 sts from cn back to left needle, p2, (k1, p1, k1) from cn.

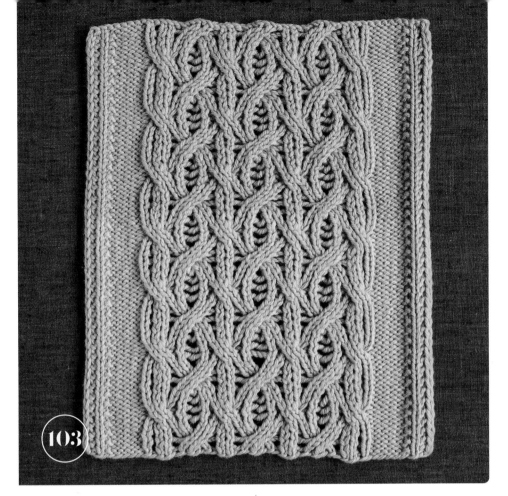

Perforated Rib Share GROUP 8

To create Perforated Rib Share from Rib Share Lattice (#99), I added a 4-stitch lace pattern and inserted ladders made of double yarnovers to open up the fabric. Watch for the stitch-count changes within the row repeat. See reverse side on page 131.

(multiple of 10 sts + 6; increases to 12 sts + 6; decreases back to 10 sts + 6; 14-row repeat)

NOTE: You will increase 2 sts per repeat on Row 3; original st count is restored on Row 13.

TOTAL SSE: 12.5 sts

REPEAT SSE: 8 sts

ROW 1 (WS): P1, yo, ssp, p2tog, yo, p1, *k1, p2, k1, p1, yo, ssp, p2tog, yo, p1; repeat from * to end.

ROW 2: K5; *slip 3 sts to cn, hold to back, k1, p1, k1, (k1, p1, k1) from cn, k5; repeat from * to end.

ROW 3: P1, yo, ssp, p2tog, yo, p1, *k1, p1, yo2, p1, k1, p1, yo, ssp, p2tog, yo, p1; repeat from * to end —2 sts increased per repeat.

ROW 4: *K6, p1, k1, (k1, p1) into yo2, k1, p1; repeat from * to last 6 sts, k6.

ROW 5: P1, yo, ssp, p2tog, yo, p1,

*k1, ssp, yo2, p2tog, k1, p1, yo, ssp, p2tog, yo, p1; repeat from * to end.

ROWS 6–9: Repeat Rows 4 and 5 twice.

ROW 10: Slip 3 sts to cn, hold to front, k1, p1, k1, (k1, p1, k1) from cn; *p1, k1, (k1, p1) into yo2, k1, p1; slip 3 sts to cn, hold to front, k1, p1, k1, (k1, p1, k1) from cn; repeat from * to end.

ROWS 11 AND 12: Repeat Rows 5 and 6.

ROW 13: P1, yo, ssp, p2tog, yo, p1, *k1, ssp, p2tog, k1, p1, yo, ssp, p2tog, yo, p1; repeat from * to end—2 sts decreased per repeat.

ROW 14: Repeat Row 2.
Repeat Rows 1–14 for pattern.

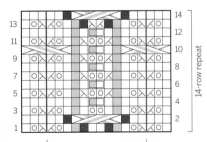

10-st repeat; increases to 12 sts; decreases back to 10 sts

☐ Knit on RS, purl on WS.

▨ Purl on RS, knit on WS.

⊙ Yo

⊙⊙ Yo2

▭ (K1, p1) into yo2.

⧄ K2tog on RS, p2tog on WS.

⧅ Ssk on RS, ssp on WS.

■ No stitch

❘ Pattern repeat

Slip 3 sts to cn, hold to back, k1, p1, k1, (k1, p1, k1) from cn.

Slip 3 sts to cn, hold to front, k1, p1, k1, (k1, p1, k1) from cn.

1/1 Diamonds GROUP 9

The setup for this cable is similar to Rib Share Lattice (#99), but with the addition of a few p2 ribs. These additional stitches mean that the k1 rib on each end of the initial k1, p1, k1 over k1, p1, k1 cable needs to travel farther diagonally before it becomes part of a similar shared cable. This is an expanded version of 1/1 Travel Share (#76) from Chapter 3. Check out the interesting wrong side of 1/1 Diamonds on page 131.

(multiple of 16 sts + 6; 16-row repeat)

TOTAL SSE: 14.5 sts

REPEAT SSE: 11 sts

ROW 1 (WS): *P1, k1, p2, k1, p1, k2; repeat from * to last 6 sts, p1, k1, p2, k1, p1.

ROWS 2 AND 3: Knit the knit sts and purl the purl sts as they face you.

ROW 4: K1, p1, k2, *p1, k1, p2; slip 3 sts to cn, hold to back, k1, p1, k1, (k1, p1, k1) from cn; p2, k1, p1, k2; repeat from * to last 2 sts, p1, k1.

ROWS 5–7: Repeat Row 2.

ROW 8: K1, p1, k2; *slip 3 sts to cn, hold to back, p1, k1, p1, (p1, k1, p1) from cn; k2; slip 3 sts to cn, hold to front, p1, k1, p1, (p1, k1, p1) from cn; k2; repeat from * to last 2 sts, p1, k1.

ROWS 9–11: Repeat Row 2.

ROW 12: Slip 3 sts to cn, hold to front, k1, p1, k1, (k1, p1, k1) from cn; *p2, k1, p1, k2, p1, k1, p2; slip 3 sts to cn hold to front, k1, p1, k1, (k1, p1, k1) from cn; repeat from * to end.

ROWS 13–15: Repeat Row 2.

ROW 16: K1, p1, k2; *slip 3 sts to cn, hold to front, p1, k1, p1, (p1, k1, p1) from cn; k2; slip 3 sts to cn, hold to back, p1, k1, p1, (p1, k1, p1) from cn; k2; repeat from * to last 2 sts, p1, k1.

Repeat Rows 1–16 for pattern.

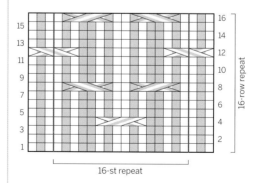

☐ Knit on RS, purl on WS.

▨ Purl on RS, knit on WS.

❘ Pattern repeat

▨ Slip 3 sts to cn, hold to back, k1, p1, k1, (k1, p1, k1) from cn.

▨ Slip 3 sts to cn, hold to front, k1, p1, k1, (k1, p1, k1) from cn.

▨ Slip 3 sts to cn, hold to back, p1, k1, p1, (p1, k1, p1) from cn.

▨ Slip 3 sts to cn, hold to front, p1, k1, p1, (p1, k1, p1) from cn.

1/1 Diamond Twist GROUP 9

Two simple changes transform 1/1 Diamonds (#104) into 1/1 Diamond Twist. Right twists are added to one of the k2 ribs, and left twists are added to the other k2 ribs in the repeat. This is an expanded version of Twist 1/1 Travel Share (#77) from Chapter 3.

(multiple of 16 sts + 6; 16-row repeat)

TOTAL SSE: 14.5 sts

REPEAT SSE: 11 sts

ROW 1 (WS): *P1, k1, p2, k1, p1, k2; repeat from * to last 6 sts, p1, k1, p2, k1, p1.

ROW 2: K1, p1, LT, *p1, k1, p2, k1, p1, RT, p1, k1, p2, k1, p1, LT; repeat from * to last 2 sts, p1, k1.

ROW 3 AND ALL FOLLOWING WS ROWS: Knit the knit sts and purl the purl sts as they face you.

ROW 4: K1, p1, LT, *p1, k1, p2; slip 3 sts to cn, hold to back, k1, p1, k1, (k1, p1, k1) from cn; p2, k1, p1, LT; repeat from * to last 2 sts, p1, k1.

ROW 6: Repeat Row 2.

ROW 8: K1, p1, LT; * slip 3 sts to cn, hold to back, p1, k1, p1, (p1, k1, p1) from cn; RT; slip 3 sts to cn, hold

to front, p1, k1, p1, (p1, k1, p1) from cn; LT; repeat from * to last 2 sts, p1, k1.

ROW 10: Repeat Row 2.

ROW 12: Slip 3 sts to cn, hold to front, k1, p1, k1, (k1, p1, k1) from cn; *p2, k1, p1, RT, p1, k1, p2; slip 3 sts to cn, hold to front, k1, p1, k1, (k1, p1, k1) from cn; repeat from * to end.

ROW 14: Repeat Row 2.

ROW 16: K1, p1, LT; * slip 3 sts to cn, hold to front, p1, k1, p1, (p1, k1, p1) from cn; RT; slip 3 sts to cn, hold to back, p1, k1, p1, (p1, k1, p1) from cn; LT; repeat from * to last 2 sts, p1, k1.

Repeat Rows 1–16 for pattern.

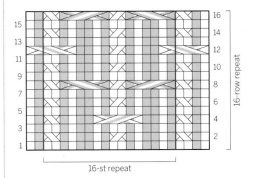

☐ Knit on RS, purl on WS. ▨ Purl on RS, knit on WS.

❙ Pattern repeat

RT (right twist): K2tog, but do not drop sts from left needle; insert right needle between 2 sts just worked and knit first st again, slip both sts from left needle together.

LT (left twist): Insert needle from back to front between first and second sts on left needle and knit the second st through the front loop; knit first st, slip both sts from left needle together.

Slip 3 sts to cn, hold to back, k1, p1, k1, (k1, p1, k1) from cn.

Slip 3 sts to cn, hold to front, k1, p1, k1, (k1, p1, k1) from cn.

Slip 3 sts to cn, hold to back, p1, k1, p1, (p1, k1, p1) from cn.

Slip 3 sts to cn, hold to front, p1, k1, p1, (p1, k1, p1) from cn.

1/1 Diamond Fancy GROUP 9

1/1 Diamond Twist (#105) becomes 1/1 Diamond Fancy when several of the cable crosses are repeated a second time. As is true of all three 1/1 Diamond variations, the finished result looks much more complicated than it is to knit. 1/1 Diamond Fancy is an expanded version of Fancy 1/1 Travel Share (#78) in Chapter 3.

(multiple of 16 sts + 6; 34-row repeat)

TOTAL SSE: 14.5 sts

REPEAT SSE: 11 sts

ROW 1 (WS): *P1, k1, p2, k1, p1, k2; repeat from * to last 6 sts, p1, k1, p2, k1, p1.

ROW 2: K1, p1, LT, *p1, k1, p2, k1, p1, RT, p1, k1, p2, k1, p1, LT; repeat from * to last 2 sts, p1, k1.

ROW 3 AND ALL FOLLOWING WS ROWS: Knit the knit sts and purl the purl sts as they face you.

ROW 4: K1, p1, LT, *p1, k1, p2; slip 3 sts to cn, hold to back, k1, p1, k1, (k1, p1, k1) from cn; p2, k1, p1, LT; repeat from * to last 2 sts, p1, k1.

ROW 6: Repeat Row 2.

ROW 8: K1, p1, LT; * slip 3 sts to cn, hold to back, p1, k1, p1, (p1, k1, p1) from cn; RT; slip 3 sts to cn, hold to front, p1, k1, p1, (p1, k1, p1) from cn; LT; repeat from * to last 2 sts, p1, k1.

ROWS 10 AND 12: Repeat Row 2.

ROW 14: Repeat Row 8.

ROW 16: Repeat Row 2.

ROW 18: Slip 3 sts to cn, hold to front, k1, p1, k1, (k1, p1, k1) from cn; *p2, k1, p1, RT, p1, k1, p2; slip 3 sts to cn, hold to front, k1, p1, k1, (k1, p1, k1) from cn; repeat from * to end.

ROW 20: Repeat Row 2.

ROW 22: K1, p1, LT; * slip 3 sts to cn, hold to front, p1, k1, p1, (p1, k1, p1) from cn; RT; slip 3 sts to cn, hold to back, p1, k1, p1, (p1, k1, p1) from cn; LT; repeat from * to last 2 sts, p1, k1.

ROWS 24 AND 26: Repeat Row 2.

ROW 28: Repeat Row 22.

ROW 30: Repeat Row 2.

ROW 32: Repeat Row 4.

ROW 34: Repeat Row 2

Repeat Rows 1–34 for pattern.

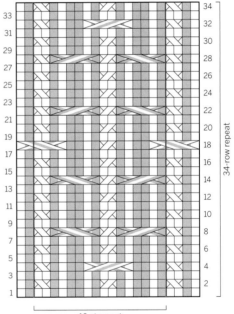

16-st repeat

34-row repeat

☐ Knit on RS, purl on WS.

▨ Purl on RS, knit on WS.

| Pattern repeat

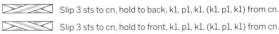 RT (right twist): K2tog, but do not drop sts from left needle; insert right needle between 2 sts just worked and knit first st again, slip both sts from left needle together.

LT (left twist): Insert needle from back to front between first and second sts on left needle and knit the second st through the front loop; knit first st, slip both sts from left needle together.

Slip 3 sts to cn, hold to back, k1, p1, k1, (k1, p1, k1) from cn.

Slip 3 sts to cn, hold to front, k1, p1, k1, (k1, p1, k1) from cn.

Slip 3 sts to cn, hold to back, p1, k1, p1, (p1, k1, p1) from cn.

Slip 3 sts to cn, hold to front, p1, k1, p1, (p1, k1, p1) from cn.

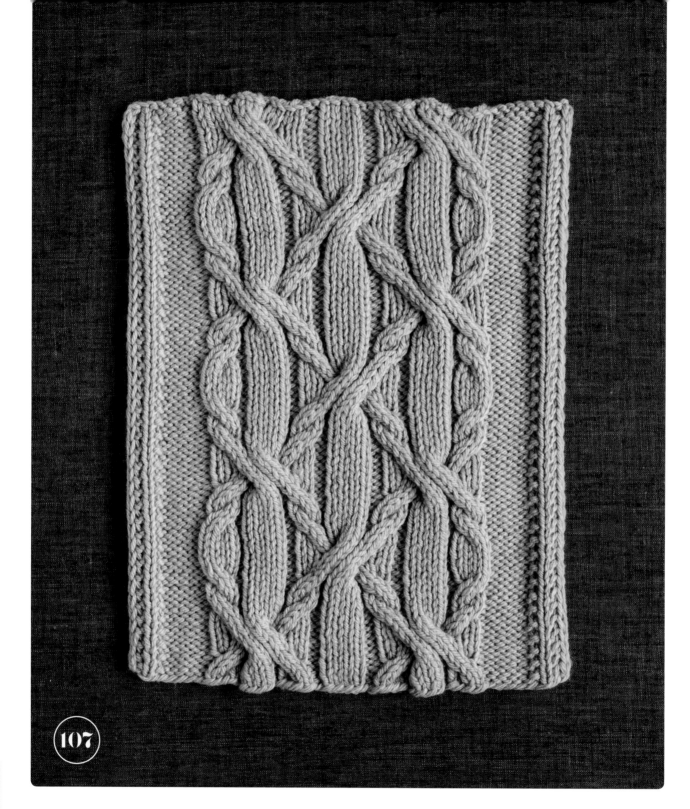

Medallion Expansion

This is the expanded version of Medallion (#74) from Chapter 3. Two of the original Medallion cables are set side by side with p2, k4, p2 between them. A center cable cross in the opposite direction is then added to unite them into 1 panel.

(multiple of 24 sts + 16; 24-row repeat)
TOTAL SSE: 28 sts
REPEAT SSE: 18 sts

ROW 1 (WS): P4, *k2, p4; repeat from * to end.

ROWS 2 AND 3: Knit the knit sts and purl the purl sts as they face you.

ROW 4: 2/2 LC, p2, k4, p2, 2/2 RC, *p2, k4, p2, 2/2 LC, p2, k4, p2, 2/2 RC; repeat from * to end.

ROWS 5–7: Repeat Row 2.

ROW 8: K2; slip 6 sts to cn, hold to front, k2, p2, k2, (k2, p2, k2) from cn; k2, *p2, k4, p2, k2; slip 6 sts to cn, hold to front, k2, p2, k2, (k2, p2, k2) from cn; k2; repeat from * to end.

ROWS 9–11: Repeat Row 2.

ROW 12: 2/2 RC, p2, k4, p2, 2/2 LC, *p2, k4, p2, 2/2 RC, p2, k4, p2, 2/2 LC; repeat from * to end.

ROWS 13–15: Repeat Row 2.

ROW 16: Repeat Row 12.

ROWS 17–19: Repeat Row 2.

ROW 20: K4, *p2, k4, p2, k2; slip 6 sts to cn, hold to back, k2, p2, k2, (k2, p2, k2) from cn; k2; repeat from * to last 14 sts, [p2, k4] twice.

ROWS 21–23: Repeat Row 2.

ROW 24: Repeat Row 4.
Repeat Rows 1–24 for pattern.

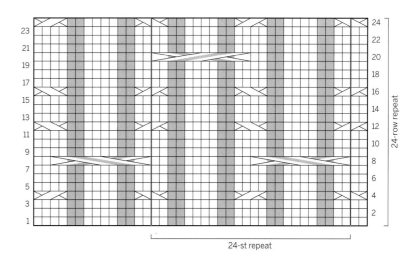

24-st repeat

□ Knit on RS, purl on WS.

▨ Purl on RS, knit on WS.

| Pattern repeat

⬲ 2/2 RC (2 over 2 right cross): Slip 2 sts to cn, hold to back, k2, k2 from cn.

⬳ 2/2 LC (2 over 2 left cross): Slip 2 sts to cn, hold to front, k2, k2 from cn.

⬲ Slip 6 sts to cn, hold to back, k2, p2, k2, (k2, p2, k2) from cn.

⬳ Slip 6 sts to cn, hold to front, k2, p2, k2, (k2, p2, k2) from cn.

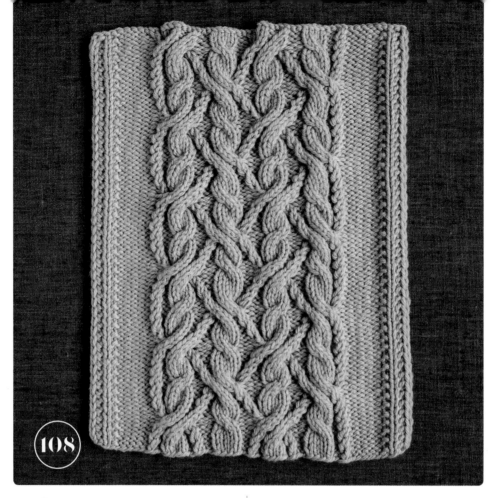

Dolled-Up Share GROUP 11

This is an expanded and more elaborate version of 2/2 Share (#65) in Chapter 3. Here the k2 ribs become right twists and the k4 centers become 2/2 ropes.

(multiple of 20 sts + 22; 16-row repeat)
TOTAL SSE: 27 sts
REPEAT SSE: 12.5 sts

ROW 1 (WS): *P2, k2, p4, k2; repeat from * to last 2 sts, p2.
ROW 2: *RT, p2, k4, p2; repeat from * to last 2 sts, RT.
ROW 3 AND ALL FOLLOWING WS ROWS: Knit the knit sts and purl the purl sts as they face you.

ROWS 4 AND 6: Repeat Row 2.
ROW 8: RT, *p2, 2/2 LC, p2; slip 6 sts to cn, hold to back, k2, p2, k2, (k2, p2, k2) from cn; repeat from * to end.
ROWS 10, 12, AND 14: Repeat Row 2.
ROW 16: *Slip 6 sts to cn, hold to front, k2, p2, k2, (k2, p2, k2) from cn; p2, 2/2 RC, p2; repeat from * to last 2 sts, RT.
Repeat Rows 1–16 for pattern.

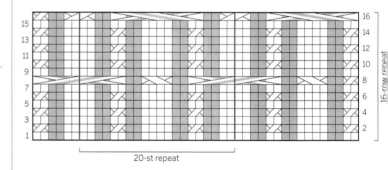

20-st repeat

16-row repeat

☐ Knit on RS, purl on WS.   ▨ Purl on RS, knit on WS.

| Pattern repeat

▧ RT (right twist): K2tog, but do not drop sts from left needle; insert right needle between 2 sts just worked and knit first st again, slip both sts from left needle together.

▨ 2/2 RC (2 over 2 right cross): Slip 2 sts to cn, hold to back, k2, k2 from cn.

▨ 2/2 LC (2 over 2 left cross): Slip 2 sts to cn, hold to front, k2, k2 from cn.

▨ Slip 6 sts to cn, hold to back, k2, p2, k2, (k2, p2, k2) from cn.

▨ Slip 6 sts to cn, hold to front, k2, p2, k2, (k2, p2, k2) from cn.

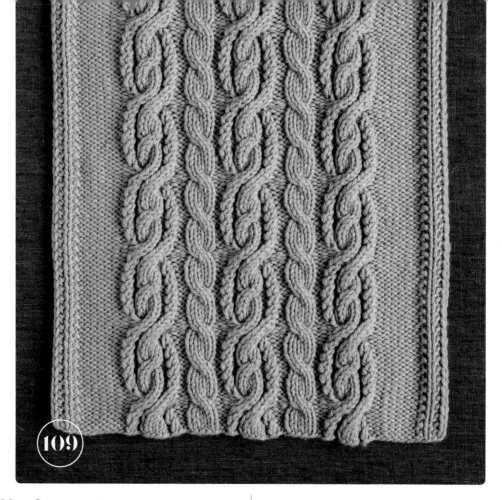

(109)

Dolled-Up Separates GROUP 11

To create Dolled-Up Separates, I divided the elements of Dolled-Up Share (#108) into distinct columns, which eliminated the shared diagonals. I used the same technique to create O Knot Singles (#94). The first 12 stitches of Dolled-Up Separates can also be used as a stand-alone cable column.

(multiple of 20 sts + 12;
16-row repeat)
TOTAL SSE: 20 sts
REPEAT SSE: 13.5 sts

ROW 1 (WS): *P2, k2, p4, k2; repeat from * to last 2 sts, p2.
ROW 2: *RT, p2, k4, p2; repeat from * to last 2 sts, RT.
ROW 3 AND ALL FOLLOWING WS ROWS: Knit the knit sts and purl the purl sts as they face you.
ROWS 4 AND 6: Repeat Row 2.

ROW 8: *Slip 6 sts to cn, hold to back, k2, p2, k2, (k2, p2, k2) from cn; p2, 2/2 LC, p2; repeat from * to last 12 sts; slip 6 sts to cn, hold to back, k2, p2, k2, (k2, p2, k2) from cn.
ROWS 10, 12, AND 14: Repeat Row 2.
ROW 16: RT, p2, 2/2 RC, p2, RT, *p2, 2/2 LC, p2, RT, p2, 2/2 RC, p2, RT; repeat from * to end.
Repeat Rows 1–16 for pattern.

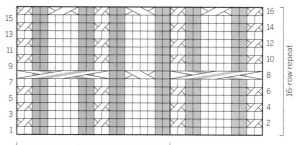

20-st repeat

16-row repeat

☐ Knit on RS, purl on WS.   ▨ Purl on RS, knit on WS.

▮ Pattern repeat

⬚ **RT (right twist):** K2tog, but do not drop sts from left needle; insert right needle between 2 sts just worked and knit first st again, slip both sts from left needle together.

⬚ **2/2 RC (2 over 2 right cross):** Slip 2 sts to cn, hold to back, k2, k2 from cn.

⬚ **2/2 LC (2 over 2 left cross):** Slip 2 sts to cn, hold to front, k2, k2 from cn.

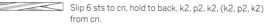 Slip 6 sts to cn, hold to back, k2, p2, k2, (k2, p2, k2) from cn.

Slip 6 sts to cn, hold to front, k2, p2, k2, (k2, p2, k2) from cn.

Balaclava

FINISHED
MEASUREMENTS
Approximately 18"
(45.5 cm) wide x 22"
(56 cm) long

YARN
Woolfolk Får [100%
Ovis 21 ultimate merino;
142 yards (130 meters)/
50 grams): 4 hanks #7

NEEDLES
One 16–24" (40–60 cm)
long circular needle size
US 9 (5.5 mm)

One double-pointed
needle size US 9 (5.5 mm),
for joining

Change needle size if
necessary to obtain cor-
rect gauge.

NOTIONS
Stitch markers [including
2 of a different color
(optional)]; cable needle

GAUGE
28 sts and 24 rows = 4"
(10 cm) in Cable Pattern

Steam or wet block your
swatch before taking the
measurements.

STITCH PATTERN
Cable: Twist Share Lattice
(#101).

PATTERN NOTES
The Balaclava is worked
back and forth in one
piece to the front neck
opening, where the two
halves are separated; a
new ball of yarn is joined
and stitches are cast on
for the left half, and the
two pieces are worked sep-
arately for a few inches,
then joined again at the
back neck, then worked in
one piece to the end, with
decreases to shape the
back and top of the hood.

If you'd like to make
a cable substitution, see
page 162.

Balaclava

CO 123 sts. Do not join.

SET-UP ROW 1 (WS): [K1, p1] 4 times, k2, pm, work Cable Pattern over 46 sts, pm, k2, [p1, k1] 3 times, p1, k2, pm, work Cable Pattern over 46 sts, pm, k2, [p1, k1] 4 times.

SET-UP ROW 2: K2, [p1, k1] 3 times, p2, sm, work Cable Pattern, sm, p2, [k1, p1] 3 times, k1, p2, sm, work Cable Pattern, sm, p2, [k1, p1] 3 times, k2.

Work even until piece measures 9" (23 cm) from the beginning, ending with a RS row.

DIVIDE FOR FRONT NECK

ROW 1 (RS): Work to second marker, sm, p1, join a second ball of yarn, k2, [p1, k1] 3 times, p2, sm, work to end.

ROW 2: Working both sides at the same time with separate balls of yarn, on right neck edge, work to second marker, sm, k2, [p1, k1] 4 times; on left neck edge, CO 9 sts using Knitted CO, work-ing across CO sts, [k1, p1] 4 times, k2, sm, work to end—66 sts each side.

ROW 3: On left neck edge, work to second marker, sm, p2, [k1, p1] 3 times, k2; on right neck edge, k2, [p1, k1] 3 times, p2, sm, work to end.

ROW 4: On right neck edge, work to second marker, k2, [p1, k1] 4 times; on left neck edge, [k1, p1] 4 times, k2, sm, work to end. Work even until piece measures 3" (7.5 cm) from division, end-ing with a RS row. Do not turn.

JOIN BACK NECK

With RS still facing, slip last 66 sts worked (right neck edge) back to left needle so that needle tips are now between sides; cut yarn for right neck edge.

NEXT ROW (WS): Turn and work across left neck edge sts to last 9 sts, slip these 9 sts to dpn, hold to front of first 9 sts of right neck edge; k2tog (1 st on dpn together with 1 st on back needle), [p2tog (1 st on back needle together with 1 st on dpn), k2tog (1 st on dpn together with 1 st on back needle)] 4 times, p1, sm, work to end of right neck edge—123 sts remain.

Work even until piece measures 5" (12.5 cm) from join, ending with a WS row.

SHAPE BACK OF HOOD

Note: You will now remove the 4 original markers and place 2 new markers for shaping. If you prefer to keep the original markers in place, use markers of a different color for shaping.

SET-UP ROW (RS): Work to second marker, removing original markers as you come to them, p2, pm for shaping, work to 2 sts before third marker, pm for shaping, work to end, removing original markers.

DECREASE ROW (WS): Continuing in patterns as established, work to 2 sts before first shaping marker, k2tog, sm, work to next shaping marker, sm, ssk, work to end—2 sts decreased.

Repeat Decrease Row every 6 rows 3 times, then every 4 rows twice, then every WS row 3 times—105 sts remain.

SHAPE TOP OF HOOD

DECREASE ROW 1 (RS): Work to second shaping marker, sm, p3tog, turn—2 sts decreased.

DECREASE ROW 2 (WS): Slip 1, sm, work to next marker, sm, sssk, turn—2 sts decreased.

DECREASE ROW 3: Slip 1, sm, work to next marker, sm, p3tog, turn—2 sts decreased.

Repeat Decrease Rows 2 and 3 twenty-two times, then repeat Decrease Row 3 once—9 sts remain.

BO all sts in pattern.

Sew CO sts at base of front neck to WS, being careful not to let sts show on RS.

Block as desired.

8 Cable Substitution

Before getting started, review Stockinette Stitch Equivalent System on page 20.

CHOOSING CABLES

Use cables with an SSE of 31.5 or less and add reverse stockinette stitch to make up any difference. You can cheat a little by adding some width to the cable panel, but don't add more than an SSE of 5 or 6 stitches. If you add width, you'll need to repeat Decrease Row 3 when you shape the top of the hood until only the 9 rib stitches in the center remain.

MANAGING A CHANGE IN STITCH COUNT

If, after substituting, your stitch count has changed, adjust the number of stitches to cast on to accommodate the new stitch count. Any change will also affect the number of times you have to repeat the last Decrease Row.

CABLE PATTERN

(multiple of 10 sts + 6; 8-row repeat)
SSE: 10.5 sts
REPEAT SSE: 7 sts

ROW 1 AND ALL WS ROWS (WS):
*P1, k1, p2, k1; repeat from * to last st, p1.
ROW 2: K1, p1, k2, *p1, k1, p1, RT, p1, k1, p1, k2; repeat from * to last 2 sts, p1, k1.

ROW 4: K1, p1, k2, *p1; slip 3 sts to cn, hold to back, k1, p1, k1, (k1, p1, k1) from cn; p1, k2; repeat from * to last 2 sts, p1, k1.
ROW 6: Repeat Row 2.
ROW 8: Slip 3 sts to cn, hold to front, k1, p1, k1, (k1, p1, k1) from cn; *p1, RT, p1; slip 3 sts to cn, hold to front, k1, p1, k1, (k1, p1, k1) from cn; repeat from * to end. Repeat Rows 1–8 for pattern.

CABLE PATTERN

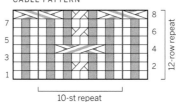

10-st repeat

☐ Knit on RS, purl on WS.

▧ Purl on RS, knit on WS.

❘ Pattern repeat

⧅ RT (right twist): K2tog, but do not drop sts from left needle; insert right needle between 2 sts just worked and knit first st again, slip both sts from left needle together.

▱ Slip 3 sts to cn, hold to back, k1, p1, k1, (k1, p1, k1) from cn.

▱ Slip 3 sts to cn, hold to front, k1, p1, k1, (k1, p1, k1) from cn.

Wrap/Poncho

FINISHED MEASUREMENTS

Approximately 15 (30)" [38 (76) cm] wide x 60 (30)" [152.5 (76) cm] long

Note: Instructions are given for Wrap first, with Poncho in parentheses. Where only 1 number is given, it applies to both versions.

YARN

Quince & Co. Owl [50% American wool/ 50% alpaca; 120 yards (110 meters)/50 grams]: 10 hanks Abyssinian

NEEDLES

One pair straight needles size US 7 (4.5 mm)

Change needle size if necessary to obtain correct gauge.

NOTIONS

Cable needle; crochet hook G-6 (4 mm) (for Poncho only)

GAUGE

20 sts and 28 rows = 4" (10 cm) in St st

30 sts and 30 rows = 4" (10 cm) in Cable B

Steam or wet block your swatch before taking the measurements.

STITCH PATTERNS

Cable A: Basic Flat Braid (#12)
Cable B: Ribbon Weave (#96)

If you'd like to make a cable substitution, see page 165.

Wrap

Cast on 113 sts.

ROW 1 (WS): Slip 2 wyif, k2, work Cable A over 8 sts, k1, work Cable B over 87 sts, k1, work Cable A to last 4 sts, k2, p2.

ROW 2: Slip 2 wyib, p2, work Cable A as established, p1, work Cable B as established, p1, work Cable A as established, p2, k2.

Work even until piece measures approximately 60" [152.5 cm], ending with Row 4 of Cable B.

BIND-OFF ROW (RS): S2kp2, BO in pattern to last 2 sts, p2tog, BO remaining st. Fasten off.

Finishing

Steam or wet-block piece to finished measurements.

For Poncho Variation

Fold piece in half lengthwise and hold WSs of one edge together. Beginning 6" [15 cm] up from bottom edge and ending approximately 14" [35.5 cm] down from fold, join edges using crochet hook and crochet slip st as follows: Make slip knot and place on crochet hook. With RS facing and holding edges to be joined with WSs together, *insert crochet hook into third st in from edge, going through both layers of fabric; yo hook and draw loop back through both layers, then through st on hook; repeat from * for length to be joined. Fasten off last st. *Note: You may need to skip 1 or more rows along edge to keep seam smooth.*

✂ Cable Substitution

Before getting started, review Stockinette Stitch Equivalent System on page 20.

CHOOSING CABLES

To maintain wrap proportions, aim for a cable panel that has an SSE between 80 and 110 (including whatever stitches you use to separate the cables.) Work the first and last 4 stitches as written. If you go narrower, you'll have a scarf.

MANAGING A CHANGE IN STITCH COUNT

If, after substituting, your stitch count has changed, adjust the number of stitches to cast on to accommodate this change.

Chapter 5

Finding Motifs

Sometimes you can look at a cable pattern and see an interesting motif formed by the lines and curves. This motif can then become the basis for a new cable pattern, or as is often the case for me, a whole new series. More than 20 years ago, I started riffing on a motif that I have come to call Fave. When knit on its own,

Fave doesn't look all that unusual; however, I have found it to be a fascinating and useful building block when I'm designing. While it's not in every cable in this chapter, it is the basis for the majority.

Introducing Fave

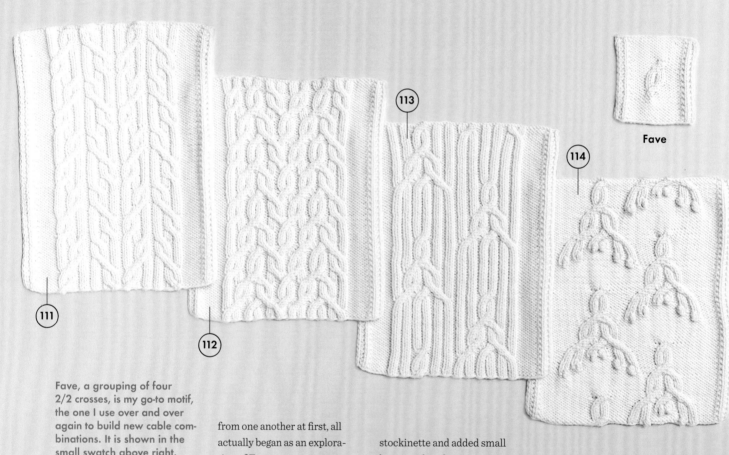

113

114

Fave

111

112

Fave, a grouping of four 2/2 crosses, is my go-to motif, the one I use over and over again to build new cable combinations. It is shown in the small swatch above right.

Two crosses form the diagonal line at the bottom of the motif and after 3 straight rows another 2 crosses cap off the top. If made with right crosses, the motif slants to the right; if made with left crosses, it slants to the left.

These 4 cables from Group 1, which might look very different

from one another at first, all actually began as an exploration of Fave.

INCLINE FAVE (#111) is built from a combination of 2 Fave motifs on the diagonal. To create **FUSION (#112)** from Incline Fave, I added a few new crosses. **RIB BLOSSOM (#113)** is an exploration of a motif that I found within Fusion. Finally, I replaced the rib that joins the motifs in Rib Blossom with reverse

stockinette and added small knots at their bases to create **WEEPING BLOSSOM (#114).**

I am presenting this progression here because I think it demonstrates very well why I love exploring Fave so much.

To & Fro Fave GROUP 1

In this pattern, Fave grows out of 2 x 2 ribbing. The motif slants to the right when made with right crosses and to the left when made with left crosses. Each column alternates right- and left-slanting Faves. The cable panel shown here is one column repeated 4 times.

(multiple of 12 sts + 10; 20-row repeat)

TOTAL SSE: 15 sts

REPEAT SSE: 8.5 sts

ROW 1 (WS): P2, *k2, p2; repeat from * to end.

ROW 2: K2, p2, k2, 2/2 RC, *[p2, k2] twice, 2/2 RC; repeat from * to end.

ROW 3 AND ALL FOLLOWING WS ROWS: Knit the knit sts and purl the purl sts as they face you.

ROW 4: K2, p2, 2/2 RPC, *[k2, p2] twice, 2/2 RPC; repeat from * to last 2 sts, k2.

ROW 6: Repeat Row 3.

ROW 8: Repeat Row 2.

ROW 10: Repeat Row 4.

ROW 12: 2/2 LC, *[k2, p2] twice, 2/2 LC; repeat from * to last 6 sts, k2, p2, k2.

ROW 14: K2, 2/2 LPC, *[p2, k2] twice, 2/2 LPC; repeat from * to last 4 sts, p2, k2.

ROW 16: Repeat Row 3.

ROW 18: Repeat Row 12.

ROW 20: Repeat Row 14.

Repeat Rows 1–20 for pattern.

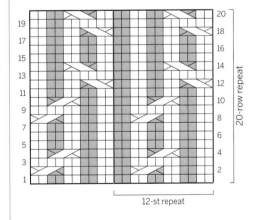

12-st repeat

20-row repeat

□ Knit on RS, purl on WS.

▨ Purl on RS, knit on WS.

| Pattern repeat

2/2 RC (2 over 2 right cross): Slip 2 sts to cn, hold to back, k2, k2 from cn.

2/2 LC (2 over 2 left cross): Slip 2 sts to cn, hold to front, k2, k2 from cn.

2/2 RPC (2 over 2 right purl cross): Slip 2 sts to cn, hold to back, k2, p2 from cn.

2/2 LPC (2 over 2 left purl cross): Slip 2 sts to cn, hold to front, p2, k2 from cn.

Incline Fave GROUP 1

Still built on 2×2 ribbing, like To & Fro Fave (#110), here 2 motifs in a row share the same slant and one leads directly into the next. This panel also has 4 columns. These columns are not identical this time; each one is a mirror image of the one next to it and, as a result, the motifs form horizontal zigzags when they come together.

(multiple of 24 sts + 22; 20-row repeat)

TOTAL SSE: 30 sts
REPEAT SSE: 15 sts
SINGLE COLUMN SSE: 8.5 sts

ROW 1 (WS): P2, *k2, p2; repeat from * to end.
ROW 2: 2/2 LC, k2, [p2, k2] 3 times, 2/2 RC, *p2, 2/2 LC, k2, [p2, k2] 3 times, 2/2 RC; repeat from * to end.
ROW 3 AND ALL FOLLOWING WS ROWS: Knit the knit sts and purl the purl sts as they face you.
ROW 4: K2, 2/2 LPC, p2, [k2, p2] twice, 2/2 RPC, *k2, p2, k2, 2/2 LPC, p2, [k2, p2] twice, 2/2 RPC; repeat from * to last 2 sts, k2.

ROW 6: Repeat Row 3.
ROW 8: Repeat Row 2.
ROW 10: Repeat Row 4.
ROW 12: K2, p2, 2/2 LC, k2, p2, k2, 2/2 RC, *p2, [k2, p2] twice, 2/2 LC, k2, p2, k2, 2/2 RC; repeat from * to last 4 sts, p2, k2.
ROW 14: K2, p2, k2, 2/2 LPC, p2, 2/2 RPC, *k2, [p2, k2] 3 times, 2/2 LPC, p2, 2/2 RPC; repeat from * to last 6 sts, k2, p2, k2.
ROW 16: Repeat Row 3.
ROW 18: Repeat Row 12.
ROW 20: Repeat Row 14.
Repeat Rows 1–20 for pattern.

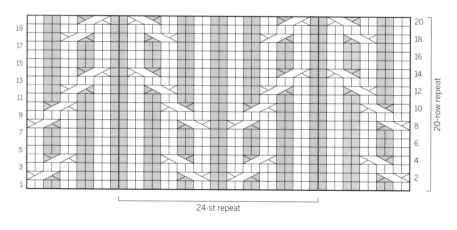

24-st repeat

20-row repeat

☐ Knit on RS, purl on WS.

▨ Purl on RS, knit on WS.

❙ Pattern repeat

2/2 RC (2 over 2 right cross): Slip 2 sts to cn, hold to back, k2, k2 from cn.

2/2 LC (2 over 2 left cross): Slip 2 sts to cn, hold to front, k2, k2 from cn.

2/2 RPC (2 over 2 right purl cross): Slip 2 sts to cn, hold to back, k2, p2 from cn.

2/2 LPC (2 over 2 left purl cross): Slip 2 sts to cn, hold to front, p2, k2 from cn.

Fusion GROUP 1

The addition of a few center stable crosses fuses all 4 of the columns from Incline Fave (#111) into one intertwined panel in Fusion.

(multiple of 24 sts + 22; 20-row repeat)

TOTAL SSE: 30 sts

REPEAT SSE: 15 sts

ROW 1 (WS): P2, *k2, p2; repeat from * to end.

ROW 2: Knit the knit sts and purl the purl sts as they face you.

ROW 3 AND ALL FOLLOWING WS ROWS: Repeat Row 2.

ROW 4: 2/2 LC, k2, [p2, k2] 3 times, 2/2 RC, *p2, 2/2 LC, k2, [p2, k2] 3 times, 2/2 RC; repeat from * to end.

ROW 6: K2, 2/2 LPC, p2, 2/2/2 RPC, p2, 2/2 RPC, *k2, k2, 2/2 LPC, p2, 2/2/2 RPC, p2, 2/2 RPC; repeat from * to last 2 sts, k2.

ROW 8: K2, p2, 2/2 LC, k2, p2, k2, 2/2 RC, *p2, 2/2/2 RPC, p2, 2/2 LC, k2, p2, k2, 2/2 RC; repeat from * to last 4 sts, p2, k2.

ROW 10: K2, p2, k2, 2/2 LPC, p2, 2/2 RPC, *k2, [p2, k2] 3 times, 2/2 LPC, p2, 2/2 RPC; repeat from * to last 6 sts, k2, p2, k2.

ROW 12: Repeat Row 2.

ROW 14: K2, p2, 2/2 LC, k2, p2, k2, 2/2 RC, *p2, [k2, p2] twice, 2/2 LC, k2, p2, k2, 2/2 RC; repeat from * to last 4 sts, p2, k2.

ROW 16: K2, p2, k2, 2/2 LPC, p2, 2/2 RPC, *k2, p2, 2/2/2 RPC, p2, k2, 2/2 LPC, p2, 2/2 RPC; repeat from * to last 6 sts, k2, p2, k2.

ROW 18: 2/2 LC, k2, p2, 2/2/2 RPC, p2, k2, 2/2 RC, *p2, 2/2 LC, k2, p2, 2/2/2 RPC, p2, k2, 2/2 RC; repeat from * to end.

ROW 20: K2, 2/2 LPC, p2, [k2, p2] twice, 2/2 RPC, *k2, p2, k2, 2/2 LPC, p2, [k2, p2] twice, 2/2 RPC; repeat from * to last 2 sts, k2. Repeat Rows 1–20 for pattern.

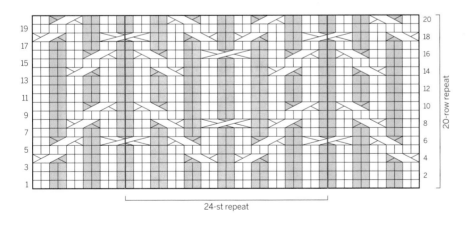

24-st repeat

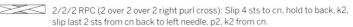

☐ Knit on RS, purl on WS.

▨ Purl on RS, knit on WS.

❘ Pattern repeat

2/2 RC (2 over 2 right cross): Slip 2 sts to cn, hold to back, k2, k2 from cn.

2/2 LC (2 over 2 left cross): Slip 2 sts to cn, hold to front, k2, k2 from cn.

2/2 RPC (2 over 2 right purl cross): Slip 2 sts to cn, hold to back, k2, p2 from cn.

2/2 LPC (2 over 2 left purl cross): Slip 2 sts to cn, hold to front, p2, k2 from cn.

2/2/2 RPC (2 over 2 over 2 right purl cross): Slip 4 sts to cn, hold to back, k2, slip last 2 sts from cn back to left needle, p2, k2 from cn.

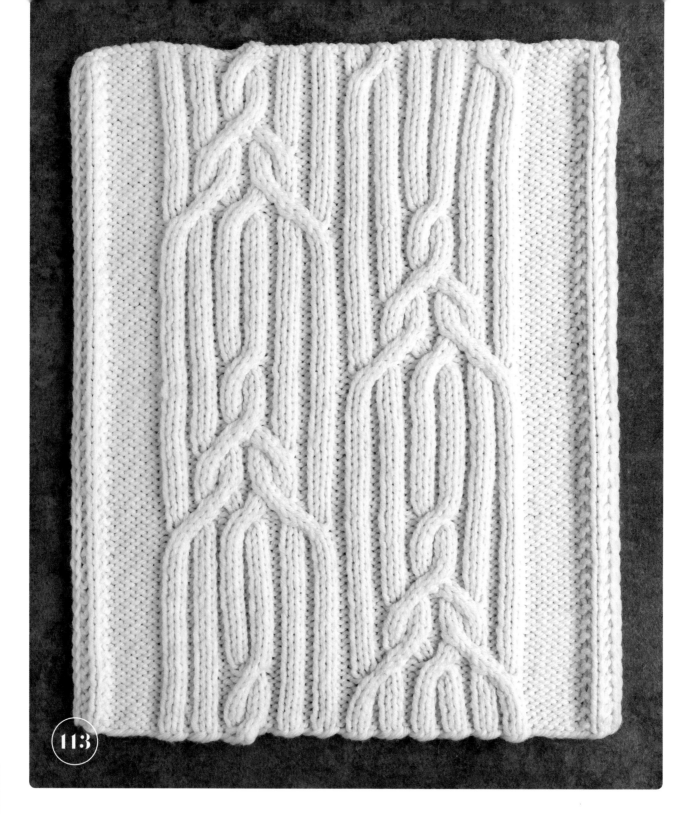

Rib Blossom

Removing some of the cable crosses from Fusion (#112) allows for the transition from a kinetic allover cable pattern to a calmer Rib Blossom (in which blossom shapes emerge from a rib ground).

(panel of 46 sts; 40-row repeat)
SSE: 31 sts

ROW 1 (WS): P2, [k2, p2] eleven times.

ROW 2: [K2, p2] 8 times, 2/2/2 RPC, [p2, k2] twice.

ROW 3 AND ALL FOLLOWING WS ROWS: Knit the knit sts and purl the purl sts as they face you.

ROWS 4 AND 6: Repeat Row 3.

ROW 8: 2/2 LC, k2, [p2, k2] 3 times, 2/2 RC, [p2, k2] 6 times.

ROW 10: K2, 2/2 LPC, p2, 2/2/2 RPC, p2, 2/2 RPC, [k2, p2] 3 times, 2/2/2 RPC, [p2, k2] twice.

ROW 12: K2, p2, 2/2 LC, k2, p2, k2, 2/2 RC, [p2, k2] 7 times.

ROW 14: K2, p2, k2, 2/2 LPC, p2, 2/2 RPC, k2, [p2, k2] 7 times.

ROW 16: Repeat Row 3.

ROW 18: Repeat Row 12.

ROW 20: Repeat Row 14.

ROW 22: [K2, p2] twice, 2/2/2 RPC, [p2, k2] 8 times.

ROWS 24 AND 26: Repeat Row 3.

ROW 28: [K2, p2] 6 times, 2/2 LC, k2, [p2, k2] 3 times, 2/2 RC.

ROW 30: [K2, p2] twice, 2/2/2 RPC, [p2, k2] 3 times, 2/2 LPC, p2, 2/2/2 RPC, p2, 2/2 RPC, k2.

ROW 32: [K2, p2] 7 times, 2/2 LC, k2, p2, k2, 2/2 RC, p2, k2.

ROW 34: K2, [p2, k2] 7 times, 2/2 LPC, p2, 2/2 RPC, k2, p2, k2.

ROW 36: Repeat Row 3.

ROW 38: Repeat Row 32.

ROW 40: Repeat Row 34.
Repeat Rows 1–40 for pattern.

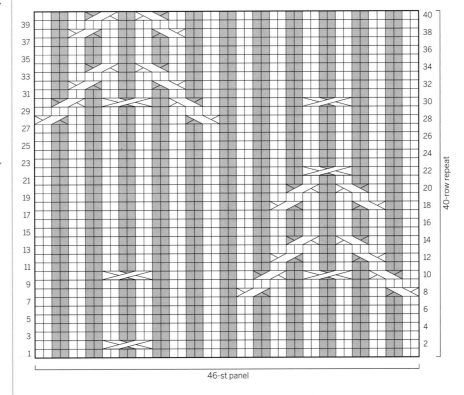

46-st panel

☐ Knit on RS, purl on WS.

▨ Purl on RS, knit on WS.

▧ 2/2 RC (2 over 2 right cross): Slip 2 sts to cn, hold to back, k2, k2 from cn.

▧ 2/2 LC (2 over 2 left cross): Slip 2 sts to cn, hold to front, k2, k2 from cn.

▧ 2/2 RPC (2 over 2 right purl cross): Slip 2 sts to cn, hold to back, k2, p2 from cn.

▧ 2/2 LPC (2 over 2 left purl cross): Slip 2 sts to cn, hold to front, p2, k2 from cn.

▧ 2/2/2 RPC (2 over 2 over 2 right purl cross): Slip 4 sts to cn, hold to back, k2, slip last 2 sts from cn back to left needle, p2, k2 from cn.

Weeping Blossom GROUP 1

Two simple changes—the elimination of the ribbed background and the addition of knots—turn Rib Blossom (#113) into Weeping Blossom. Without the rib to pull them in, the blossoms become wider at the bottom and appear more curved. The addition of little knots gives a logical ending point to the weeping lines.

(panel of 42 sts; 40-row repeat)
SSE: 33 sts

ROW 1 (WS): K8, p2, k2, p2, k6, p2, k18, p2.

ROW 2: K2, p2, k1, MK, p10, MK, k1, p2, k2, p6, 2/2/2 RPC, p8.

ROWS 3–5: Knit the knit sts and purl the purl sts as they face you; purl knots.

ROW 6: [K2, p2] twice, k1, MK, p2, MK, k1, [p2, k2] twice, p6, k2, p2, k2, p8.

ROW 7: Repeat Row 3.

ROW 8: 2/2 LPC, k2, [p2, k2] 3 times, 2/2 RPC, p6, k2, p2, k2, p8.

ROW 9: Repeat Row 3.

ROW 10: P2, 2/2 LPC, p2, [k2, p2] twice, 2/2 RPC, p8, 2/2/2 RPC, p8.

ROW 11: K24, p2, [k2, p2] 3 times, k4.

ROW 12: P4, 2/2 LC, 2/2/2 RPC, 2/2 RC, p24.

ROW 13: Repeat Row 3.

ROW 14: P4, k2, 2/2 LPC, p2, 2/2 RPC, k2, p24.

ROWS 15–17: Repeat Row 3.

ROW 18: P4, 2/2 LPC, k2, p2, k2, 2/2 RPC, p24.

ROW 19: Repeat Row 3.

ROW 20: P6, 2/2 LPC, p2, 2/2 RPC, p4, k1, MK, p18, MK, k1.

ROW 21: Repeat Row 3.

ROW 22: P8, 2/2/2 RPC, p6, k2, p2, k1, MK, p10, MK, k1, p2, k2.

ROWS 23–25: Repeat Row 3.

ROW 26: P8, k2, p2, k2, p6, [k2, p2] twice, k1, MK, p2, MK, k1, [p2, k2] twice.

ROW 27: P2, [k2, p2] 5 times, p6, k2, p2, k2, p8.

ROW 28: P8, k2, p2, k2, p6, 2/2 LPC, k2, [p2, k2] 3 times, 2/2 RPC.

ROW 29: Repeat Row 3.

ROW 30: P8, 2/2/2 RPC, p8, 2/2 LPC, p2, [k2, p2] twice, 2/2 RPC, p2.

ROW 31: K4, p2, [k2, p2] 3 times, k24.

ROW 32: P24, 2/2 LC, 2/2/2 RPC, 2/2 RC, p4.

ROW 33: Repeat Row 3.

ROW 34: P24, k2, 2/2 LPC, p2, 2/2 RPC, k2, p4.

ROWS 35–37: Repeat Row 3.

ROW 38: P24, 2/2 LPC, k2, p2, k2, 2/2 RPC, p4.

ROW 39: Repeat Row 3.

ROW 40: K1, MK, p18, MK, k1, p4, 2/2 LPC, p2, 2/2 RPC, p6.
Repeat Rows 1–40 for pattern.

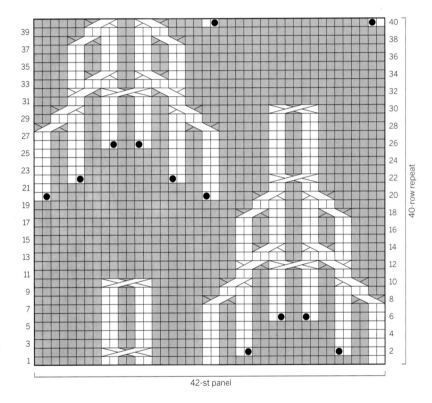

42-st panel

40-row repeat

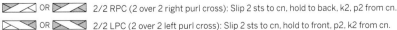

Knit on RS, purl on WS.

Purl on RS, knit on WS.

MK (make knot): [K1-f/b] twice, slip these 4 sts back to left needle and k4; pass fourth, third, then second sts over first.

2/2 RC (2 over 2 right cross): Slip 2 sts to cn, hold to back, k2, k2 from cn.

2/2 LC (2 over 2 left cross): Slip 2 sts to cn, hold to front, k2, k2 from cn.

OR 2/2 RPC (2 over 2 right purl cross): Slip 2 sts to cn, hold to back, k2, p2 from cn.

OR 2/2 LPC (2 over 2 left purl cross): Slip 2 sts to cn, hold to front, p2, k2 from cn.

2/2/2 RPC (2 over 2 over 2 right purl cross): Slip 4 sts to cn, hold to back, k2, slip last 2 sts from cn back to left needle, p2, k2 from cn.

Finding Motifs

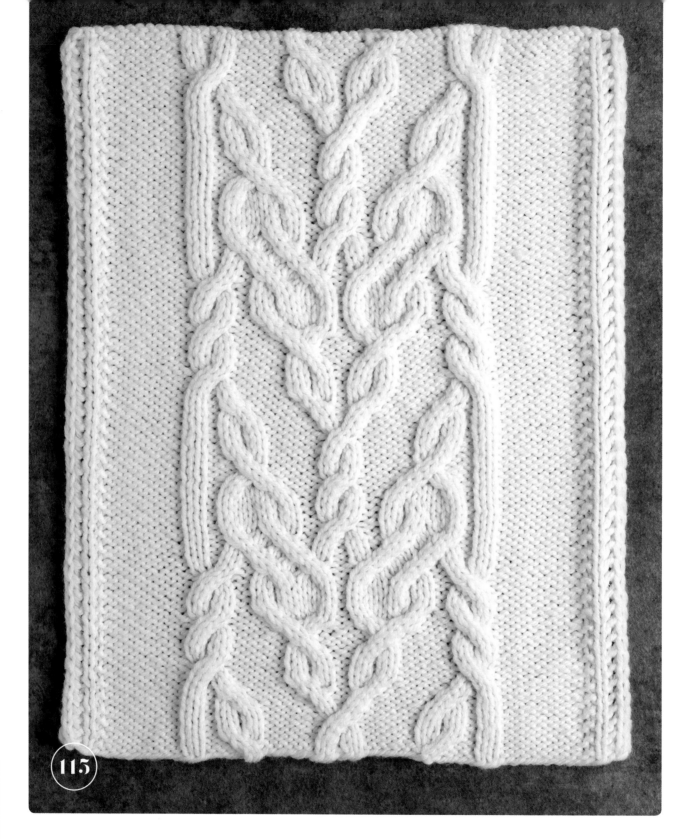

Cruller Chevron

Cruller Chevron is a fanciful expansion of Incline Fave (#111). Several of the diagonals combine to make a new larger motif that looks like an ornate S. The motifs are mirrored and combined with rib and center stable crosses. This new cruller motif is also used in Diverge (#150) in Chapter 6.

(panel of 38 sts; 40-row repeat)
SSE: 26 sts

ROW 1 (WS): P2, k4, p4, k6, p2, k2, p2, k6, p4, k4, p2.

ROW 2: K2, p4, 2/2 RC, p6, k2, p2, k2, p6, 2/2 LC, p4, k2.

ROW 3 AND ALL FOLLOWING WS ROWS: Knit the knit sts and purl the purl sts as they face you.

ROW 4: K2, p2, 2/2 RPC, k2, p6, k2, p2, k2, p6, k2, 2/2 LPC, p2, k2.

ROW 6: K2, [p2, k2] twice, p6, 2/2/2 RPC, p6, k2, [p2, k2] twice.

ROW 8: K2, p2, k2, 2/2 RPC, p6, k2, p2, k2, p6, 2/2 LPC, k2, p2, k2.

ROW 10: K2, p2, 2/2 RPC, p6, 2/2 RC, p2, 2/2 LC, p6, 2/2 LPC, p2, k2.

ROW 12: K2, p2, k2, p6, 2/2 RPC, k2, p2, k2, 2/2 LPC, p6, k2, p2, k2.

ROW 14: 2/2/2 LPC, p6, k2, [p2, k2] 3 times, p6, 2/2/2 RPC.

ROW 16: K2, p2, k2, p6, k2, 2/2 RPC, p2, 2/2 LPC, k2, p6, k2, p2, k2.

ROW 18: K2, p2, k2, p6, 2/2 RC, p6, 2/2 LC, p6, k2, p2, k2.

ROW 20: 2/2/2 LPC, p4, 2/2 RC, 2/2 LC, p2, 2/2 RC, 2/2 LC, p4, 2/2/2 RPC.

ROW 22: [K2, p2] twice, 2/2 RPC, k6, p2, k6, 2/2 LPC, [p2, k2] twice.

ROW 24: Repeat Row 3.

ROW 26: 2/2/2 LPC, p2, k2, 2/2 RC, k4, p2, k4, 2/2 LC, k2, p2, 2/2/2 RPC.

ROW 28: [K2, p2] twice, 2/2 RC, k2, 2/2 RC, p2, 2/2 LC, k2, 2/2 LC, [p2, k2] twice.

ROW 30: K2, p2, k2, 2/2 RC, k2, 2/2 RPC, k2, p2, k2, 2/2 LPC, k2, 2/2 LC, k2, p2.

ROW 32: K2, p2, 2/2 RC, k2, 2/2 RC, p2, [k2, p2] twice, 2/2 LC, k2, 2/2 LC, p2, k2.

ROW 34: K2, p2, k4, 2/2 RPC, k2, p2, 2/2/2 RPC, p2, k2, 2/2 LPC, k4, p2, k2.

ROW 36: Repeat Row 3.

ROW 38: K2, p2, k6, 2/2 RPC, p2, [k2, p2] twice, 2/2 LPC, k6, p2, k2.

ROW 40: K2, p2, 2/2 LPC, 2/2 RPC, p4, 2/2/2 RPC, p4, 2/2 LPC, 2/2 RPC, p2, k2.

Repeat Rows 1–40 for pattern.

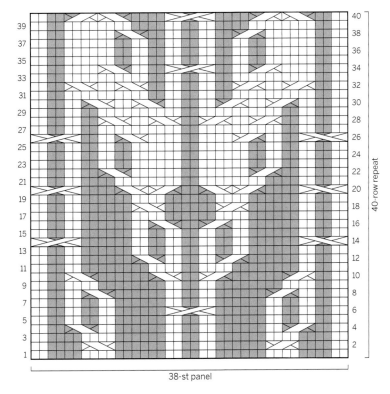

38-st panel

40-row repeat

□ Knit on RS, purl on WS.

▨ Purl on RS, knit on WS.

2/2 RC (2 over 2 right cross): Slip 2 sts to cn, hold to back, k2, k2 from cn.

2/2 LC (2 over 2 left cross): Slip 2 sts to cn, hold to front, k2, k2 from cn.

2/2 RPC (2 over 2 right purl cross): Slip 2 sts to cn, hold to back, k2, p2 from cn.

2/2 LPC (2 over 2 left purl cross): Slip 2 sts to cn, hold to front, p2, k2 from cn.

2/2/2 RPC (2 over 2 over 2 right purl cross): Slip 4 sts to cn, hold to back, k2, slip last 2 sts from cn back to left needle, p2, k2 from cn.

2/2/2 LPC (2 over 2 over 2 left purl cross): Slip 4 sts to cn, hold to front, k2, slip last 2 sts from cn back to left needle, p2, k2 from cn.

Left Bias Weave GROUP 2

For Left Bias Weave, I began with a series of left-slanting Fave motifs, then connected them with diagonal lines running in the opposite direction, creating what looks like a bias plaid.

(panel of 46 sts; 26-row repeat)
SSE: 30 sts

ROW 1 (WS): P2, k2, p2, k6, p6, k2, p6, k6, p2, k2, p2, k6, p2.

ROW 2: 2/2 LC, p4, 2/2 LPC, k2, p6, k2, 2/2 LPC, p2, k2, 2/2 LPC, p6, k2, p2, k2.

ROW 3 AND ALL FOLLOWING WS ROWS: Knit the knit sts and purl the purl sts as they face you.

ROW 4: K2, [2/2 LPC, p4] twice, 2/2 RC, p2, k2, 2/2 RPC, p2, 2/2 LC, p4, 2/2 LPC, k2.

ROW 6: K2, p2, k2, p6, [2/2 LC, 2/2 RPC] twice, p4, k2, 2/2 LPC, p4, 2/2 LPC.

ROW 8: 2/2 LPC, k2, p6, k2, 2/2 LPC, p2, k2, 2/2 LPC, p6, k2, p2, k2, p6, k2.

ROW 10: P2, 2/2 LPC, p4, 2/2 RC, p2, k2, 2/2 RPC, p2, 2/2 LPC, p4, 2/2 LPC, k2, p6, k2.

ROW 12: P4, [2/2 LC, 2/2 RPC] twice, p4, k2, 2/2 LPC, p4, 2/2 LPC, p4, 2/2 RC.

ROW 14: P4, k2, 2/2 LPC, p2, k2, 2/2 LPC, p6, k2, p2, k2, p6, 2/2 LC, 2/2 RPC, k2.

ROW 16: P2, 2/2 RC, p2, k2, 2/2 RPC, p2, 2/2 LC, p4, 2/2 LPC, k2, p6, k2, 2/2 LPC, p2, k2.

ROW 18: 2/2 RPC, 2/2 LC, 2/2 RPC, p4, k2, [2/2 LPC, p4] twice, 2/2 RC, p2, k2, 2/2 RPC.

ROW 20: K2, p2, k2, 2/2 LPC, p6, k2, p2, k2, p6, [2/2 LC, 2/2 RPC] twice, p2.

ROW 22: K2, 2/2 RPC, p2, 2/2 LC, p4, 2/2 LPC, k2, p6, k2, 2/2 LPC, p2, k2, 2/2 LPC, p4.

ROW 24: 2/2 RPC, p4, k2, [2/2 LPC, p4] twice, 2/2 RC, p2, k2, 2/2 RPC, p2, 2/2 LC, p2.

ROW 26: K2, p6, k2, p2, k2, p6, [2/2 LC, 2/2 RPC] twice, p4, k2, 2/2 LPC.

Repeat Rows 1–26 for pattern.

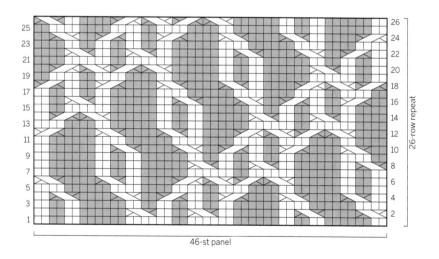

46-st panel

26-row repeat

☐ Knit on RS, purl on WS.

▨ Purl on RS, knit on WS.

2/2 RC (2 over 2 right cross): Slip 2 sts to cn, hold to back, k2, k2 from cn.

2/2 LC (2 over 2 left cross): Slip 2 sts to cn, hold to front, k2, k2 from cn.

OR 2/2 RPC (2 over 2 right purl cross): Slip 2 sts to cn, hold to back, k2, p2 from cn.

OR 2/2 LPC (2 over 2 left purl cross): Slip 2 sts to cn, hold to front, p2, k2 from cn.

Right Bias Weave GROUP 2
Right Bias Weave is a mirror image of Left Bias Weave (#116).

(panel of 46 sts; 26-row repeat)
SSE: 30 sts

ROW 1 (WS): P2, k6, p2, k2, p2, k6, p6, k2, p6, k6, p2, k2, p2.

ROW 2: K2, p2, k2, p6, 2/2 RPC, k2, p2, 2/2 RPC, k2, p6, k2, 2/2 RPC, p4, 2/2 RC.

ROW 3 AND ALL FOLLOWING WS ROWS: Knit the knit sts and purl the purl sts as they face you.

ROW 4: K2, 2/2 RPC, p4, 2/2 RC, p2, 2/2 LPC, k2, p2, 2/2 LC, p4, 2/2 RPC, p4, 2/2 RPC, k2.

ROW 6: 2/2 RPC, p4, 2/2 RPC, k2, p4, [2/2 LPC, 2/2 RC] twice, p6, k2, p2, k2.

ROW 8: K2, p6, k2, p2, k2, p6, 2/2 RPC, k2, p2, 2/2 RPC, k2, p6, k2, 2/2 RPC.

ROW 10: K2, p6, k2, 2/2 RPC, p4, 2/2 RC, p2, 2/2 LPC, k2, p2, 2/2 LC, p4, 2/2 RPC, p2.

ROW 12: 2/2 LC, p4, 2/2 RPC, p4, 2/2 RPC, k2, p4, [2/2 LPC, 2/2 RC] twice, p4.

ROW 14: K2, 2/2 LPC, 2/2 RC, p6, k2, p2, k2, p6, 2/2 RPC, k2, p2, 2/2 RPC, k2, p4.

ROW 16: K2, p2, 2/2 RPC, k2, p6, k2, 2/2 RPC, p4, 2/2 RC, p2, 2/2 LPC, k2, p2, 2/2 LC, p2.

ROW 18: 2/2 LPC, k2, p2, 2/2 LC, p4, 2/2 RPC, p4, 2/2 RPC, k2, p4, 2/2 LPC, 2/2 RC, 2/2 LPC.

ROW 20: P2, [2/2 LPC, 2/2 RC] twice, p6, k2, p2, k2, p6, 2/2 RPC, k2, p2, k2.

ROW 22: P4, 2/2 RPC, k2, p2, 2/2 RPC, k2, p6, k2, 2/2 RPC, p4, 2/2 RC, p2, 2/2 LPC, k2.

ROW 24: P2, 2/2 RC, p2, 2/2 LPC, k2, p2, 2/2 LC, p4, 2/2 RPC] twice, k2, p4, 2/2 LPC.

ROW 26: 2/2 RPC, k2, p4, [2/2 LPC, 2/2 RC] twice, p6, k2, p2, k2, p6, k2.
Repeat Rows 1–26 for pattern.

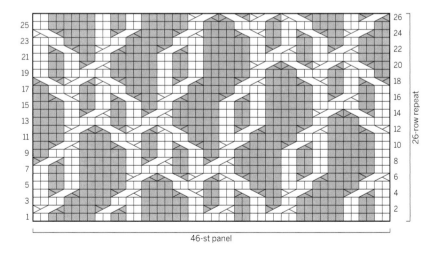

46-st panel

☐ Knit on RS, purl on WS.

▨ Purl on RS, knit on WS.

2/2 RC (2 over 2 right cross): Slip 2 sts to cn, hold to back, k2, k2 from cn.

2/2 LC (2 over 2 left cross): Slip 2 sts to cn, hold to front, k2, k2 from cn.

OR 2/2 RPC (2 over 2 right purl cross): Slip 2 sts to cn, hold to back, k2, p2 from cn.

OR 2/2 LPC (2 over 2 left purl cross): Slip 2 sts to cn, hold to front, p2, k2 from cn.

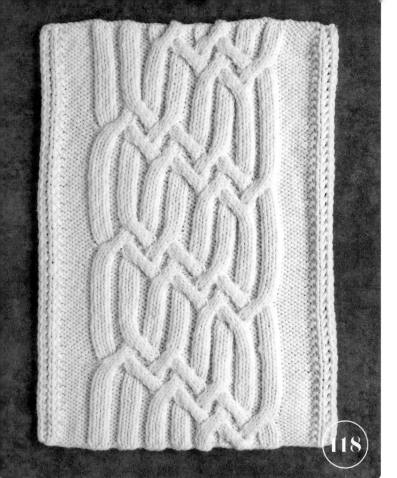

Crosshatch Bias GROUP 2

For Crosshatch Bias, I borrowed the crosshatch motif from Right Bias Weave (#117), but used a 3 x 3 instead of 2 x 2 rib.

(panel of 45 sts; 28-row repeat)
SSE: 30 sts

ROW 1 (WS): P3, [k3, p3] 7 times.

ROW 2: K3, p3, 3/3 LC, k3, [p3, k3] 5 times.

ROW 3 AND ALL FOLLOWING WS ROWS: Knit the knit sts and purl the purl sts as they face you.

ROW 4: K3, p3, k3, 3/3 LPC, [p3, k3] 5 times.

ROW 6: K3, 3/3 RC, p3, k3, 3/3 RC, [p3, k3] 4 times.

ROW 8: 3/3 RPC, k3, p3, 3/3 RPC, k3, [p3, k3] 4 times.

ROW 10: [K3, p3, 3/3 LC] twice, k3, [p3, k3] 3 times.

ROW 12: K3, [p3, k3, 3/3 LPC] twice, [p3, k3] 3 times.

ROW 14: K3, [p3, k3] twice, 3/3 RC, p3, k3, 3/3 RC, [p3, k3] twice.

ROW 16: [K3, p3] twice, 3/3 RPC, k3, p3, 3/3 RPC, k3, [p3, k3] twice.

ROW 18: [K3, p3] 3 times, [3/3 LC, k3, p3] twice, k3.

ROW 20: K3, [p3, k3] 3 times, [3/3 LPC, p3, k3] twice.

ROW 22: K3, [p3, k3] 4 times, 3/3 RC, p3, k3, 3/3 RC.

ROW 24: [K3, p3] 4 times, 3/3 RPC, k3, p3, 3/3 RPC, k3.

ROW 26: [K3, p3] 5 times, 3/3 LC, k3, p3, k3.

ROW 28: K3, [p3, k3] 5 times, 3/3 LPC, p3, k3.

Repeat Rows 1–28 for pattern.

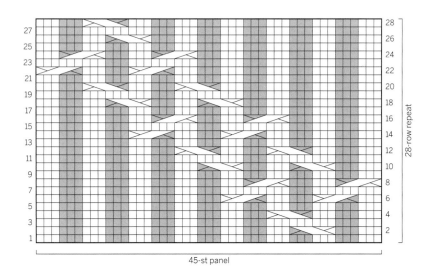

45-st panel

28-row repeat

☐ Knit on RS, purl on WS.

▨ Purl on RS, knit on WS.

⬲ 3/3 RC (3 over 3 right cross): Slip 3 sts to cn, hold to back, k3, k3 from cn.

⬲ 3/3 LC (3 over 3 left cross): Slip 3 sts to cn, hold to front, k3, k3 from cn.

⬲ 3/3 RPC (3 over 3 right purl cross): Slip 3 sts to cn, hold to back, k3, p3 from cn.

⬲ 3/3 LPC (3 over 3 left purl cross): Slip 3 sts to cn, hold to front, p3, k3 from cn.

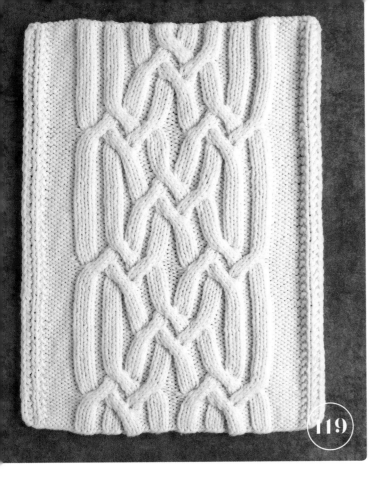

Crosshatch Weave GROUP 2

Here I placed the crosshatch motif from Crosshatch Bias (#118) on a rib background in a checkerboard arrangement. Ribs flow smoothly from one motif up into the next.

(panel of 45 sts; 32-row repeat)
SSE: 30 sts

ROW 1 (WS): P3, [k3, p3] 7 times.

ROW 2: Knit the knit sts and purl the purl sts as they face you.

ROW 3 AND ALL FOLLOWING WS ROWS: Repeat Row 2.

ROW 4: Repeat Row 2.

ROW 6: K3, p3, 3/3 LC, [k3, p3] 3 times, 3/3 LC, k3, p3, k3.

ROW 8: K3, p3, k3, 3/3 LPC, [p3, k3] 3 times, 3/3 LPC, p3, k3.

ROW 10: K3, 3/3 RC, [p3, k3, 3/3 RC] 3 times.

ROW 12: [3/3 RPC, k3, p3] 3 times, 3/3 RPC, k3.

ROW 14: Repeat Row 6.

ROW 16: Repeat Row 8.

ROWS 18 AND 20: Repeat Row 2.

ROW 22: [K3, p3] 3 times, 3/3 LC, k3, [p3, k3] 3 times.

ROW 24: K3, [p3, k3] 3 times, 3/3 LPC, [p3, k3] 3 times.

ROW 26: K3, [p3, k3] twice, 3/3 RC, p3, k3, 3/3 RC, [p3, k3] twice.

ROW 28: [K3, p3] twice, 3/3 RPC, k3, p3, 3/3 RPC, k3, [p3, k3] twice.

ROW 30: Repeat Row 22.

ROW 32: Repeat Row 24.

Repeat Rows 1–32 for pattern.

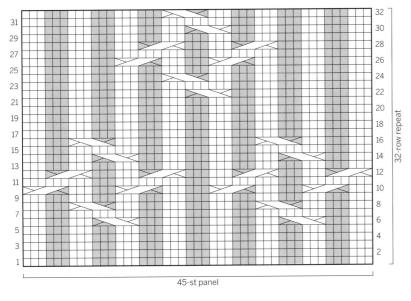

45-st panel

☐ Knit on RS, purl on WS.

▨ Purl on RS, knit on WS.

▱▱ 3/3 RC (3 over 3 right cross): Slip 3 sts to cn, hold to back, k3, k3 from cn.

▱▱ 3/3 LC (3 over 3 left cross): Slip 3 sts to cn, hold to front, k3, k3 from cn.

▱▱ 3/3 RPC (3 over 3 right purl cross): Slip 3 sts to cn, hold to back, k3, p3 from cn.

▱▱ 3/3 LPC (3 over 3 left purl cross): Slip 3 sts to cn, hold to front, p3, k3 from cn.

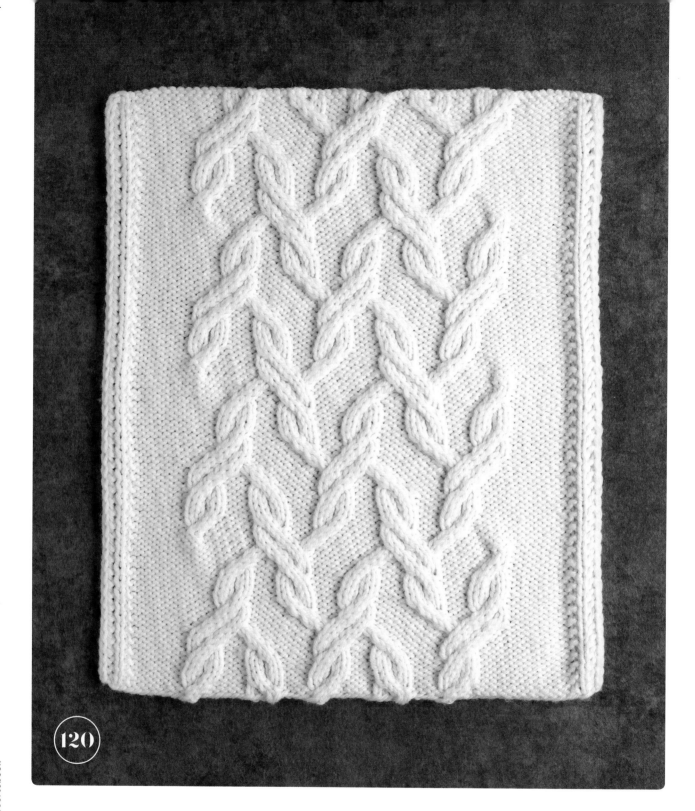

Alternate Taffy GROUP 3

Like Incline Fave (#111), this is another example of joining 2 Fave motifs to create a new form. In this case, the new form is placed in rows that slant to the right and rows that slant to the left and are also nestled together.

(multiple of 20 sts + 30; 28-row repeat)
TOTAL SSE: 34 sts
REPEAT SSE: 14 sts

ROW 1 (WS): P2, k8, *p6, k4, p2, k8; repeat from * to end.

ROW 2: P6, 2/2 RC, *p4, 2/2 LC, k2, p6, 2/2 RC; repeat from * to end.

ROW 3 AND ALL FOLLOWING WS ROWS: Knit the knit sts and purl the purl sts as they face you.

ROW 4: P4, 2/2 RPC, k2, *p4, k2, 2/2 LPC, p4, 2/2 RPC, k2; repeat from * to end.

ROW 6: *P4, k2, p2, k2; repeat from * to end.

ROW 8: P4, k2, 2/2 RC, *p4, 2/2 LPC, k2, p4, k2, 2/2 RC; repeat from * to end.

ROW 10: P4, 2/2 RC, k2, *p6, 2/2 LPC, p4, 2/2 RC, k2; repeat from * to end.

ROW 12: P2, [2/2 RC] twice, *p8, 2/2 LPC, [2/2 RC] twice; repeat from * to end.

ROW 14: 2/2 RC, 2/2 RPC, 2/2 LPC, p8, *2/2 RC, 2/2 RPC, 2/2 LPC, p8; repeat from * to last 10 sts, 2/2 RC, 2/2 RPC, p2.

ROW 16: K2, 2/2 RC, p4, *2/2 LC, p6, k2, 2/2 RC, p4; repeat from * to end.

ROW 18: 2/2 RPC, k2, p4, *k2, 2/2 LPC, p4, 2/2 RPC, k2, p4; repeat from * to end.

ROW 20: *K2, p2, k2, p4; repeat from * to end.

ROW 22: K2, 2/2 RPC, p4, *2/2 LC, k2, p4 k2, 2/2 RPC, p4; repeat from * to end.

ROW 24: 2/2 RPC, p6, *k2, 2/2 LC, p4, 2/2 RPC, p6; repeat from * to end.

ROW 26: P10, *[2/2 LC] twice, 2/2 RPC, p8; repeat from * to end.

ROW 28: P8, *2/2 RPC, 2/2 LPC, 2/2 LC, p8; repeat from * to last 2 sts, p2.

Repeat Rows 1–28 for pattern.

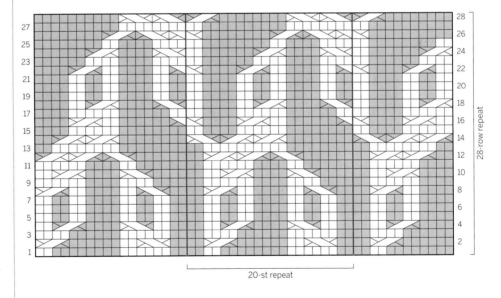

28-row repeat

20-st repeat

☐ Knit on RS, purl on WS.

▨ Purl on RS, knit on WS.

❘ Pattern repeat

▷◁ OR ▷◁ 2/2 RC (2 over 2 right cross): Slip 2 sts to cn, hold to back, k2, k2 from cn.

▷◁ OR ▷◁ 2/2 LC (2 over 2 left cross): Slip 2 sts to cn, hold to front, k2, k2 from cn.

▷◁ OR ▷◁ 2/2 RPC (2 over 2 right purl cross): Slip 2 sts to cn, hold to back, k2, p2 from cn.

▷◁ OR ▷◁ 2/2 LPC (2 over 2 left purl cross): Slip 2 sts to cn, hold to front, p2, k2 from cn.

Roofline GROUP 3

I expanded the diagonal forms in Alternate Taffy (#120) to create Roofline. The point where the 2 diagonals meet is capped with a rounded peak that transitions into 4-stitch ropes.

(multiple of 28 sts + 32; 36-row repeat)

TOTAL SSE: 41 sts

REPEAT SSE: 24 sts

ROW 1 (WS): P8, k6, p4, k6, *p12, k6, p4, k6; repeat from * to last 8 sts, p8.

ROW 2: 2/2 LC, 2/2 RC, p6, k4, p6, *[2/2 LC] twice, 2/2 RC, p6, k4, p6; repeat from * to last 8 sts, [2/2 LC] twice.

ROW 3 AND ALL FOLLOWING WS ROWS: Knit the knit sts and purl the purl sts as they face you.

ROW 4: K2, *2/2 RPC, k2, p6, 2/2 RC, p6, k2, 2/2 LPC; repeat from * to last 2 sts, k2.

ROW 6: *2/2 LC, p2, k2, p6, k4, p6, k2, p2; repeat from * to last 4 sts, 2/2 LC.

ROW 8: K4, *2/2 RPC, p6, 2/2 RC, p6, 2/2 LPC, k4; repeat from * to end.

ROW 10: K2, *2/2 RPC, p6, 2/2 RC, 2/2 LC, p6, 2/2 LPC; repeat from * to last 2 sts, k2.

ROW 12: 2/2 LC, *p6, 2/2 RPC, k4, 2/2 LPC, p6, 2/2 LPC; repeat from * to end.

ROW 14: K4, *p6, k2, p2, 2/2 RC, p2, k2, p6, k4; repeat from * to end.

ROW 16: 2/2 LC, *p6, k2, 2/2 RC, 2/2 LC, k2, p6, 2/2 LC; repeat from * to end.

ROW 18: K4, *p6, [2/2 RC] twice, 2/2 LC, p6, k4; repeat from * to end.

ROW 20: 2/2 LC, *p4, [2/2 RC] twice, [2/2 LC] twice, p4, 2/2 LC; repeat from * to end.

ROW 22: K4, *p4, k2, 2/2 RPC, k4, 2/2 LPC, k2, p4, k4; repeat from * to end.

ROW 24: 2/2 LC, p4, [2/2 RC, p2] twice, *[2/2 LC, p4] twice, [2/2 RC, p2] twice; repeat from * to last 12 sts, 2/2 LC, p4, 2/2 LC.

ROW 26: K4, *p2, 2/2 RPC, k2, p2, k4, p2, k2, 2/2 LPC, p2, k4; repeat from * to end.

ROW 28: 2/2 LC, *p2, [k2, p2] twice, 2/2 RC, p2, [k2, p2] twice, 2/2 LC; repeat from * to end.

ROW 30: K4, *p2, k2, 2/2 RPC, p2, k4, p2, 2/2 LPC, k2, p2, k4; repeat from * to end.

ROW 32: 2/2 LC, *p2, [2/2 RC, p4] twice, 2/2 LC, p2, 2/2 LC; repeat from * to end.

ROW 34: K4, *2/2 RC, k2, p4, k4, p4, k2, 2/2 LC, k4; repeat from * to end.

ROW 36: K2, *2/2 RC, 2/2 RPC, p4, 2/2 RC, p4, 2/2 LPC, 2/2 LC; repeat from * to last 2 sts, k2.
Repeat Rows 1–36 for pattern.

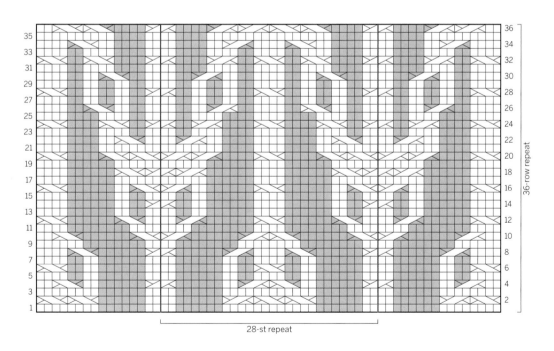

28-st repeat

36-row repeat

☐ Knit on RS, purl on WS.   ▨ Purl on RS, knit on WS.

❘ Pattern repeat

2/2 RC (2 over 2 right cross): Slip 2 sts to cn, hold to back, k2, k2 from cn.

2/2 LC (2 over 2 left cross): Slip 2 sts to cn, hold to front, k2, k2 from cn.

2/2 RPC (2 over 2 right purl cross): Slip 2 sts to cn, hold to back, k2, p2 from cn.

2/2 LPC (2 over 2 left purl cross): Slip 2 sts to cn, hold to front, p2, k2 from cn.

Free Ogee <small>GROUP 4</small>

For Free Ogee, 4 Fave motifs are joined to form the interior "flower" and 4 Fave motifs are joined to form the outer frame. While the diagonal lines stand out nicely from the stockinette stitch ground, 2 reverse stockinette stitches are needed on each side of the motif so its vertical lines won't meld into the background. The motif has a much tighter stitch gauge than the stockinette stitch ground, so increases and decreases are added to compensate.

(panel of 24 sts; increases to 34 sts; decreases back to 24 sts; 46-row repeat)

SSE: 24 sts

ROW 1 (WS): Purl.

ROW 2: K11, M1R, k1, M1R, k12—2 sts increased.

ROW 3: Purl.

ROW 4: K10, 2/2/2 RPC, k10.

ROWS 5–7: Knit the knit sts and purl the purl sts as they face you.

ROW 8: K8, M1R, 2/2 RPC, p2, 2/2 LPC, M1L, k8—2 sts increased.

ROW 9: P11, k6, p11.

ROW 10: K6, M1R, k1, M1R, 2/2 RPC, p6, 2/2 LPC, M1L, k1, M1L, k6—4 sts increased.

ROW 11: P11, k10, p11.

ROW 12: K5, 2/2/2 RPC, p10, 2/2/2 LPC, k5.

ROW 13: Repeat Row 5.

ROW 14: K3, M1R, 2/2 RC, p2, 2/2 LC, p6, 2/2 RC, p2, 2/2 LC, M1L, k3—2 sts increased.

ROW 15: Repeat Row 5.

ROW 16: P2, 2/2 RPC, k2, p2, k2, 2/2 LPC, p2, 2/2 RPC, k2, p2, k2, 2/2 LPC, p2.

ROWS 17–19: Repeat Row 5.

ROW 20: P2, k2, 2/2 RPC, p2, 2/2 LPC, k2, p2, k2, 2/2 RPC, p2, 2/2 LPC, k2, p2.

ROW 21: Repeat Row 5.

ROW 22: P2, 2/2 RPC, p6, 2/2 LPC, p2, 2/2 RPC, p6, 2/2 LPC, p2.

ROW 23: Repeat Row 5.

ROW 24: P2, k2, p10, 2/2/2 RPC, p10, k2, p2.

ROW 25: Repeat Row 5.

ROW 26: P2, 2/2 LC, p6, 2/2 RC, p2, 2/2 LC, p6, 2/2 RC, p2.

ROW 27: Repeat Row 5.

ROW 28: P2, k2, 2/2 LPC, p2, 2/2 RPC, k2, p2, k2, 2/2 LPC, p2, 2/2 RPC, k2, p2.

ROWS 29–31: Repeat Row 5.

ROW 32: K2, 2/2 LC, k2, p2, k2, 2/2 RPC, p2, 2/2 LPC, k2, p2, k2, 2/2 RC, k2.

ROW 33: P2, p2tog, p4, k2, p4, k6, p4, k2, p4, p2tog, p2—2 sts decreased.

ROW 34: K3, 2/2 LC, p2, 2/2 RPC, p6, 2/2 LPC, p2, 2/2 RC, k3.

ROW 35: Repeat Row 5.

ROW 36: K5, 2/2/2 LC, p10, 2/2/2 RC, k5.

ROW 37: P5, [p2tog] twice, p2, k10, p2, [p2tog] twice, p5—4 sts decreased.

ROW 38: K7, 2/2 LC, p6, 2/2 RC, k7.

ROW 39: P7, p2tog, p2, k6, p2, p2tog, p7—2 sts decreased.

ROW 40: K8, 2/2 LPC, p2, 2/2 RPC, k8.

ROWS 41–43: Repeat Row 5.

ROW 44: K10, 2/2/2 RC, k10.

ROW 45: P12, [p2tog] twice, p10—2 sts decreased.

ROW 46: Knit.

Repeat Rows 1–46 for pattern.

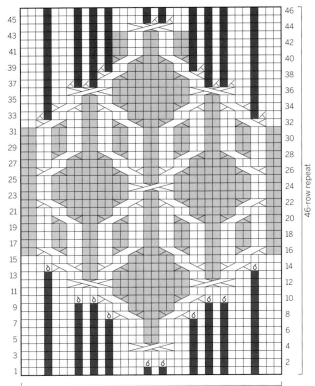

24-st panel; increases to 34 sts; decreases back to 24 sts

46-row repeat

☐ Knit on RS, purl on WS.

▨ Purl on RS, knit on WS.

⬠ M1L

⬡ M1R

☒ K2tog on RS, p2tog on WS.

■ No stitch

 OR 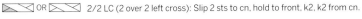 2/2 RC (2 over 2 right cross): Slip 2 sts to cn, hold to back, k2, k2 from cn.

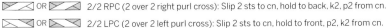 OR 2/2 LC (2 over 2 left cross): Slip 2 sts to cn, hold to front, k2, k2 from cn.

OR 2/2 RPC (2 over 2 right purl cross): Slip 2 sts to cn, hold to back, k2, p2 from cn.

OR 2/2 LPC (2 over 2 left purl cross): Slip 2 sts to cn, hold to front, p2, k2 from cn.

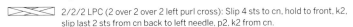 OR 2/2/2 RPC (2 over 2 over 2 right purl cross): Slip 4 sts to cn, hold to back, k2, slip last 2 sts from cn back to left needle, p2, k2 from cn.

 2/2/2 LPC (2 over 2 over 2 left purl cross): Slip 4 sts to cn, hold to front, k2, slip last 2 sts from cn back to left needle, p2, k2 from cn.

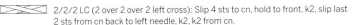 2/2/2 RC (2 over 2 over 2 right cross): Slip 4 sts to cn, hold to back, k2, slip last 2 sts from cn back to left needle, k2, k2 from cn.

2/2/2 LC (2 over 2 over 2 left cross): Slip 4 sts to cn, hold to front, k2, slip last 2 sts from cn back to left needle, k2, k2 from cn.

(123)

Ogee X GROUP 4

Here the large motif of Free Ogee (#122) is placed on a background of 2 x 2 rib to create a panel. None of the increasing and decreasing of Free Ogee is necessary in this case because the rib compacts naturally and allows for a smooth transition from one ogee to the next.

(panel of 46 sts; 64-row repeat)
SSE: 30 sts

ROW 1 (WS): P2, [k2, p2] eleven times.

ROW 2: Knit the knit sts and purl the purl sts as they face you.

ROW 3 AND ALL FOLLOWING WS ROWS: Repeat Row 2.

ROW 4: K2, p2, 2/2 LPC, k2, p2, k2, 2/2 RPC, p2, [k2, p2] twice, 2/2 LPC, k2, p2, k2, 2/2 RPC, p2, k2.

ROW 6: K2, p4, 2/2 LPC, p2, 2/2 RPC, p4, k2, p2, k2, p4, 2/2 LPC, p2, 2/2 RPC, p4, k2.

ROW 8: K2, p6, [2/2/2 RPC, p6] twice, 2/2/2 LPC, p6, k2.

ROW 10: K2, p4, 2/2 RPC, p2, k2, p6, k2, p2, k2, p6, k2, p2, 2/2 LPC, p4, k2.

ROW 12: K2, p2, 2/2 RPC, p4, k2, p4, 2/2 RPC, p2, 2/2 LPC, p4, k2, p4, 2/2 LPC, p2, k2.

ROW 14: K2, p2, k2, p6, k2, p2, 2/2 RPC, p6, 2/2 LPC, p2, k2, p6, k2, p2, k2.

ROW 16: 2/2/2 RPC, p6, 2/2/2 RPC, p10, 2/2/2 LPC, p6, 2/2/2 LPC.

ROW 18: K2, p2, k2, p4, 2/2 RC, p2, 2/2 LC, p6, 2/2 RC, p2, 2/2 LC, p4, k2, p2, k2.

ROW 20: [K2, p2] twice, [2/2 RPC, k2, p2, k2, 2/2 LPC, p2] twice, k2, p2, k2.

ROW 22: Repeat Row 2.

ROW 24: K2, [p2, k2] twice, [2/2 RPC, p2, 2/2 LPC, k2, p2, k2] twice, p2, k2.

ROW 26: [K2, p2] twice, [2/2 RPC, p6, 2/2 LPC, p2] twice, k2, p2, k2.

ROW 28: K2, [p2, k2] twice, p10, 2/2/2 RPC, p10, k2, [p2, k2] twice.

ROW 30: [K2, p2] twice, [2/2 LC, p6, 2/2 RC, p2] twice, k2, p2, k2.

ROW 32: K2, [p2, k2] twice, [2/2 LPC, p2, 2/2 RPC, k2, p2, k2] twice, p2, k2.

ROW 34: Repeat Row 2.

ROW 36: [K2, p2] twice, [2/2 LPC, k2, p2, k2, 2/2 RPC, p2] twice, k2, p2, k2.

ROW 38: K2, p2, k2, p4, 2/2 LPC, p2, 2/2 RPC, p6, 2/2 LPC, p2, 2/2 RPC, p4, k2, p2, k2.

ROW 40: 2/2/2 RPC, p6, 2/2/2 LPC, p10, 2/2/2 RPC, p6, 2/2/2 LPC.

ROW 42: K2, p2, k2, p6, k2, p2, 2/2 LPC, p6, 2/2 RPC, p2, k2, p6, k2, p2, k2.

ROW 44: K2, p2, 2/2 LPC, p4, k2, p4, 2/2 LPC, p2, 2/2 RPC, p4, k2, p4, 2/2 RPC, p2, k2.

ROW 46: K2, p4, 2/2 LPC, p2, k2, p6, k2, p2, k2, p6, k2, p2, 2/2 RPC, p4, k2.

ROW 48: K2, p6, 2/2/2 LPC, p6, [2/2/2 RPC, p6] twice, k2.

ROW 50: K2, p4, 2/2 RC, p2, 2/2 LC, p4, k2, p2, k2, p4, 2/2 RC, p2, 2/2 LC, p4, k2.

ROW 52: K2, p2, 2/2 RPC, k2, p2, k2, 2/2 LPC, p2, [k2, p2] twice, 2/2 RPC, k2, p2, k2, 2/2 LPC, p2, k2.

ROW 54: Repeat Row 2.

ROW 56: K2, p2, k2, 2/2 RPC, p2, 2/2 LPC, k2, [p2, k2] 3 times, 2/2 RPC, p2, 2/2 LPC, k2, p2, k2.

ROW 58: K2, p2, 2/2 RPC, p6, 2/2 LPC, p2, [k2, p2] twice, 2/2 RPC, p6, 2/2 LPC, p2, k2.

ROW 60: 2/2/2 RPC, p10, k2, [p2, k2] 3 times, p10, 2/2/2 LPC.

ROW 62: K2, p2, 2/2 LC, p6, 2/2 RC, p2, [k2, p2] twice, 2/2 LC, p6, 2/2 RC, p2, k2.

ROW 64: K2, p2, k2, 2/2 LPC, p2, 2/2 RPC, k2, [p2, k2] 3 times, 2/2 LPC, p2, 2/2 RPC, k2, p2, k2.
Repeat Rows 1–64 for pattern.

46-st panel

64-row repeat

☐ Knit on RS, purl on WS.

▨ Purl on RS, knit on WS.

2/2 RC (2 over 2 right cross): Slip 2 sts to cn, hold to back, k2, k2 from cn.

2/2 LC (2 over 2 left cross): Slip 2 sts to cn, hold to front, k2, k2 from cn.

OR 2/2 RPC (2 over 2 right purl cross): Slip 2 sts to cn, hold to back, k2, p2 from cn.

OR 2/2 LPC (2 over 2 left purl cross): Slip 2 sts to cn, hold to front, p2, k2 from cn.

2/2/2 RPC (2 over 2 over 2 right purl cross): Slip 4 sts to cn, hold to back, k2, slip last 2 sts from cn back to left needle, p2, k2 from cn.

2/2/2 LPC (2 over 2 over 2 left purl cross): Slip 4 sts to cn, hold to front, k2, slip last 2 sts from cn back to left needle, p2, k2 from cn.

Open Medallion GROUP 4

For Open Mediallion, I isolated and expanded an oval motif within Free Ogee (#122) and Ogee X (#123) and filled it with lace. Because the lace begins as the cable is being crossed, it is clearly delineated from the stockinette-stitch cables around it.

(panel of 33 sts; increases to 36 sts; decreases back to 33 sts; 34-row repeat)

SSE: 33 sts

ROW 1 (WS): Purl.
ROW 2: K16, M1L, k17—1 st increased.
ROW 3: Purl.
ROW 4: K15, 2/2 RC, k15.
ROW 5: Purl.
ROW 6: K13; slip 2 sts to cn, hold to back, k2, (yo, p2tog) from cn; slip 2 sts to cn, hold to front, yo, p2tog, k2 from cn; k13.
ROW 7: P15, [yo, p2tog] twice, p15.
ROW 8: K11, 2/2 RC, [yo, p2tog] twice, 2/2 LC, k11.
ROW 9: Repeat Row 7.
ROW 10: K7, p2, 2/2 RPC, k2, [yo, p2tog] twice, k2, 2/2 LPC, p2, k7.
ROW 11: P7, [k2, p2] twice, [yo, p2tog] twice, [p2, k2] twice, p7.
ROW 12: K6, M1R, k1, [p2, k2] twice, [yo, p2tog] twice, [k2, p2] twice, k1, M1L, k6—2 sts increased.
ROW 13: P8, [k2, p2] twice, [yo, p2tog] twice, [p2, k2] twice, p8.
ROW 14: K4, 2/2 LC, p2, k2; slip 2 sts to cn, hold to back, k2, (yo, p2tog) from cn; [yo, p2tog] twice; slip 2 sts to cn, hold to front, yo, p2tog, k2 from cn; k2, p2, 2/2 RC, k4.
ROW 15: P8, k2, p4, [yo, p2tog] 4 times, p4, k2, p8.
ROW 16: K2; slip 2 sts to cn, hold to back, k2, (yo, p2tog) from cn; slip 2 sts to cn, hold to front, yo, p2tog, k2 from cn; slip 2 sts to cn, hold to back, k2, (yo, p2tog) from cn; [yo, p2tog] 4 times; slip 2 sts to cn, hold to front, yo, p2tog, k2 from cn; slip 2 sts to cn, hold to back, k2, (yo, p2tog) from cn; slip 2 sts to cn, hold to front, yo, p2tog, k2 from cn; k2.

ROW 17: P4, [yo, p2tog] twice, p4, [yo, p2tog] 6 times, p4, [yo, p2tog] twice, p4.
ROW 18: 2/2 RC, [yo, p2tog] twice, 2/2 RC, [yo, p2tog] 6 times, 2/2 LC, [yo, p2tog] twice, 2/2 LC.
ROW 19: Repeat Row 17.
ROW 20: K2, 2/2 LC, 2/2 RPC, 2/2 LC, [yo, p2tog] 4 times, 2/2 RC, 2/2 LPC, 2/2 RC, k2.
ROW 21: Repeat Row 15.
ROW 22: K4, 2/2 LC, p2, k2, 2/2 LPC, [yo, p2tog] twice, 2/2 RPC, k2, p2, 2/2 RC, k4.
ROW 23: P4, p2tog, p2, [k2, p2] twice, [yo, p2tog] twice, p2, [k2, p2] twice, p2tog, p4—2 sts decreased.
ROW 24: K7, [p2, k2] twice, [yo, p2tog] twice, [k2, p2] twice, k7.
ROW 25: Repeat Row 11.
ROW 26: K9, 2/2 LC, k2, [yo, p2tog] twice, k2, 2/2 RC, k9.
ROW 27: Repeat Row 7.
ROW 28: K11, 2/2 LC, [yo, p2tog] twice, 2/2 RC, k11.
ROW 29: Repeat Row 7.
ROW 30: K13, 2/2 LC, 2/2 RC, k13.
ROW 31: Purl.
ROW 32: Repeat Row 4.
ROW 33: P16, p2tog, p16.
ROW 34: Knit.
Repeat Rows 1–34 for pattern.

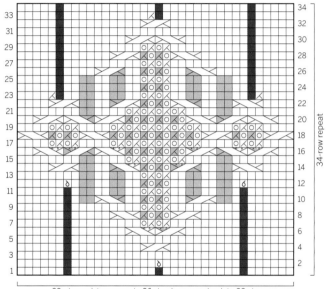

33-st panel; increases to 36 sts; decreases back to 33 sts

☐ Knit on RS, purl on WS.

▨ Purl on RS, knit on WS.

◖ M1L

◗ M1R

◯ Yo

◺ K2tog on RS, p2tog on WS.

◣ P2tog on RS, k2tog on WS.

■ No stitch

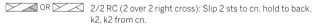 2/2 RC (2 over 2 right cross): Slip 2 sts to cn, hold to back, k2, k2 from cn.

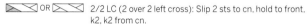 2/2 LC (2 over 2 left cross): Slip 2 sts to cn, hold to front, k2, k2 from cn.

2/2 RPC (2 over 2 right purl cross): Slip 2 sts to cn, hold to back, k2, p2 from cn.

2/2 LPC (2 over 2 left purl cross): Slip 2 sts to cn, hold to front, p2, k2 from cn.

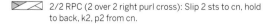 Slip 2 sts to cn, hold to back, k2, (yo, p2tog) from cn.

Slip 2 sts to cn, hold to front, yo, p2tog, k2 from cn.

Twist Argyle

GROUP 5

I worked the Fave motif in right twists this time and used it as the diagonal connector between columns of tight cable braids punctuated with circles. Additional right twists form a loose lattice within the circles.

(multiple of 44 sts + 8; 40-row repeat)

SSE: 35 sts

ROW 1 (WS): P2, k4, *p4, k2, p2, k8, p8, k8, p2, k2, p4, k4; repeat from * to last 2 sts, p2.

ROW 2: RT, p4, *slip 2 sts to cn, hold to front, k2, RT from cn; p2, k2, p8, k2, 2/2 LC, k2, p8, k2, p2; slip 2 sts to cn, hold to front, k2, RT from cn; p4; repeat from * to last 2 sts, RT.

ROW 3 AND ALL FOLLOWING WS ROWS: Knit the knit sts and purl the purl sts as they face you.

ROW 4: Slip 2 sts to cn, hold to front, p2, RT from cn; slip 2 sts to cn, hold to back, RT, p2 from cn; *slip 2 sts to cn, hold to front, p2, RT from cn; k2, p8, [2/2 RC] twice, p8, k2; slip 2 sts to cn, hold to back, RT, p2 from cn; slip 2 sts to cn, hold to front, p2, RT from cn; slip 2 sts to cn, hold to back, RT, p2 from cn; repeat from * to end.

ROW 6: P2; slip 2 sts to cn, hold to back, RT, k2 from cn; *p4, 2/2 RC, p8, k2, 2/2 LC, k2, p8; slip 2 sts to cn, hold to back, RT, k2 from cn; p4; slip 2 sts to cn, hold to back, RT, k2 from cn; repeat from * to last 2 sts, p2.

ROW 8: Slip 2 sts to cn, hold to back, RT, p2 from cn; slip 2 sts to cn, hold to front, p2, RT from cn; *2/2 RPC; slip 2 sts to cn, hold to front, k2, RT from cn; p6, [2/2 RC] twice, p6; slip 2 sts to cn, hold to back, RT, k2 from cn; 2/2 LPC; slip 2 sts to cn, hold to back, RT, p2 from cn; slip 2 sts to cn, hold to front, p2, RT from cn; repeat from * to end.

ROW 10: RT, p4, *2/2 RPC, p2, RT; slip 2 sts to cn, hold to front, p2, RT from cn; p4, k2, 2/2 LC, k2, p4; slip 2 sts to cn, hold to back, RT, p2 from cn; RT, p2, 2/2 LPC, p4; repeat from * to last 2 sts; RT.

ROW 12: 2/2 LC, 2/2 RC, *p4, RT, p2, RT, p4, 2/2 RPC, 2/2 LPC, p4, RT, p2, RT, p4, 2/2 LC, 2/2 RC; repeat from * to end.

ROW 14: K2, 2/2 RC, k2, *p4; slip 2 sts to cn, hold to front, p2, RT from cn; RT, p2, 2/2 RC, p4, 2/2 LC, p2, RT; slip 2 sts to cn, hold to back, RT, p2 from cn; p4, k2, 2/2 RC, k2; repeat from * to end.

ROW 16: [2/2 LC] twice, *p6; slip 2 sts to cn, hold to front, p2, RT from cn; 2/2 RPC; slip 2 sts to cn, hold to front, p2, RT from cn; slip 2 sts to cn, hold to back, RT, p2 from cn; 2/2 LPC; slip 2 sts to cn, hold to back, RT, p2 from cn; p6, [2/2 LC] twice; repeat from * to end.

ROW 18: K2, 2/2 RC, k2, *p8, 2/2 RC, [p4; slip 2 sts to cn, hold to back, RT, k2 from cn] twice, p8, k2, 2/2 RC, k2; repeat from * to end.

ROW 20: [2/2 LC] twice, *p8, k2; [slip 2 sts to cn, hold to front, p2, RT from cn; slip 2 sts to cn, hold to back, RT, p2 from cn] twice, k2, p8, [2/2 LC] twice; repeat from * to end.

ROW 22: K2, 2/2 RC, k2, *p8, k2, p2; slip 2 sts to cn, hold to front, k2, RT from cn; p4; slip 2 sts to cn, hold to front, k2, RT from cn; p2, k2, p8, k2, 2/2 RC, k2; repeat from * to end.

ROW 24: [2/2 LC] twice, *p8, k2; [slip 2 sts to cn, hold to back, RT, p2 from cn; slip 2 sts to cn, hold to front, p2, RT from cn] twice, k2, p8, [2/2 LC] twice; repeat from * to end.

ROW 26: K2, 2/2 RC, k2, *p8; [slip 2 sts to cn, hold to back, RT, k2 from cn; p4] twice, 2/2 RC, p8, k2, 2/2 RC, k2; repeat from * to end.

ROW 28: 2/2 LPC, *2/2 LC, p6; slip 2 sts to cn, hold to back, RT, k2 from cn; 2/2 LPC; slip 2 sts to cn, hold to back, RT, p2 from cn; slip 2 sts to cn, hold to front, p2, RT from cn; 2/2 RPC; slip 2 sts to cn, hold to front, k2, RT from cn; p6, 2/2 LC; repeat from * to last 4 sts, 2/2 RPC.

ROW 30: P2, 2/2 RC, *k2, p4; slip 2 sts to cn, hold to back, RT, p2 from cn; RT, p2, 2/2 LPC, p4, 2/2 RPC, p2, RT; slip 2 sts to cn, hold to front, k2, RT from cn; p4, k2, 2/2 RC; repeat from * to last 2 sts, p2.

ROW 32: 2/2 RPC, 2/2 LPC, *p4, RT, p2, RT, p4, 2/2 LC, 2/2 RC, p4, RT, p2, RT, p4, 2/2 RPC, 2/2 LPC; repeat from * to end.

ROW 34: RT, p4, *2/2 LC, p2, RT; slip 2 sts to cn, hold to back, RT, p2 from cn; p4, k2, 2/2 LC, k2, p4; slip 2 sts to cn, hold to front, p2, RT from cn; RT, p2, 2/2 RC, p4; repeat from * to last 2 sts; RT.

ROW 36: Slip 2 sts to cn, hold to front, p2, RT from cn; slip 2 sts to cn, hold to back, RT, p2 from cn; *2/2 LPC; slip 2 sts to cn, hold to back, RT, p2 from cn; p6, [2/2 RC] twice, p6; slip 2 sts to cn, hold to front, p2, RT from cn; 2/2 RPC; slip 2 sts to cn, hold to front, p2, RT from cn; slip 2 sts to cn, hold to back, RT, p2 from cn; repeat from * to end.

ROW 38: P2; slip 2 sts to cn, hold to back, RT, k2 from cn; *p4; slip 2 sts to cn, hold to back, RT, k2 from cn; p8, k2, 2/2 LC, k2, p8, 2/2 RC, p4; slip 2 sts to cn, hold to back, RT, k2 from cn; repeat from * to last 2 sts, p2.

ROW 40: Slip 2 sts to cn, hold to back, RT, p2 from cn; slip 2 sts to cn, hold to front, p2, RT from cn; *slip 2 sts to cn, hold to back, RT, p2 from cn; k2, p8, [2/2 RC] twice, p8, k2; slip 2 sts to cn, hold to front, p2, RT from cn; slip 2 sts to cn, hold to back, RT, p2 from cn; slip 2 sts to cn, hold to front, p2, RT from cn; repeat from * to end. Repeat Rows 1–40 for pattern.

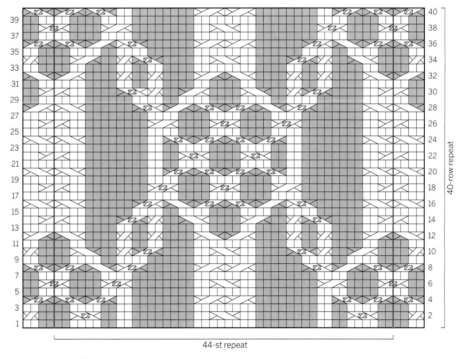

44-st repeat

40-row repeat

☐   Knit on RS, purl on WS.

▦   Purl on RS, knit on WS.

❘   Pattern repeat

    RT (right twist): K2tog, but do not drop sts from left needle; insert right needle between 2 sts just worked and knit first st again, slip both sts from left needle together.

    OR   2/2 RC (2 over 2 right cross): Slip 2 sts to cn, hold to back, k2, k2 from cn.

    OR   2/2 LC (2 over 2 left cross): Slip 2 sts to cn, hold to front, k2, k2 from cn.

    OR   2/2 RPC (2 over 2 right purl cross): Slip 2 sts to cn, hold to back, k2, p2 from cn.

    OR   2/2 LPC (2 over 2 left purl cross): Slip 2 sts to cn, hold to front, p2, k2 from cn.

    OR   Slip 2 sts to cn, hold to back, RT, k2 from cn.

    OR   Slip 2 sts to cn, hold to front, k2, RT from cn.

    OR   Slip 2 sts to cn, hold to back, RT, p2 from cn.

    OR   Slip 2 sts to cn, hold to front, p2, RT from cn.

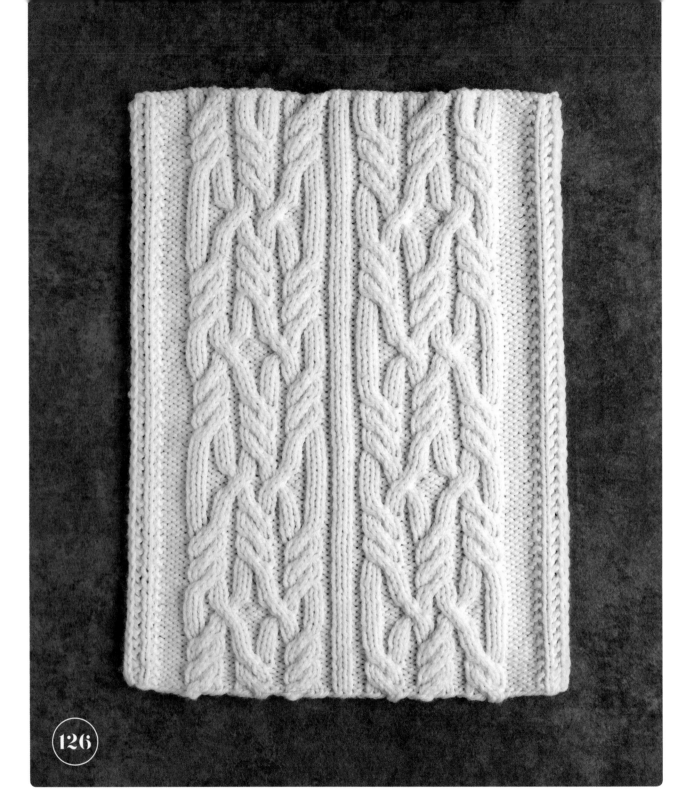

Encase Diamond GROUP 6

In this cable, 3 columns featuring a compressed version of Fave exchange ribs with their adjacent columns and in doing so combine to form a wider cable. After the exchange, the Fave motifs resume, leaving both small and large diamond shapes in the center of the wider cable. The 2 wider cables shown in the swatch are mirror images of each other, and each starts at a different point in the pattern, creating a staggered effect.

(panel of 50 sts; 44-row repeat)
SSE: 32.5 sts

ROW 1 (WS): P2, [k2, p2] 12 times.
ROW 2: 2/2 LC, k2, p2, k2, 2/2 RC, p2, 2/2 LC, k2, [p2, k2] twice, 2/2 RC, p2, 2/2 LC, k2, p2, k2, 2/2 RC.
ROW 3 AND ALL FOLLOWING WS ROWS: Knit the knit sts and purl the purl sts as they face you.
ROW 4: K2, 2/2 LPC, p2, 2/2 RPC, k2, p2, k2, 2/2 LPC, p2, k2, p2, 2/2 RPC, k2, p2, k2, 2/2 LPC, p2, 2/2 RPC, k2.
ROW 6: Repeat Row 2.
ROW 8: Repeat Row 4.
ROW 10: K2, [p2, k2] twice, 2/2 RC, [p2, k2] 4 times, 2/2 RC, [p2, k2] 3 times, 2/2 RC.
ROW 12: [K2, p2] twice, 2/2 RPC, [k2, p2] 4 times, 2/2 RPC, [k2, p2] 3 times, 2/2 RPC, k2.
ROW 14: K2, p2, 2/2 LPC, k2, p2, k2, 2/2 RPC, [p2, k2] 4 times, 2/2 RPC, p2, 2/2 LPC, k2, p2, k2.
ROW 16: K2, p4, 2/2 LC, p2, 2/2 LC, p4, [k2, p2] 3 times, 2/2 RC, p6, 2/2 LC, p2, k2.
ROW 18: K2, p2, 2/2 RPC, k2, p2, k2, 2/2 LPC, [p2, k2] 4 times, 2/2 LPC, p2, 2/2 RPC, k2, p2, k2.
ROW 20: Repeat Row 10.
ROW 22: Repeat Row 12.
ROW 24: Repeat Row 2.
ROW 26: Repeat Row 4.
ROW 28: Repeat Row 2.
ROW 30: Repeat Row 4.
ROW 32: 2/2 LC, [k2, p2] 3 times, 2/2 LC, [k2, p2] 4 times, 2/2 LC, k2, [p2, k2] twice.
ROW 34: K2, 2/2 LPC, [p2, k2] 3 times, 2/2 LPC, [k2, p2] 4 times, 2/2 LPC, [p2, k2] twice.

ROW 36: K2, p2, k2, 2/2 RPC, p2, 2/2 LPC, [k2, p2] 4 times, 2/2 LPC, k2, p2, k2, 2/2 RPC, p2, k2.
ROW 38: K2, p2, 2/2 RC, p6, 2/2 LC, [p2, k2] 3 times, p4, 2/2 RC, p2, 2/2 RC, p4, k2.
ROW 40: K2, p2, k2, 2/2 LPC, p2, 2/2 RPC, [k2, p2] 4 times, 2/2 RPC, k2, p2, k2, 2/2 LPC, p2, k2.
ROW 42: Repeat Row 32.
ROW 44: Repeat Row 34.
Repeat Rows 1–44 for pattern.

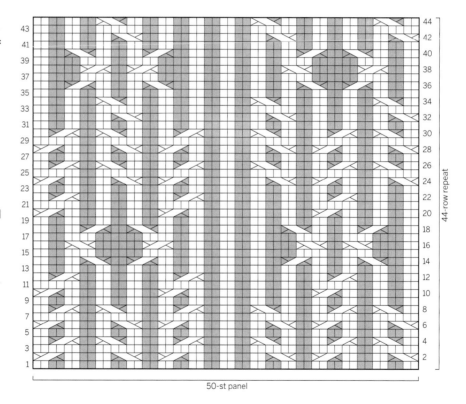

50-st panel

44-row repeat

☐ Knit on RS, purl on WS.

▨ Purl on RS, knit on WS.

2/2 RC (2 over 2 right cross): Slip 2 sts to cn, hold to back, k2, k2 from cn.

2/2 LC (2 over 2 left cross): Slip 2 sts to cn, hold to front, k2, k2 from cn.

2/2 RPC (2 over 2 right purl cross): Slip 2 sts to cn, hold to back, k2, p2 from cn.

2/2 LPC (2 over 2 left purl cross): Slip 2 sts to cn, hold to front, p2, k2 from cn.

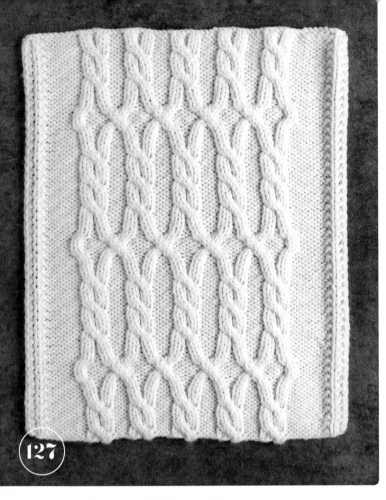

Diamond Stretch GROUP 6

Here the larger diamond shape from Encase Diamond (#126) repeats horizontally. The diamonds are connected vertically with Fave.

(multiple of 10 sts + 20; 30-row repeat)
TOTAL SSE: 22.5 sts
REPEAT SSE: 7.5 sts

ROW 1 (WS): *K2, [p2, k2] twice; repeat from * to end.
ROW 2: *P2, 2/2 LC, k2, p2; repeat from * to end.
ROW 3: Knit the knit sts and purl the purl sts as they face you.
ROW 4: *P2, k2, 2/2 LPC, p2; repeat from * to end.
ROWS 5–7: Repeat Row 3.
ROW 8: Repeat Row 2.
ROW 9: Repeat Row 3.
ROW 10: Repeat Row 4.

ROWS 11–15: Repeat Row 3.
ROW 16: *2/2 RPC, p2, 2/2 LPC; repeat from * to end.
ROW 17: Repeat Row 3.
ROW 18: K2, p6, *2/2 LC, p6; repeat from * to last 2 sts, k2.
ROW 19: Repeat Row 3.
ROW 20: *2/2 LPC, p2, 2/2 RPC; repeat from * to end.
ROWS 21–25: Repeat Row 3.
ROW 26: Repeat Row 2.
ROW 27: Repeat Row 3.
ROW 28: Repeat Row 4.
ROW 29: Repeat Row 3.
ROW 30: Repeat Row 3.
Repeat Rows 1–30 for pattern.

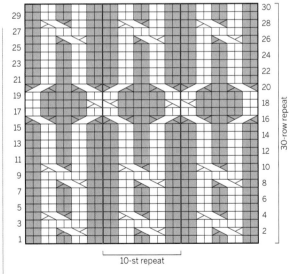

□ Knit on RS, purl on WS.

▨ Purl on RS, knit on WS.

❘ Pattern repeat

 OR 2/2 LC (2 over 2 left cross): Slip 2 sts to cn, hold to front, k2, k2 from cn.

 2/2 RPC (2 over 2 right purl cross): Slip 2 sts to cn, hold to back, k2, p2 from cn.

▨ OR ▨ 2/2 LPC (2 over 2 left purl cross): Slip 2 sts to cn, hold to front, p2, k2 from cn.

30-row repeat

10-st repeat

Knitted Cable Sourcebook

127

Hexa Variations

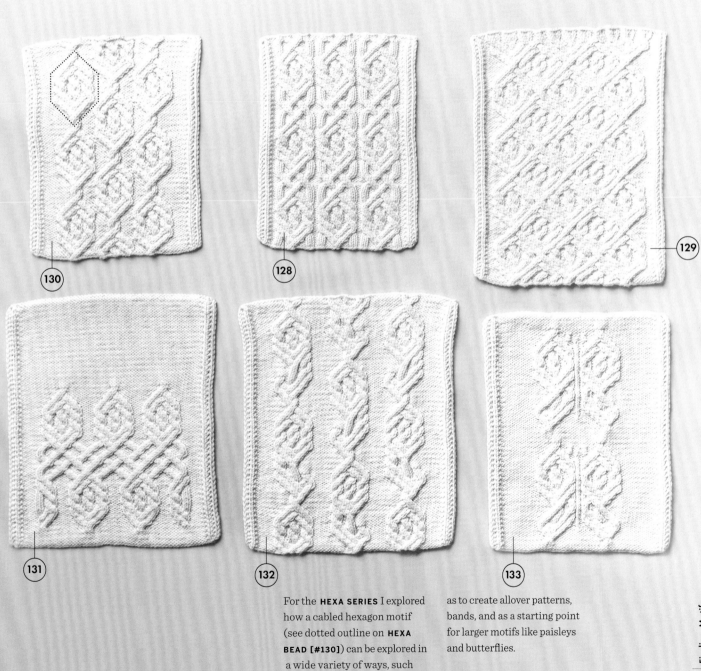

(130)

(128)

(129)

(131)

(132)

(133)

For the **HEXA SERIES** I explored how a cabled hexagon motif (see dotted outline on **HEXA BEAD [#130]**) can be explored in a wide variety of ways, such as to create allover patterns, bands, and as a starting point for larger motifs like paisleys and butterflies.

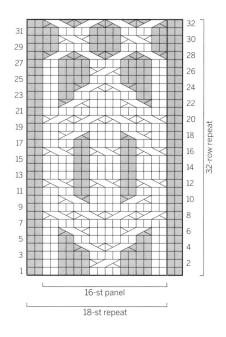

Hexa Grid GROUP 7

Hexa Grid is a melding of 2 motifs: a hexagon and a braided X. I also used the hexagon motif to create the Compact (#129), Bead (#130), Frieze (#131), Paisley (#132), and Butterfly (#133) variations, and the X to create Moss X (#134) and Wobble X (#135).

(multiple of 18 sts + 2; 32-row repeat)

NOTE: Pattern may also be worked in panels of 16 sts (see Chart).

TOTAL SSE: 12.5 sts

REPEAT SSE: 11 sts

ROW 1 (WS): K2, *p2, k4, p4, k4, p2, k2; repeat from * to end.

ROW 2: P2, *k2, p4, 2/2 RC, p4, k2, p2; repeat from * to end.

ROW 3 AND ALL FOLLOWING WS ROWS: Knit the knit sts and purl the purl sts as they face you.

ROW 4: P2, *k2, p2, 2/2 RC, 2/2 LC, p2, k2, p2; repeat from * to end.

ROW 6: P2, *k2, 2/2 RC, k4, 2/2 LC, k2, p2; repeat from * to end.

ROW 8: P2, *[2/2 RC] twice, [2/2 LC] twice, p2; repeat from * to end.

ROW 10: P2, *k2, 2/2 RPC, k4, 2/2 LPC, k2, p2; repeat from * to end.

ROW 12: P2, *2/2 LC, p2; repeat from * to end.

ROW 14: Repeat Row 3.

ROW 16: Repeat Row 12.

ROW 18: P2, *k2, 2/2 LC, k4, 2/2 RC, k2, p2; repeat from * to end.

ROW 20: P2, *[2/2 LC] twice, [2/2 RC] twice, p2; repeat from * to end.

ROW 22: P2, *k2, 2/2 LPC, k4, 2/2 RPC, k2, p2; repeat from * to end.

ROW 24: P2, *k2, p2, 2/2 LPC, 2/2 RPC, p2, k2, p2; repeat from * to end.

ROW 26: Repeat Row 2.

ROW 28: P2, *[2/2 LPC, 2/2 RPC] twice, p2; repeat from * to end.

ROW 30: P4, *2/2 LC, p4; repeat from * to end.

ROW 32: P2, *[2/2 RPC, 2/2 LPC] twice, p2; repeat from * to end.
Repeat Rows 1–32 for pattern.

16-st panel

18-st repeat

32-row repeat

☐ Knit on RS, purl on WS.

▦ Purl on RS, knit on WS.

| Pattern repeat

OR — 2/2 RC (2 over 2 right cross): Slip 2 sts to cn, hold to back, k2, k2 from cn.

OR — 2/2 LC (2 over 2 left cross): Slip 2 sts to cn, hold to front, k2, k2 from cn.

OR — 2/2 RPC (2 over 2 right purl cross): Slip 2 sts to cn, hold to back, k2, p2 from cn.

OR — 2/2 LPC (2 over 2 left purl cross): Slip 2 sts to cn, hold to front, p2, k2 from cn.

Hexa Compact GROUP 7

I created Hexa Compact by compressing the hexagon motif of Hexa Grid (#128) until the outside edges overlapped, then changing the direction of some of the crosses.

(multiple of 24 sts + 16; 24-row repeat)
TOTAL SSE: 29 sts
REPEAT SSE: 15 sts

ROW 1 (WS): K6, p4, *[k2, p4]; repeat from * to last 6 sts, k6.

ROW 2: P6, 2/2 RC, *p2, [k4, p2] 3 times, 2/2 RC; repeat from * to last 6 sts, p6.

ROW 3 AND ALL FOLLOWING WS ROWS: Knit the knit sts and purl the purl sts as they face you.

ROW 4: P4, 2/2 RC, 2/2 LC, *[2/2 RC, p2] twice, [2/2 RC] twice, 2/2 LC; repeat from * to last 4 sts, p4.

ROW 6: P2, [2/2 RC] twice, *[2/2 LC] twice, k4, [2/2 RC] 3 times; repeat from * to last 6 sts, 2/2 LC, p2.

ROW 8: [2/2 RC] twice, *[2/2 LC] 3 times, [2/2 RC] 3 times; repeat from * to last 8 sts, [2/2 LC] twice.

ROW 10: K2, 2/2 RPC, k4, *2/2 LPC, [2/2 LC] twice, 2/2 RC, 2/2 RPC, k4; repeat from * to last 6 sts, 2/2 LPC, k2.

ROW 12: 2/2 LC, [p2, 2/2 LC] twice, *2/2 LPC, 2/2 RPC, 2/2 LC, [p2, 2/2 LC] twice; repeat from * to end.

ROW 14: K4, [p2, k4] twice, *p2, 2/2 LC, [p2, k4] 3 times; repeat from * to end.

ROW 16: 2/2 LC, [p2, 2/2 LC] twice, *2/2 RC, [2/2 LC] twice, [p2, 2/2 LC] twice; repeat from * to end.

ROW 18: K2, 2/2 LC, k4, *[2/2 RC] twice, [2/2 LC] 3 times, k4; repeat from * to last 6 sts, 2/2 RC, k2.

ROW 20: 2/2 LPC, 2/2 LC, *[2/2 RC] 3 times, [2/2 LC] 3 times; repeat from * to last 8 sts, 2/2 RC, 2/2 RPC.

ROW 22: P2, 2/2 LPC, 2/2 RC, *2/2 RC, 2/2 RPC, k4, 2/2 LPC, 2/2 LC, 2/2 RC; repeat from * to last 6 sts, 2/2 RPC, p2.

ROW 24: P4, 2/2 LPC, *2/2 RPC, 2/2 RC, [p2, 2/2 RC] twice, 2/2 LPC; repeat from * to last 8 sts, 2/2 RPC, p4.

Repeat Rows 1–24 for pattern.

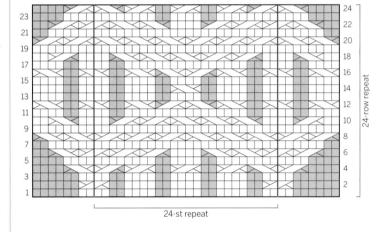

24-st repeat

24-row repeat

☐ Knit on RS, purl on WS.

▨ Purl on RS, knit on WS.

| Pattern repeat

⬳ OR ⬳ 2/2 RC (2 over 2 right cross): Slip 2 sts to cn, hold to back, k2, k2 from cn.

⬳ OR ⬳ 2/2 LC (2 over 2 left cross): Slip 2 sts to cn, hold to front, k2, k2 from cn.

⬳ 2/2 RPC (2 over 2 right purl cross): Slip 2 sts to cn, hold to back, k2, p2 from cn.

⬳ 2/2 LPC (2 over 2 left purl cross): Slip 2 sts to cn, hold to front, p2, k2 from cn.

Hexa Bead

GROUP 7

For Hexa Bead, I isolated the hexagon motif from Hexa Grid (#128) and stacked it to form a column. A few rows of stockinette between the last cross of one hexagon and the first cross of the next creates the illusion that the hexagons are a string of beads.

(multiple of 32 sts + 16; 28-row repeat)
TOTAL SSE: 30 sts
REPEAT SSE: 20 sts

ROW 1 (WS): K6, p4, k6, *[p4, k2] twice, [p4, k6] twice; repeat from * to end.

ROW 2: P6, 2/2 RC, p6, *2/2 LC, [p2, 2/2 LC] twice, p6, 2/2 RC, p6; repeat from * to end.

ROW 3 AND ALL FOLLOWING WS ROWS: Knit the knit sts and purl the purl sts as they face you.

ROW 4: P4, 2/2 RC, 2/2 LC, p4, *k2, 2/2 LC, k4, 2/2 RC, k2, p4, 2/2 RC, 2/2 LC, p4; repeat from * to end.

ROW 6: P2, [2/2 RC] twice, 2/2 LC, p2, *2/2 LPC, 2/2 LC, 2/2 RC, 2/2 RPC, p2, [2/2 RC] twice, 2/2 LC, p2; repeat from * to end.

ROW 8: [2/2 RC] twice, [2/2 LC] twice, *p2, 2/2 LPC, 2/2 RC, 2/2 RPC, p2, [2/2 RC] twice, [2/2 LC] twice; repeat from * to end.

ROW 10: K2, 2/2 RPC, k4, 2/2 LPC, k2, *p4, 2/2 LPC, 2/2 RPC, p4, k2, 2/2 RPC, k4, 2/2 LPC, k2; repeat from * to end.

ROW 12: 2/2 LC, [p2, 2/2 LC] twice, *p6, 2/2 RC, p6, 2/2 LC, [p2, 2/2 LC] twice; repeat from * to end.

ROW 14: Repeat Row 3.

ROW 16: Repeat Row 12.

ROW 18: K2, 2/2 LC, k4, 2/2 RC, k2, *p4, 2/2 RC, 2/2 LC, p4, k2, 2/2 LC, k4, 2/2 RC, k2; repeat from * to end.

ROW 20: 2/2 LPC, 2/2 LC, 2/2 RC, 2/2 RPC, *p2, [2/2 RC] twice, 2/2 LC, p2, 2/2 LPC, 2/2 LC, 2/2 RC, 2/2 RPC; repeat from * to end.

ROW 22: P2, 2/2 LPC, 2/2 RC, 2/2 RPC, p2, *[2/2 RC] twice, [2/2 LC] twice, p2, 2/2 LPC, 2/2 RC, 2/2 RPC, p2; repeat from * to end.

ROW 24: P4, 2/2 LPC, 2/2 RPC, p4, *k2, 2/2 RPC, k4, 2/2 LPC, k2, p4, 2/2 LPC, 2/2 RPC, p4; repeat from * to end.

ROW 26: Repeat Row 2.

ROW 28: Repeat Row 3.

Repeat Rows 1–28 for pattern.

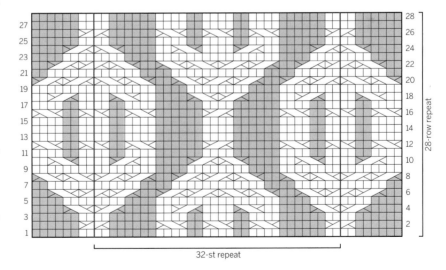

32-st repeat

□ Knit on RS, purl on WS.

▨ Purl on RS, knit on WS.

❙ Pattern repeat

2/2 RC (2 over 2 right cross): Slip 2 sts to cn, hold to back, k2, k2 from cn.

2/2 LC (2 over 2 left cross): Slip 2 sts to cn, hold to front, k2, k2 from cn.

2/2 RPC (2 over 2 right purl cross): Slip 2 sts to cn, hold to back, k2, p2 from cn.

2/2 LPC (2 over 2 left purl cross): Slip 2 sts to cn, hold to front, p2, k2 from cn.

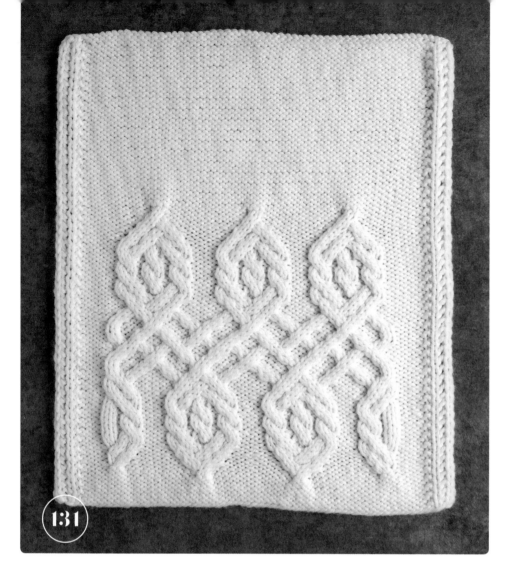

Hexa Frieze GROUP 7

Two rows of the hex motifs from Hexa Grid (#128) are set in alternating positions and joined with diagonal lines of 2/2 cables in Hexa Frieze. The diagonal lines form the illusion of lattice. Careful inspection of the chart reveals that the lines are not actually interwoven, nor do they meet up perfectly at each intersection. Placing the motifs closer together would have resulted in a "perfect" lattice, but I preferred the look of the original spacing.

(multiple of 15 sts + 14; increases to 20 sts + 20; decreases back to 15 sts + 14; 70-row repeat)
TOTAL SSE: 26 sts
REPEAT SSE: 14 sts

ROW 1 (WS): Knit.
ROW 2: Purl.
ROWS 3–6: Repeat Rows 1 and 2 twice.
ROW 7: K13, *p3, k12; repeat from * to last st, k1.
ROW 8: P13, *slip 1 st to cn, hold to back, k2, (yo, k1) from cn; p12; repeat from * to last st, p1—1 st increased per repeat.
ROW 9: P2, k5, *k6, p1, p1-tbl, p2, k6; repeat from * to last 7 sts, k5, p2.
ROW 10: Slip 2 sts to cn, hold to front, k1, yo, k2 from cn; p8, *2/2 RC, 2/2 LC, p8; repeat from * to last 3 sts; slip 1 st to cn, hold to back, k2, (yo, k1) from cn—2 sts increased outside of repeats.
ROW 11: P1, p1-tbl, p2, k8, *p8, k8; repeat from * to last 4 sts, p2, p1-tbl, p1.

ROW 12: K2; slip 2 sts to cn, hold to front, k1, yo, k2 from cn; p6, *slip 1 st to cn, hold to back, k2, (yo, k1) from cn; 2/2 RC; slip 2 sts to cn, hold to front, k1, yo, k2 from cn; p6; repeat from * to last 5 sts; slip 1 st to cn, hold to back, k2, (yo, k1) from cn; k2—2 sts increased per repeat; 2 sts increased outside of repeats.
ROW 13: P3, p1-tbl, p2, k6, *p2, p1-tbl, p6, p1-tbl, p2, k6; repeat from * to last 6 sts, p2, p1-tbl, p3.
ROW 14: 2/2 LC; slip 2 sts to cn, hold to front, k1, yo, k2 from cn; p4, *slip 1 st to cn, hold to back, k2, (yo, k1) from cn; 2/2 RC, 2/2 LC; slip 2 sts to cn, hold to front, k1, yo, k2 from cn; p4; repeat from * to last 7 sts; slip 1 st to cn, hold to back, k2, (yo, k1) from cn; 2/2 RC—2 sts increased per repeat; 2 sts increased outside of repeats.
ROW 15: P5, p1-tbl, p2, k4, *p2, p1-tbl, p10, p1-tbl, p2, k4; repeat from * to last 8 sts, p2, p1-tbl, p5.
ROW 16: K2, 2/2 LPC, k2, p4, *k2, 2/2 RPC, k4, 2/2 LPC, k2, p4; repeat from * to last 8 sts, k2, 2/2 RPC, k2.
ROW 17 AND ALL FOLLOWING WS ROWS: Knit the knit sts and purl the purl sts as they face you.
ROW 18: K2, p2, 2/2 LC, p4, *[2/2 LC, p2] twice, 2/2 LC, p4; repeat from * to last 8 sts, 2/2 LC, p2, k2.
ROW 20: Repeat Row 17.
ROW 22: Repeat Row 18.
ROW 24: K2, 2/2 RC, k2, p4, *k2, 2/2 LC, k4, 2/2 RC, k2, p4; repeat from * to last 8 sts, k2, 2/2 LC, k2.
ROW 26: 2/2 RC, 2/2 RPC, p4, *2/2 LPC, 2/2 LC, 2/2 RC, 2/2 RPC, p4; repeat from * to last 8 sts, 2/2 LPC, 2/2 LC.
ROW 28: K2, 2/2 RC, p8, *2/2 LC, [2/2 RC] twice, p8; repeat from * to last 6 sts, 2/2 LC, k2.
ROW 30: *2/2 RPC, 2/2 LPC, p4, 2/2 RPC, 2/2 LPC; repeat from * to end.
ROW 32: K2, p4, 2/2 LPC, 2/2 RPC, p4, *2/2 RC, p4, 2/2 LPC, 2/2 RPC, p4; repeat from * to last 2 sts, k2.
ROW 34: *2/2 LPC, p4, 2/2 RC, p4, 2/2 RPC; repeat from * to end.
ROW 36: *P2, 2/2 LC, 2/2 RPC, 2/2 LPC, 2/2 RC, p2; repeat from * to end.
ROW 38: Repeat Row 30.
ROW 40: Repeat Row 32.
ROW 42: Repeat Row 34.

ROW 44: *P2, 2/2 LPC, 2/2 RC, 2/2 LC, 2/2 RPC, p2; repeat from * to end.

ROW 46: *P4, [2/2 RC] twice, 2/2 LC, p4; repeat from * to end.

ROW 48: *P2, [2/2 RC] twice, [2/2 LC] twice, p2; repeat from * to end.

ROW 50: *P2, k2, 2/2 RPC, k4, 2/2 LPC, k2, p2; repeat from * to end.

ROW 52: *P2, [2/2 LC, p2] 3 times; repeat from * to end.

ROW 54: Repeat Row 17.

ROW 56: Repeat Row 52.

ROW 58: *P2, k2, 2/2 LC, k4, 2/2 RC, k2, p2; repeat from * to end.

ROW 60: *P2; slip 2 sts to cn, hold to front, p2tog, k2 from cn; 2/2 LC, 2/2 RC; slip 2 sts to cn, hold to back, k2, p2tog from cn; p2; repeat from * to end—2 sts decreased per repeat; 2 sts decreased outside of repeats.

ROW 62: *P3; slip 2 sts to cn, hold to front, p2tog, k2 from cn; 2/2 RC; slip 2 sts to cn, hold to back, k2, p2tog from cn; p3; repeat from * to end—2 sts decreased per repeat; 2 sts decreased outside of repeats.

ROW 64: P4; slip 2 sts to cn, hold to front, p2tog, k2 from cn; *2/2 RPC, p8, 2/2 LPC; repeat from * to last 8 sts, 2/2 RPC, p4—1 st decreased outside of repeats.

ROW 66: P5; *slip 2 sts to cn, hold to back, k2, ssk from cn; p12; repeat from * to last 10 sts; slip 2 sts to cn, hold to back, k2, ssk from cn, p6—1 st decreased per repeat, 1 st decreased outside of repeats.

ROWS 68 AND 70: Purl.

Repeat Rows 1–70 for pattern.

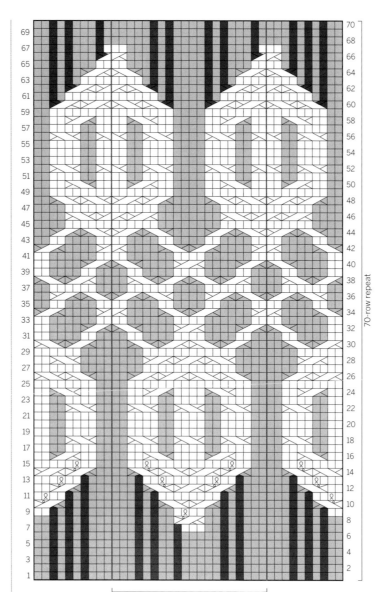

15-st repeat; increases to 20 sts; decreases back to 15 sts

70-row repeat

NOTE: No-st columns will shift when going from Row 70 to Row 1, but sts will still line up correctly.

☐ Knit on RS, purl on WS. ▨ Purl on RS, knit on WS. ■ No stitch.

Ⓠ K1-tbl on RS, p1-tbl on WS.

| Pattern Repeat.

OR 2/2 RC (2 over 2 right cross): Slip 2 sts to cn, hold to back, k2, k2 from cn.

OR 2/2 LC (2 over 2 left cross): Slip 2 sts to cn, hold to front, k2, k2 from cn.

OR 2/2 RPC (2 over 2 right purl cross): Slip 2 sts to cn, hold to back, k2, p2 from cn.

OR 2/2 LPC (2 over 2 left purl cross): Slip 2 sts to cn, hold to front, p2, k2 from cn.

OR Slip 1 st to cn, hold to back, k2, (yo, k1) from cn—1 st increased.

Slip 2 sts to cn, hold to front, k1, yo, k2 from cn—1 st increased.

Slip 2 sts to cn, hold to back, k2, p2tog from cn—1 st decreased.

Slip 2 sts to cn, hold to front, p2tog, k2 from cn—1 st decreased.

Slip 2 sts to cn, hold to back, k2, ssk from cn—1 st decreased.

Hexa Paisley GROUP 7

I added paisley tails to the hexagon shapes from Hexa Grid (#128) to make Hexa Paisley.

ORIGINAL VERSION (CENTER)
(panel of 16 sts; 80-row repeat)
SSE: 10 sts

ROW 1 (WS): K6, p4, k6.
ROW 2: P4, 2/2 RC, k2, p6.
ROW 3 AND ALL FOLLOWING WS ROWS: Knit the knit sts and purl the purl sts as they face you.
ROW 4: P2, 2/2 RC, 2/2 LC, p6.
ROW 6: 2/2 RC, [2/2 LC] twice, p4.
ROW 8: K2, 2/2 RPC, [2/2 LC] twice, p2.
ROW 10: 2/2 LPC, p2, k2, 2/2 LPC, 2/2 LC.
ROW 12: P6, k2, p2, 2/2 LPC, k2.
ROW 14: P6, k2, p4, 2/2 LC.
ROW 16: P6, 2/2 LC, p2, k4.
ROW 18: P4, 2/2 RC, [2/2 LC] twice.

ROW 20: P2, 2/2 RC, [2/2 LC] twice, k2.
ROW 22: [2/2 RC] twice, [2/2 LC] twice.
ROW 24: K2, 2/2 RPC, k4, 2/2 LPC, k2.
ROW 26: 2/2 RC, [p2, 2/2 RC] twice.
ROW 28: Repeat Row 3.
ROW 30: Repeat Row 26.
ROW 32: K2, 2/2 LC, k4, 2/2 RC, k2.
ROW 34: 2/2 LPC, 2/2 LC, 2/2 RC, 2/2 RPC.
ROW 36: P2, 2/2 LPC, 2/2 LC, 2/2 RPC, p2.
ROW 38: P4, 2/2 LPC, 2/2 RPC, p4.
ROW 40: P6, 2/2 RC, p6.
ROW 42: P6, k2, 2/2 LC, p4.

ROW 44: P6, 2/2 RC, 2/2 LC, p2.
ROW 46: P4, [2/2 RC] twice, 2/2 LC.
ROW 48: P2, [2/2 RC] twice, 2/2 LPC, k2.
ROW 50: 2/2 RC, 2/2 RPC, k2, p2, 2/2 RPC.
ROW 52: K2, 2/2 RPC, p2, k2, p6.
ROW 54: 2/2 RC, p4, k2, p6.
ROW 56: K4, p2, 2/2 RC, p6.
ROW 58: [2/2 RC] twice, 2/2 LC, p4.
ROW 60: K2, [2/2 RC] twice, 2/2 LC, p2.
ROW 62: [2/2 RC] twice, [2/2 LC] twice.
ROW 64: K2, 2/2 RPC, k4, 2/2 LPC, k2.
ROW 66: 2/2 LC, [p2, 2/2 LC] twice.
ROW 68: Repeat Row 3.
ROW 70: Repeat Row 66.
ROW 72: K2, 2/2 LC, k4, 2/2 RC, k2.
ROW 74: 2/2 LPC, 2/2 LC, 2/2 RC, 2/2 RPC.
ROW 76: P2, 2/2 LPC, 2/2 RC, 2/2 RPC, p2.
ROW 78: P4, 2/2 LPC, 2/2 RPC, p4.
ROW 80: P6, 2/2 LC, p6.
Repeat Rows 1–80 for pattern.

HALF-DROP VERSION (LEFT AND RIGHT)
(panel of 16 sts; 80-row repeat)
SSE: 10 sts

ROW 1 (WS): K4, p12.
ROW 2: K2, [2/2 RC] twice, 2/2 LC, p2.
ROW 3 AND ALL FOLLOWING WS ROWS: Knit the knit sts and purl the purl sts as they face you.
ROW 4: [2/2 RC] twice, [2/2 LC] twice.
ROW 6: K2, 2/2 RPC, k4, 2/2 LPC, k2.
ROW 8: 2/2 LC, [p2, 2/2 LC] twice.
ROW 10: Repeat Row 3.
ROW 12: Repeat Row 8.
ROW 14: K2, 2/2 LC, k4, 2/2 RC, k2.
ROW 16: 2/2 LPC, 2/2 LC, 2/2 RC, 2/2 RPC.
ROW 18: P2, 2/2 LPC, 2/2 RC, 2/2 RPC, p2.
ROW 20: P4, 2/2 LPC, 2/2 RPC, p4.
ROW 22: P6, 2/2 LC, p6.
ROW 24: P4, 2/2 RC, k2, p6.
ROW 26: P2, 2/2 RC, 2/2 LC, p6.
ROW 28: 2/2 RC, [2/2 LC] twice, p4.
ROW 30: K2, 2/2 RPC, [2/2 LC] twice, p2.
ROW 32: 2/2 LPC, p2, k2, 2/2 LPC, 2/2 LC.
ROW 34: P6, k2, p2, 2/2 LPC, k2.
ROW 36: P6, k2, p4, 2/2 LC.

ROW 38: P6, 2/2 LC, p2, k4.

ROW 40: P4, 2/2 RC, [2/2 LC] twice.

ROW 42: P2, 2/2 RC, [2/2 LC] twice, k2.

ROW 44: [2/2 RC] twice, [2/2 LC] twice.

ROW 46: K2, 2/2 RPC, k4, 2/2 LPC, k2.

ROW 48: 2/2 RC, [p2, 2/2 RC] twice.

ROW 50: Repeat Row 3.

ROW 52: Repeat Row 48.

ROW 54: K2, 2/2 LC, k4, 2/2 RC, k2.

ROW 56: 2/2 LPC, 2/2 LC, 2/2 RC, 2/2 RPC.

ROW 58: P2, 2/2 LPC, 2/2 LC, 2/2 RPC, p2.

ROW 60: P4, 2/2 LPC, 2/2 RPC, p4.

ROW 62: P6, 2/2 RC, p6.

ROW 64: P6, k2, 2/2 LC, p4.

ROW 66: P6, 2/2 RC, 2/2 LC, p2.

ROW 68: P4, [2/2 RC] twice, 2/2 LC.

ROW 70: P2, [2/2 RC] twice, 2/2 LPC, k2.

ROW 72: 2/2 RC, 2/2 RPC, k2, p2, 2/2 RPC.

ROW 74: K2, 2/2 RPC, p2, k2, p6.

ROW 76: 2/2 RC, p4, k2, p6.

ROW 78: K4, p2, 2/2 RC, p6.

ROW 80: [2/2 RC] twice, 2/2 LC, p4.

Repeat Rows 1–80 for pattern.

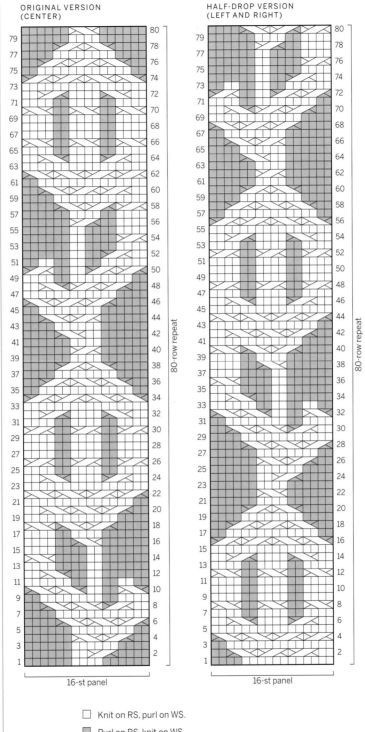

ORIGINAL VERSION (CENTER)

HALF-DROP VERSION (LEFT AND RIGHT)

80-row repeat

16-st panel

☐ Knit on RS, purl on WS.

▨ Purl on RS, knit on WS.

│ Pattern repeat

OR 2/2 RC (2 over 2 right cross): Slip 2 sts to cn, hold to back, k2, k2 from cn.

OR 2/2 LC (2 over 2 left cross): Slip 2 sts to cn, hold to front, k2, k2 from cn.

2/2 RPC (2 over 2 right purl cross): Slip 2 sts to cn, hold to back, k2, p2 from cn.

2/2 LPC (2 over 2 left purl cross): Slip 2 sts to cn, hold to front, p2, k2 from cn.

Hexa Butterfly GROUP 7

By removing the curlicue from the base of a Hexa Paisley (#132) motif and making a few other minor changes, I created a butterfly wing. By mirror-imaging the wing around a line of twisted rib and tiny knots, I created the full butterfly form of Hexa Butterfly.

(panel of 25 sts; increases to 35 sts; decreases back to 25 sts; 46-row repeat)

SSE: 22.5 sts

ROW 1 (WS): Knit.

ROW 2: Purl.

ROWS 3 AND 4: Repeat Rows 1 and 2.

ROW 5: K2, p3, k15, p3, k2.

ROW 6: P2; slip 2 sts to cn, hold to front, k1, yo, k2 from cn; p15; slip 1 st to cn, hold to back, k2, (yo, k1) from cn; p2—27 sts.

ROW 7: K2, p1, p1-tbl, p2, k15, p2, p1-tbl, p1, k2.

ROW 8: P1; slip 1 st to cn, hold to back, k2, (yo, k1) from cn; 2/2 LC, p11, 2/2 RC; slip 2 sts to cn, hold to front, k1, yo, k2 from cn; p1—29 sts.

ROW 9: K1, p2, p1-tbl, p5, k11, p5, p1-tbl, p2, k1.

ROW 10: Slip 1 st to cn, hold to back, k2, (yo, k1) from cn; 2/2 LC; slip 2 sts to cn, hold to front, k1, yo, k2 from cn; p4, k1-tbl, p4; slip 1 st to cn, hold to back, k2, (yo, k1) from cn; 2/2 RC; slip 2 sts to cn, hold to front, k1, yo, k2 from cn—33 sts.

ROW 11: P2, p1-tbl, p6, p1-tbl, p2, k4, p1-tbl, k4, p2, p1-tbl, p6, p1-tbl, p2.

ROW 12: K2, 2/2 RC, [2/2 LC] twice, p2, k1-tbl, p2, [2/2 RC] twice, 2/2 LC, k2.

ROW 13: P14, k2, p1-tbl, k2, p14.

ROW 14: 2/2 LPC, k4, 2/2 LC; slip 2 sts to cn, hold to front, k1, yo, k2 from cn; p1, k1-tbl, p1; slip 1 st to cn, hold to back, k2, (yo, k1) from cn; 2/2 RC, k4, 2/2 RPC—35 sts.

ROW 15: K2, p11, p1-tbl, p2, k1, p1-tbl, k1, p2, p1-tbl, p11, k2.

ROW 16: P2, 2/2 LPC, 2/2 LC, 2/2 LPC, k2, p1, k1-tbl, p1, k2, 2/2 RPC, 2/2 RC, 2/2 RPC, p2.

ROW 17: K4, p6, k2, p4, k1, p1-tbl, k1, p4, k2, p6, k4.

ROW 18: P4, 2/2 LPC, k2, p2, 2/2 LC, p1, k1-tbl, p1, 2/2 RC, p2, k2, 2/2 RPC, p4.

ROW 19: K6, p4, k2, p4, k1, p1-tbl, k1, p4, k2, p4, k6.

ROW 20: P6, 2/2 LC, p2, k4, p1, k1-tbl, p1, k4, p2, 2/2 RC, p6.

ROW 21: K6, p4, k2, p4, k1, p1-tbl, k1, p4, k2, p4, k6.

ROW 22: P4, 2/2 RC, 2/2 LC, 2/2 RC, p1, k1-tbl, p1, 2/2 LC, 2/2 RC, 2/2 LC, p4.

ROW 23: K4, p12, k1, p1-tbl, k1, p12, k4.

ROW 24: P2, 2/2 RC, [2/2 LC] twice, k2, p1, k1-tbl, p1, k2, [2/2 RC] twice, 2/2 LC, p2.

ROW 25: K2, p14, k1, p1-tbl, k1, p14, k2.

ROW 26: [2/2 RC] twice, [2/2 LC] twice, p1, k1-tbl, p1, [2/2 RC] twice, [2/2 LC] twice.

ROW 27: P16, k1, p1-tbl, k1, p16.

ROW 28: K2, 2/2 RPC, k4, 2/2 LPC, k2, p1, k1-tbl, p1, k2, 2/2 RPC, k4, 2/2 LPC, k2.

ROW 29: P4, [k2, p4] twice, k1, p1-tbl, k1, p4, [k2, p4] twice.

ROW 30: [2/2 RC, p2] twice, 2/2 LC, p1, k1-tbl, p1, 2/2 RC, [p2, 2/2 LC] twice.

ROW 31: Repeat Row 29.

ROW 32: K4, [p2, k4] twice, p1, k1-tbl, p1, k4, [p2, k4] twice.

ROWS 33 AND 34: Repeat Rows 29 and 30.

ROW 35: Repeat Row 29.

ROW 36: K2, 2/2 LC, k4, 2/2 RC, k2, p1, k1-tbl, p1, k2, 2/2 LC, k4, 2/2 RC, k2.

ROW 37: Repeat Row 27.

ROW 38: Slip 2 sts to cn, hold to front, p2tog, k2 from cn; 2/2 LC, 2/2 RC; slip 2 sts to cn, hold to back, k2, p2tog from cn; p1, k1-tbl, p1; slip 2 sts to cn, hold to front, p2tog, k2 from cn; 2/2 LC, 2/2 RC; slip 2 sts to cn, hold to back, k2, p2tog from cn—31 sts remain.

ROW 39: K1, p12, k2, p1-tbl, k2, p12, k1.

ROW 40: P1; slip 2 sts to cn, hold to front, p2tog, k2 from cn; 2/2 LC, 2/2 RPC, p5, 2/2 LPC, 2/2 RC; slip 2 sts to cn, hold to back, k2, p2tog from cn; p1—29 sts remain.

ROW 41: K2, p8, k9, p8, k2.

ROW 42: P2, 2/2 LPC; slip 2 sts to cn, hold to back, k2, p2tog from cn; p2, MK, p3, MK, p2; slip 2 sts to cn, hold to front, p2tog, k2 from cn; 2/2 RPC, p2—27 sts remain.

ROW 43: K4, p4, k11, p4, k4.

ROW 44: P4; slip 2 sts to cn, hold to front, k2tog, k2 from cn; p11; slip 2 sts to cn, hold to back, k2, k2tog from cn; p4—25 sts remain.

ROW 45: K4, p3, k11, p3, k4.

ROW 46: Purl.

Repeat Rows 1–46 for pattern.

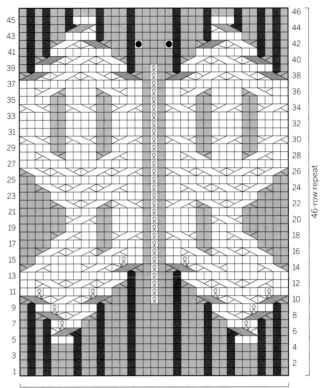

25-st panel; increases to 35 sts; decreases back to 25 sts

NOTE: No-st columns will shift when going from Row 46 to Row 1, but sts will still line up correctly.

☐ Knit on RS, purl on WS.

▨ Purl on RS, knit on WS.

⧜ K1-tbl on RS, p1-tbl on WS.

● MK (make knot): Knit into front, back, then front of st, slip these 3 sts back to left needle and k3; pass third, then second sts over first.

■ No stitch

OR 2/2 RC (2 over 2 right cross): Slip 2 sts to cn, hold to back, k2, k2 from cn.

OR 2/2 LC (2 over 2 left cross): Slip 2 sts to cn, hold to front, k2, k2 from cn.

2/2 RPC (2 over 2 right purl cross): Slip 2 sts to cn, hold to back, k2, p2 from cn.

2/2 LPC (2 over 2 left purl cross): Slip 2 sts to cn, hold to front, p2, k2 from cn.

OR Slip 1 st to cn, hold to back, k2, (yo, k1) from cn—1 st increased.

OR Slip 2 sts to cn, hold to front, k1, yo, k2 from cn—1 st increased.

Slip 2 sts to cn, hold to back, k2, p2tog from cn—1 st decreased.

Slip 2 sts to cn, hold to front, p2tog, k2 from cn—1 st decreased.

Slip 2 sts to cn, hold to front, k2tog, k2 from cn.

Slip 2 sts to cn, hold to back, k2, k2tog from cn—1 st decreased.

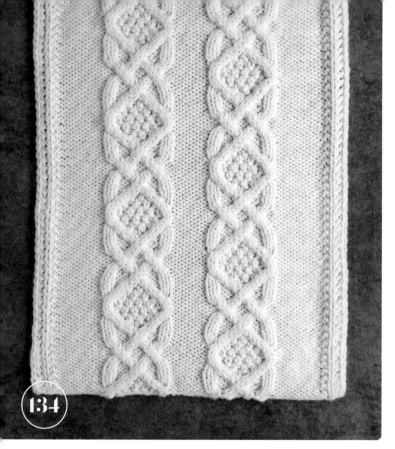

134

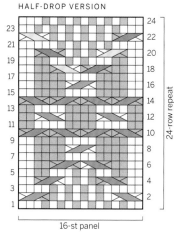

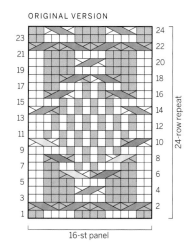

16-st panel   16-st panel

☐ Knit on RS, purl on WS.

▦ Purl on RS, knit on WS.

⬚⬚ OR ⬚⬚ 2/2 RC (2 over 2 right cross): Slip 2 sts to cn, hold to back, k2, k2 from cn.

⬚⬚ OR ⬚⬚ 2/2 LC (2 over 2 left cross): Slip 2 sts to cn, hold to front, k2, k2 from cn.

⬚⬚ OR ⬚⬚ OR ⬚⬚ 2/2 RPC (2 over 2 right purl cross): Slip 2 sts to cn, hold to back, k2, p2 from cn.

⬚⬚ OR ⬚⬚ OR ⬚⬚ 2/2 LPC (2 over 2 left purl cross): Slip 2 sts to cn, hold to front, p2, k2 from cn.

⬚⬚ OR ⬚⬚ Slip 2 sts to cn, hold to back, k2, (k1, p1) from cn.

⬚⬚ Slip 2 sts to cn, hold to front, p1, k1, k2 from cn.

⬚⬚ Slip 2 sts to cn, hold to back, k2, (p1, k1) from cn.

⬚⬚ OR ⬚⬚ Slip 2 sts to cn, hold to front, k1, p1, k2 from cn.

Moss X GROUP 8

The large X motif isolated from Hexa Grid (#128) is stacked up to form a column of Xs in Moss X. The adjacent columns would be identical except they start at different points in the pattern, which staggers them. Moss stitch fills the void between the stacked Xs, adding a solidity to each column.

ORIGINAL VERSION (RIGHT)
(panel of 16 sts; 24-row repeat)
SSE: 11 sts

ROW 1 (WS): K2, p4, k4, p4, k2.
ROW 2: [2/2 RPC, 2/2 LPC] twice.
ROW 3 AND ALL FOLLOWING WS ROWS: Knit the knit sts and purl the purl sts as they face you.
ROW 4: K2, p4, 2/2 RC, p4, k2.
ROW 6: K2, p2; slip 2 sts to cn, hold to back, k2, (k1, p1) from cn; slip 2 sts to cn, hold to front, k1, p1, k2 from cn; p2, k2.
ROW 8: K2; slip 2 sts to cn, hold to back, k2, (p1, k1) from cn; [p1, k1] twice; slip 2 sts to cn, hold to front, p1, k1, k2 from cn; k2.
ROW 10: Slip 2 sts to cn, hold to back, k2, (k1, p1) from cn; [k1, p1] 4 times; slip 2 sts to cn, hold to front, k1, p1, k2 from cn.
ROW 12: K2, [p1, k1] 5 times, p1, k3.
ROW 14: 2/2 LC, [k1, p1] 4 times, 2/2 RC.

ROW 16: K2, 2/2 LPC, [p1, k1] twice, 2/2 RPC, k2.
ROW 18: K2, p2, 2/2 LPC, 2/2 RPC, p2, k2.
ROW 20: K2, p4, 2/2 RC, p4, k2.
ROW 22: [2/2 LPC, 2/2 RPC] twice.
ROW 24: P2, 2/2 LC, p4, 2/2 LC, p2.
Repeat Rows 1–24 for pattern.

HALF-DROP VERSION (LEFT)
(panel of 16 sts; 24-row repeat)
SSE: 16 sts

ROW 1 (WS): P3, [k1, p1] 5 times, k1, p2.
ROW 2: 2/2 LC, [k1, p1] 4 times, 2/2 RC.
ROW 3 AND ALL FOLLOWING WS ROWS: Knit the knit sts and purl the purl sts as they face you.
ROW 4: K2, 2/2 LPC, [p1, k1] twice, 2/2 RPC, k2.
ROW 6: K2, p2, 2/2 LPC, 2/2 RPC, p2, k2.

ROW 8: K2, p4, 2/2 RC, p4, k2.
ROW 10: [2/2 LPC, 2/2 RPC] twice.
ROW 12: P2, 2/2 LC, p4, 2/2 LC, p2.
ROW 14: [2/2 RPC, 2/2 LPC] twice.
ROW 16: K2, p4, 2/2 RC, p4, k2.
ROW 18: K2, p2; slip 2 sts to cn, hold to back, k2, (k1, p1) from cn; slip 2 sts to cn, hold to front, k1, p1, k2 from cn; p2, k2.
ROW 20: K2; slip 2 sts to cn, hold to back, k2, (p1, k1) from cn; [p1, k1] twice; slip 2 sts to cn, hold to front, p1, k1, k2 from cn; k2.
ROW 22: Slip 2 sts to cn, hold to back, k2, (k1, p1) from cn; [k1, p1] 4 times; slip 2 sts to cn, hold to front, k1, p1, k2 from cn.
ROW 24: K2, [p1, k1] 5 times, p1, k3.
Repeat Rows 1–24 for pattern.

Rearranging Xs

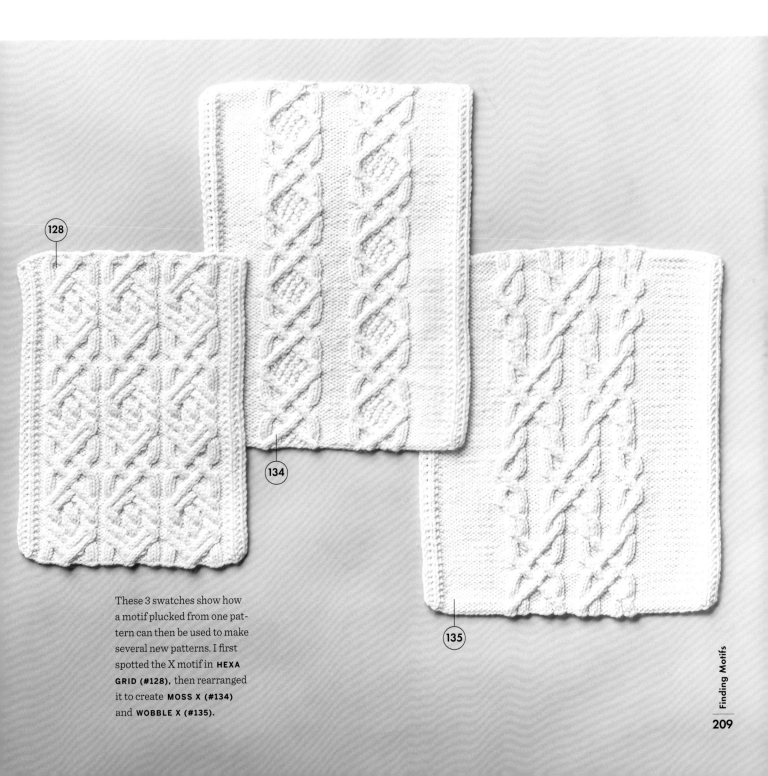

These 3 swatches show how a motif plucked from one pattern can then be used to make several new patterns. I first spotted the X motif in **HEXA GRID (#128)**, then rearranged it to create **MOSS X (#134)** and **WOBBLE X (#135)**.

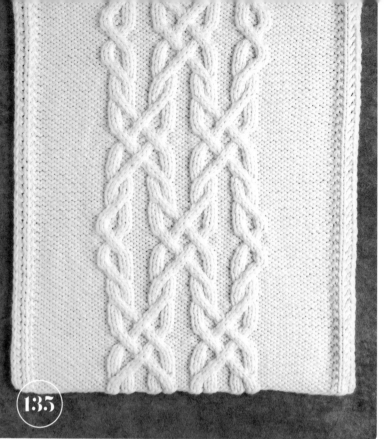

48-row repeat

20-st repeat

Wobble X GROUP 8

While the Xs in Moss X (#134) are stacked one on top of the other, the Xs in Wobble X are joined diagonally with Fave.

(multiple of 20 sts + 20; 48-row repeat)

TOTAL SSE: 26 sts

REPEAT SSE: 14.5 sts

ROW 1 (WS): *K2, [p2, k2] twice; repeat from * to end.

ROW 2: Knit the knit sts and purl the purl sts as they face you.

ROW 3 AND ALL FOLLOWING WS ROWS: Repeat Row 2.

ROW 4: *P2, 2/2 LC, k2, p4, k2, 2/2 RC, p2; repeat from * to end.

ROW 6: *P2, k2, 2/2 LPC, p4, 2/2 RPC, k2, p2; repeat from * to end.

ROW 8: *P2, k2, p2, 2/2 LPC, 2/2 RPC, p2, k2, p2; repeat from * to end.

ROW 10: *P2, k2, p4, 2/2 RC, p4, k2, p2; repeat from * to end.

ROW 12: *P2, [2/2 LPC, 2/2 RPC] twice, p2; repeat from * to end.

ROW 14: *P4, [2/2 LC, p4] twice; repeat from * to end.

ROW 16: *P2, [2/2 RPC, 2/2 LPC] twice, p2; repeat from * to end.

ROW 18: Repeat Row 10.

ROW 20: *P2, k2, p2, 2/2 RPC, 2/2 LPC, p2, k2, p2; repeat from * to end.

ROW 22: *P2, k2, 2/2 RC, p4, 2/2 LC, k2, p2; repeat from * to end.

ROW 24: *P2, 2/2 RPC, k2, p4, k2, 2/2 LPC, p2; repeat from * to end.

ROW 26: Repeat Row 2.

ROW 28: Repeat Row 22.

ROW 30: Repeat Row 24.

ROW 32: *2/2 RPC, p2, k2, p4, k2, p2, 2/2 LPC; repeat from * to end.

ROW 34: [K2, p4] 3 times, *2/2 RC, p4, [k2, p4] twice; repeat from * to last 2 sts, k2.

ROW 36: *2/2 LPC, 2/2 RPC, p4, 2/2 LPC, 2/2 RPC; repeat from * to end.

ROW 38: *P2, 2/2 LC, p8, 2/2 LC, p2; repeat from * to end.

ROW 40: *2/2 RPC, 2/2 LPC, p4, 2/2 RPC, 2/2 LPC; repeat from * to end.

ROW 42: Repeat Row 34.

ROW 44: *2/2 LPC, p2, k2, p4, k2, p2, 2/2 RPC; repeat from * to end.

ROW 46: *P2, 2/2 LC, k2, p4, k2, 2/2 RC, p2; repeat from * to end.

ROW 48: *P2, k2, 2/2 LPC, p4, 2/2 RPC, k2, p2; repeat from * to end.

Repeat Rows 1–48 for pattern.

☐ Knit on RS, purl on WS.

▨ Purl on RS, knit on WS.

❘ Pattern repeat

⬨ OR ⬨ 2/2 RC (2 over 2 right cross): Slip 2 sts to cn, hold to back, k2, k2 from cn.

⬨ OR ⬨ 2/2 LC (2 over 2 left cross): Slip 2 sts to cn, hold to front, k2, k2 from cn.

⬨ OR ⬨ 2/2 RPC (2 over 2 right purl cross): Slip 2 sts to cn, hold to back, k2, p2 from cn.

⬨ OR ⬨ 2/2 LPC (2 over 2 left purl cross): Slip 2 sts to cn, hold to front, p2, k2 from cn.

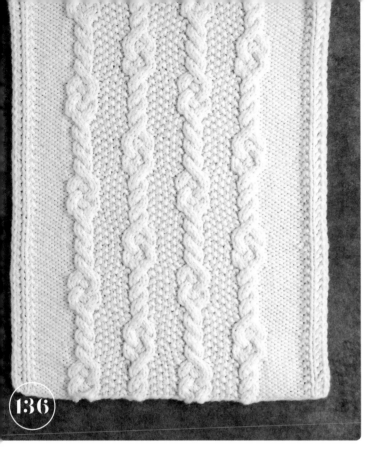

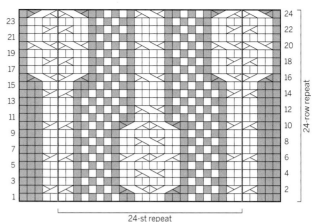

☐ Knit on RS, purl on WS.

▨ Purl on RS, knit on WS.

Ⅰ Pattern repeat

◩◪ OR ◩◪ 2/2 RC (2 over 2 right cross): Slip 2 sts to cn, hold to back, k2, k2 from cn.

◪◩ OR ◪◩ 2/2 LC (2 over 2 left cross): Slip 2 sts to cn, hold to front, k2, k2 from cn.

◩◪ 2/2 RPC (2 over 2 right purl cross): Slip 2 sts to cn, hold to back, k2, p2 from cn.

◪◩ 2/2 LPC (2 over 2 left purl cross): Slip 2 sts to cn, hold to front, p2, k2 from cn.

Knots GROUP 9

Here tightly braided cables look like knots in a rope. To create this panel, I staggered 4 knotted ropes on a seed-stitch ground.

(multiple of 24 sts + 10; 24-row repeat)

TOTAL SSE: 22.5 sts

REPEAT SSE: 16 sts

ROW 1 (WS): K3, p4, *[k1, p1] 3 times, k2, p4, k3, p1, k1, p1, k2, p4; repeat from * to last 3 sts, k3.

ROW 2: P3, 2/2 RC, *[p1, k1] twice, p2, 2/2 RC, 2/2 LC, [p1, k1] twice, p2, 2/2 RC; repeat from * to last 3 sts, p3.

ROW 3: K3, p4, *[k1, p1] twice, k2, p8, [k1, p1] twice, k2, p4; repeat from * to last 3 sts, k3.

ROW 4: P3, k4, *[p1, k1] twice, p2, k2, 2/2 LC, k2, [p1, k1] twice, p2, k4; repeat from * to last 3 sts, p3.

ROW 5: Repeat Row 3.

ROW 6: P3, 2/2 RC, *[p1, k1] twice, p2, [2/2 RC] twice, [p1, k1] twice, p2, 2/2 RC; repeat from * to last 3 sts, p3.

ROWS 7 AND 8: Repeat Rows 3 and 4.

ROW 9: Repeat Row 3.

ROW 10: P3, 2/2 RC, *[p1, k1] twice, p2, 2/2 LPC, 2/2 RPC, [p1, k1] twice, p2, 2/2 RC; repeat from * to last 3 sts, p3.

ROW 11: K3, p4, *[k1, p1] 3 times, k2, p4, [k1, p1] 3 times, k2, p4; repeat from * to last 3 sts, k3.

ROW 12: P3, k4, *[p1, k1] 3 times, p2, 2/2 LC, [p1, k1] 3 times, p2, k4; repeat from * to last 3 sts, p3.

ROW 13: Repeat Row 11.

ROW 14: P3, 2/2 RC, *[p1, k1] 3 times, p2, k4, [p1, k1] 3 times, p2, 2/2 RC; repeat from * to last 3 sts, p3.

ROW 15: K3, p4, k3, *p1, k1, p1, k2, p4, [k1, p1] 3 times, k2, p4, k3; repeat from * to end.

ROW 16: P1, 2/2 RC, 2/2 LC, *[p1, k1] twice, p2, 2/2 LC, [p1, k1] twice, p2, 2/2 RC, 2/2 LC; repeat from * to last st, k1.

ROW 17: K1, p8, *[k1, p1] twice, k2, p4, [k1, p1] twice, k2, p8; repeat from * to last st, k1.

ROW 18: P1, k2, 2/2 RC, k2, *[p1, k1] twice, p2, k4, [p1, k1] twice, p2, k2, 2/2 RC, k2; repeat from * to last st, p1.

ROW 19: Repeat Row 17.

ROW 20: P1, [2/2 LC] twice, *[p1, k1] twice, p2, 2/2 LC, [p1, k1] twice, p2, [2/2 LC] twice; repeat from * to last st, k1.

ROWS 21 AND 22: Repeat Rows 17 and 18.

ROW 23: Repeat Row 17.

ROW 24: P1, 2/2 LPC, 2/2 RPC, *[p1, k1] twice, p2, 2/2 LC, [p1, k1] twice, p2, 2/2 LPC, 2/2 RPC; repeat from * to last st, k1.

Repeat Rows 1–24 for pattern.

137

X Knot Evolution

This swatch shows 3 related cable patterns side by side so you can see how one idea leads to the next. On the left, knotted center X shapes are stacked. In the center column, the same X shapes are moved farther apart, then joined with 2/2 rope cables. On the right, the rope has been cut in the center, the motifs separated further, and a new combination of rib and cables is inserted to reunite the elements into a column.

LEFT

(panel of 12 sts; 14-row repeat
SSE: 7.5 sts

ROW 1 (WS): P4, k4, p4.
ROW 2: 2/2 LC, p4, 2/2 LC.
ROW 3 AND ALL FOLLOWING WS ROWS: Knit the knit sts and purl the purl sts as they face you.
ROW 4: K2, 2/2 LC, 2/2 RC, k2.
ROW 6: 2/2 LPC, 2/2 RC, 2/2 RPC.
ROW 8: P2, [2/2 LC] twice, p2.
ROW 10: [2/2 RC] twice, 2/2 LC.
ROW 12: K2, 2/2 RPC, 2/2 LPC, k2.
ROW 14: Repeat Row 2.
Repeat Rows 1–14 for pattern.

CENTER

(panel of 12 sts; 20-row repeat)
SSE: 8 sts

ROW 1 (WS): P4, k4, p4.
ROW 2: 2/2 LC, p4, 2/2 LC.
ROW 3 AND ALL FOLLOWING WS ROWS: Knit the knit sts and purl the purl sts as they face you.
ROW 4: Repeat Row 3.
ROW 6: Repeat Row 2.
ROW 8: K2, 2/2 LC, 2/2 RC, k2.
ROW 10: 2/2 LPC, 2/2 RC, 2/2 RPC.
ROW 12: P2, [2/2 LC] twice, p2.
ROW 14: [2/2 RC] twice, 2/2 LC.
ROW 16: K2, 2/2 RPC, 2/2 LPC, k2.
ROW 18: Repeat Row 2.
ROW 20: Repeat Row 3.
Repeat Rows 1–20 for pattern.

RIGHT

(panel of 16 sts; 36-row repeat)
SSE: 11 sts

ROW 1 (WS): P2, k4, p4, k4, p2.
ROW 2: K2, p4, 2/2 RC, p4, k2.
ROW 3 AND ALL FOLLOWING WS ROWS: Knit the knit sts and purl the purl sts as they face you.
ROW 4: [2/2 LPC, 2/2 RPC] twice.
ROW 6: [P2, 2/2 LC, p2] twice.
ROW 8: Repeat Row 3.
ROW 10: Repeat Row 6.
ROW 12: P2, k2, 2/2 LC, 2/2 RC, k2, p2.
ROW 14: P2, 2/2 LPC, 2/2 RC, 2/2 RPC, p2.
ROW 16: P4, [2/2 LC] twice, p4.
ROW 18: P2, [2/2 RC] twice, 2/2 LC, p2.
ROW 20: P2, k2, 2/2 RPC, 2/2 LPC, k2, p2.
ROW 22: Repeat Row 6.
ROW 24: Repeat Row 3.
ROW 26: Repeat Row 6.
ROW 28: [2/2 RPC, 2/2 LPC] twice.
ROW 30: Repeat Row 2.
ROW 32: K2, p2, 2/2 RPC, 2/2 LPC, p2, k2.
ROW 34: Repeat Row 3.
ROW 36: K2, p2, 2/2 LPC, 2/2 RPC, p2, k2.
Repeat Rows 1–36 for pattern.

LEFT

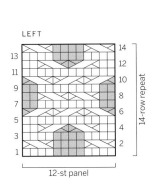

12-st panel

CENTER

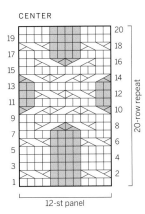

12-st panel

RIGHT

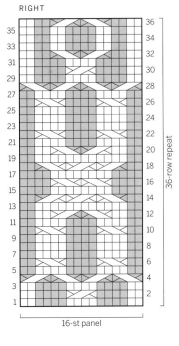

16-st panel

☐ Knit on RS, purl on WS.

▨ Purl on RS, knit on WS.

⬚ OR ⬚ 2/2 RC (2 over 2 right cross): Slip 2 sts to cn, hold to back, k2, k2 from cn.

⬚ OR ⬚ 2/2 LC (2 over 2 left cross): Slip 2 sts to cn, hold to front, k2, k2 from cn.

⬚ OR ⬚ 2/2 RPC (2 over 2 right purl cross): Slip 2 sts to cn, hold to back, k2, p2 from cn.

⬚ OR ⬚ 2/2 LPC (2 over 2 left purl cross): Slip 2 sts to cn, hold to front, p2, k2 from cn.

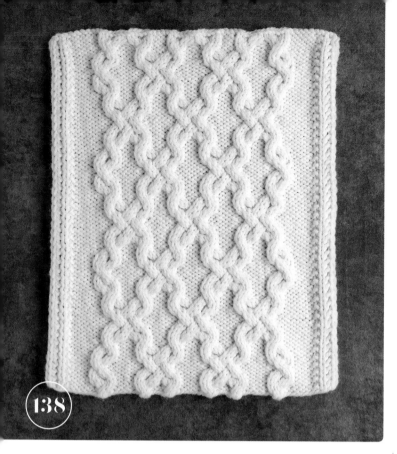

X Knot Curve GROUP 9

The knotted center X shapes from X Knot Evolution (#137) are repeated in a checkerboard to form X Knot Curve. Rather than weaving the crosses in and out of each other as they do in the center of the X (and as is more expected), I chose to leave them as they were in X Knot Evolution; I like the serpentine curves that are formed as the legs of the Xs connect to each other.

(multiple of 16 sts + 16; 24-row repeat)
TOTAL SSE: 20 sts
REPEAT SSE: 10 sts

ROW 1 (WS): K2, p4, *k4, p4; repeat from * to last 2 sts, k2.
ROW 2: *P2, 2/2 LC, p4, 2/2 RC, p2; repeat from * to end.
ROW 3 AND ALL FOLLOWING WS ROWS: Knit the knit sts and purl the purl sts as they face you.
ROW 4: *2/2 RC, k2, p4, k2, 2/2 LC; repeat from * to end.
ROW 6: K2, 2/2 RPC, p4, *2/2 LPC, 2/2 RC, 2/2 RPC, p4; repeat from * to last 6 sts, 2/2 LPC, k2.
ROW 8: *2/2 LC, p8, 2/2 LC; repeat from * to end.
ROW 10: K2, 2/2 LC, p4, *[2/2 RC] twice, 2/2 LC, p4; repeat from * to last 6 sts, 2/2 RC, k2.

ROW 12: *2/2 LPC, k2, p4, k2, 2/2 RPC; repeat from * to end.
ROW 14: *P2, 2/2 RC, p4, 2/2 LC, p2; repeat from * to end.
ROW 16: *P2, k2, 2/2 LC, 2/2 RC, k2, p2; repeat from * to end.
ROW 18: *P2, 2/2 LPC, 2/2 RC, 2/2 RPC, p2; repeat from * to end.
ROW 20: *P4, [2/2 LC] twice, p4; repeat from * to end.
ROW 22: *P2, [2/2 RC] twice, 2/2 LC, p2; repeat from * to end.
ROW 24: *P2, k2, 2/2 RPC, 2/2 LPC, k2, p2; repeat from * to end.
Repeat Rows 1–24 for pattern.

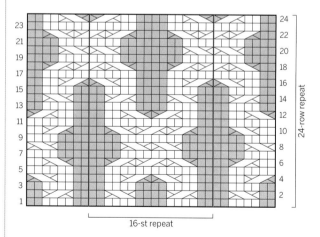

☐ Knit on RS, purl on WS.

▨ Purl on RS, knit on WS.

❘ Pattern repeat

⬓ OR ⬓ 2/2 RC (2 over 2 right cross): Slip 2 sts to cn, hold to back, k2, k2 from cn.

⬓ OR ⬓ 2/2 LC (2 over 2 left cross): Slip 2 sts to cn, hold to front, k2, k2 from cn.

⬓ 2/2 RPC (2 over 2 right purl cross): Slip 2 sts to cn, hold to back, k2, p2 from cn.

⬓ 2/2 LPC (2 over 2 left purl cross): Slip 2 sts to cn, hold to front, p2, k2 from cn.

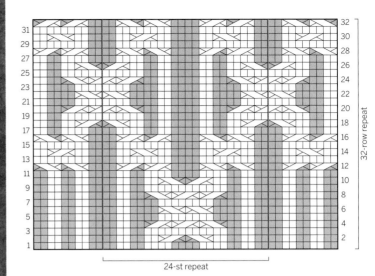

Rib X Knot GROUP 9

The motifs in X Knot Curve (#138) are moved away from each other in both directions in Rib X Knot. In the space created by that shift, I added rib and reverse stockinette stitch. A second kind of knot forms where the rib interacts with the diagonals between Xs.

(multiple of 24 sts + 20; 32-row repeat)

TOTAL SSE: 22.5 sts

REPEAT SSE: 15 sts

ROW 1 (WS): [K2, p2] twice, k4, *p2, k2, p4, k4, p4, k2, p2, k4; repeat from * to last 8 sts, [p2, k2] twice.

ROW 2: [P2, k2] twice, p4, *k2, p2, k2, 2/2 LC, 2/2 RC, k2, p2, k2, p4; repeat from * to last 8 sts, [k2, p2] twice.

ROW 3 AND ALL FOLLOWING WS ROWS: Knit the knit sts and purl the purl sts as they face you.

ROW 4: [P2, k2] twice, p4, *k2, p2, 2/2 LPC, 2/2 RC, 2/2 RPC, p2, k2, p4; repeat from * to last 8 sts, [k2, p2] twice.

ROW 6: [P2, k2] twice, p4, *k2, p4, [2/2 LC] twice, p4, k2, p4; repeat from * to last 8 sts, [k2, p2] twice.

ROW 8: [P2, k2] twice, p4, *k2, p2, [2/2 RC] twice, 2/2 LC, p2, k2, p4; repeat from * to last 8 sts, [k2, p2] twice.

ROW 10: [P2, k2] twice, p4, *k2, p2, k2, 2/2 RPC, 2/2 LPC, k2, p2, k2, p4; repeat from * to last 8 sts, [k2, p2] twice.

ROW 12: [2/2 RC] twice, p4, [2/2 LC] twice, *p4, [2/2 RC] twice, p4, [2/2 LC] twice; repeat from * to end.

ROW 14: K2, 2/2 LC, k2, p4, k2, 2/2 RC, k2, *p4, k2, 2/2 LC, k2, p4, k2, 2/2 RC, k2; repeat from * to end.

ROW 16: 2/2 RPC, 2/2 RC, p4, 2/2 LC, 2/2 LPC, *p4, 2/2 RPC, 2/2 RC, p4, 2/2 LC, 2/2 LPC; repeat from * to end.

ROW 18: K2, p2, k2, 2/2 LC, 2/2 RC, k2, p2, k2, *p4, k2, p2, k2, 2/2 LC, 2/2 RC, k2, p2, k2; repeat from * to end.

ROW 20: K2, p2, 2/2 LPC, 2/2 RC, 2/2 RPC, p2, k2, *p4, k2, p2, 2/2 LPC, 2/2 RC, 2/2 RPC, p2, k2; repeat from * to end.

ROW 22: K2, p4, [2/2 LC] twice, p4, k2, *p4, k2, p4, [2/2 LC] twice, p4, k2; repeat from * to end.

ROW 24: K2, p2, [2/2 RC] twice, 2/2 LC, p2, k2, *p4, k2, p2, [2/2 RC] twice, 2/2 LC, p2, k2; repeat from * to end.

ROW 26: K2, p2, k2, 2/2 RPC, 2/2 LPC, k2, p2, k2, *p4, k2, p2, k2, 2/2 RPC, 2/2 LPC, k2, p2, k2; repeat from * to end.

ROW 28: [2/2 LC] twice, p4, [2/2 RC] twice, *p4, [2/2 LC] twice, p4, [2/2 RC] twice; repeat from * to end.

ROW 30: K2, 2/2 RC, p4, k2, 2/2 LC, k2, *p4, k2, 2/2 RC, k2, p4, k2, 2/2 LC, k2; repeat from * to end.

ROW 32: [2/2 LPC] twice, p4, 2/2 RPC, 2/2 RC, *p4, 2/2 LC, 2/2 LPC, p4, [2/2 RPC] twice; repeat from * to end.

Repeat Rows 1–32 for pattern.

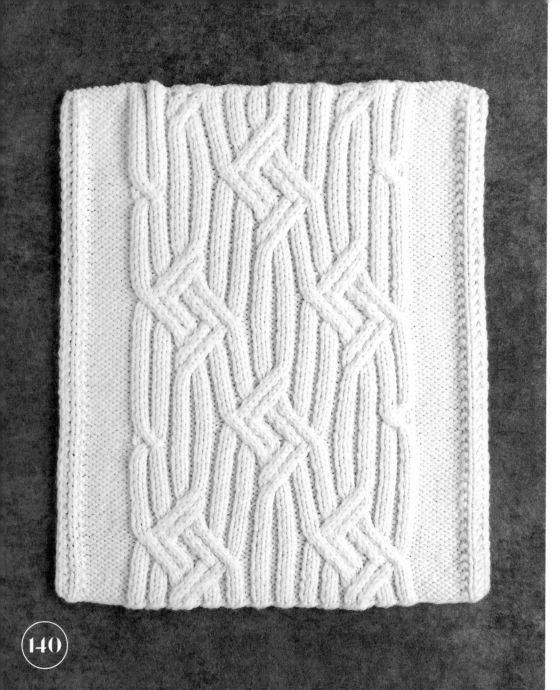

Tilted Cube

GROUP 10

This is an enlarged version of the crosshatch in Right Bias Weave (#117), with each line of the crosshatch doubled, then lengthened. The tilted cube motif flows in and out of a 2 x 2 rib background.

(multiple of 32 sts + 22; 48-row repeat)

TOTAL SSE: 33.5 sts

REPEAT SSE: 20 sts

ROW 1 (WS): [P2, k2] twice, p6, *k2, [p2, k2] 6 times, p6; repeat from * to last 8 sts, [k2, p2] twice.

ROW 2: [K2, p2] twice, 2/2 RC, *[k2, p2] 7 times, 2/2 RC; repeat from * to last 10 sts, k2, [p2, k2] twice.

ROW 3 AND ALL FOLLOWING WS ROWS: Knit the knit sts and purl the purl sts as they face you.

ROW 4: K2, p2, k2, [2/2 RC] twice, *[p2, k2] 6 times, [2/2 RC] twice; repeat from * to last 8 sts, [p2, k2] twice.

ROW 6: K2, p2, [2/2 RC] twice, *[k2, p2] 6 times, [2/2 RC] twice; repeat from * to last 10 sts, k2, [p2, k2] twice.

ROW 8: K2, 2/2 RC, 2/2 RPC, k2, 2/2 LC, *k2, [p2, k2] 4 times, 2/2 RC, 2/2 RPC, k2, 2/2 LC; repeat from * to last 6 sts, k2, p2, k2.

ROW 10: [2/2 LC] twice, p2, 2/2 LPC, 2/2 LC, *p2, [k2, p2] 3 times, [2/2 LC] twice, p2, 2/2 LPC, 2/2 LC; repeat from * to last 4 sts, p2, k2.

ROW 12: K2, 2/2 LPC, 2/2 LC, p2, 2/2 LPC, 2/2 LC, *k2, [p2, k2] 3 times, 2/2 LPC, 2/2 LC, p2, 2/2 LPC, 2/2 LC; repeat from * to last 2 sts, k2.

ROW 14: K2, p2, [2/2 LC] twice, p2, [2/2 LC] twice, *p2, [k2, p2] 3 times, [2/2 LC] twice, p2, [2/2 LC] twice; repeat from * to end.

ROW 16: K2, p2, k2, 2/2 LPC, k2, 2/2 RC, 2/2 RPC, *k2, [p2, k2] 4 times, 2/2 LPC, k2, 2/2 RC, 2/2 RPC; repeat from * to last 2 sts, k2.

ROW 18: K2, [p2, k2] twice, [2/2 RC] twice, *[p2, k2] 6 times, [2/2 RC] twice; repeat from * to last 4 sts, p2, k2.

ROW 20: [K2, p2] twice, 2/2 RC, 2/2 RPC, *[k2, p2] 6 times, 2/2 RC, 2/2 RPC; repeat from * to last 6 sts, k2, p2, k2.

ROW 22: K2, [p2, k2] twice, 2/2 RC, *[p2, k2] 7 times, 2/2 RC; repeat from * to last 8 sts, [p2, k2] twice.

ROW 24: [K2, p2] twice, 2/2 RPC, *k2, [p2, k2] 3 times, 2/2 RC, p2, [k2, p2] twice, 2/2 RPC; repeat from * to last 10 sts, k2, [p2, k2] twice.

ROW 26: [K2, p2] 5 times, *k2, p2, 2/2 RC, [k2, p2] 6 times; repeat from * to last 2 sts, k2.

ROW 28: K2, [p2, k2] 5 times, *[2/2 RC] twice, [p2, k2] 6 times; repeat from * to end.

ROW 30: [K2, p2] 5 times, *[2/2 RC] twice, [k2, p2] 6 times; repeat from * to last 2 sts, k2.

ROW 32: K2, [p2, k2] 4 times, *2/2 RC, 2/2 RPC, k2, 2/2 LC, k2, [p2, k2] 4 times; repeat from * to last 4 sts, 2/2 RC.

ROW 34: [K2, p2] 4 times, *[2/2 LC] twice, p2, 2/2 LPC, 2/2 LC, p2, [k2, p2] 3 times; repeat from * to last 6 sts, 2/2 LC, k2.

ROW 36: 2/2 LC, k2, [p2, k2] 3 times, *2/2 LPC, 2/2 LC, p2, 2/2 LPC, 2/2 LC, k2, [p2, k2] 3 times; repeat from * to last 4 sts, 2/2 LPC.

ROW 38: K2, 2/2 LC, p2, [k2, p2] 3 times, *[(2/2 LC) twice, p2] twice, [k2, p2] 3 times; repeat from * to last 2 sts, k2.

ROW 40: 2/2 RPC, k2, [p2, k2] 4 times, *2/2 LPC, k2, 2/2 RC, 2/2 RPC, k2, [p2, k2] 4 times; repeat from * to end.

ROW 42: K2, *[p2, k2] 6 times, [2/2 RC] twice; repeat from * to last 20 sts, [p2, k2] 5 times.

ROW 44: *[K2, p2] 6 times, 2/2 RC, 2/2 RPC; repeat from * to last 22 sts, [p2, k2] 5 times, k2.

ROW 46: K2, [p2, k2] 5 times, *p2, k2, 2/2 RC, [p2, k2] 6 times; repeat from * to end.

ROW 48: K2, [p2, k2] twice, 2/2 RC, *p2, [k2, p2] twice, 2/2 RPC, k2, [p2, k2] 3 times, 2/2 RC; repeat from * to last 8 sts, [p2, k2] twice. Repeat Rows 1–48 for pattern.

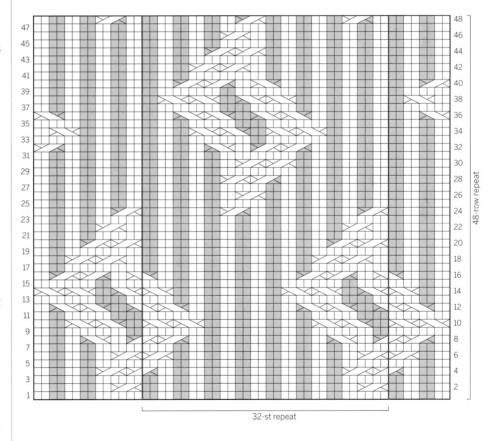

48-row repeat

32-st repeat

☐ Knit on RS, purl on WS.

▨ Purl on RS, knit on WS.

❘ Pattern repeat

OR 2/2 RC (2 over 2 right cross): Slip 2 sts to cn, hold to back, k2, k2 from cn.

OR 2/2 LC (2 over 2 left cross): Slip 2 sts to cn, hold to front, k2, k2 from cn.

 2/2 RPC (2 over 2 right purl cross): Slip 2 sts to cn, hold to back, k2, p2 from cn.

 2/2 LPC (2 over 2 left purl cross): Slip 2 sts to cn, hold to front, p2, k2 from cn.

Tilted Cube Grid GROUP 10

Tilted Cube (#140) is placed in a grid formation and connected with 2/2 ropes, ribs, and Fave to form Tilted Cube Grid.

(multiple of 22 sts + 8; 28-row repeat)

TOTAL SSE: 24 sts
REPEAT SSE: 13 sts

ROW 1 (WS): K2, p4, *[k2, p2] 4 times, k2, p4; repeat from * to last 2 sts, k2.

ROW 2: Knit the knit sts and purl the purl sts as they face you.

ROW 3 AND ALL FOLLOWING WS ROWS: Repeat Row 2.

ROW 4: P2, 2/2 LC, *[p2, k2] twice, 2/2 RC, p2, k2, p2, 2/2 LC; repeat from * to last 2 sts, p2.

ROW 6: P2, k4, *p2, k2, p2, 2/2 RC, [k2, p2] twice, k4; repeat from * to last 2 sts, p2.

ROW 8: P2, 2/2 LC, *p2, k2, [2/2 RC] twice, p2, k2, p2, 2/2 LC; repeat from * to last 2 sts, p2.

ROW 10: P2, k4, *p2, [2/2 RC] twice, [k2, p2] twice, k4; repeat from * to last 2 sts, p2.

ROW 12: P2, 2/2 LC, *2/2 RC, 2/2 RPC, k2, 2/2 LC, k2, p2, 2/2 LC; repeat from * to last 2 sts, p2.

ROW 14: 2/2 RPC, 2/2 LPC, *2/2 LC, p2, 2/2 LPC, 2/2 LC, 2/2 RPC, 2/2 LPC; repeat from * to end.

ROW 16: K2, p4, *[2/2 LC] twice, p2, 2/2 LPC, 2/2 LC, p4; repeat from * to last 2 sts, k2.

ROW 18: 2/2 LPC, 2/2 RPC, *[2/2 LC] twice, p2, [2/2 LC] twice, 2/2 RPC; repeat from * to end.

ROW 20: P2, 2/2 LC, p2, *k2, 2/2 LPC, k2, 2/2 RC, 2/2 RPC, 2/2 LC, p2; repeat from * to end.

ROW 22: P2, k4, *[p2, k2] twice, [2/2 RC] twice, p2, k4; repeat from * to last 2 sts, p2.

ROW 24: P2, 2/2 LC, p2, *k2, 2/2 RC, 2/2 RPC, k2, p2, 2/2 LC, p2; repeat from * to end.

ROW 26: P2, k4, *[p2, k2] twice, 2/2 RC, p2, k2, p2, k4; repeat from * to last 2 sts, p2.

ROW 28: P2, 2/2 LC, p2, *k2, p2, 2/2 RPC, [k2, p2] twice, 2/2 LC, p2; repeat from * to end.

Repeat Rows 1–28 for pattern.

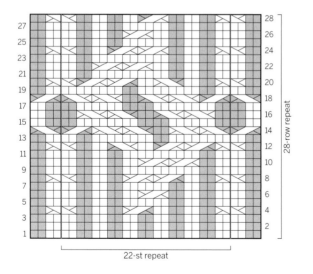

22-st repeat

28-row repeat

☐ Knit on RS, purl on WS.

▨ Purl on RS, knit on WS.

| Pattern repeat

2/2 RC (2 over 2 right cross): Slip 2 sts to cn, hold to back, k2, k2 from cn.

2/2 LC (2 over 2 left cross): Slip 2 sts to cn, hold to front, k2, k2 from cn.

2/2 RPC (2 over 2 right purl cross): Slip 2 sts to cn, hold to back, k2, p2 from cn.

2/2 LPC (2 over 2 left purl cross): Slip 2 sts to cn, hold to front, p2, k2 from cn.

Tilted Argyle GROUP 11

A seemingly insignificant shape from the lower portion of the Hexa Butterfly (#133) wing is repeated, joined, and filled with an X, like the center of an argyle pattern, to create Tilted Argyle. The 2 columns shown are mirror images of each other and each starts at a different part of the pattern.

(panel of 50 sts; 32-row repeat)
SSE: 31 sts

ROW 1 (WS): [K4, p2] twice, k6, p2, k10, p2, [k4, p4] twice, k2.

ROW 2: 2/2 RC, 2/2 LC, 2/2 RPC, 2/2 LPC, 2/2 RC, p10, k2, p4, 2/2 RPC, p4, k2, p4.

ROW 3 AND ALL FOLLOWING WS ROWS: Knit the knit sts and purl the purl sts as they face you.

ROW 4: K6, 2/2 LC, p4, 2/2 RPC, k2, p10, k2, p2, 2/2 RC, p6, k2, p4.

ROW 6: 2/2 LPC, k4, 2/2 LC, 2/2 RPC, p2, k2, p10, k2, 2/2 RC, 2/2 LC, p4, k2, p4.

ROW 8: P2, 2/2 LPC, k4, 2/2 LC, p4, k2, p10, 2/2 RC, k6, p4, k2, p4.

ROW 10: P4, 2/2 LC, k6, p4, k2, p8, 2/2 RC, k4, 2/2 RC, p4, k2, p4.

ROW 12: P4, k2, 2/2 LPC, 2/2 RPC, p4, k2, p6, 2/2 RC, k4, 2/2 RPC, 2/2 LPC, p2, k2, p4.

ROW 14: P4, k2, p2, 2/2 LPC, p6, k2, p6, k6, 2/2 RC, p4, 2/2 LC, k2, p4.

ROW 16: P4, k2, p4, 2/2 LPC, p4, k2, p6, [2/2 LPC, 2/2 RPC] twice, 2/2 LPC, p4.

ROW 18: P4, k2, p6, 2/2 LC, p2, k2, p8, 2/2 LPC, p4, 2/2 LC, p4, 2/2 LC, p2.

ROW 20: P4, k2, p4, 2/2 RC, 2/2 LC, k2, p10, 2/2 LC, 2/2 RPC, 2/2 LPC, 2/2 RC, 2/2 LC.

ROW 22: P4, k2, p4, k6, 2/2 LC, p10, k2, 2/2 LPC, p4, 2/2 RC, k6.

ROW 24: P4, k2, p4, 2/2 LC, k4, 2/2 LC, p8, k2, p2, 2/2 LPC, 2/2 RC, k4, 2/2 RPC.

ROW 26: P4, k2, p2, 2/2 RPC, 2/2 LPC, k4, 2/2 LC, p6, k2, p4, 2/2 RC, k4, 2/2 RPC, p2.

ROW 28: P4, k2, 2/2 RC, p4, 2/2 LC, k6, p6, k2, p4, k6, 2/2 RC, p4.

ROW 30: P4, [2/2 RPC, 2/2 LPC] twice, 2/2 RPC, p6, k2, p4, 2/2 LPC, 2/2 RPC, k2, p4.

ROW 32: P2, [2/2 RC, p4] twice, 2/2 RPC, p8, k2, p6, 2/2 RPC, p2, k2, p4.

Repeat Rows 1–32 for pattern.

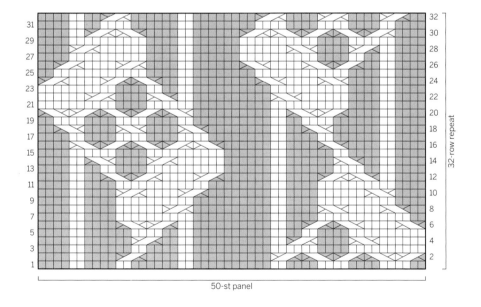

32-row repeat

50-st panel

☐ Knit on RS, purl on WS.

▨ Purl on RS, knit on WS.

2/2 RC (2 over 2 right cross): Slip 2 sts to cn, hold to back, k2, k2 from cn.

2/2 LC (2 over 2 left cross): Slip 2 sts to cn, hold to front, k2, k2 from cn.

2/2 RPC (2 over 2 right purl cross): Slip 2 sts to cn, hold to back, k2, p2 from cn.

2/2 LPC (2 over 2 left purl cross): Slip 2 sts to cn, hold to front, p2, k2 from cn.

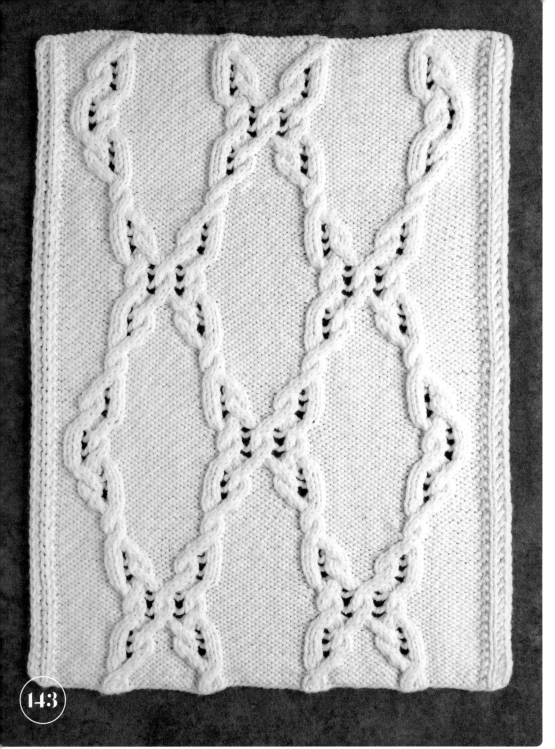

Open Butterfly GROUP 11

The outline of a butterfly is formed by combining 2/2 ropes and lines made with 2/2 cables. Double yarnover ladders worked on wrong-side rows add an airy, summery feeling while not interrupting the cable pattern.

(multiple of 32 sts + 32; 64-row repeat)

TOTAL SSE: 52.5 sts

REPEAT SSE: 26 sts

ROW 1 (WS): K6, p4, *k12, p4; repeat from * to last 6 sts, k6.

ROWS 2 AND 3: Knit the knit sts and purl the purl sts as they face you.

ROW 4: *P6, 2/2 RC, p6; repeat from * to end.

ROW 5: Repeat Row 2.

ROW 6: *P6, k2, 2/2 LC, p8, 2/2 RC, k2, p6; repeat from * to end.

ROW 7: *K6, p1, p2tog, yo2, ssp, p1, k8, p1, p2tog, yo2, ssp, p1, k6; repeat from * to end.

ROW 8: *P6, k2, (k1, p1) into yo2, 2/2 LC, p4, 2/2 RC, (k1, p1) into yo2, k2, p6; repeat from * to end.

ROW 9: *K6, p1, p2tog, yo2, ssp, p3, k4, p3, p2tog, yo2, ssp, p1, k6; repeat from * to end.

ROW 10: *P6, k2, (k1, p1) into yo2, k4, p4, k4, (k1, p1) into yo2, k2, p6; repeat from * to end.

ROW 11: Repeat Row 9.

ROW 12: Repeat Row 8.

ROW 13: *K6, p8, k4, p8, k6; repeat from * to end.

ROW 14: *P6, 2/2 LPC, k2, 2/2 LC, 2/2 RC, k2, 2/2 RPC, p6; repeat from * to end.

ROW 15: *K8, p3, p2tog, yo2, ssp, p2, p2tog, yo2, ssp, p3, k8; repeat from * to end.

ROW 16: *P8, 2/2 RC, [(k1, p1) into yo2, 2/2 RC] twice, p8; repeat from * to end.

ROW 17: Repeat Row 15.

ROW 18: *P8, k4, [(k1, p1) into yo2, k4] twice, p8; repeat from * to end.

ROWS 19 AND 20: Repeat Rows 15 and 16.

ROW 21: *K8, p16, k8; repeat from * to end.

ROW 22: *P6, 2/2 RC, k2, 2/2 RPC, 2/2 LPC, k2, 2/2 LC, p6; repeat from * to end.

ROW 23: Repeat Row 9.

ROW 24: *P6, k2, (k1, p1) into yo2, 2/2 RC, p4, 2/2 LC, (k1, p1) into yo2, k2, p6; repeat from * to end.

ROWS 25 AND 26: Repeat Rows 9 and 10.

ROW 27: Repeat Row 9.

ROW 28: *P6, k2, (k1, p1) into yo2, 2/2 RPC, p4, 2/2 LPC, (k1, p1) into yo2, k2, p6; repeat from * to end.

ROW 29: *K6, p6, k8, p6, k6; repeat from * to end.

ROW 30: *P6, k2, 2/2 RPC, p8, 2/2 LPC, k2, p6; repeat from * to end.

ROW 31: *K6, p4, k6; repeat from * to end.

ROW 32: *P6, 2/2 RC, p6; repeat from * to end.

ROWS 33–35: Knit the knit sts and purl the purl sts as they face you.

ROW 36: Repeat Row 32.

ROW 37: Repeat Row 33.

ROW 38: *P4, 2/2 RC, k2, p12, k2, 2/2 LC, p4; repeat from * to end.

ROW 39: *K4, p1, p2tog, yo2, ssp, p1, k12, p1, p2tog, yo2, ssp, p1, k4; repeat from * to end.

ROW 40: *P2, 2/2 RC, (k1, p1) into yo2, k2, p12, k2, (k1, p1) into yo2, 2/2 LC, p2; repeat from * to end.

ROW 41: *K2, p3, p2tog, yo2, ssp, p1, k12, p1, p2tog, yo2, ssp, p3, k2; repeat from * to end.

ROW 42: *P2, k4, (k1, p1) into yo2, k2, p12, k2, (k1, p1) into yo2, k4, p2; repeat from * to end.

ROW 43: Repeat Row 41.

ROW 44: Repeat Row 40.

ROW 45: *K2, p8, k12, p8, k2; repeat from * to end.

ROW 46: *2/2 RC, k2, 2/2 RPC, p12, 2/2 LPC, k2, 2/2 LC; repeat from * to end.

ROW 47: *P1, p2tog, yo2, ssp, p3, k16, p3, p2tog, yo2, ssp, p1; repeat from * to end.

ROW 48: K2, (k1, p1) into yo2, 2/2 RC, p16, *2/2 RC, [(k1, p1) into yo2, 2/2 RC] twice, p16; repeat from * to last 8 sts, 2/2 RC, (k1, p1) into yo2, k2.

ROW 49: Repeat Row 47.

ROW 50: *K2, (k1, p1) into yo2, k4, p16, k4, [(k1, p1) into yo2, k2; repeat from * to end.

ROWS 51 AND 52: Repeat Rows 47 and 48.

ROW 53: P8, k16, *p16, k16; repeat from * to last 8 sts, p8.

ROW 54: *2/2 LPC, k2, 2/2 LC, p12, 2/2 RC, k2, 2/2 RPC; repeat from * to end.

ROW 55: *K2, p3, p2tog, yo2, ssp, p1, k12, p1, p2tog, yo2, ssp, p3, k2; repeat from * to end.

ROW 56: *P2, 2/2 LC, (k1, p1) into yo2, k2, p12, k2, (k1, p1) into yo2, 2/2 RC, p2; repeat from * to end.

ROW 57: Repeat Row 55.

ROW 58: Repeat Row 42.

ROW 59: Repeat Row 55.

ROW 60: *P2, 2/2 LPC, (k1, p1) into yo2, k2, p12, k2, (k1, p1) into yo2, 2/2 RPC, p2; repeat from * to end.

ROW 61: *K4, p6, k12, p6, k4; repeat from * to end.

ROW 62: *P4, 2/2 LPC, k2, p12, k2, 2/2 RPC, p4; repeat from * to end.

ROW 63: Knit the knit sts and purl the purl sts as they face you.

ROW 64: P6, 2/2 RC, *p12, 2/2 RC; repeat from * to last 6 sts, p6. Repeat Rows 1–64 for pattern.

□ Knit on RS, purl on WS.

▨ Purl on RS, knit on WS.

 Yo2

▭ (K1, p1) into yo2.

◹ K2tog on RS, p2tog on WS.

◸ Ssk on RS, ssp on WS.

| Pattern repeat

OR 2/2 RC (2 over 2 right cross): Slip 2 sts to cn, hold to back, k2, k2 from cn.

OR 2/2 LC (2 over 2 left cross): Slip 2 sts to cn, hold to front, k2, k2 from cn.

 2/2 RPC (2 over 2 right purl cross): Slip 2 sts to cn, hold to back, k2, p2 from cn.

 2/2 LPC (2 over 2 left purl cross): Slip 2 sts to cn, hold to front, p2, k2 from cn.

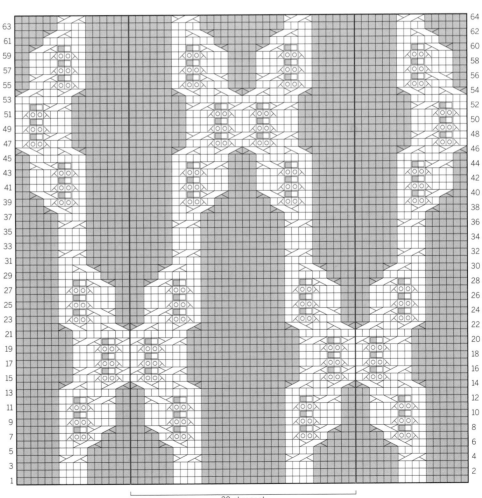

32-st repeat

64-row repeat

Batwing Pullover

Yoke

Using larger 24" (60 cm) long circular needle, CO 202 sts. Join for working in the rnd; pm for beginning of rnd. Beginning of rnd will be at beginning of Left Sleeve.

SET-UP RND 1: *P2, work Cable Pattern over 96 sts, p2, pm, k1, pm; repeat from * once.

SET-UP RND 2 (INCREASE RND): *P2, work to 2 sts before marker, p2, sm, yo, k1, yo, sm; repeat from * once—206 sts.

SET-UP RND 3: *P2, work to 2 sts before marker, p2, sm, knit to marker, sm; repeat from * once.

SET-UP RND 4 (INCREASE RND): *P2, work to 2 sts before marker, p2, sm, [yo, k1] 3 times, yo, sm]; repeat from * once—214 sts.

RND 5: Repeat Set-Up Rnd 3.

SHAPE YOKE
Note: Change to larger 32" (80 cm) long circular needle when desired for number of sts on needle.

RND 1 (INCREASE RND): *P2, work to 2 sts before marker, p2, sm, yo, k1, yo, k2tog, knit to 3 sts before next marker, ssk, yo, k1, yo, sm; repeat from * once—4 sts increased.

RND 2: *P2, work to 2 sts before marker, p2, sm, knit to marker, sm; repeat from * once.

RND 3 (INCREASE RND): *P2, work to 2 sts before marker, p2, sm, yo, k1, yo, knit to 1 st before next marker, yo, k1, yo, sm; repeat from * once—8 sts increased.

RND 4: Repeat Rnd 2.

SIZES 50 AND 54" [127 AND 137 CM] ONLY
Repeat Rnds 3 and 4 - (-, -, -, -, 2, 8) times.

ALL SIZES
Repeat Rnds 1–4 two (9, 16, 22, 29, 34, 33) times, then Repeat Rnds 1 and 2 fifty-five (43, 31, 22, 10, 0, 0) times—470 (506, 542, 578, 614, 650, 686) sts; 135 (153, 171, 189, 207, 225, 243) sts each for Front and Back, 100 sts each Sleeve.

DIVIDE FOR FRONT AND BACK
NEXT RND: *BO 100 sts in pattern, remove marker, knit to next marker, sm; repeat from * once—270 (306, 342, 378, 414, 450, 486) sts remain.

Body

Continuing in St st, knit 1 rnd.

SHAPE BODY

RND 1 (DECREASE RND): *K2, k2tog, knit to 4 sts before marker, ssk, k2, sm; repeat from * once—4 sts decreased.

RND 2: Knit.

SIZES 30 AND 34" (76 AND 86.5 CM) ONLY

Repeat Rnds 1 and 2 thirteen (16, -, -, -, -, -) times—214 (238, -, -, -, -) sts remain.

SIZES 38, 42, 46, 50, AND 54" (96.5, 106.5, 117, 127, AND 137 CM) ONLY

RND 3 (DECREASE RND): K2, k3tog, knit to 5 sts before marker, sssk, k2, sm; repeat from * once—8 sts decreased.

RND 4: Knit.

SIZES 50 AND 54" (127 AND 137 CM) ONLY

RNDS 5 AND 6: Repeat Rnds 3 and 4—8 sts decreased.

SIZES 38, 42, 46, 50, AND 54" (96.5, 106.5, 117, 127, AND 137 CM) ONLY

Repeat Rnds - (-, 1–4, 1–4, 1–4, 1–6, 1–6) - (-, 2, 4, 7, 4, 5) times, then Repeat Rnds 1 and 2 - (-, 11, 8, 2, 4, 2) times— - (-, 262, 286, 310, 334, 358) sts remain.

ALL SIZES

Change to smaller 24" (60 cm) long circular needle.

NEXT RND: k12 (0, 15, 12, 0, 19, 12), [k9 (9, 8, 9, 9, 8, 9) M1L] 22 (26, 30, 30, 34, 38, 38) times, k4 (4, 7, 4, 4, 11, 4)—236 (264, 292, 316, 344, 372, 396) sts.

Begin 2 x 2 Rib; work even for 2" (5 cm). BO all sts in pattern using larger needle.

Finishing

BACK NECK INSERT

With RS facing, using larger 24" (60 cm) long circular needle, pick up and knit 34 sts from center of Right Sleeve to center of neck, place removable marker on next-to-last st picked up, pick up and knit 34 sts to center of Left Sleeve—68 sts.

Purl 1 row.

ROW 1 (RS): K1, k2tog, knit to 3 sts before marked st, [ssk] twice, sm, yo2, [k2tog] twice, knit to last 3 sts, ssk, k1—4 sts decreased.

ROW 2: Purl, working (p1, k1) into yo2.

ROW 3: K1, [k2tog] twice, knit to 4 sts before marked st, [ssk] 3 times, yo2, [k2tog] 3 times, knit to last 5 sts, [ssk] twice, k1—8 sts decreased.

ROW 4: Repeat Row 2.

ROW 5: K1, k2tog, knit to 2 sts before marked st, [ssk] twice, sm, yo2, [k2tog] twice, knit to last 3 sts, ssk, k1—4 sts decreased.

ROW 6: Repeat Row 2.

Repeat Rows 3–6 three times, then Repeat Rows 3 and 4 once—8 sts remain.

NEXT ROW (RS): [K2tog, ssk] twice—4 sts remain.

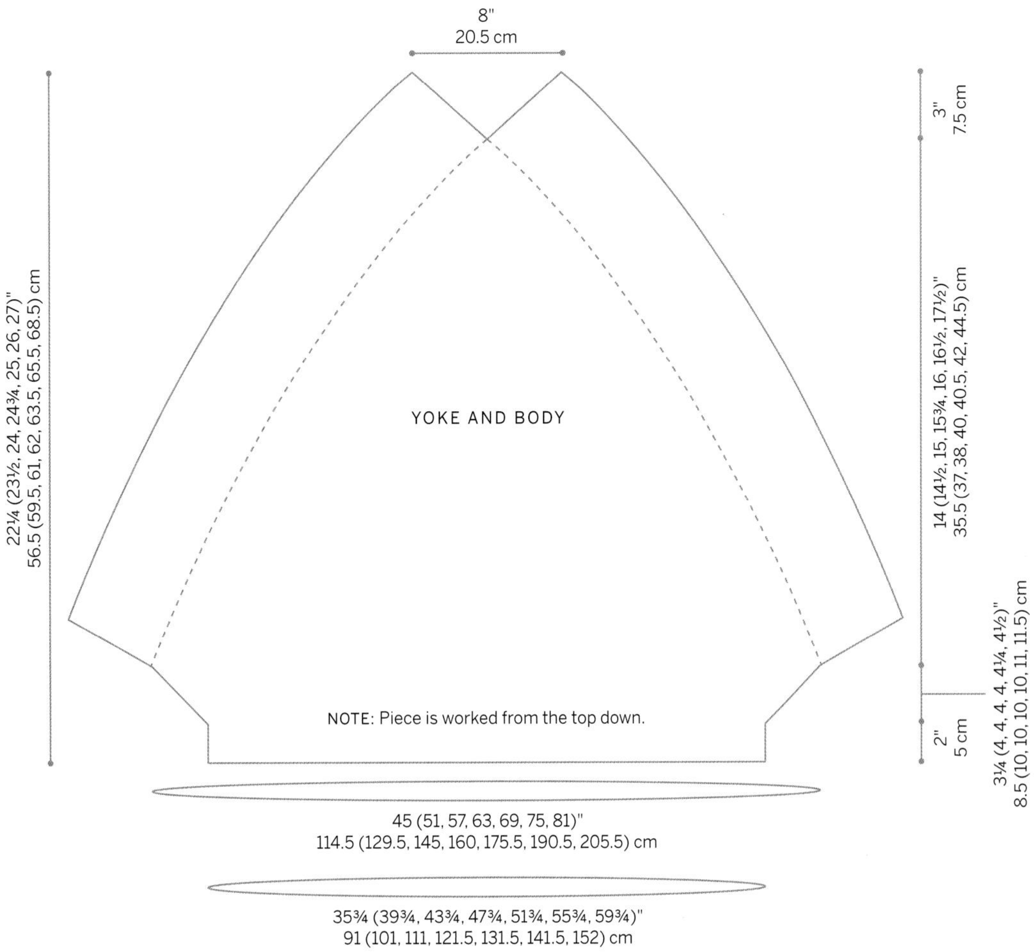
8"
20.5 cm
22¼ (23½, 24, 24¾, 25, 26, 27)"
56.5 (59.5, 61, 62, 63.5, 65.5, 68.5) cm
3"
7.5 cm
14 (14½, 15, 15¾, 16, 16½, 17½)"
35.5 (37, 38, 40, 40.5, 42, 44.5) cm
YOKE AND BODY
3¼ (4, 4, 4, 4¼, 4¼, 4½)"
8.5 (10, 10, 10, 10, 11, 11.5) cm
NOTE: Piece is worked from the top down.
2"
5 cm
45 (51, 57, 63, 69, 75, 81)"
114.5 (129.5, 145, 160, 175.5, 190.5, 205.5) cm
35¾ (39¾, 43¾, 47¾, 51¾, 55¾, 59¾)"
91 (101, 111, 121.5, 131.5, 141.5, 152) cm

NEXT ROW: [P2tog] twice, pass first st over second st. Fasten off. Block piece as desired.

CUFFS

Beginning at Body, sew bottom edge of Sleeve closed for 2 (2, 1½, 1½, 1½, 1, 1)" [5 (5, 4, 4, 4, 2.5, 2.5) cm], leaving 8¾ (8¾, 9¾, 9¾ 9¾, 10¾, 10¾)" [22 (22, 25, 25, 25, 27.5, 27.5) cm] opening. Using needles in preferred style for small circumference knitting in the rnd, and beginning at seam, pick up and knit 52 (52, 60, 60, 60, 68, 68) sts around opening. Join for working in the rnd; pm for beginning of rnd. Begin 2 x 2 Rib; work even for 5" (12.5 cm).

BO RND: K2, *insert left needle into fronts of sts just knit, then knit them again through the back loops, k1; repeat from * until 1 st remains, omitting final k1. Fasten off.

TURTLENECK

Using smaller 16" (40 cm) long circular needle and beginning at left shoulder, pick up and knit 112 sts around neck shaping. Join for working in the rnd; pm for beginning of rnd. Begin 2 x 2 Rib; work even for 8" (20.5 cm).

BO RND: K2, *insert left needle into fronts of sts just knit, then knit them again through the back loops, k1; repeat from * until 1 st remains, omitting final k1. Fasten off.

8 Cable Substitution

Before getting started, review Stockinette Stitch Equivalent System on page 20.

CHOOSING CABLES

The original cable—with a total SSE of 78 (3 repeats of 26)—uses up all of the possible space. You can use any size cable or combination of cables and spacers that add up to a total SSE of 78 or less. Make up any difference with reverse stockinette stitch at each end.

MANAGING A CHANGE IN STITCH COUNT

If, after substituting, your stitch count has changed, make note of the difference between your cast-on numbers and the cast-on called for in the pattern and remember to add or subtract this difference for the cast-on. The cast-on includes the stitches for 2 cable panels; each panel forms half of the yoke, from center front over the shoulder to center back. You will work all of the yoke increases between the charts at the center back or center front. Adjust all of the stitch counts until you divide for front and back. At this point, you will be binding off all of the chart stitches, leaving the remaining stockinette stitches for the body. Where the pattern calls you to "BO 100 sts in pattern," BO all of the chart sts on each side of the increased yoke stitches, plus the 2 reverse stockinette stitches on either side of each chart.

Poncho

FINISHED
MEASUREMENTS
Approximately 38"
(96.5) cm wide x 20"
(51 cm) long

YARN
Berroco Indigo [95% cot-
ton/5% other; 219 yards
(200 meters)/100 grams)]:
7 hanks #6410 Relaxed

NEEDLES
One 32" (80 cm) long
circular needle size US 7
(4.5 mm)

One 32" (80 cm) long
circular needle size US 5
(3.75 mm)

One 16" (40 cm) long
circular needle size US 5
(3.75 mm), for Neckband

One spare size US 7
(4.5 mm) needle, for
Three-Needle BO

Change needle size if
necessary to obtain cor-
rect gauge.

NOTIONS
Stitch markers; cable
needle; stitch holders or
waste yarn

GAUGE
20 sts and 27 rows = 4"
(10 cm) in St st, using
larger needle

46-st panel from Left Bias
Weave (#116) or Right
Bias Weave (#117) mea-
sures 6¾" (17 cm) wide,
using larger needle

6-st panel from Small
Center Stable (#47) mea-
sures 1" (2.5 cm), using
larger needle

Steam or wet block your
swatch before taking the
measurements.

STITCH PATTERNS
2 x 2 Rib
(multiple of 4 sts + 2)
ROW 1 (WS): Slip 2, *k2,
p2; repeat from * to end.
ROW 2: Slip 2, *p2, k2;
repeat from * to end.
Repeat Rows 1 and 2 for
pattern.

Cable A: Left Bias
Weave (#116)

Cable B: Small Center
Stable (#47)

Cable C: Right Bias
Weave (#117)

⚭ If you'd like to make
a cable substitution, see
page 228.

Front

Using smaller circular needle, cast on 234 sts. Begin 2 x 2 Rib; work even until piece measures 2" (5 cm) from the beginning, ending with a RS row.

Change to larger needle.

DECREASE ROW (WS): Slip 2, k2, p2, k2, [p5, p2tog] 8 times, pm, k2, work Cable C over 46 sts, k2, work Cable B over 6 sts, k2, work Cable A over 46 sts, k2, pm, [p2tog, p5] 8 times, [k2, p2] twice—218 sts remain.

NEXT ROW: Slip 2, p2, k2, p2, knit to marker, sm, p2, work Cable A over 46 sts, p2, work Cable B over 6 sts, p2, work Cable C over 46 sts, p2, sm, knit to last 8 sts, [p2, k2] twice.

NEXT ROW: Slip 2, k2, p2, k2, purl to marker, sm, work in patterns as established to next marker, sm, purl to last 8 sts, [k2, p2] twice. Work even until piece measures 17" (43 cm) from the beginning, ending with a WS row.

Change to smaller needle.

DECREASE ROW (RS): Slip 2, p2, k2, p2, knit to marker, sm, [k2, k2tog] 26 times, knit to last 8 sts, [p2, k2] twice—192 sts remain.

NEXT ROW: Slip 2, k2, p2, k2, k79 (removing marker), pm, k18, pm, knit to last 8 sts (removing marker), [k2, p2] twice.

SHAPE NECK

NEXT ROW (RS): Continuing to work 8 sts at each edge in Rib pattern, and remaining sts in Garter st, work to marker, join a second ball of yarn, BO center sts (removing markers), work to end—87 sts remain each side.

Working both sides at the same time, BO 4 sts at each neck edge once, 3 sts once, then 2 sts twice, then decrease 1 st at each neck edge every RS row 5 times, as follows: On left neck edge, knit to last 3 sts, ssk, k1; on right neck edge, k1, k2tog, knit to end—71 sts remain each side. Work even until piece measures 20" (51 cm) from the beginning, ending with a WS row. Cut yarn and place sts on st holders or waste yarn.

Back

Work as for Front until piece measures 2" (5 cm) from beginning of Garter st, ending with a WS row.

SHAPE NECK

NEXT ROW (RS): Work to marker, join a second ball of yarn, BO center sts (removing markers), work to end—87 sts remain each side. Working both sides at the same time, BO 4 sts at each neck edge 4

times—71 sts remain each side. Work even until piece measures 20" (51 cm) from the beginning, ending with a WS row. Do not cut yarn.

Finishing

Steam or wet-block pieces to finished measurements.

With WSs together (seam will be on the outside), and using Three-Needle BO, join Front and Back shoulders, working the first 4 sts together (2 sts from each needle) to prevent flaring; work the last 4 sts the same.

NECKBAND

With RS facing, using 16" (40 cm) long circular needle, and beginning at left shoulder, pick up and knit approximately 110 sts around neck opening (exact st count is not essential). Join for working in the rnd; pm for beginning of rnd. Purl 3 rnds. BO all sts purlwise.

⅄ Cable Substitution

Before getting started, review Stockinette Stitch Equivalent System on page 20.

CHOOSING CABLES

Cables A and C are mirror images of each other; each has an SSE of 30. Cable B has an SSE of 5 and is unique to this pattern. Cable B has the same number of rows as Cables A and C. If you replace Cables A and C, you can adjust the number of rows between cable crosses in Cable B to make it coordinate with any cable you choose. The easiest substitution would be to keep the cable panel the same width and replace the entire panel (leaving the 2 reverse stockinette stitches at each outside edge of the panel in place); SSE = 69 (30 + p2 + 5 + p2 + 30). As currently written, there are 48 stockinette stitches on either side of the original panel; if you'd like to use a wider panel of cables, you can replace any number of the stockinette stitches with cables. So, if you want to keep the Poncho the same width as the original, the maximum SSE that you have to work with would be 165.

MANAGING A CHANGE IN STITCH COUNT

If, after substituting, your stitch count has changed, make note of the difference between your cast-on numbers and the cast-on called for in the pattern and remember to add or subtract this difference during the decrease row after the ribbing is complete. When you get to the top of each piece, split any difference in stitch count between the center of the neck and the shoulders. The neck finishing may need a little adjustment as well.

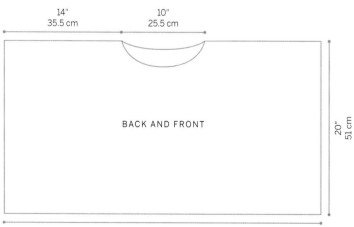

14"
35.5 cm

10"
25.5 cm

BACK AND FRONT

20"
51 cm

38"
96.5 cm

Chunky Cardigan

SIZES
To fit bust 30 (34, 38, 42, 46, 50, 54)" [76 (86.5, 96.5, 106.5, 117, 127, 137) cm]

FINISHED MEASUREMENTS
39 (42¾, 46¾, 51½, 55, 58¾, 62¾)" [99 (108.5, 118.5, 131, 139.5, 149, 159.5) cm] bust, buttoned

YARN
Quince & Co. Puffin [100% American wool; 112 yards (102 meters)/100 grams]: 11 (12, 13, 14, 15, 16, 17) hanks Audouin

NEEDLES
One pair straight needles size US 10½ (6.5 mm)

One pair straight needles size US 9 (5.5 mm)

One 32" (80 cm) long or longer circular needle size 9 (5.5 mm), for Front Bands/Collar

Change needle size if necessary to obtain correct gauge.

NOTIONS
Stitch markers; stitch holder or waste yarn; five 1" (25 mm) buttons

GAUGE
13 sts and 18 rows = 4" (10 cm) in St st, using larger needles

16-st panel from Hexa Paisley original and half-drop versions (#132) measure 3¾" (9.5 cm) wide, using larger needles

Steam or wet block your swatch before taking the measurements.

STITCH PATTERNS
1 x 1 Rib
(odd number of sts; 1-row repeat)
ROW 1 (RS): K1, *p1, k1; repeat from * to end.
ROW 2: Knit the knit sts and purl the purl sts as they face you.
Repeat Row 2 for pattern.

Texture Pattern
(panel of 4 sts; 2-row repeat)
ROW 1 (WS): K1, p2, k1.
ROW 2: Purl.
Repeat Rows 1 and 2 for pattern.

Cable A: Hexa Paisley (Original) (#132)

Cable B: Hexa Paisley (Half-drop) (#132)

⅜ If you'd like to make a cable substitution, see page 233.

Back

Using smaller needles, CO 79 (85, 91, 99, 105, 111, 117) sts. Begin 1 x 1 Rib; work even for 3" (7.5 cm), ending with a WS row.
Change to larger needles. Knit 1 row, decreasing 1 st at center of row—78 (84, 90, 98, 104, 110, 116) sts remain.

SET-UP ROW 1 (WS): P7 (10, 13, 17, 20, 23, 26), pm, work Texture Pattern over 4 sts, work Cable A over 16 sts, work Texture Pattern over 4 sts, work Cable B over 16 sts, work Texture Pattern over 4 sts, work Cable A over 16 sts, work Texture Pattern over 4 sts, pm, purl to end.
SET-UP ROW 2: Knit to marker, sm, work in patterns as established to next marker, sm, knit to end.
Work even until piece measures 7½" (19 cm) from the beginning, ending with a WS row.

SHAPE SIDES

DECREASE ROW (RS): K2, k2tog, work to last 4 sts, ssk, k2—2 sts decreased.
Repeat Decrease Row on RS every 4 (4, 4, 4½, 4½, 4½, 4½)" [10 (10, 10, 11.5, 11.5, 11.5, 11.5) cm] twice—72 (78, 84, 92, 98, 104, 110) sts remain.
Work even until piece measures 18 (18, 18, 18½, 18½, 18½, 19)" [45.5 (45.5, 45.5, 47, 47, 47, 48.5) cm] from the beginning, ending with a WS row.

SHAPE ARMHOLES

Continuing in patterns as established, BO 2 (3, 4, 5, 6, 7, 8) sts at beginning of next 2 rows, then 2 sts at beginning of next 2 (2, 2, 4, 4, 6, 6) rows—64 (68, 72, 74, 78, 78, 82) sts remain.
DECREASE ROW (RS): K1, k2tog, work to last 3 sts, ssk, k1—2 sts decreased.
Repeat Decrease Row every RS row 3 (3, 3, 3, 4, 3, 4) times—56 (60, 64, 66, 68, 70, 72) sts remain.
Work even until armholes measure 8 (8, 8½, 8½, 9, 9½, 10)" [20.5 (20.5, 21.5, 21.5, 23, 24, 25.5) cm], ending with a WS row.

SHAPE SHOULDERS

BO 5 (6, 6, 7, 7, 7, 7) sts at beginning of next 4 rows, then 6 (6, 7, 6, 6, 7, 7) sts at beginning of next 2 rows. Place remaining 24 (24, 26, 26, 28, 28, 30) sts on holder or waste yarn for neck.

Left Front

Using smaller needles, CO 37 (41, 43, 47, 51, 53, 57) sts. Begin 1 x 1 Rib; work even for 3" (7.5 cm), ending with a WS row.

Change to larger needles. Knit 1 row, decreasing 0 (1, 0, 0, 1, 0, 1) st(s)—37 (40, 43, 47, 50, 53, 56) sts remain.

SET-UP ROW 1 (WS): P6, pm, work Texture Pattern over 4 sts, work Cable A over 16 sts, work Texture Pattern over 4 sts, pm, purl to end.

SET-UP ROW 2: Knit to marker, sm, work in patterns as established to next marker, sm, knit to end.

Work even until piece measures 7½" (19 cm) from the beginning, ending with a WS row.

SHAPE SIDE, NECK, AND ARMHOLE

Note: Side, neck, and armhole shaping are worked at the same time; please read entire section through before beginning. Neck shaping will not be completed until after armhole shaping is complete.

SIDE DECREASE ROW (RS): Continuing in patterns as established, k2, k2tog, work to end—1 st decreased.

Repeat Side Decrease Row on RS every 4 (4, 4, 4½, 4½, 4½, 4½)" [10 (10, 10, 11.5, 11.5, 11.5, 11.5) cm] twice. AT THE SAME TIME, when piece measures 16 (16, 16, 16½, 16, 16, 16½)" [40.5 (40.5, 40.5, 42, 40.5, 40.5, 42) cm] from the beginning, ending with a WS row, shape neck as follows:

NECK DECREASE ROW (RS): Continuing to work side shaping if necessary, work to last 4 sts, ssk, k2—1 st decreased.

Repeat Neck Decrease Row [every 6 rows once, then every 4 rows once] 3 (3, 3, 3, 3, 4, 3) times, then every 4 rows 3 (3, 4, 4, 5, 3, 6) times. AT THE SAME TIME, when piece measures 18 (18, 18, 18½, 18½, 18½, 19)" [45.5 (45.5, 45.5, 47, 47, 47, 48.5) cm] from the beginning, ending with a WS row, shape armhole as follows:

Continuing to work neck shaping, BO 2 (3, 4, 5, 6, 7, 8) sts at armhole edge once, then 2 sts 1 (1, 1, 2, 2, 3, 3) time(s).

ARMHOLE DECREASE ROW (RS): Continuing to work neck shaping, k1, k2tog, work to end—1 st decreased.

Repeat Armhole Decrease Row every RS row 3 (3, 3, 4, 3, 4) times—16 (18, 19, 20, 20, 21, 21) sts remain when all shaping is complete.

Work even until armhole measures 8 (8, 8½, 8½, 9, 9½, 10)" [20.5 (20.5, 21.5, 21.5, 23, 24, 25.5) cm], ending with a WS row.

SHAPE SHOULDERS

BO 5 (6, 6, 7, 7, 7, 7) sts at armhole edge twice, then 6 (6, 7, 6, 6, 7, 7) sts once.

Right Front

Using smaller needles, CO 37 (41, 43, 47, 51, 53, 57) sts. Begin 1 x 1 Rib; work even for 3" (7.5 cm), ending with a WS row.

Change to larger needles. Knit 1 row, decreasing 0 (1, 0, 0, 1, 0, 1) st(s)—37 (40, 43, 47, 50, 53, 56) sts remain.

SET-UP ROW 1 (WS): P7 (10, 13, 17, 20, 23, 26), pm, work Texture Pattern over 4 sts, work Cable A over 16 sts, work Texture Pattern over 4 sts, pm, purl to end.

SET-UP ROW 2: Knit to marker, sm, work in patterns as established to next marker, sm, knit to end.

Work even until piece measures 7½" (19 cm) from the beginning, ending with a WS row.

SHAPE SIDE, NECK, AND ARMHOLE

Note: Side, neck, and armhole shaping are worked at the same time; please read entire section through before beginning. Neck shaping will not be completed until after armhole shaping is complete.

SIDE DECREASE ROW (RS): Continuing in patterns as established, work to last 4 sts, ssk, k2—1 st decreased.

Repeat Side Decrease Row on RS every 4 (4, 4, 4½, 4½, 4½, 4½)" [10 (10, 10, 11.5, 11.5, 11.5, 11.5) cm] twice. AT THE SAME TIME, when piece measures 16 (16, 16, 16½, 16, 16, 16½)" [40.5 (40.5, 40.5, 42, 40.5, 40.5, 42) cm] from the beginning, ending with a WS row, shape neck as follows:

NECK DECREASE ROW (RS): Continuing to work side shaping if necessary, k2, k2tog, work to end—1 st decreased.

Repeat Neck Decrease Row [every 6 rows once, then every 4 rows once] 3 (3, 3, 3, 3, 4, 3) times, then every 4 rows 3 (3, 4, 4, 5, 3, 6) times. AT THE SAME TIME, when piece measures 18 (18, 18, 18½, 18½, 18½, 19)" [45.5 (45.5, 45.5, 47, 47, 47, 48.5) cm] from the beginning, ending with a RS row, shape armhole as follows:

Continuing to work neck shaping, BO 2 (3, 4, 5, 6, 7, 8) sts at armhole edge once, then 2 sts 1 (1, 1, 2, 2, 3, 3) time(s).

ARMHOLE DECREASE ROW (RS): Continuing to work neck shaping, work to last 3 sts, ssk, k1—1 st decreased.

Repeat Armhole Decrease Row every RS row 3 (3, 3, 3, 4, 3, 4) times—16 (18, 19, 20, 20, 21, 21) sts remain when all shaping is complete.

Work even until armhole measures 8 (8, 8½, 8½, 9, 9½, 10)" [20.5 (20.5, 21.5, 21.5, 23, 24, 25.5) cm], ending with a RS row.

SHAPE SHOULDERS

BO 5 (6, 6, 7, 7, 7, 7) sts at armhole edge twice, then 6 (6, 7, 6, 6, 7, 7) sts once.

Sleeves

Using smaller needles, CO 39 (39, 39, 41, 41, 43, 43) sts. Begin 1 x 1 Rib; work even for 3" (7.5 cm), ending with a WS row.

Change to larger needles. Knit 1 row, decreasing 1 st—38 (38, 38, 40, 40, 42, 42) sts remain.

SET-UP ROW 1 (WS): P7 (7, 7, 8, 8, 9, 9), pm, work Texture Pattern over 4 sts, work Cable B over 16 sts, work Texture Pattern over 4 sts, pm, purl to end.

SET-UP ROW 2: Knit to marker, sm, work in patterns as established to next marker, sm, knit to end.

Work even until piece measures 5" (12.5 cm), ending with a WS row.

SHAPE SLEEVE

INCREASE ROW (RS): K2, M1R, work to last 2 sts, M1L, k2—2 sts increased.

Repeat Increase Row every 10 (8, 6, 6, 4, 4, 4) rows 4 (4, 5, 9, 2, 5, 10) times, then every 12 (10, 8, 0, 6, 6, 6) rows 1 (2, 3, 0, 8, 6, 3) time(s), working new sts in St st—50 (52, 56, 60, 62, 66, 70) sts.

Work even until piece measures 18 (18, 18½, 18½, 19, 19, 19½)" [45.5 (45.5, 47, 47, 48.5, 48.5, 49.5) cm] from the beginning, ending with a WS row.

SHAPE CAP

Continuing in patterns as established, BO 2 sts at beginning of next 2 (2, 4, 6, 6, 8, 10) rows—46 (48, 48, 48, 50, 50, 50) sts remain.

DECREASE ROW (RS): K1, k2tog, work to last 3 sts, ssk, k1—2 sts decreased.

Repeat Decrease Row every RS row 2 (2, 2, 3, 3, 3, 3) times, every 4 rows 3 (3, 3, 3, 3, 3, 2) times, then every RS row 3 (4, 4, 2, 3, 3, 4) times—28 (28, 28, 30, 30, 30, 30) sts remain.

BO 2 sts at beginning of next 2 rows, then 3 sts at beginning of next 2 rows.

BO remaining 18 (18, 18, 20, 20, 20, 20) sts.

Finishing

Block pieces as desired. Sew shoulder seams.

FRONT BANDS/COLLAR

With RS facing, using 32" (80 cm) long circular needle, and beginning at lower Right Front edge, pick up and knit 58 (58, 58, 60, 58, 58, 60) sts to base of neck shaping, pm, 43 (43, 45, 45, 49, 49, 51) sts to shoulder seam, knit across 24 (24, 26, 26, 28, 28, 30) back neck sts from holder, picking up and knitting 1 st at center back neck, pick up and knit 43 (43, 45, 45, 49, 49, 51) sts to base of neck shaping, pm, then 58 (58, 58, 60, 58, 58, 60) sts to lower Left Front edge—227 (227, 233, 237, 243, 243, 253) sts.

NEXT ROW (WS): P1, *k1, p1; repeat from * to end.

SHAPE COLLAR

SHORT ROW 1 (RS): Continuing in rib pattern as established, work to second marker, turn.

SHORT ROW 2 (WS): Yo, work to marker, turn.

SHORT ROW 3: Yo, work to 1 st before yo from previous RS row, turn.

SHORT ROW 4: Yo, work to 1 st before yo from previous WS row, turn.

SHORT ROWS 5–22: Repeat Short Rows 3 and 4 nine times.

SHORT ROW 23: Yo, work to end, working yos together with adjacent sts as you come to them, as follows: If st following yo is a knit st, work k2tog on yo and following st; if st following yo is a purl st, work ssp on yo and following st.

ROW 24: Work to end, working remaining yos together with adjacent sts. Work even for 2 rows.

BUTTONHOLE ROW (RS): Work 3 sts, yo, k2tog, [work 11 sts, yo, work 2 sts together (k2tog if second st is a knit st, p2tog if second st is a purl st)] 4 times, work to end.

Work even until band measures 1¾" (4.5 cm) from pick-up row, measured at lower edge.

BO all sts in pattern using larger needle.

Set in Sleeves. Sew side and Sleeve seams, working seam ½ st in from edge, to minimize bulk of seams.

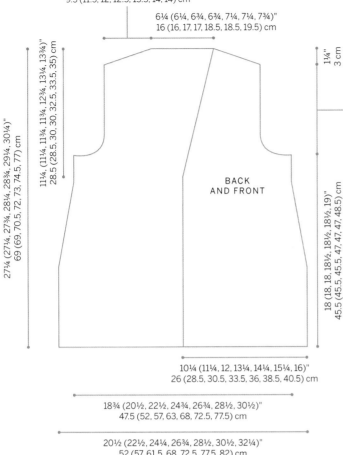

3¾ (4½, 4¾, 5, 5¼, 5½, 5½)"
9.5 (11.5, 12, 12.5, 13.5, 14, 14) cm

6¼ (6¼, 6¾, 6¾, 7¼, 7¼, 7¾)"
16 (16, 17, 17, 18.5, 18.5, 19.5) cm

1¼"
3 cm

11¼, (11¼, 11¾, 11¾, 12¾, 13¼, 13¾)"
28.5 (28.5, 30, 30, 32.5, 33.5, 35) cm

BACK
AND FRONT

27¼ (27¼, 27¾, 28¼, 28¾, 29¼, 30¼)"
69 (69, 70.5, 72, 73, 74.5, 77) cm

8 (8, 8½, 8½, 9, 9½, 10)"
20.5 (20.5, 21.5, 21.5, 23, 24, 25.5) cm

18 (18, 18, 18½, 18½, 18½, 19)"
45.5 (45.5, 45.5, 47, 47, 47, 48.5) cm

10¼ (11¼, 12, 13¼, 14¼, 15¼, 16)"
26 (28.5, 30.5, 33.5, 36, 38.5, 40.5) cm

18¾ (20½, 22½, 24¾, 26¾, 28½, 30½)"
47.5 (52, 57, 63, 68, 72.5, 77.5) cm

20½ (22½, 24¼, 26¾, 28½, 30½, 32¼)"
52 (57, 61.5, 68, 72.5, 77.5, 82) cm

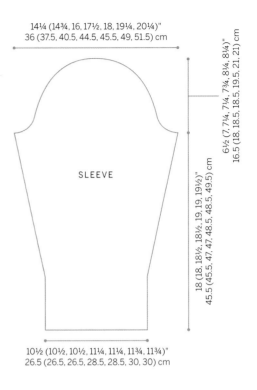

14¼ (14¾, 16, 17½, 18, 19¼, 20¼)"
36 (37.5, 40.5, 44.5, 45.5, 49, 51.5) cm

SLEEVE

6½ (7, 7¼, 7¼, 7¾, 8¼, 8¼)"
16.5 (18, 18.5, 18.5, 19.5, 21, 21) cm

18 (18, 18½, 18½, 19, 19, 19½)"
45.5 (45.5, 47, 47, 48.5, 48.5, 49.5) cm

10½ (10½, 10½, 11¼, 11¼, 11¾, 11¾)"
26.5 (26.5, 26.5, 28.5, 28.5, 30, 30) cm

🔗 Cable Substitution

Before getting started, review Stockinette Stitch Equivalent System on page 20.

CHOOSING CABLES

On the fronts, the original cable has an SSE of 10. If you'd like to keep the textured stitch, you'll need a cable with an SEE of 10 or smaller. If you are willing to ditch the textured stitch, the cable can be as wide as SSE 16.

The back has 3 columns of cables, each with an SSE of 10. You can replace each column with another of the same size, or you might want to use an unrelated wider cable panel to fill the space. If you want to eliminate the texture stitch, you can go as wide as a total SSE of 44, keeping 1 reverse stockinette stitch on either outside edge of the panel.

MANAGING A CHANGE IN STITCH COUNT

If, after substituting, your required stitch count is different from the stitch count at the end of the ribbing, remember to add or subtract the difference while working the knit row following the ribbing. The difference in stitch count will remain throughout each piece and may require you to adjust the shoulder shaping.

Chapter 6

Drawing

For the cables in this chapter, I used straight and sinuous lines of cable crosses to draw abstract or representational shapes that combine to make larger compositions. Within the cabled line drawings are textural stitches, such as ribs, seed, reverse stockinette, and lace, as well as smaller allover cable patterns.

The patterns in this chapter fall into four categories. The allover Bulb (#144) can be made infi-nitely wider and longer (like the rest of the allover cable patterns in this book). Macramé (#145) and Paisley Shadow (#146) are wide panels whose rows can be repeated but whose width is fixed. Turnbuckle, Weave & Duck, Meander, Diverge, and Fennec (#147–#151) feature large, non-repeatable compositions. Starburst (#152) is a large free-floating motif that can be placed anywhere on a stockinette-stitch ground.

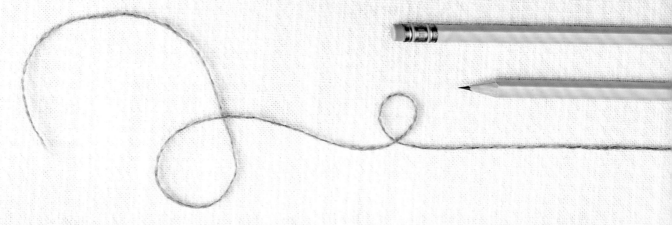

Bulb GROUP 1

The onion, or ogee, shape of Bulb is drawn with 2-stitch-wide cable lines and filled with decorative stitchwork. I approached designing this motif as if I were drawing, using a minimal number of lines and embellishments to get my idea across. The panel is made by staggering the bulb shape in repeat. As in Ogee X (#123), the addition of a few ribs between the bulbs helps compensate for the difference in gauge between the cable and the stockinette stitch.

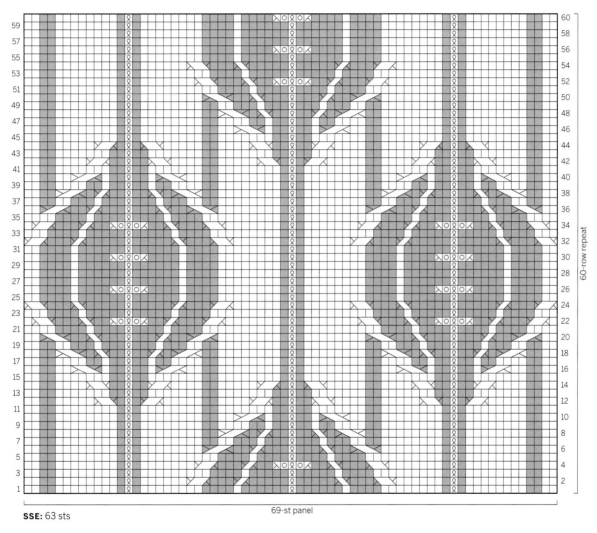

SSE: 63 sts

69-st panel

60-row repeat

□ Knit on RS, purl on WS.	▨ Purl on RS, knit on WS.
⊠ K2tog on RS, p2tog on WS.	⊠ K1-tbl on RS, p1-tbl on WS.
⊠ Ssk on RS, ssp on WS.	○ Yo

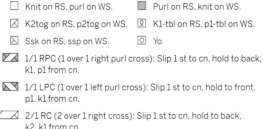 1/1 RPC (1 over 1 right purl cross): Slip 1 st to cn, hold to back, k1, p1 from cn.

1/1 LPC (1 over 1 left purl cross): Slip 1 st to cn, hold to front, p1, k1 from cn.

OR 2/1 RC (2 over 1 right cross): Slip 1 st to cn, hold to back, k2, k1 from cn.

OR 2/1 LC (2 over 1 left cross): Slip 2 sts to cn, hold to front, k1, k2 from cn.

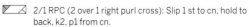 2/1 RPC (2 over 1 right purl cross): Slip 1 st to cn, hold to back, k2, p1 from cn.

2/1 LPC (2 over 1 left purl cross): Slip 2 sts to cn, hold to front, p1, k2 from cn.

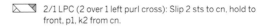 2/2 RC (2 over 2 right cross): Slip 2 sts to cn, hold to back, k2, k2 from cn.

2/2 LC (2 over 2 left cross): Slip 2 sts to cn, hold to front, k2, k2 from cn.

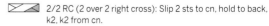 OR 2/2 RPC (2 over 2 right purl cross): Slip 2 sts to cn, hold to back, k2, p2 from cn.

 OR 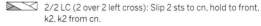 2/2 LPC (2 over 2 left purl cross): Slip 2 sts to cn, hold to front, p2, k2 from cn.

Macramé GROUP 2

Cabled diagonal lines made entirely of 2/2 crosses and vertical ribbing combine to look a lot like macramé here. Rows 1–6 of the cabled rib at the bottom can be repeated as many times as you like. Or you can skip it entirely and start with Row 9. While this panel is only 46 stitches wide, it is 80 rows long, so it's best used in a long project like a scarf, afghan, or skirt (see page 265). If you want to use it on a sweater, I suggest you try it with a finer gauge yarn in order to fit in more than one vertical repeat.

☐ Knit on RS, purl on WS.

▨ Purl on RS, knit on WS.

I Pattern repeat

⬚ OR ⬚ 2/2 RC (2 over 2 right cross): Slip 2 sts to cn, hold to back, k2, k2 from cn.

⬚ OR ⬚ 2/2 LC (2 over 2 left cross): Slip 2 sts to cn, hold to front, k2, k2 from cn.

⬚ OR ⬚ 2/2 RPC (2 over 2 right purl cross): Slip 2 sts to cn, hold to back, k2, p2 from cn.

⬚ OR ⬚ 2/2 LPC (2 over 2 left purl cross): Slip 2 sts to cn, hold to front, p2, k2 from cn.

SSE: 32 sts

46-st panel

80-row repeat

6-row repeat (optional)

Drawing

Paisley Shadow

GROUP 2

Here straight and sinuous lines combine to make a loosely interwoven pattern on a simple background of reverse stockinette. For a different look, you could fill in some of the shapes with lace, seed, or moss stitch, or another stitch of your choice. I added small knots to represent the final curlicue of a traditional paisley shape.

☐ Knit on RS, purl on WS.

▨ Purl on RS, knit on WS.

◉ MK (make knot): Knit into front, back, then front of st, slip these 3 sts back to left needle and k3; pass third, then second sts over first.

▱ 2/1 RPC (2 over 1 right purl cross): Slip 1 st to cn, hold to back, k2, p1 from cn.

▱ 2/1 LPC (2 over 1 left purl cross): Slip 2 sts to cn, hold to front, p1, k2 from cn.

▱ OR ▱ 2/2 RPC (2 over 2 right purl cross): Slip 2 sts to cn, hold to back, k2, p2 from cn.

▱ OR ▱ 2/2 LPC (2 over 2 left purl cross): Slip 2 sts to cn, hold to front, p2, k2 from cn.

▱ 2/1/2 RPC (2 over 1 over 2 right purl cross): Slip 3 sts to cn, hold to back, k2, slip last st from cn back to left needle, p1, k2 from cn.

▱ 2/1/2 LPC (2 over 1 over 2 left purl cross): Slip 3 sts to cn, hold to front, k2, slip last st from cn back to left needle, p1, k2 from cn.

SSE: 42 sts

53-st panel

Sinuous Lines

151

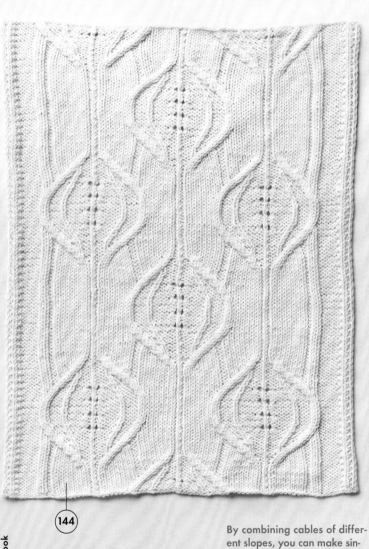

144

By combining cables of different slopes, you can make sinuous lines with which to draw cables (as in Bulb [#144] and Fennec [#151] in the photo).

Here are some guidelines for working with lines of 2 or 3 stitches, to help you if you want to give this type of drawing a try.

When a group of stitches isn't crossed, it forms a vertical line.

When a group of stitches moves over 1 stitch, the line it makes has a high slope; it's approaching vertical.

When a group of stitches moves over 2 stitches, the line it makes has a medium slope, at about a 45° angle.

When a group of stitches moves over 3 stitches or more, it has a low slope and it is as close as possible to horizontal.

Moving over 4 or more stitches tends to strain the stitches and causes gathering of the background stitches, but I do this on occasion (for example, in **FENNEC (#151),** where 2 stitches cross over 4).

You can't make a horizontal line with cables alone.

Turnbuckle GROUP 3

Turnbuckwle combines stockinette stitch and ribbed cables, creating fine and broad lines that make an interesting composition. The first 24 rows on the bottom and the last 6 rows at the top can each be repeated as many times as necessary in order to finesse the placement of the more elaborately cabled middle section on a project. When designing this cable, I was imagining it on a sweater, with the simpler top section easily adaptable to different neckline treatments.

TURNBUCKLE

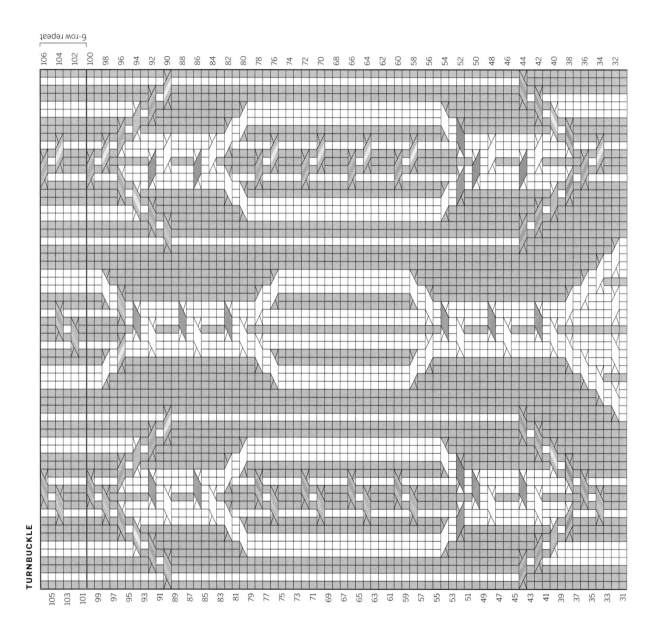

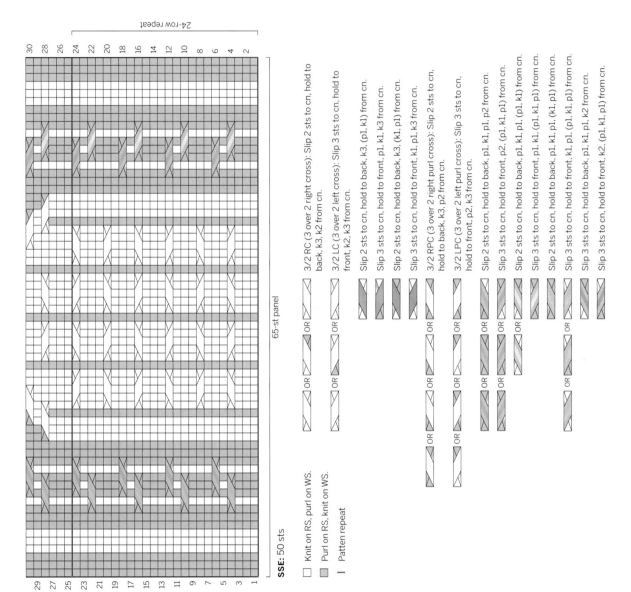

24-row repeat

65-st panel

SSE: 50 sts

☐ Knit on RS, purl on WS.

▨ Purl on RS, knit on WS.

❙ Pattern repeat

◹ OR ◸ 3/2 RC (3 over 2 right cross): Slip 2 sts to cn, hold to back, k3, k2 from cn.

◸ OR ◹ 3/2 LC (3 over 2 left cross): Slip 3 sts to cn, hold to front, k2, k3 from cn.

◸ Slip 2 sts to cn, hold to back, k3, (p1, k1) from cn.

◸ Slip 3 sts to cn, hold to front, p1, k1, k3 from cn.

◸ Slip 2 sts to cn, hold to back, k3, (k1, p1) from cn.

◸ Slip 3 sts to cn, hold to front, k1, p1, k3 from cn.

◸ OR ◹ 3/2 RPC (3 over 2 right purl cross): Slip 2 sts to cn, hold to back, k3, p2 from cn.

◸ OR ◹ 3/2 LPC (3 over 2 left purl cross): Slip 3 sts to cn, hold to front, p2, k3 from cn.

◸ OR ◹ Slip 2 sts to cn, hold to back, p1, k1, p1, p2 from cn.

◸ OR ◹ Slip 3 sts to cn, hold to front, p2, (p1, k1, p1) from cn.

◸ Slip 2 sts to cn, hold to back, p1, k1, p1, (p1, k1, k1) from cn.

◸ Slip 3 sts to cn, hold to front, p1, k1, p1, (k1, p1, p1) from cn.

◸ OR ◹ Slip 2 sts to cn, hold to back, k1, p1, p1, (p1, k1, p1) from cn.

◸ Slip 3 sts to cn, hold to back, p1, k1, p1, k2 from cn.

◸ Slip 3 sts to cn, hold to front, k2, (p1, k1, p1) from cn.

Drawing

245

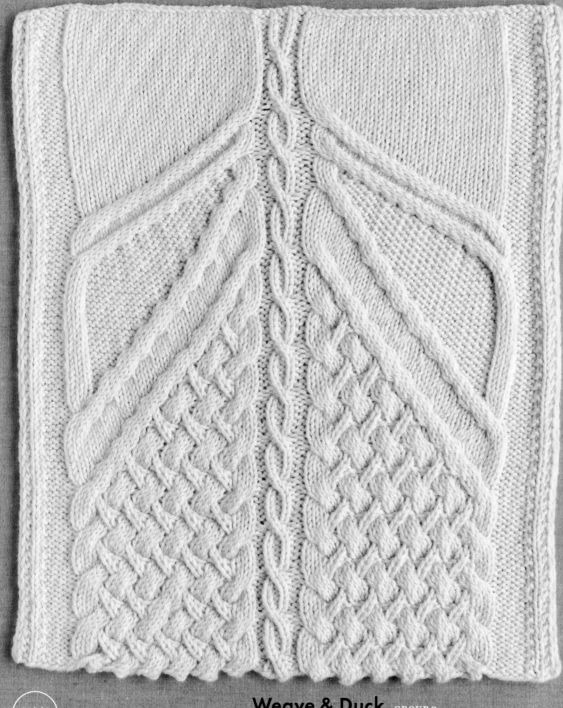

Weave & Duck GROUP 3

Typically I make diagonal lines by crossing stitches as evenly as possible every right-side row, but for this riff on Uneven Weave (#97), I made steeper diagonal lines by crossing 3 stitches every 4th row to coordinate with the crosses of Uneven Weave. Later in the pattern, when it switches from being cabled to stockinette stitch, I worked special cable crosses that include decreases to compensate for the difference in gauge between the cabled section and the stockinette stitch. You can finesse the placement of the most interesting section of the pattern (Rows 10–74) by working the 8-row repeat near the bottom as many times as needed.

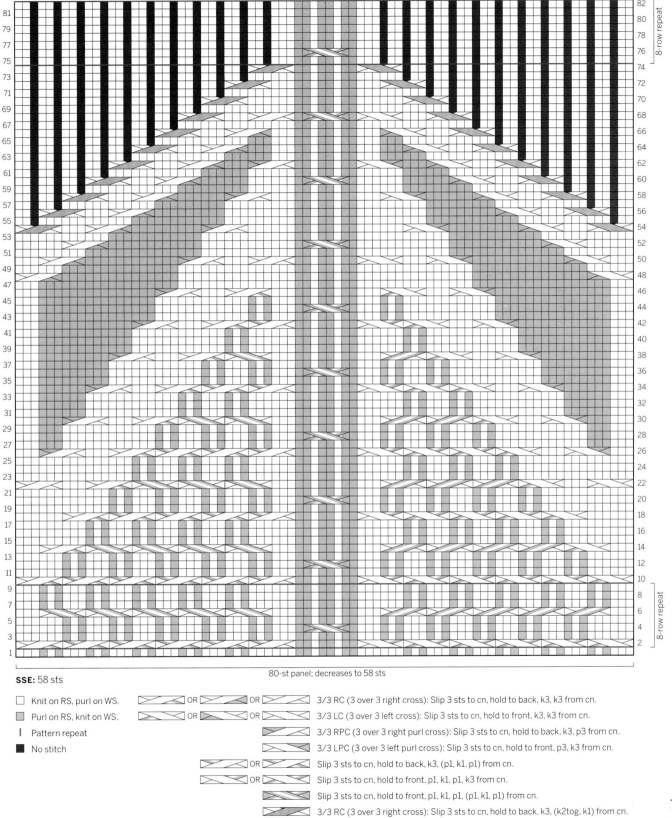

Left row numbers (bottom to top): 1, 3, 5, 7, 9, 11, 13, 15, 17, 19, 21, 23, 25, 27, 29, 31, 33, 35, 37, 39, 41, 43, 45, 47, 49, 51, 53, 55, 57, 59, 61, 63, 65, 67, 69, 71, 73, 75, 77, 79, 81

Right row numbers (bottom to top): 2, 4, 6, 8, 10, 12, 14, 16, 18, 20, 22, 24, 26, 28, 30, 32, 34, 36, 38, 40, 42, 44, 46, 48, 50, 52, 54, 56, 58, 60, 62, 64, 66, 68, 70, 72, 74, 76, 78, 80, 82

8-row repeat (top right), 8-row repeat (bottom right)

80-st panel; decreases to 58 sts

SSE: 58 sts

☐ Knit on RS, purl on WS.

▨ Purl on RS, knit on WS.

❘ Pattern repeat

■ No stitch

3/3 RC (3 over 3 right cross): Slip 3 sts to cn, hold to back, k3, k3 from cn.

3/3 LC (3 over 3 left cross): Slip 3 sts to cn, hold to front, k3, k3 from cn.

3/3 RPC (3 over 3 right purl cross): Slip 3 sts to cn, hold to back, k3, p3 from cn.

3/3 LPC (3 over 3 left purl cross): Slip 3 sts to cn, hold to front, p3, k3 from cn.

Slip 3 sts to cn, hold to back, k3, (p1, k1, p1) from cn.

Slip 3 sts to cn, hold to front, p1, k1, p1, k3 from cn.

Slip 3 sts to cn, hold to front, p1, k1, p1, (p1, k1, p1) from cn.

3/3 RC (3 over 3 right cross): Slip 3 sts to cn, hold to back, k3, (k2tog, k1) from cn.

3/3 LC (3 over 3 left cross): Slip 3 sts to cn, hold to front, (k1, k2tog), k3 from cn.

Mirroring

(149)

(146)

All of the cables in this chapter are mirrored along the vertical axis.

Most of them include a narrow vertical section that isn't part of the mirroring, where the cables from each side come together (as shown on **MEANDER [#149]** and **PAISLEY SHADOW [#146]** here). Mirroring can also be done horizontally.

Any cable chart can be easily mirrored if you draw it on your computer and manipulate from there. An old-school way of achieving the same result is to use a copy machine to copy the chart onto a piece of acetate, flip over the acetate to show the mirror image of the chart, and then make a paper copy of the "new" flipped version.

To design **STARBURST (#152),**
I double-mirrored the chart
on my computer, meaning I first
mirrored **LEFT BIAS WEAVE
(#116)** side to side (on either
side of the dotted line) and then
I mirrored it top to bottom (on
either side of the dotted line).
Then came the fun part: fig-
uring out how to merge the
quadrants and how wide and
tall to make the new motif.

Meander GROUP 4

You can vary the length of the narrow cable base of Meander by working the 6-row repeat as many times as you like before starting the V formation. The last 28 rows can also be repeated to extend the length of your panel at the top. Special cable crosses that include increases are worked as the pattern switches from stockinette to being more cabled. The increases make up for the difference in gauge between the stockinette stitch and the cabled section.

Diverge GROUP 4

The center of Diverge is formed with a column of Double O (#31) surrounded by a series of Fave motifs (page 168) joined together, then the big S motif from Cruller Chevron (#115) is used in diagonal formation. This panel can be ended gracefully at any point in the last 24 rows or, for more length, those 24 rows can be repeated as many times as needed.

MEANDER

28-row repeat

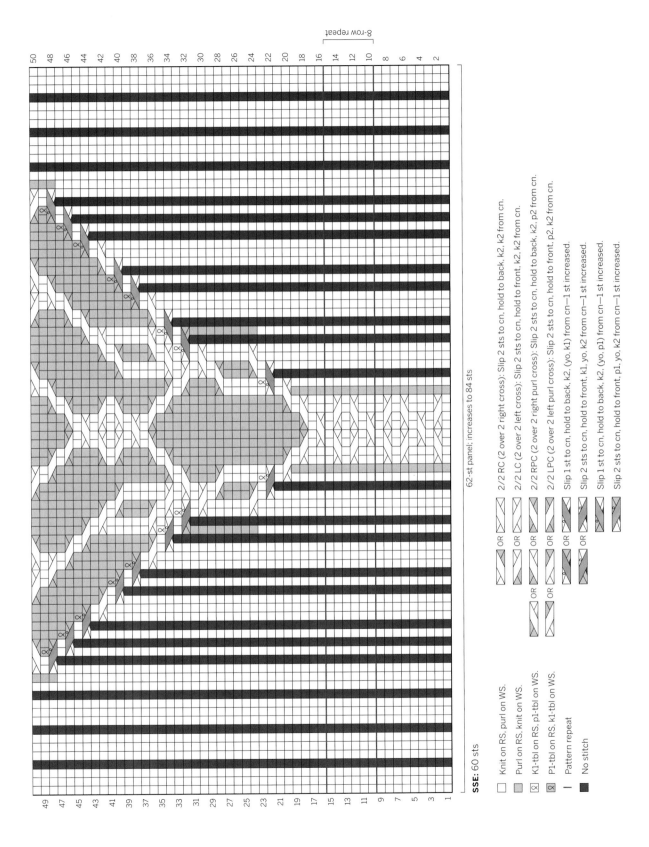

62-st panel; increases to 84 sts

SSE: 60 sts

Knit on RS, purl on WS.

Purl on RS, knit on WS.

K1-tbl on RS, p1-tbl on WS.

P1-tbl on RS, k1-tbl on WS.

| Pattern repeat

No stitch

OR 2/2 RC (2 over 2 right cross): Slip 2 sts to cn, hold to back, k2, k2 from cn.

OR 2/2 LC (2 over 2 left cross): Slip 2 sts to cn, hold to front, k2, k2 from cn.

OR 2/2 RPC (2 over 2 right purl cross): Slip 2 sts to cn, hold to back, k2, p2 from cn.

OR 2/2 LPC (2 over 2 left purl cross): Slip 2 sts to cn, hold to front, p2, k2 from cn.

OR Slip 1 st to cn, hold to back, k2, (yo, k1) from cn—1 st increased.

OR Slip 2 sts to cn, hold to front, k1, yo, k2 from cn—1 st increased.

Slip 1 st to cn, hold to back, k2, (yo, p1) from cn—1 st increased.

Slip 2 sts to cn, hold to front, p1, yo, k2 from cn—1 st increased.

DIVERGE

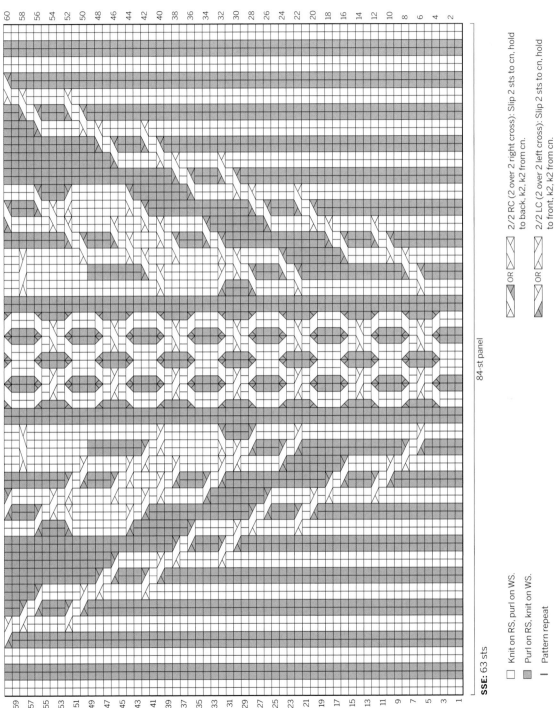

SSE: 63 sts

84-st panel

☐ Knit on RS, purl on WS.

▨ Purl on RS, knit on WS.

▮ Pattern repeat

◤ 2/1 RPC (2 over 1 right purl cross): Slip 1 st to cn, hold to back, k2, p1 from cn.

◣ 2/1 LPC (2 over 1 left purl cross): Slip 2 sts to cn, hold to front, p1, k2 from cn.

◤◥ OR ◤◥ 2/2 RC (2 over 2 right cross): Slip 2 sts to cn, hold to back, k2, k2 from cn.

◤◥ OR ◤◥ 2/2 LC (2 over 2 left cross): Slip 2 sts to cn, hold to front, k2, k2 from cn.

◤◥ OR ◤◥ 2/2 RPC (2 over 2 right purl cross): Slip 2 sts to cn, hold to back, k2, p2 from cn.

◤◥ OR ◤◥ 2/2 LPC (2 over 2 left purl cross): Slip 2 sts to cn, hold to front, p2, k2 from cn.

◤◥ OR ◤◥ 3/3 RC (3 over 3 right cross): Slip 3 sts to cn, hold to back, k3, k3 from cn.

◤◥ OR ◤◥ 3/3 LC (3 over 3 left cross): Slip 3 sts to cn, hold to front, k3, k3 from cn.

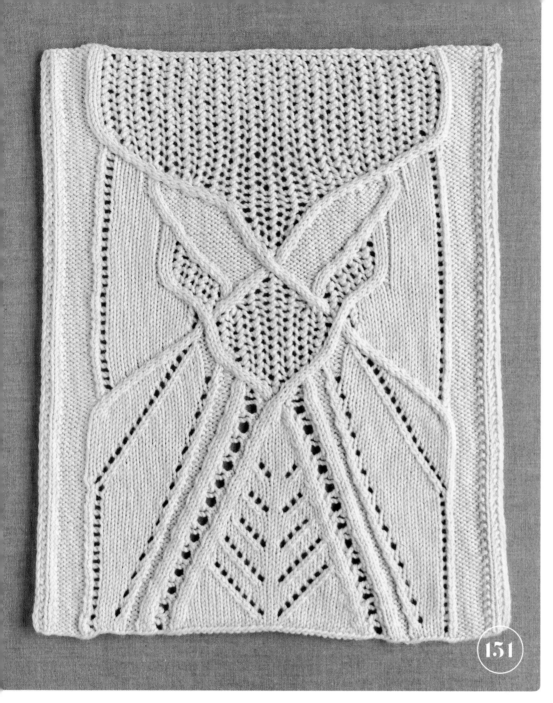

Fennec GROUP 4

My intention when designing Fennec was to make it summery-looking by combining lines of openwork and lace fills. I planned a transition from straight lines to sinuous ones and then topped it off with a graceful shape that would surround a neckline in a pretty way. It was only when I finished that I realized that the sinewy lines had taken on the look of a fennec fox.

☐ Knit on RS, purl on WS.

▨ Purl on RS, knit on WS.

▨ P1-tbl on RS, k1-tbl on WS.

⊙ Yo

⊙⊙ Yo2

▭ (P1, k1) into yo2.

▨ K2tog on RS, p2tog on WS.

▨ Ssk on RS, ssp on WS.

▨ P2tog on RS, k2tog on WS.

■ No stitch

RT (right twist): K2tog, but do not drop sts from left needle; insert right needle between 2 sts just worked and knit first st again, slip both sts from left needle together.

LT (left twist): Insert needle from back to front between first and second sts on left needle and knit the second st through the front loop; knit first st, slip both sts from left needle together.

▨ OR ▨

2/1 RPC (2 over 1 right purl cross): Slip 1 st to cn, hold to back, k2, p1 from cn.

▨ OR ▨

2/1 LPC (2 over 1 left purl cross): Slip 2 sts to cn, hold to front, p1, k2 from cn.

▨

2/2 RC (2 over 2 right cross): Slip 2 sts to cn, hold to back, k2, k2 from cn.

▨

2/2 LC (2 over 2 left cross): Slip 2 sts to cn, hold to front, k2, k2 from cn.

2/2 RPC (2 over 2 right purl cross): Slip 2 sts to cn, hold to back, k2, p2 from cn.

▨

2/2 LPC (2 over 2 left purl cross): Slip 2 sts to cn, hold to front, p2, k2 from cn.

 OR OR

Slip 2 sts to cn, hold to back, k2, (yo, p2tog) from cn.

 OR OR

Slip 2 sts to cn, hold to front, (yo, p2tog), k2 from cn.

Slip 1 st to cn, hold to back, k2, (yo, p1) from cn—1 st increased.

Slip 2 sts to cn, hold to front, p1, yo, k2 from cn—1 st increased.

 OR

Slip 2 sts to cn, hold to back, k2, p2tog from cn—1 st decreased.

 OR

Slip 2 sts to cn, hold to front, p2tog, k2 from cn—1 st decreased.

2/2/2 RPC (2 over 2 over 2 right purl cross): Slip 4 sts to cn, hold to back, k2, slip last 2 sts from cn back to left needle, p2, k2 from cn.

2/2/2 LPC (2 over 2 over 2 left purl cross): Slip 4 sts to cn, hold to front, k2, slip last 2 sts from cn back to left needle, p2, k2 from cn.

 OR OR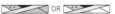

Slip 4 sts to cn, hold to back, k2, ([yo, p2tog] twice) from cn.

 OR 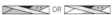 OR

Slip 2 sts to cn, hold to front, [yo, p2tog] twice, k2 from cn.

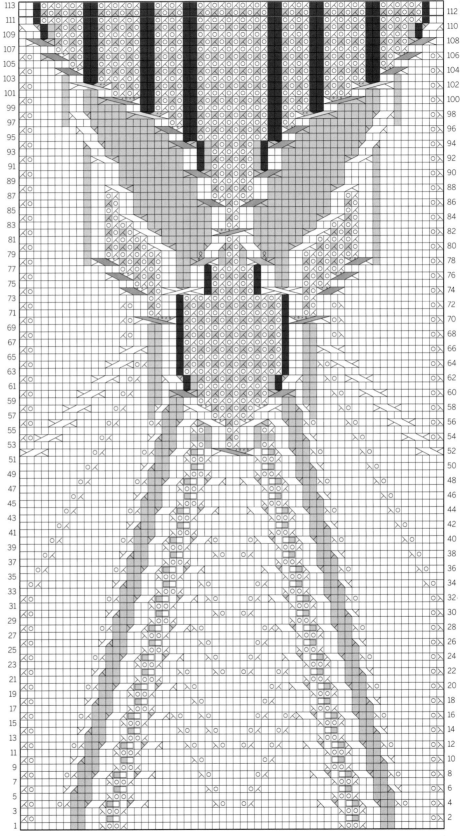 OR

Slip 4 sts to cn, hold to back, k2, ([p2tog] twice) from cn—2 sts decreased.

OR

Slip 2 sts to cn, hold to front, [p2tog] twice, k2 from cn—2 sts decreased.

2-row repeat

SSE: 54 sts

60-st panel; decreases to 46 sts

Drawing

257

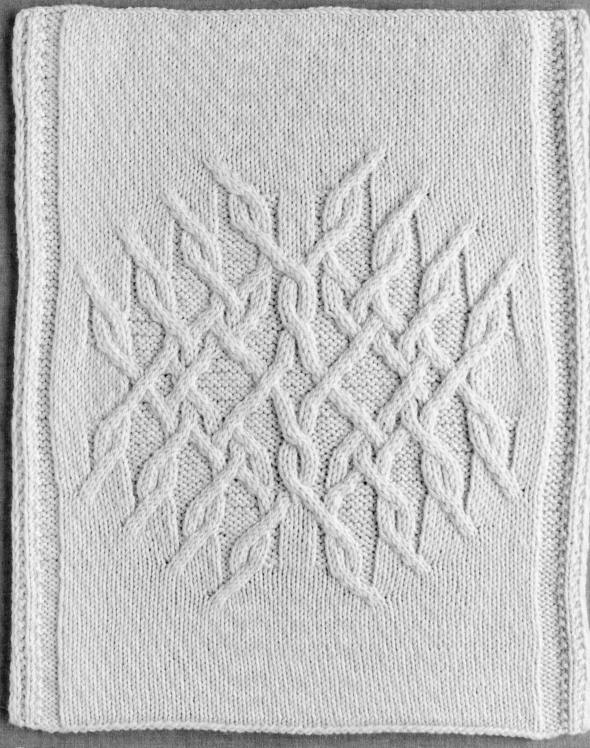

Starburst GROUP 5

Evocative of forms found on handwoven Western saddle blankets, this large, free-floating motif derived from Left Bias Weave (#116) can be used alone on the front of a sweater or in multiples, as shown on the Afghan (page 272).

SSE: 52 sts

52-st panel; increases to 78 sts

☐ Knit on RS, purl on WS.

▨ Purl on RS, knit on WS.

⧍ K1-tbl on RS, p1-tbl on WS.

⧍ P1-tbl on RS, k1-tbl on WS.

■ No stitch

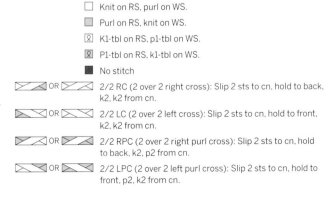 2/2 RC (2 over 2 right cross): Slip 2 sts to cn, hold to back, k2, k2 from cn.

2/2 LC (2 over 2 left cross): Slip 2 sts to cn, hold to front, k2, k2 from cn.

2/2 RPC (2 over 2 right purl cross): Slip 2 sts to cn, hold to back, k2, p2 from cn.

2/2 LPC (2 over 2 left purl cross): Slip 2 sts to cn, hold to front, p2, k2 from cn.

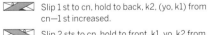 Slip 1 st to cn, hold to back, k2, (yo, k1) from cn—1 st increased.

 Slip 2 sts to cn, hold to front, k1, yo, k2 from cn—1 st increased.

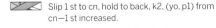 Slip 1 st to cn, hold to back, k2, (yo, p1) from cn—1 st increased.

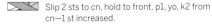 Slip 2 sts to cn, hold to front, p1, yo, k2 from cn—1 st increased.

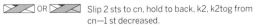 Slip 2 sts to cn, hold to back, k2, k2tog from cn—1 st decreased.

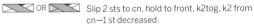 Slip 2 sts to cn, hold to front, k2tog, k2 from cn—1 st decreased.

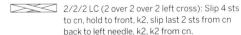 2/2/2 LC (2 over 2 over 2 left cross): Slip 4 sts to cn, hold to front, k2, slip last 2 sts from cn back to left needle, k2, k2 from cn.

 2/2/2 LPC (2 over 2 over 2 left purl cross): Slip 4 sts to cn, hold to front, k2, slip last 2 sts from cn back to left needle, p2, k2 from cn.

Flared Pullover

SIZES
To fit bust 30 (34, 38, 42, 46, 50, 54)" [76 (86.5, 96.5, 106.5, 117, 127, 137) cm]

FINISHED MEASUREMENTS
33 (37, 41, 45, 49, 53, 57)" [84 (94, 104, 114.5, 124.5, 134.5, 145) cm]

YARN
JaggerSpun Lamb DK [100% merino; 112 yards (102 meters)/100 grams]: 6 (7, 7, 8, 9, 9, 10) skeins in Pewter

NEEDLES
One pair straight needles size US 8 (5 mm)

One pair straight needles size US 6 (4 mm)

One 16" (40 cm) long circular needle size US 6 (4 mm)

Change needle size if necessary to obtain correct gauge.

NOTIONS
Stitch markers; removable markers; cable needle

GAUGE
20 sts and 28 rows = 4" (10 cm) in St st, using larger needles

12-st panel from Stable Braid (#54) measures 2" (5 cm), using larger needles

53-st panel from Paisley Shadow (#146) measures 8½" (21.5 cm) wide, using larger needles.

Steam or wet block your swatch before taking the measurements.

STITCH PATTERNS
Cable A: Stable Braid (#54)

Cable B: Paisley Shadow (#146)

PATTERN NOTES
This pullover begins with the Lower Back, which is worked from side to side, with markers placed for working the Upper Back. Once the Lower Back is complete, stitches are picked up for the Upper Back between the Lower Back markers, leaving the remainder of each end of the Lower Back to be sewn to the Front. Then the Upper Back is worked to the shoulders. Next, the Front and Sleeves are worked from the bottom up. The side edges of the Front are sewn to the remaining side edges of the Lower Back.

✂ If you'd like to make a cable substitution, see page 264.

Lower Back

Using smaller needles, CO 70 (70, 74, 74, 78, 78, 78) sts.
Note: Slip sts purlwise with yarn to WS.
SET-UP ROW 1 (WS): Slip 2, k1, p1, k1, *k2, p2; repeat from * to last 5 sts, k2, p3.
ROW 2: K3, p2, *k2, p2; repeat from * to last 5 sts, k5.
Work Rows 1 and 2 eleven more times, then work Row 1 once more.

Change to larger needles.
NEXT ROW (RS): K3, p2, [k10 (10, 9, 9, 9, 8, 8), k2tog] 5 (5, 6, 6, 6, 7, 7) times, knit to end—65 (65, 68, 68, 72, 71, 71) sts remain.
NEXT ROW: Slip 2, k1, p1, k1, purl to last 5 sts, k2, p3.
NEXT ROW: K3, p2, knit to end.
Work even until piece measures 12½ (12½, 13, 13, 13½, 13½, 14)" [32 (32, 33, 33, 34.5, 34.5, 35.5) cm] from the beginning. Place removable marker at beginning of RS row to mark right side of Back and top point of side seam.
Work even until piece measures 16½ (18½, 20½, 22½, 24½, 26½, 28½)" [42 (47, 52, 57, 62, 67.5, 72.5) cm from marker. Place second removable marker at beginning of RS row to mark left side of Back and top point of side seam.
Work even until piece measures 9½ (9½, 10, 10, 10½, 10½, 11)" [24 (24, 25.5, 25.5, 26.5, 26.5, 28) cm] from second marker, ending with a WS row.

Change to smaller needles.
NEXT ROW (RS): K3, p2, [k11 (11, 10, 10, 10, 9, 9), M1L] 5 (5, 6, 6, 6, 7, 7) times, knit to end—70 (70, 74, 74, 78, 78, 78) sts.
ROW 1 (WS): Slip 2, k1, p1, k1, *k2, p2; repeat from * to last 5 sts, k2, p3.
ROW 2: K3, p2, *k2, p2; repeat from * to last 5 sts, k5.
Work Rows 1 and 2 eleven more times, then work Row 1 once more.
BO all sts in pattern.

Upper Back

With RS of Lower Back facing, using larger needles and working along right long edge (opposite slipped-st edging), pick up and knit 82 (93, 102, 112, 123, 133, 143) sts between markers. Leave markers in place. Purl 1 row.
Continuing in St st, BO 2 (3, 5, 7, 6, 8, 10) sts at beginning of next 2 rows, then 2 sts at beginning of next 2 (2, 2, 4, 6, 8, 8) rows—74 (83, 88, 90, 99, 101, 107) sts remain.
DECREASE ROW (RS): K1, k2tog, knit to last 3 sts, ssk, k1—2 sts decreased.
Repeat Decrease Row every RS row 1 (3, 3, 2, 3, 4, 6) time(s), then every 4 rows 2 (4, 4, 3, 4, 3, 3) times—66 (67, 72, 78, 83, 85, 87) sts remain.

Work even until armholes measure 4½ (4½, 4¾, 5, 5½, 5½, 6)" [11.5 (11.5, 12, 12.5, 14, 14, 15) cm], ending with a RS row. Change to Garter st; work even until armholes measure 7¼ (7½, 8, 8¼, 8½, 9, 9½)" [18.5 (19, 20.5, 21, 21.5, 23, 24) cm], ending with a WS row. Place marker on either side of center 14 (15, 16, 18, 19, 21, 23) sts.

SHAPE NECK AND SHOULDERS

NEXT ROW (RS): BO 6 (6, 6, 6, 8, 8, 8) sts, knit to marker, join a second ball of yarn, BO center sts, knit to end. Continuing in Garter st and working both sides at the same time, BO 6 (6, 6, 6, 8, 8, 8) sts at armhole edge once, then 5 (5, 6, 7, 7, 7, 7) sts at each armhole edge twice. AT THE SAME TIME, BO 5 sts at each neck edge twice.

Front

Using smaller needles, CO 72 (72, 88, 88, 104, 104, 112) sts.

ROW 1 (WS): P1, *k2, p2; repeat from * to last 3 sts, k2, p1.

ROW 2: K1, *p2, k2; repeat from * to last 3 sts p2, k1.

ROWS 3 AND 4: Repeat Rows 1 and 2.

ROW 5: Repeat Row 1. Place marker 1 (1, 9, 9, 17, 17, 21) st(s) in from each edge.

ROW 6 (INCREASE ROW): Knit to marker, M1R, sm, work to next marker, sm, M1R, knit to end—2 sts increased.

ROW 7: Purl to marker, sm, work to next marker, sm, purl to end.

ROW 8: Knit to marker, sm, work to next marker, sm, knit to end.

ROWS 8 AND 10: Repeat Rows 7 and 8.

ROW 11: Repeat Row 7.

ROW 12: Repeat Row 6.

Repeat Rows 7–12 twice, then repeat Row 7 once—80 (80, 96, 96, 112, 112, 120) sts.

Change to larger needles.

NEXT ROW (RS): Knit to marker, sm, k3, [k4, M1L] 15 times, k7, sm, knit to end—95 (95, 111, 111, 127, 127, 135); 85 sts between markers.

SET-UP ROW 1: Purl to marker, sm, k2, work Cable A over 12 sts, k2, work Cable B over 53 sts, k2, work Cable A over 12 sts, k2, sm, purl to end.

SET-UP ROW 2: Knit to marker, sm, p2, work Cable A, p2, work Cable B, p2, work Cable A, p2, sm, knit to end.

SHAPE SIDES

INCREASE ROW (RS): Knit to marker, M1R, sm, work to next marker, sm, M1L, knit to end—2 sts increased.

Repeat Increase Row every 16 (6, 10, 4, 8, 4, 4) rows 3 (8, 4, 4, 7, 8, 9) times, then every 0 (0, 12, 6, 0, 6, 6) rows 0 (0, 1, 6, 0, 4, 4) time(s), working new sts in St st—103 (113, 123, 133, 143, 153, 163) sts; 9 (14, 19, 24, 29, 34, 39) sts outside markers on each side.

Work even until piece measures 12½ (12½, 13, 13, 13½, 13½, 14)" [32 (32, 33, 33, 34.5, 34.5, 35.5) cm] from the beginning, ending with a WS row.

SHAPE ARMHOLES

BO 2 (3, 5, 6, 7, 8, 10) sts at beginning of next 2 rows, then 2 sts at beginning of next 2 (2, 2, 4, 6, 8, 8) rows—95 (103, 109, 113, 117, 121, 127) sts remain.

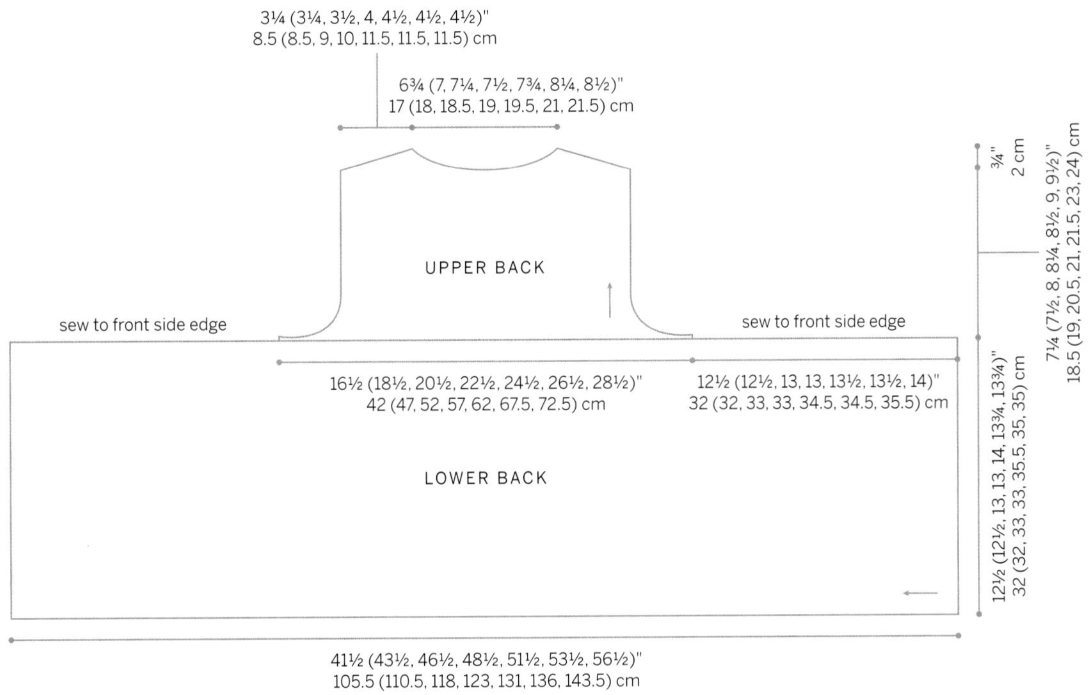
3¼ (3¼, 3½, 4, 4½, 4½, 4½)"
8.5 (8.5, 9, 10, 11.5, 11.5, 11.5) cm
6¾ (7, 7¼, 7½, 7¾, 8¼, 8½)"
17 (18, 18.5, 19, 19.5, 21, 21.5) cm
UPPER BACK
sew to front side edge
sew to front side edge
¾"
2 cm
7¼ (7½, 8, 8¼, 8½, 9, 9½)"
18.5 (19, 20.5, 21, 21.5, 23, 24) cm
16½ (18½, 20½, 22½, 24½, 26½, 28½)"
42 (47, 52, 57, 62, 67.5, 72.5) cm
12½ (12½, 13, 13, 13½, 13½, 14)"
32 (32, 33, 33, 34.5, 34.5, 35.5) cm
LOWER BACK
12½ (12½, 13, 13, 14, 13¾, 13¾)"
32 (32, 33, 33, 35.5, 35, 35) cm
41½ (43½, 46½, 48½, 51½, 53½, 56½)"
105.5 (110.5, 118, 123, 131, 136, 143.5) cm

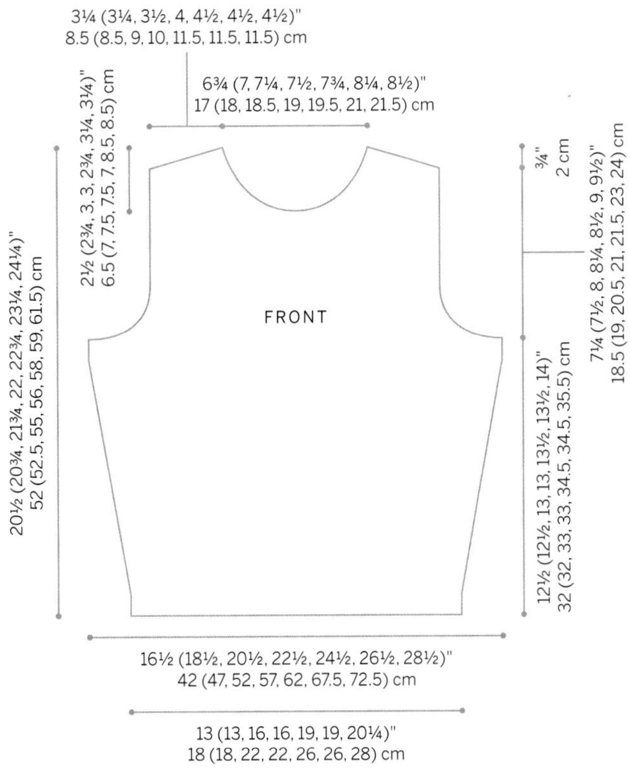
3¼ (3¼, 3½, 4, 4½, 4½, 4½)"
8.5 (8.5, 9, 10, 11.5, 11.5, 11.5) cm
6¾ (7, 7¼, 7½, 7¾, 8¼, 8½)"
17 (18, 18.5, 19, 19.5, 21, 21.5) cm
2½ (2¾, 3, 3, 2¾, 3¼, 3¼)"
6.5 (7, 7.5, 7.5, 7, 8.5, 8.5) cm
20½ (20¾, 21¾, 22, 22¾, 23¾, 24¼)"
52 (52.5, 55, 56, 58, 59, 61.5) cm
FRONT
¾"
2 cm
7¼ (7½, 8, 8¼, 8½, 9, 9½)"
18.5 (19, 20.5, 21, 21.5, 23, 24) cm
12½ (12½, 13, 13, 13½, 13½, 14)"
32 (32, 33, 33, 34.5, 34.5, 35.5) cm
16½ (18½, 20½, 22½, 24½, 26½, 28½)"
42 (47, 52, 57, 62, 67.5, 72.5) cm
13 (13, 16, 16, 19, 19, 20¼)"
18 (18, 22, 22, 26, 26, 28) cm

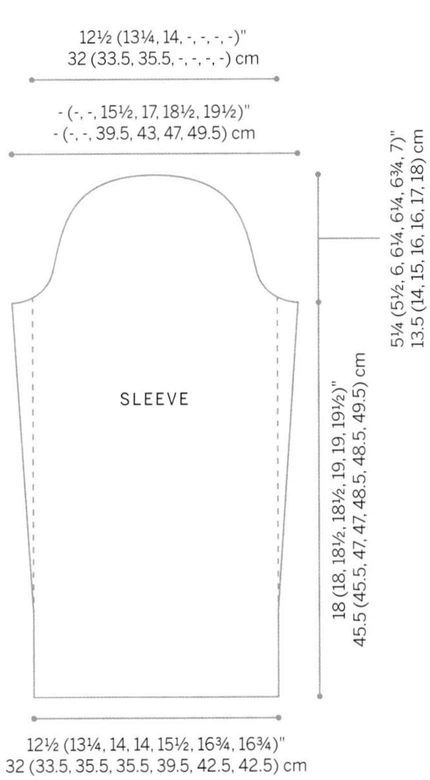
12½ (13¼, 14, -, -, -, -)"
32 (33.5, 35.5, -, -, -, -) cm
- (-, -, 15½, 17, 18½, 19½)"
- (-, -, 39.5, 43, 47, 49.5) cm
5¼ (5½, 6, 6¼, 6¼, 6¾, 7)"
13.5 (14, 15, 16, 16, 17, 18) cm
SLEEVE
18 (18, 18½, 18½, 19, 19, 19½)"
45.5 (45.5, 47, 47, 48.5, 48.5, 49.5) cm
12½ (13¼, 14, 14, 15½, 16¾, 16¾)"
32 (33.5, 35.5, 35.5, 39.5, 42.5, 42.5) cm

NOTE: The Sleeves for the first 3 sizes, denoted by the dashed lines, are not shaped; the last 4 sizes are.

DECREASE ROW (RS): K1, k2tog, work to last 3 sts, ssk, k1—2 sts decreased.

Repeat Decrease Row every RS row 0 (3, 3, 3, 2, 3, 5) time(s), then every 4 rows 4 times, removing markers if necessary to work last 1 or 2 decrease(s)—85 (87, 93, 97, 103, 105, 107) sts remain. Work even, keeping first and last sts in St st, until armholes measure 4½ (4½, 4¾, 5, 5½, 5½, 6)" [11.5 (11.5, 12, 12.5, 14, 14, 15) cm], ending with a RS row, and removing any markers on final row.

NEXT ROW (RS): K4 (2, 4, 0, 0, 1, 2), [k2 (2, 2, 3, 3, 3, 3), k2tog] 19 (20, 21, 19, 20, 20, 20) times, knit to end—66 (67, 72, 78, 83, 85, 87) sts remain.

Change to Garter st; work even until armholes measure 5½ (5½, 5¾, 6, 6½, 6½, 7)" [14 (14, 14.5, 15, 16.5, 16.5, 18) cm], ending with a WS row. Place markers on either side of center 10 (11, 12, 14, 15, 17, 19) sts.

SHAPE NECK

NEXT ROW (RS): Knit to marker, join a second ball of yarn, bind off center sts, knit to end. Working both sides at the same time, BO 4 sts at each neck edge once, then 3 sts once, then 2 sts once—19 (19, 21, 23, 25, 25, 25) sts remain each side.

DECREASE ROW (RS): On left neck edge, knit to last 3 sts, ssk, k1; on right neck edge, k1, k2tog, knit to end—1 st decreased each neck edge. Repeat Decrease Row every RS row twice—16 (16, 18, 20, 22, 22, 22) sts remain each side.

Work even until armholes measure 7¼ (7½, 8, 8¼, 8½, 9, 9½)" [18.5 (19, 20.5, 21, 21.5, 23, 24) cm], ending with a WS row.

SHAPE SHOULDERS

BO 6 (6, 6, 6, 8, 8, 8) sts at each armhole edge once, then 5 (5, 6, 7, 7, 7, 7) sts twice.

Sleeve

Using smaller needles, CO 70 (74, 78, 78, 86, 94, 94) sts.

ROW 1 (WS): P2, *k2, p2; repeat from * to end.
ROW 2: K2, *p2, k2; repeat from * to end.
Work even for 4" (10 cm), ending with a WS row.

Change to larger needles.
NEXT ROW (RS): K4 (2, 4, 4, 4, 4, 4), [k6, k2tog] 7 (8, 8, 8, 9, 10, 10) times, knit to end—63 (66, 70, 70, 77, 84, 84) sts remain.

SIZES 45, 49, 53, AND 57" (114.5, 124.5, 134.5, AND 145 CM) ONLY
Purl 1 row.

SHAPE SLEEVE

INCREASE ROW (RS): K1, M1R, knit to last st, M1L, k1—2 sts increased. Repeat Increase Row every - (-, -, 28, 30, 30, 16) rows - (-, -, 3, 3, 3, 6) times, working new sts in St st—- (-, -, 78, 85, 92, 98) sts.

ALL SIZES

Work even until piece measures 18 (18, 18½, 18½, 19, 19, 19½)" [45.5 (45.5, 47, 47, 48.5, 48.5, 49.5) cm] from the beginning, ending with a WS row.

SHAPE CAP

BO 2 (3, 5, 7, 6, 8, 10) sts at beginning of next 2 rows, then 2 sts at beginning of next 2 (2, 2, 2, 4, 6, 6) rows—55 (56, 56, 60, 65, 64, 66) sts remain.

DECREASE ROW (RS): K3, k2tog, knit to last 5 sts ssk, k3—2 sts decreased.

Repeat Decrease Row every RS row 2 (3, 2, 2, 5, 4, 5) times, then every 4 rows 4 (4, 6, 6, 3, 4, 4) times, then every RS row 3 (3, 2, 3, 5, 4, 4) times, ending with a RS row—35 (34, 34, 36, 37, 38, 38) sts remain. Knit 1 row.
Repeat Decrease Row once—33 (32, 32, 34, 35, 36, 36) sts remain. Knit 1 row.
Continuing in Garter st, BO 2 sts at beginning of next 2 rows, then 3 sts at beginning of next 2 rows.
BO remaining 23 (22, 22, 24, 25, 26, 26) sts.

Finishing

Block pieces as desired. Sew shoulder seams.

NECKBAND

With RS facing, using circular needle and beginning at left shoulder, pick up and knit 96 (100, 104, 108, 112, 116, 120) sts around neck opening. Join for working in the rnd; pm for beginning of rnd.
NEXT RND: *K2, p2; repeat from * to end.
Work even for 1" (2.5 cm). BO all sts in pattern.

Set in Sleeves. Sew Sleeve seam from cuff to underarm, then sew side seam, sewing side edge of Front to Back from marker to base of ribbing; sew Sleeve seams.

✂ Cable Substitution

Before getting started, please review Stockinette Stitch Equivalent System on page 20.

CHOOSING CABLES

The cable panel shown has a total SSE of 65 (Cable A = 9.5 each, Cable B = 42, 2 reverse stockinette stitches between cables). You can use any cable or combination of cables and spacers giving you an SSE of 65 or less, not including the 2 reverse stockinette stitches on either side of the cable panel. Make up any difference with stockinette or reverse stockinette stitch at each side of the cable panel.

MANAGING A CHANGE IN STITCH COUNT

If, after substituting, your required stitch count is different from the stitch count at the end of the ribbing, remember to add or subtract the difference while working the knit row above the ribbing, before working Set-Up Row 1. The difference in stitch count will be carried throughout the front until the row right before changing to garter stitch, when you may need to adjust the decreases in order to end with the required stitch counts for garter stitch.

Skirt

SIZES
To fit hip 30 (34, 38, 42, 46, 50)" [76 (86.5, 96.5, 106.5, 117, 127) cm]

FINISHED MEASUREMENTS
Low waist: 25½ (30¾, 34¼, 38¾, 42¼, 46)" [65 (78, 87, 98.5, 107.5, 117) cms]
Length: 26 (26, 27, 27, 28, 28)" [66 (66, 68.5, 68.5, 71, 71) cm]

YARNS
Valley Yarns Northfield [70% merino wool/20% baby alpaca/10% silk; 124 yards (113 meters)/50 grams): 9 (10, 12, 13, 14, 15) balls Medium Gray

NEEDLES
One 24" (60 cm) long circular needle size US 4 (3.5 mm)

One 32" (80 cm) long circular needle size US 4 (3.5 mm)

One 24" (60 cm) long circular needle size US 6 (4 mm)

One 32" (80 cm) long circular needle size US 6 (4 mm)

Change needle size if necessary to obtain correct gauge.

NOTIONS
Stitch markers, cable needle

GAUGES
22 sts and 32 rows = 4" (10 cm) in St st, using larger needle

25 sts and 32 rows = 4" (10 cm) in 2 x 2 Rib, using larger needle

46 sts over Cable Chart = 6¼" (16 cm) wide, using larger needle

Steam or wet block your swatch before taking the measurements

STITCH PATTERN
2 x 2 Rib
(multiple of 4 sts; 1-rnd repeat)
ALL RNDS: *K2, p2; repeat from * to end.

Cable: Macramé (#145)

If you'd like to make a cable substitution, see page 266.

Using smaller 32" (80 cm) long needle, cast on 352 (384, 416, 448, 480, 512) sts. Join for working in the rnd, being careful not to twist sts; pm for beginning of rnd.

SET-UP RND: *P2, [k2, p2] 32 (36, 40, 44, 48, 52) times, pm, work Cable Chart over 46 sts, pm; repeat from * once.

Working patterns as established, work even through Rnd 11 of Chart, working Rnds 1–6 as indicated in Chart.

Change to larger 32" (80 cm) long circular needle.

NEXT RND: *P2, [k2, p2] 10 (10, 11, 11, 12, 13) times, pm, [k3 (5, 6, 8, 9, 10), k2tog] 8 times, k6, pm, [p2, k2] 10 (10, 11, 11, 12, 13) times, p2, sm, work Cable Chart as established, sm]; repeat from * once—336 (368, 400, 432, 464, 496) sts remain

NEXT RND: *[Work to marker, sm, knit to next marker, sm, [work to next marker, sm] twice; repeat from * once.

Repeat last rnd once.

SHAPE SKIRT

Note: Change to larger 24" (60 cm) long circular needle when necessary for number of sts on needle.

DECREASE RND 1: Continuing in patterns as established, *p2, k1, ssk, work to marker, sm, knit to next marker, sm, work to 5 sts before next marker, k2tog, k1, p2, sm, work to next marker, sm; repeat from * once—4 sts decreased.

Repeat Decrease Rnd 1 every 4 (3, 3, 3, 3, 3) rnds 2 (37, 38, 36, 36, 30) times, then every 3 (0, 2, 2, 2, 2) rnds 35 (0, 3, 5, 9, 19) times—184 (216, 232, 264, 280, 296) sts remain; 42 (58, 66, 82, 90, 98) sts in each St st section, 2 purl sts on either side of each cable panel.

NEXT RND: *P2, k2, remove marker, knit to next marker, remove marker, k2, p2, sm, work to next marker, sm; repeat from * once.

NEXT RND: *P2, knit to 2 sts before next marker, p2, sm, work to next marker; sm; repeat from * once.

Repeat last rnd 4 times.

DECREASE RND 2: *P2, k1, ssk, knit to 5 sts before next marker, k2tog, k1, p2, sm, work to next marker, sm; repeat from * once—4 sts decreased.

Repeat Decrease Rnd 2 every 7 (6, 7, 5, 6, 7) rnds 4 (5, 4, 6, 5, 4) times—164 (192, 212, 236, 256, 276) sts remain; 32 (46, 56, 68, 78, 88) in each St st section.

Work even until piece measures 23 (23, 24, 24, 25, 25)" [58.5 (58.5, 61, 61, 63.5, 63.5) cm], ending with an odd-numbered rnd of Cable Chart.

Change to smaller 24" (60 cm) circular needle.

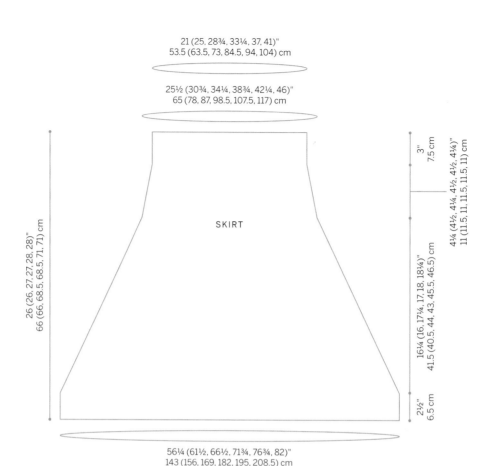

21 (25, 28¾, 33¼, 37, 41)"
53.5 (63.5, 73, 84.5, 94, 104) cm

25½ (30¾, 34¼, 38¾, 42¼, 46)"
65 (78, 87, 98.5, 107.5, 117) cm

SKIRT

26 (26, 27, 27, 28, 28)"
66 (66, 68.5, 68.5, 71, 71) cm

3"
7.5 cm

4¼ (4½, 4¼, 4½, 4½, 4¼)"
11 (11.5, 11, 11.5, 11.5, 11) cm

16¼ (16, 17¼, 17, 18, 18¼)"
41.5 (40.5, 44, 43, 45.5, 46.5) cm

2½"
6.5 cm

56¼ (61½, 66½, 71¾, 76¾, 82)"
143 (156, 169, 182, 195, 208.5) cm

NEXT RND: *[K3 (3, 4, 6, 8, 11), k2tog] 8 (9, 8, 7, 6, 5) times, k1 (3, 5, 3, 4, 4); repeat from * 3 times—132 (156, 180, 208, 232, 256) sts remain.

Change to 2x2 Rib; work even for 3" (7.5 cm).

BO RND: K2, *insert left needle into fronts of sts just knit, then knit them again through the back loops, k1; repeat from * until 1 st remains, omitting final k1. Fasten off.

Finishing

Steam or wet-block piece to finished measurements.

ℬ Cable Substitution

Before getting started, please review Stockinette Stitch Equivalent System on page 20.

CHOOSING CABLES

EASY SUBSTITUTION: Keep the cable panel the same width and replace the entire panel (leaving 2 reverse stockinette stitches at each outside edge of the panel). The cables you choose need to add up to an SSE of 32.

ADVANCED SUBSTITUTION: If you'd like to make your cable panel wider, you can borrow stitches from the stockinette stitches on either side of the cable panel. I'd recommend replacing up to 6 stockinette

stitches from each side with cables to keep the look of the finished garment similar, but you can replace more. Make sure you have at least 30 stockinette stitches between the markers after the final repeat of Decrease Rnd 1.

MANAGING A CHANGE IN STITCH COUNT

FOR THE EASY SUBSTITUTION: If, after substituting, your stitch count has changed in the cable section, make note of the difference between your cable section numbers and the cable section numbers called for in the pattern and remember to add or subtract the difference in your cast-on.

FOR THE ADVANCED SUBSTITUTION: If you have replaced any stockinette stitches with cables, the above note applies, plus you'll need to calculate how many rib stitches to cast on under the remaining stockinette stitch. I like about 15 percent more rib than stockinette stitch when the rib needs to lay flat. You may need to adjust your cast-on to accommodate the rib multiple of 4 stitches + 2. Your cast-on total should include stitches for 2 cable panels + 4 rib godets (the ribbed triangular insert panels on either side of the cable panels) + rib for under each stockinette stitch section between the markers.

Fitted Pullover

SIZES
To fit bust 30 (34, 38, 42, 46, 50, 54)" [76 (86.5, 96.5, 106.5, 117, 127, 137) cm]

FINISHED MEASUREMENTS
35½ (39½, 44, 48, 52, 56½, 60½)" [90 (100.5, 112, 122, 132, 143.5, 153.5) cm] bust

MATERIALS
Zealana Kiwi Fingering Weight [40% fine New Zealand merino/30% organic cotton/30% brush-tail possum; 135 yards (123 meters) / 40 grams]: 7 (8, 9, 10, 12, 13, 14) balls #16 Storm Blue

NEEDLES
One pair straight needles size US 4 (3.5 mm)

One pair straight needles size US 2 (2.75 mm)

One 16" (40 cm) long circular needle size 2 (2.75 mm), for Neckband

Change needle size if necessary to obtain correct gauge.

NOTIONS
Stitch markers, cable needle

GAUGE
23 sts and 34 rows = 4" in St st, using larger needles

60-st panel from Fennec (#151) measures 9¼" (23.5 cm) wide, using larger needles

Steam or wet block your swatch before taking the measurements

STITCH PATTERNS
Twisted Rib
(worked in rnds over an even number of sts; 1-rnd repeat)
ALL RNDS: *P1, k1-tbl; repeat from * to end.

Twisted Rib
(worked in rows over an even number of sts; 2-row repeat)
ROW 1: *P1, k1-tbl; repeat from * to end.
ROW 2: *P1-tbl, k1; repeat from * to end.
Repeat Rows 1 and 2 for pattern.

Cable: Fennec (#151)

PATTERN NOTES
Stitch counts change within the Fennec Cable Chart. After each Front shaping element, you will be given stitch counts for the stitches outside the Chart markers, rather than for the entire row.

🔗 If you'd like to make a cable substitution, see page 271.

Back
Using smaller needles, CO 84 (96, 108, 120, 132, 144, 156) sts. Begin Twisted Rib; work even for 2¾" (7 cm).

Change to larger needles.
SET-UP ROW 1 (RS): K16 (22, 28, 34, 40, 46, 52), p2, k2, p5, [M1P, p11] 3 times, M1P, p6, k2, p2, knit to end—88 (100, 112, 124, 136, 148, 160) sts.
SET-UP ROW 2: P16 (22, 28, 34, 40, 46, 52), k2, p2, k48, p2, k2, purl to end.
Work even for 1" (2.5 cm), ending with a WS row.

SHAPE SIDES
INCREASE ROW (RS): K3, M1R, work to last 3 sts, M1L, k3—2 sts increased.
Repeat Increase Row every 8 rows 6 times—102 (114, 126, 138, 150, 162, 174) sts.
Work even until piece measures 11 (11, 11½, 12, 12½, 12¾, 13)" 28 (28, 29, 30.5, 32, 32.5, 33) cm] from the beginning, ending with a WS row.

SHAPE ARMHOLES
BO 3 (4, 5, 7, 9, 11, 13) sts at beginning of next 2 rows, 3 sts at beginning of next 2 (2, 2, 2, 2, 4, 6) rows, then 2 sts at beginning of next 2 (4, 6, 6, 8, 6, 8) rows—86 (92, 98, 106, 110, 116, 114) sts remain.
DECREASE ROW (RS): K3, k2tog, work to last 5 sts, ssk, k3—2 sts decreased.
Repeat Decrease Row every RS row 2 (3, 3, 5, 3, 7, 3) times, then every 4 rows 3 (4, 4, 3, 4, 2, 3) times—74 (76, 82, 88, 94, 96, 100) sts remain.
Work even until armholes measure 6½ (7, 7½, 8, 8½, 9, 9½)" [16.5 (18, 19, 20.5, 21.5, 23, 24) cm], ending with a WS row. Place marker on either side of center 20 (22, 24, 24, 26, 28, 30) sts.

SHAPE SHOULDERS AND NECK
NEXT ROW (RS): BO 5 (5, 7, 8, 8, 8, 9) sts, work to marker, join a second ball of yarn, BO center sts, work to end. Working both sides at the same time, BO 5 (5, 7, 8, 8, 8, 9) sts at each armhole edge once, then 6 (6, 6, 7, 8, 8, 8) sts twice, and AT THE SAME TIME, BO 5 sts at each neck edge twice.

Front
Using smaller needles, CO 84 (96, 108, 120, 132, 144, 156) sts. Begin Twisted Rib; work even for 2¾" (7 cm).

Change to larger needles.

SET-UP ROW 1 (WS): K16 (22, 28, 34, 40, 46, 52), p2, [k4, M1L] 12 times, p2, knit to end—96 (108, 120, 132, 144, 156, 168) sts.

SET-UP ROW 2: P16 (22, 28, 34, 40, 46, 52), k2, pm, work Cable Pattern over 60 sts, pm, k2, purl to end.

Work even for 1" (2.5 cm), ending with a WS row.

SHAPE SIDES

INCREASE ROW (RS): K3, M1R, work to last 3 sts, M1L, k3—2 sts increased.

Repeat Increase Row every 8 rows 6 times—25 (31, 37, 43, 49, 55, 61) sts outside of markers on either side.

Work even until piece measures 11 (11, 11½, 12, 12½, 12¾, 13)" 28 (28, 29, 30.5, 32, 32.5, 33) cm] from the beginning, ending with a WS row.

SHAPE ARMHOLES

BO 3 (4, 5, 7, 9, 11, 13) sts at beginning of next 2 rows, 3 sts at beginning of next 2 (2, 2, 2, 2, 4, 6) rows, then 2 sts at beginning of next 2 (4, 6, 6, 8, 6, 8) rows—17 (20, 23, 27, 29, 32, 31) sts remain outside of markers on either side.

DECREASE ROW (RS): K3, k2tog, work to last 5 sts, ssk, k3—2 sts decreased.

Repeat Decrease Row every RS row 2 (3, 3, 5, 3, 7, 3) times, then every 4 rows 3 (4, 4, 3, 4, 2, 3) times—11 (12, 15, 18, 21, 22, 24) sts remain outside of markers on either side.

Work even until armholes measure approximately 4½ (4½, 5, 5, 5½, 5½, 6)" [11.5 (11.5, 12.5, 12.5, 14, 14, 15) cm], ending with a WS row—68 (70, 76, 82, 88, 90, 94) sts remain after Row 108 of Chart. Place marker on either side of center 10 (12, 14, 14, 16, 18, 20) sts.

SHAPE NECK

NEXT ROW (RS): Work to marker, join a second ball of yarn, BO center sts, work to end. Working both sides at the same time, BO 6 sts at each neck edge twice—17 (17, 19, 22, 24, 24, 25) sts remain each shoulder.

Work even until armholes measure 6½ (7, 7½, 8, 8½, 9, 9½)" [16.5 (18, 19, 20.5, 21.5, 23, 24) cm], ending with a WS row.

SHAPE SHOULDERS

BO 5 (5, 7, 8, 8, 8, 9) sts at each armhole edge once, then 6 (6, 6, 7, 8, 8, 8) sts twice.

Sleeve

Using smaller needles, CO 58 (60, 64, 68, 70, 74, 78) sts. Begin Twisted Rib; work even for 2¾" (7 cm).

Change to larger needles and St st, beginning with a RS row; work even for 1" (2.5 cm), ending with a WS row.

SHAPE SLEEVE

INCREASE ROW (RS): K3, M1R, knit to last 3 sts, M1L, k3—2 sts increased.

Repeat Increase Row every 10 (8, 8, 6, 4, 4, 4) rows 10 (8, 8, 6, 4, 4, 4) times, then every 0 (0, 0, 8, 6, 0, 0) rows 0 (0, 0, 3, 6, 0, 0) times—68 (72, 78, 86, 92, 102, 108) sts.

Work even until piece measures 12 (12, 13, 13¼, 13¼, 13½, 13¾)" [30.5 (30.5, 33, 33.5, 33.5, 34.5, 35) cm], ending with a WS row.

SHAPE CAP

BO 2 (3, 4, 6, 8, 10, 12) sts at beginning of next 2 rows, then 2 sts at beginning of next 2 (4, 4, 4, 4, 6, 6) rows—60 (58, 62, 66, 68, 70, 72) sts remain.

DECREASE ROW (RS): K3, k2tog, work to last 5 sts, ssk, k3—2 sts decreased.

Repeat Decrease Row every RS row 4 (2, 3, 4, 4, 4, 4) times, then every 4 rows 4 (7, 7, 7, 8, 8, 9) times, then every RS row 5 (3, 4, 4, 4, 5, 5) times—32 (32, 32, 34, 34, 34, 34) sts remain.

BO 2 sts at beginning of next 4 rows, then 3 sts at beginning of next 2 rows.

Purl 1 row.

BO remaining 18 (18, 18, 20, 20, 20, 20) sts.

Finishing

Block pieces as desired. Sew shoulder seams.

NECKBAND

With RS facing, using smaller circular needle, and beginning at left shoulder, pick up and knit 102 (106, 112, 112, 118, 122, 128) sts around neck opening. Join for working in the rnd; pm for beginning of rnd. Begin Twisted Rib; work even for 1" (2.5 cm). BO all sts in pattern.

Set in Sleeves. Sew side and Sleeve seams.

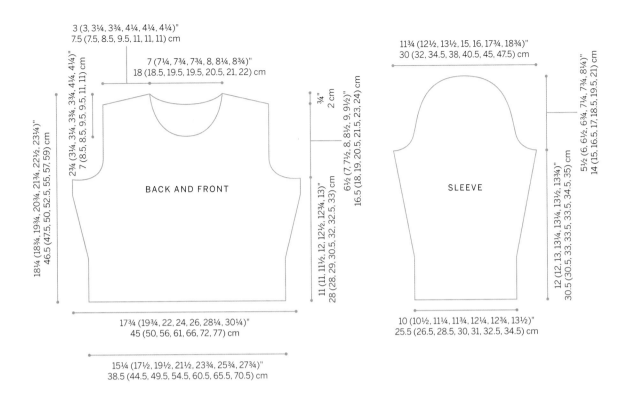

BACK AND FRONT

3 (3, 3¼, 3¾, 4¼, 4¼, 4¼)"
7.5 (7.5, 8.5, 9.5, 11, 11, 11) cm

7 (7¼, 7¾, 7¾, 8, 8¼, 8¾)"
18 (18.5, 19.5, 19.5, 20.5, 21, 22) cm

2¾ (3¼, 3¼, 3¾, 3¾, 4¼, 4¼)"
7 (8.5, 8.5, 9.5, 9.5, 11, 11) cm

18¼ (18¾, 19¾, 20¾, 21¾, 22½, 23¾)"
46.5 (47.5, 50, 52.5, 55, 57, 59) cm

17¾ (19¾, 22, 24, 26, 28¼, 30¼)"
45 (50, 56, 61, 66, 72, 77) cm

15¼ (17½, 19½, 21½, 23¾, 25¾, 27¾)"
38.5 (44.5, 49.5, 54.5, 60.5, 65.5, 70.5) cm

¾"
2 cm

6½ (7, 7½, 8, 8½, 9, 9½)"
16.5 (18, 19, 20.5, 21.5, 23, 24) cm

11 (11, 11½, 12, 12½, 12¾, 13)"
28 (28, 29, 30.5, 32, 32.5, 33) cm

SLEEVE

11¾ (12½, 13½, 15, 16, 17¾, 18¾)"
30 (32, 34.5, 38, 40.5, 45, 47.5) cm

5½ (6, 6½, 6¾, 7¼, 7¾, 8¼)"
14 (15, 16.5, 17, 18.5, 19.5, 21) cm

12 (12, 13, 13¼, 13¼, 13½, 13¾)"
30.5 (30.5, 33, 33.5, 33.5, 34.5, 35) cm

10 (10½, 11¼, 11¾, 12¼, 12¾, 13½)"
25.5 (26.5, 28.5, 30, 31, 32.5, 34.5) cm

⑧ Cable Substitution

Before getting started, please review Stockinette Stitch Equivalent System on page 20.

CHOOSING CABLES

The cable panel shown has a total SSE of 54. If you'd like to change the width of the cable, you can add as much as 20 (22, 28, 34, 40, 42, 46) SSE, depending on the size you are knitting. The number of stitches available after the armholes is the deciding factor. The widest possible cable combination for each size is an SSE of 74 (76, 82, 88, 94, 96, 100).

MANAGING A CHANGE IN STITCH COUNT

If, after substituting, your required stitch count is different from the stitch count at the end of the ribbing, remember to add or subtract the difference while working the knit row above the ribbing and in the stitch counts throughout the piece. In addition, this cable panel is special because it ends with fewer stitches than when it began, since decreases are worked within the cable panel to accommodate the drastic change in stitch gauge. Starburst (#152) and Weave & Duck (#148) are similar. To use any other cables in the book, the front neck shaping below, based on the gauge at the bottom of the Fennec cable panel, will be a better starting point. You may still need to add or subtract a few stitches, sharing them evenly between the neck and shoulder shaping.

More universal neck shaping for Fennec:
Place marker on either side of center 14 (16, 19, 19, 20, 22, 25) sts.

SHAPE NECK

NEXT ROW (RS): Work to marker, join a second ball of yarn, BO center sts, work to end. Working both sides at the same time, BO 6 sts at each neck edge once, 4 sts once, 3 sts once, then 2 sts once. Work even...

Afghan

FINISHED
MEASUREMENTS
Approximately 60"
(152.5 cm) wide x 50¼"
(127.5 cm) long

YARN
Brooklyn Tweed Shelter
[100% Targhee-Columbia
wool; 140 yards (128
meters)/50 grams]:
17 skeins Foothills

Note: Fringe used nearly
1 skein of yarn.

NEEDLES
One 40" (100 cm) long or
longer circular needle size
US 8 (5 mm)

One needle any style size
US 9 (5.5 mm) for BO
(optional)

Change needle size if
necessary to obtain cor-
rect gauge.

NOTIONS
Crochet hook size US H-8
(5 mm) for fringe, stitch
markers, removable
marker, cable needle

GAUGE
16 sts and 24 rows = 4"
(10 cm) in St st

78 sts over Cable Pattern
measures 11½" (29 cm),
measured over Row 40 of
pattern

Steam or wet block your
swatch before taking the
measurements.

STITCH PATTERNS
Cable: Starburst (#152)

If you'd like to make
a cable substitution, see
page 273.

Afghan

Using Long-Tail CO, CO 252 sts.

HORIZONTAL RIBBING

Purl 1 row; place removable marker at beginning of this row to indicate RS.

*Purl 1 row. Knit 2 rows. Purl 1 row.

Repeat from * 6 times.

ROW 30 (WS): Purl.

ROW 31: Knit.

ROW 32: K10, purl to last 10 sts, knit to end.

ROW 33: P10, knit to last 10 sts, purl to end.

ROWS 34–49: Repeat Rows 30–33 four times.

SECTION A

NEXT ROW (WS): Continuing to work first and last 10 sts in pattern as established, work 10 sts, p30, pm, work Cable Pattern over 52 sts, pm, p68, pm, work Cable Pattern over 52 sts, pm, purl to last 10 sts, work in pattern as established to end.

Work even, working first and last 10 sts and Cable Patterns as established, and St st on remaining sts, until Row 70 of Cable Pattern is complete, ending with a RS row.

SECTION B

NEXT ROW (WS): Continuing to work first and last 10 sts in pattern as established, work 10 sts, p90, pm, work Cable Pattern over 52 sts, pm, purl to last 10 sts, work in pattern as established to end.

Work even, working first and last 10 sts and Cable Patterns as established, and St st on remaining sts, until Row 70 of Cable Pattern is complete, ending with a RS row.

Repeat Section A once.

Work even for 20 rows, working first and last 10 sts as established, and remaining sts in St st.

HORIZONTAL RIBBING

*Knit 1 row. Purl 2 rows. Knit 1 row.

Repeat from * 6 times.

Knit 1 row.

BO all sts loosely purlwise, using a larger needle for BO if necessary to keep edge from pulling in.

Finishing

Block piece as desired.

FRINGE

Work 1 fringe on each side edge in each St st stripe, as follows:
For each fringe, cut 3 lengths of yarn 9" (23 cm) long. Holding all 3 strands together, fold in half. With WS facing, insert crochet hook into edge st between 2 purl rows, catch loop of folded strands and pull through to WS, then insert ends through loop and pull to tighten. Holding 3 of the 6 strands together, twist them clockwise until the triple strand begins to twist back on itself. Holding onto this first twisted strand, twist the remaining 3 strands counter clockwise. Twist the 2 triple strands around each other, then tie a knot at the base and trim the ends neatly.

Cable Substitution

Before getting started, review Stockinette Stitch Equivalent System on page 20.

CHOOSING CABLES

You have an SSE of 232 to work with, whether to change to cables or reverse stockinette stitch, or to leave stockinette stitch as you please. After Row 29 is complete, continue working the first and last 10 sts as established (as for Section A), with your chosen cables and fillers in between.

MANAGING A CHANGE IN STITCH COUNT

The original cable is unique in this book in that it begins and ends as stockinette stitch. When you substitute cables, the stitch count will change. Increase the additional stitches you need for your cables while working the last knit row before the numbered rows of your chosen cable begin. Work in your pattern for about 210 rows [35" (89 cm)], ignoring the references to Sections A and B, and ending with a wrong-side row. Knit 1 row, decreasing the number of stitches needed to get back to the total of 252 stitches. Work 20 rows even, then work the final horizontal ribbing.

Abbreviations

BO: Bind off

CN: Cable needle

CO: Cast on

DPN: Double-pointed needle(s)

K1-F/B: Knit into the front loop and back loop of the same stitch to increase 1 stitch.

K1-TBL: Knit 1 stitch through the back loop.

K2TOG: Knit 2 stitches together.

K3TOG: Knit 3 stitches together.

K: Knit

M1 OR M1L (MAKE 1-LEFT SLANTING): With the tip of the left needle inserted from front to back, lift the strand between the 2 needles onto the left needle; knit the strand through the back loop to increase 1 stitch.

M1P OR M1P-R (MAKE 1 PURLWISE-RIGHT SLANTING): With the tip of the left needle inserted from back to front, lift the strand between the 2 needles onto the left needle; purl the strand through the front loop to increase 1 stitch.

M1R (MAKE 1-RIGHT SLANTING): With the tip of the left needle inserted from back to front, lift the strand between the 2 needles onto the left needle; knit the strand through the front loop to increase 1 stitch.

MK: Make knot (as instructed).

P2TOG: Purl 2 stitches together.

P3TOG: Purl 3 stitches together.

PM: Place marker

P: Purl

PSSO (PASS SLIPPED STITCH OVER): Pass the slipped stitch on the right needle over the stitch(es) indicated in the instructions, as in binding off.

P2SSO (PASS 2 SLIPPED STITCHES OVER): Pass the 2 slipped stitches on the right needle over the stitch(es) indicated in the instructions, as in binding off.

RND(S): Round(s)

RS: Right side

S2KP2: Slip the next 2 stitches together to the right needle as if to knit 2 together, k1, pass the 2 slipped stitches over.

SSE: Stockinette stitch equivalent (see page 20)

SM: Slip marker

SSK (SLIP, SLIP, KNIT): Slip the next 2 stitches to the right needle one at a time as if to knit; return them to the left needle one at a time in their new orientation; knit them together through the back loops.

SSSK: Same as ssk, but worked on the next 3 stitches.

SSP (SLIP, SLIP, PURL): Slip the next 2 stitches to the right needle one at a time as if to knit; return them to the left needle one at a time in their new orientation; purl them together through the back loops.

ST(S): Stitch(es)

TBL: Through the back loop

TOG: Together

WS: Wrong side

WYIB: With yarn in back

WYIF: With yarn in front

YO: Yarnover

YO2: Yarnover twice

Acknowledgments

This book is the culmination of many years of work and countless relationships.

To begin, I must thanks my parents, whose bravery in pursuing the life of freelance artists showed me that it could be done.

My mom, Phoebe Adams Gaughan, a talented how-to illustrator and ceramic artist, shared her love of good fiber and fabric, taught me how to sew, and helped me learn to be (more) patient with instructions. Thanks for buying me *Knitting Without Tears* to thwart my tears of frustration; that was a genius move. And thanks for being, to this day, my ultimate cheerleader.

My dad, Jack Gaughan, set the artistic bar high with his science-fiction illustrations and covers. His fluency with ink and paint were admired by many. Thank you for letting me sit in your studio watching you for hours while listening to classical music, and for all of the creative projects we did together from the time I could walk.

These important people in my childhood shared invaluable knowledge:

Gram, Susan Reiber Adams, taught me how to crochet and embroider and instilled in me a love for perfectly finished work, inside and out.

My friend Grace Judson taught me how to knit during that fateful hot summer.

I owe much to these knitting greats whose books were formative:

Elizabeth Zimmermann, whose book *Knitting Without Tears* demystified knit design for me and formed the foundation of my career.

Barbara Walker, whose Treasury of Knitting Patterns series taught me so much about stitch patterns.

How fortunate I was to meet new friends and colleagues as I started my adult life. A million thanks to:

Margery Winter, for being my friend and mentor for more than 20 years and for pushing me to stretch my boundaries, think outside of the box, and think big. Special thanks also to Milo Winter for sitting through so many dinner conversations about knitting.

Deborah Newton, for generously sharing contacts in the beginning and remaining a friend for so many years.

So many people I have worked with over the years have contributed to my growth and success, including:

John Maxim, who pounded the pavement with my newly minted swatches in the 1990s. His persistent salesmanship allowed me to focus on the creative aspect of making up new stitch patterns during one of my most artistically productive periods.

Barbara Khouri, who has written and sized so many patterns for me over the past 20 years that she knows how my designer's mind works better than anyone, and has been a good friend as well.

The multitude of knitters who have worked with me throughout my career, creating pieces for yarn companies and magazine editorials and swatches. Many have become my dearest friends.

Warren and Caroline Wheelock, who for nine years helped me to grow and thrive as part of the Berroco team.

Many thanks to those who contributed directly to this book:

The knitters who diligently worked on swatches and sweaters and asked great questions so we could get the instructions right: Elke Probst, Donna Yacino, Martha Wissing, Lynn Marlow, Pat McMullen, Nancy Brown, and Sarah Gray. I couldn't have done it without you!

Sue McCain, for tech editing the entire book and developing the modern, clean, and readable cable symbol system to illustrate the wide variety of stitches and crosses. Her enviable patience, tenacity, and brainpower have made all the difference for this book. Therese Cheynoweth, for checking all of the instructions with keen attention to detail.

Melanie Falick, for being a very hands-on editor when needed, while allowing me the freedom to pursue my vision. For keeping the writing true to me but making it so much better. For believing in my potential way back when.

Graphic designer Mary Jane Callister, who brought all the pieces together to make this volume both beautiful and useable.

Jared Flood, for his amazing photography as well as his friendship and enthusiasm.

And last, for emphasis, thanks to John Ranta, who is not only a loving and supportive husband, but also boundlessly generous with his time and energy. His gardening, chicken-raising, weekly shopping, and daily cooking have kept me well fed, his house-building has kept me warmly sheltered, and his presence in my life has kept me well loved and happy.

Editor: Melanie Falick
Designer: Mary Jane Callister
Production Manager: True Sims

Library of Congress Control Number: 2016956329

ISBN: 978-1-4197-2239-4

Text copyright © 2016 Norah Gaughan
Photographs copyright © 2016 Jared Flood

Printed and bound in China

10 9 8 7 6 5 4 3 2

Abrams books are available at special discounts when purchased in quantity for premiums and promotions as well as fundraising or educational use. Special editions can also be created to specification. For details, contact specialsales@abramsbooks.com or the address below.

ABRAMS
The Art of Books

115 West 18th Street
New York, NY 10011
abramsbooks.com